THE DRAGON AND THE FOREIGN DEVILS

Australia, Britain and the EEC 1961–1963

The Coming of the Second World War

The Australian–American Alliance

Problems of Australian Defence (ed.)

Nuclear Weapons and Chinese Policy, Adelphi Paper No. 99

The Strategic Balance (ed.)

Technology, Defense and External Relations in China 1975–1978

Sovereignty through Interdependence

Nations out of Empires

Opium, Soldiers and Evangelicals

The Dragon

and the

Foreign Devils

China and the World, 1100 BC to the Present

Harry G. Gelber

BLOOMSBURY

First published in Great Britain 2007

Copyright © Harry G. Gelber 2007

Maps by John Gilkes

The right of Harry G. Gelber to be identified as author
of this work has been asserted by him in accordance with
the Copyright, Designs and Patents Act 1988

Every reasonable effort has been made to trace copyright holders of material
reproduced in this book, but if any have been inadvertently overlooked the publishers
would be glad to hear from them. For legal purposes the acknowledgements on
page xi and the list of illustrations on page ix constitute an extension of
the copyright page

No part of this book may be used or reproduced in any manner
whatsoever without written permission from the Publisher except in the
case of brief quotations embodied in critical articles or reviews

Bloomsbury Publishing Plc
36 Soho Square
London W1D 3QY

www.bloomsbury.com

Bloomsbury Publishing, London, New York and Berlin

A CIP catalogue record for this book is available from the British Library

ISBN 9780747577959 (hardback)
10 9 8 7 6 5 4 3 2 1

ISBN 9780747590712 (trade paperback)
10 9 8 7 6 5 4 3 2 1

Typeset by Hewer Text UK Ltd, Edinburgh
Printed in the United States of America by Quebecor World Fairfield

Dedicated to Isabelle, Gabriel, Simon and Jocelyn,
who were not there last time

Contents

ILLUSTRATIONS

Founding emperor Qin Shi Huangdi. (*British Library*)

Wine vessel bronze, *c*.800 BC. (*Collection of the National Palace Museum, Taipei*)

Wine vessel bronze, 10–11th century BC. (*Collection of the National Palace Museum, Taipei*)

Illuminated letter from William Rubruck's (1220–1324) manuscript of his journey to Karakorum. (*Corpus Christi College, Cambridge University*)

Possible portrait of Marco Polo (1254–1324). (*Hulton Archive*)

Kublai Khan, the first Yuan emperor, on horseback, 1280. (*Collection of the National Palace Museum, Taipei*)

Founding Ming emperor Hongwu (1328–1398). (*Collection of the National Palace Museum, Taipei*)

Covered bowl with dragon design, early to mid-1400s (Ming dynasty). (*Collection of the National Palace Museum, Taipei*)

Dish with three immortals, *c*.1600 (Ming dynasty). (*Collection of the National Palace Museum, Taipei*)

Vase with floral scrolls, Hongwu reign, 1368–98 (Ming dynasty). (*Collection of the National Palace Museum, Taipei*)

Floral globe vase, Yongle reign, 1403–24 (Ming dynasty). (*Collection of the National Palace Museum, Taipei*)

Ming emperor Xiao Zong (1488–1505). (*Collection of the National Palace Museum, Taipei*)

The first Western atlas map of China (with an East West orientation), from the *Ortelius Theatrum* atlas, 1584. (*Private Collection, © Bonhams, London, UK / The Bridgeman Art Library*)

A senior civil servant collecting taxes, 1690. (*Private Collection, The Stapleton Collection / The Bridgeman Art Library*)

The first great leader of the united Manchus, Nurhaci (1558–1626), looks on as two Mongol leaders are put to death outside a city wall. (*British Library*)

Portrait of the first major Jesuit figure in China, Matteo Ricci (1552–1626). (*Gesu, Rome, Italy / The Bridgeman Art Library*)

Ferdinand Verbiest (1623–1688). (*Hulton Archive, Getty Images*)

The German Jesuit, Adam Schall von Bell (1591–1666). (*Athanasius Kircher, China momumentis qua sacris qua profanis . . . aliarumque rerum memorabilium argumentis illustrata, Amsterdam 1649, plate 11. Photo: Oldenbourg Wissenschaftsverlag, Munich*)

Qing emperor Kangxi (1654–1722). (*From an.haiguinet.com*)

Passport from the Qing dynasty. (*From www.ecf.caltech.edu*)

Count Fyodor Golovin (1650–1706), Russian negotiator of the 1689 Treaty of Nerchinsk. (*From www.diplomatrus.ru*)

View of the summer palace, Peking (Chinese artist, date unknown). (*Bibliothèque Nationale, Paris, France / The Bridgeman Art Library*)

ACKNOWLEDGEMENTS

T HIS BOOK IS a study of how foreign states and people have seen and dealt with China over many centuries and of how China has dealt with them. Needless to say, no such work could have been attempted without the advice and help of a number of places and people. I owe the warmest gratitude to Harvard University and especially its Center of European Studies, and to the Fairbank Center, both of which became my academic home for the two years 2004–6; to the Department of International Relations and the Asia Centre of the London School of Economics and Political Science, and the School of Government of the University of Tasmania. The Harvard and London School of Economics libraries and the British Library have, between them, offered extraordinarily rich and indispensable resources. A number of friends and colleagues have also helped in various ways or were kind enough to read and comment on parts or even the whole of the draft. I am immensely grateful to them all: they have saved me from more errors, even howlers, than I care to remember. They include Caitlin Anderson, Christopher Andrew, Christopher Coker, James Cronin, Mark Elvin, Christopher Gelber, Merle Goldman, Peter Hall, Fred Halliday, Bill Hamilton, Christopher Hill, Stanley Hoffmann, Christopher Hughes, Philip Kuhn,

Roderick MacFarquhar, Charles Maier, Jeff Makholm, Jonathan Mirsky, Robert Ross, Razeen Sally, John Schulz, Ross Terrill and Ezra Vogel. At the end of that process Bill Swainson and his colleagues at Bloomsbury Publishing were admirably, even awesomely, efficient in picking up any flaws of style or substance that might have been overlooked.

I am of course alone responsible for any errors, misunderstandings, omissions and infelicities that might have escaped all these eagle eyes.

HARRY G. GELBER
Cambridge, MA, 2006

MAPS

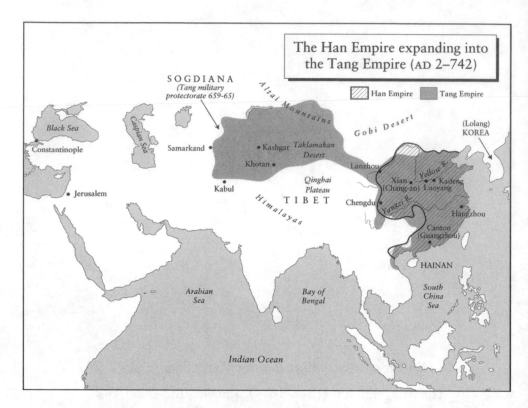

The Han Empire expanding into the Tang Empire (AD 2–742)

Han Empire   Tang Empire

SOGDIANA
(Tang military protectorate 659-65)

Black Sea

Constantinople

Caspian Sea

Altai Mountains

Gobi Desert

(Lolang) KOREA

Samarkand

Kashgar   Taklamakan Desert

Khotan

Lanzhou

Yellow R.

Xian (Chang-an)   Kaifeng   Luoyang

Jerusalem

Kabul

Qinghai Plateau
TIBET

Himalayas

Chengdu

Yangzi R.

Hangzhou

Canton (Guangzhou)

HAINAN

Arabian Sea

Bay of Bengal

South China Sea

Indian Ocean

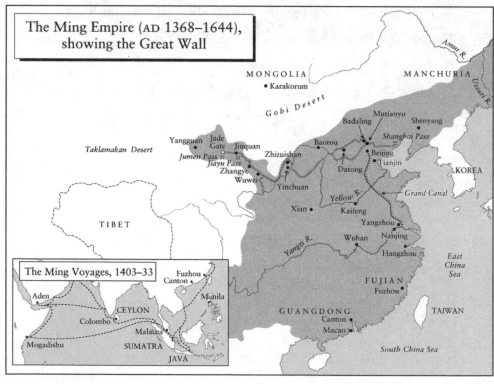

The Ming Empire (AD 1368–1644), showing the Great Wall

MONGOLIA
• Karakorum

MANCHURIA

Amur R.

Ussuri R.

Gobi Desert

Mutianyu

Badaling

Shenyang

Shanghai Pass

Taklamakan Desert

Yangguan   Jade Gate   Jiuquan

Baotou

Beijing

Jumen Pass   Jiayu Pass   Zhizuishan

Tianjin

KOREA

Zhangye

Datong

Wuwei

Yinchuan

Yellow R.

Grand Canal

Xian

Kaifeng

TIBET

Yangzhou

Wuhan

Nanjing

Yangzi R.

Hangzhou

East China Sea

The Ming Voyages, 1403–33

Fuzhou
Canton

Manila

Aden

CEYLON

Colombo

Malacca

Mogadishu

SUMATRA

JAVA

FUJIAN

Fuzhou

GUANGDONG

Canton

Macao

TAIWAN

South China Sea

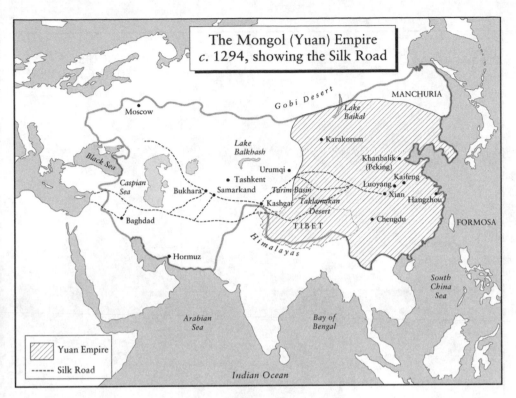

The Mongol (Yuan) Empire
c. 1294, showing the Silk Road

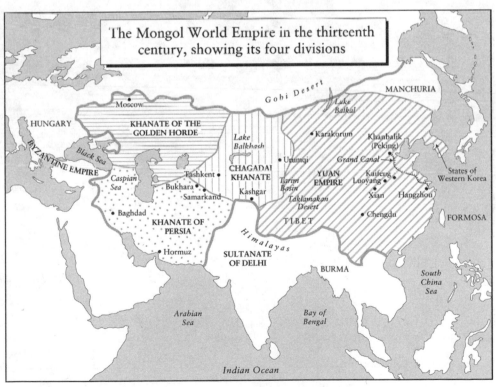

The Mongol World Empire in the thirteenth
century, showing its four divisions

RUSSIAN
FEDERATION

M O

Frontier 1689–1859 settled
by Treaty of Nerchinsk

RUSSIA

Sino-Russian borders,
1680–1859

Chinese until 1859
Russian after 1859

Nerchinsk

Albazin

CHINA

Amur R.

Khabarovsk

Kiakhta

HEILUNGKIANG

Ussuri R.

KIRIN

JAPAN

KOREA

• Urumqi
(Urumchi)

XINJIANG

QINGHAI

T I B E T

Himalayas

SICHUAN

N E P A L

Lhasa

BHUTAN

I N D I A

BANGLA-
DESH

YUNNAN

M Y A N M A R
(BURMA)

*Bay of
Bengal*

THAILAND

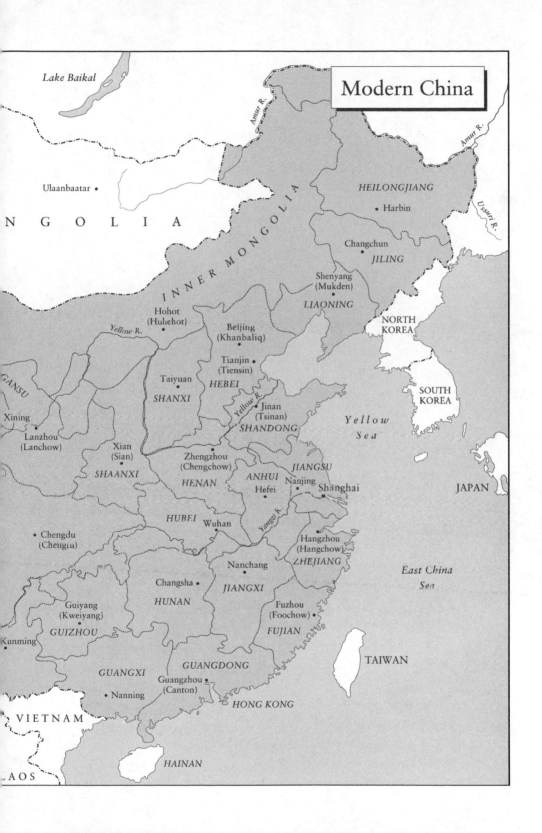

Modern China

Lake Baikal

Amur R.

Amur R.

Ussuri R.

Ulaanbaatar •

HEILONGJIANG

• Harbin

M O N G O L I A

I N N E R   M O N G O L I A

Changchun
•

JILING

Shenyang
(Mukden)
•

LIAONING

NORTH
KOREA

Hohot
(Huhehot)
•

Yellow R.

Beijing
(Khanbaliq)
•

Tianjin
(Tiensin)
•

HEBEI

SOUTH
KOREA

GANSU

Taiyuan
•

SHANXI

Yellow R.

Jinan
(Tsinan)
•

SHANDONG

*Yellow
Sea*

Xining
•

Lanzhou
(Lanchow)
•

Xian
(Sian)
•

SHAANXI

Zhengzhou
(Chengchow)
•

HENAN

ANHUI

Hefei
•

JIANGSU

Nanjing
•

Shanghai
•

JAPAN

HUBEI

Wuhan
•

Yangzi R.

Hangzhou
(Hangchow)
•

ZHEJIANG

*East China
Sea*

Chengdu
(Chengtu)
•

Nanchang
•

Changsha •

JIANGXI

HUNAN

Fuzhou
(Foochow) •

FUJIAN

Guiyang
(Kweiyang)
•

GUIZHOU

TAIWAN

Kunming
•

GUANGXI

GUANGDONG

Guangzhou
(Canton) •

• Nanning

HONG KONG

VIETNAM

HAINAN

LAOS

INTRODUCTION

C HINA IS THE most exciting rising power in the world today. The explosive growth of China's economy and the possibility that the People's Republic might soon become the next superpower, dominant in East Asia and influential in every part of the world, have attracted universal interest, admiration and envy – or alarm. It is a dramatic change from China's position a mere half century ago, when she was war-torn, poverty-stricken and the object, instead of the subject, of great power politics.

These changes, which seem so sudden, nevertheless have deep roots, reaching far back into China's history. And not just China's, but the history of the many tribes, kingdoms, nations and states that have interacted with the Chinese over long periods, with results that have helped to shape the China of today. This book traces that history of relations between the Chinese and the rest of the world, and does so with strong emphasis on the interests and world views of the other peoples and states, not only of the Chinese themselves and their ruling dynasties. It tells that story from its beginnings 3,000 or more years ago. I start with the question of how and when there arose a 'China' that was identifiable and cohesive enough for other peoples to deal with it as a single sovereign entity. The story then continues to the very beginning of the twenty-first century.

The great advantage of telling it in this way is that I can do so in a narrative that does three things. First, it can give a sense of the sweep of the relationships involved, from the incursions into China of steppe horsemen around 200 BC to the Mongol conquests of the thirteenth century AD, from the first arrival of European travellers to China's decline, after 1911, into an object of the policies of the major powers, and on to later foreign reactions to the Tiananmen affair of 1989. Second, I have tried to explain what moved these minor and major foreign societies, how concerns with China fitted into their own major interests and views of the world. And thirdly, I outline some intriguing recurrent themes in this long period. China has gone through recurring cycles, from turmoil and disorder to strong central government and back to turmoil. Each cycle has apparently been driven by three major problems for the Chinese state: population growth, overly personalised central administration and volatile borders. The book discusses each in greater detail. Foreign attitudes, too, have moved in waves or cycles, from admiration or greed to disappointment, impatience, even contempt, and back again.

When a particular person, topic, or key moment needs more explanation than the main narrative allows, I have introduced mini-essays, or 'intermezzos', to elaborate on the main text. They can deal with anything from 'Confucius' to 'concubines'; from the last nine-teenth-century empress, Cixi, to the decisive influence on the 1941–5 Pacific War of the US Navy's ability to read 'Japanese naval codes'; or some character sketches on significant figures like 'Madame Chiang' or 'Deng Xiaoping'; all without, I hope, disrupting the unfolding of the main story.

The book therefore begins with a slow development rather than a specific date, but the end is the year AD 2001. That is because, while it concludes with a glance at the future, it is meant to deal with the cycles of the past, rather than current headlines about twenty-first-century politics and economics. At the same time, the tale which the book tells has, precisely because of the recurrence of some of its major themes, an – occasionally surprising – relevance to the contemporary world. For the dramatic rise of China in our own day, even the way in which it is dealing with its domestic problems, continues to be clearly interwoven with the economic and political relations between China and other countries and powers.

In the West, the whole story and culture of China has in recent times become a major literary industry. To be sure, fascination with China, and with the graces of Chinese architecture, art, ceramics and poetry, is hardly new. But the recent history of revolution and turmoil, plus explosive economic and demographic expansion, has sharpened more than cultural interest. It has created admiration, but also cacophonous worries about the growth of China's economic influence and potential global power. That has produced a large and varied body of writing, from travellers' tales, or writings on business and finance, to first-class academic studies of Chinese history, or to policy-oriented writings about how to deal with China in the future. Yet the ebb and flow of other states' and societies' interest, in the context of their own politics and outlook, in China, as well as of China's interest or lack of interest in them, has been relatively neglected.

That is the gap which this book tries to fill.

1

CREATION

From Origins to the Qin
1100 BC to 206 BC

T HE CREATION OF China is one of the more confusing and
turbulent stories in the history of the world. From its dimly
understood beginnings as a collection of tribes in the Yellow River
valley, it has grown to be perhaps the largest state of the globe,
comprising one-quarter of the human race; and one that has fasci-
nated the outside world for twenty centuries. It is a story of violence,
philosophical and political invention, shining artistic achievement,
and of often complex and subtle relations with outsiders.

Traditional Chinese views about the origins of China, of the
'Middle Kingdom', even of mankind itself, have been surrounded
by myths and legends. Human fossils have recently been found, in
China's west, that appear to be over 3 million years old; others can be
traced back to 1.7 million years ago. Yet others appeared in or near
the fertile Yellow River valley. Beijing man lived some half a million
years ago in north China, while Neolithic man came along around
10,000 BC.

How, from scattered fragments such as these, did a group, a
society, emerge that had enough cohesion to be given the collective
name of China? Modern estimates suggest that the societies we know
by that name started to emerge from perhaps 6500 BC, when early

Neolithic farming techniques came to the Yellow River valley – possibly from the Middle East. Population and settlements of course depended on food supply: dry millet and sorghum culture in the northern plains and, even more important, the rice culture of the south. Rice has always had special importance and in time has come to provide the staple of Chinese life and to shape its culture. In many places, folklore has rice as part of the creation myth. Both Hindu and Buddhist scriptures have much to say about rice and use it as a major offering to the Gods. In China, even today, tradition has it that 'the precious things are not pearls and jade but the five grains', rice being the first. It was an ancient saying, used even long after rice became the major grain among more than five.[1]

So food like sorghum and especially rice were available as a basis for the slow merging and amalgamation of ethnic and cultural groups that took – depending on how one counts these things – at least a couple of thousand years. No one thought of himself as 'Chinese' until, at the earliest, the first millennium BC. There was an 'empire' long before there was a coherent 'Chinese people', let alone a 'China' in a modern sense. China's political geography, too, has been a process of continuing change. From its earliest days there have been constant changes of space, borders – such as they were – ethnic groupings, even names. As late as 200 BC or so, in the first unification under the Qin dynasty, 'China's' territory was only about one-quarter of its modern area.

Cultivation was for long quite primitive, with villages established for food production, hunting or defence, and simply shifted to new sites as the local soil became exhausted. Houses were of stamped clay or, in the north, could be in warm and comfortable caves cut into loess cliffs. Wheat and barley seem to have arrived in the second millennium BC, probably again from Western Asia. Peasants raised pigs and dogs for meat and over time moved away from slash-and-burn agriculture and learned how to fire pottery and store crops. Only once crops could be stored did people create more permanent villages, surrounded by mud walls. In time they became socially stratified, with some families owning land, others remaining small farmers and yet others becoming slaves. Their people learned to use tools and ornaments, including rings and axes made of polished stone and jade, which became symbols of a chief's power and of his contacts with heaven.

Settlements gradually became larger, and acquired separate living and working areas. It used to be thought that China's first city was formed around 2000 BC in what is now Shandong province, a time when statelets first appeared too. But in AD 2002 Chinese archaeologists found the ruins of a city in Anhui province dating back to 5500 BC and containing complicated houses, some large buildings, a moat, workshops as well as pottery and jewels.[2] In most places, however, it may only have been after 2500 BC that villagers began to live in more permanent settlements and people began to move into Manchuria and central and south China. By then, too, came the beginnings of ancestor worship, probably to deal with the everyday gods among whom people lived. Furthermore, from maybe 2000 BC – some five centuries after the construction of the Great Pyramid in Egypt – a kind of painted pottery appeared that had some similarities with that found at sites in the Middle East and Eastern Europe.

At the same time, China remained largely insulated. The ultimate borders of its world were set by the surrounding deserts, oceans and mountains. Isolation, with its enormous consequences, was reinforced by constant conflicts with the warlike tribes and robber bands of Central Asia which, from perhaps 1700 BC, made travel from oasis to oasis perilous, if not impossible, while China was separated by some three or four thousand miles from the emerging civilisations of India and Greece. In any serious political sense, China was a land without neighbours.

Geography helped to shape the foundations of Chinese society in other ways. China has focused, from the start, on two colossal river valleys and their hinterlands (not unlike the connection of ancient Persia to two great river arteries, the Tigris and Euphrates). They have been central and continuing themes in China's story. In spite of occasional famines, China has managed an increasingly elaborate system of agriculture more and more based on irrigation. What the

Chinese produced was a highly labour-intensive agriculture which has been the basis of the social system ever since, producing, among other things, strong social cohesion. Even in very modern times, China has had to feed some 23 per cent of the world's population from only 7 per cent of its arable land.

The first hereditary dynasty seems to have been the Xia but it is only the second, the Shang, about which there is more solid archaeological evidence. They probably flourished from around 1700 to 1122 BC. Both they and their predecessors created the first central authorities and were able to use bronze metallurgy. In fact, by 1400 BC or so, bronze came into widespread use, for both weapons and ornaments. There is high art in the work of the Shang master craftsmen. Furthermore, the Shang cultivated silk and invented writing, which has been essential to Chinese civilisation ever since. Almost all their written records have disappeared, since they were kept on perishable strips of bamboo. But some inscriptions on bronze and elsewhere have survived, with words represented by pictures resembling their meaning.

The Shang cities were probably built in the eastern part of the Yellow river, dividing the lands into city states which were, in turn, governed from a capital that might shift from one city to another. Walled towns became normal, with those of the earliest cities some 10 metres high and possibly 20 metres wide. Buildings, whether for houses for ordinary folk, or palaces for kings, were made of adobe, or stamped earth. The kings themselves seem to have combined high priestly functions with control of the economy and leadership in war; and they were buried in subterranean cross-shaped graves, accompanied by implements and human sacrifices.

In the time of the Shang most people were farmers. People kept cattle, pigs and dogs and were keen on horses, some imported from northern nomad tribes. The rulers claimed rights over the land that these farmers used and imposed obligations, whether in the delivery of grain or service in war, or forced labour. In fact, since Neolithic times Chinese ruling groups have used massive manpower for public works like walls or canals, with little thought for the suffering of individuals.

(In the Second World War, Chiang Kai-shek was still doing much the same to build airfields.) There could also be hereditary serfs and some artisans were hired as servants of noble families. Ordinary people, on the other hand, lived in dwellings of bamboo or dried brick and typically had to spend three-quarters of their income on food, while the peasant villagers continued to live partly underground. Life expectancy was around 25–6 years and, given disease, famine, and backbreaking labour, it stayed that way as late as the nineteenth century AD. The nobles, by contrast, occupied important posts and there was a class of more or less independent lords whose lands developed into statelets, some thirty of them, even while the Shang ruler continued to be the religious leader and supreme lord. By the time the Shang period ended, their successors may have found themselves controlling some 3 million free men and 1 million slaves.

Warfare was normal. From the earliest times peoples from the north and west came into the Chinese area, where they were either absorbed or fought off. The Shang were regularly at war with their neighbours. Weapons were of bronze but the Shang period also brought a great innovation: the light, two-wheeled war chariot. The technology may also have come from outside, perhaps transmitted from the Hittites in Western Asia. At any rate, it allowed the creation of chariot armies. Fighting became fiercer and more bloody, as well as concentrated in spring and autumn, fitting in with the needs of winter, or of summer harvesting. The armies were led by aristocratic warriors followed by a simple peasantry, all threatened not only by adjacent lords but by barbarian tribes from outside.

The Shang also developed highly important ideas, including the worship of 'The Lord on High' who ruled over the lesser gods of the sun, the moon and various natural forces like wind and rain. They also nourished beliefs about ancestors that became fully-fledged ancestor worship later. The point was that after death the ancestors dwelt in heaven and would continue their active interest in the family. They were the proper people to intercede with the gods on behalf of their living descendants. In return, families had obligations to those ancestors. If such duties were neglected, the ancestors would be angry, stop their protection and disasters could ensue. This social and belief system was supported by sacrifices. In fact, human sacrifice was common, for none of these kingdoms and societies were modern humanitarians. Slaves might be killed in the inaugural ceremonies for a new temple. When a king died, dozens or hundreds of slaves or prisoners might be sacrificed in this way. Each year, too, a lovely girl would be selected and, clothed and jewelled, given as bride to the Yellow River. Frequently kings would have wives, even good friends, accompany them in death by being walled up alive in the royal tomb.

SEX, MARRIAGE AND THE UNIVERSE

From very early times, the Chinese view of the universe, and of mankind, was cyclical, like the seasons of the year. There could be order, but no teleology. The order of the universe was an eternal interaction of Yin and Yang, the negative and positive cosmic forces. They were in balance, as were the relations of heaven and earth, which mated in rain storms.

The sexual union of man and woman was a replica of this universal principle and of the interaction of the dual forces of nature. Although the Chinese family was patriarchal from very early days, it was the woman who was regarded as having special and magical powers, and as being sexually superior to man. It was she who was the guardian of sexual knowledge and the great initiator, with the man as an ignorant pupil. It is the woman who has an unlimited supply of life force and cares for her mate who, in sexual union, strengthens his life force by feeding on her plentiful supply of it. It is therefore the woman's feminine magic that binds man. Unsurprisingly, from very early days and in ordinary as well as erotic literature, woman is identified with the colour red, the colour of life, happiness and sexual potency, while the man is identified with the colour white, standing for negative influences, mourning, weak potency and even death.

Given these views it is hardly surprising that sexual relations, especially those of rulers, should have been surrounded by ceremonial and rites. Special court ladies were appointed to supervise the sexual activities of the monarch and his wives, to remain in the royal bedroom to record the timing and details of events, and keep the monarch advised of the state of health of any wife or concubine. Only wives could stay in the royal bedroom all night. Concubines had to leave before dawn. And in all classes, whatever the life of concubines or even lesser wives might have been before entering the family, virginity at marriage was essential to the prospects of a woman becoming her husband's principal wife.

Shang rule lasted some six centuries and ended when, around 1050 BC or a little later, the small state of Zhou and their allies crossed from the west into the Shang region, destroyed its army and killed the last Shang emperor. Once in control though, they adopted many of the ways of Shang life and government while greatly expanding their territory, not least towards the south and the Yangzi. Zhou kings, rather like their Shang predecessors, parcelled out land to members of their own and allied clans and to favourites. Since the Zhou were a minority group, they administered the realm by establishing Zhou garrisons around the country, in areas distributed as fiefs of the clans. The fief holder, or local lord, saw the land as belonging to his clan. The Zhou also came to form new walled towns, where their own nobility lived, separate from the indigenous folk beyond. That meant a replay of the Shang principles of government largely through city states, with the rulers seeing to it that the government of these statelets was in the hands of their kinsmen, or allies. The lords who were in charge of each city statelet commanded hereditary fighting men. There was a chivalric code of conduct, with similarly complicated rules of etiquette among civilians. The Zhou also developed further ceremonials about ancestors that amounted to full-fledged ancestor worship.

Each state claimed to control the chief elements of production: water, land and manpower. Society was sharply divided between the rich, the masses of the poor, and despotic rulers who claimed to own both land and people; but who found, as another emperor named Mao Zedong was to find in the twentieth century AD, that private plots meant higher production. Economic specialisation developed to the point where commercially based production could grow to exploit the market-places within the royal and lordly centres. Settlements and towns became larger, with a clearer separation of living areas and the workshops that were often outside the city. Iron production and urban handicrafts flourished. In time, within and alongside the priesthood there developed a social group of 'scholars', who were neither lower class nor part of the nobility. Outsiders to this society were, naturally, 'barbarians'.

Over the centuries the Zhou royal house lost power. The empire was just too big and its administration too clumsy and local lords paid less and less attention to the centre. The Zhou had always been a small group with nomadic tribes of Mongols, Turcomans and some Tibetans living around and among them, making the empire's population far from homogeneous. As Zhou allies spread around the country, they became more independent and less supportive of the centre that was busy fighting off rebels and raiders. Local lords therefore became ruling groups in their own right. Finally, in 771 BC an alliance of northern lords and nomad tribes attacked Xian and killed the ruler.

At the same time, since the modern concept of a clear frontier did not exist for another 2,000 years or more, the expansion and decline of Zhou rule raised new questions of legitimacy. In order to convince their peoples of the legitimacy of their power, rulers invented the idea of the 'Mandate of Heaven' – an idea that remained central to the underlying Chinese notions of authority into the twentieth and twenty-first centuries AD. Clearly, heaven reigned supreme among all supernatural forces, and determined human affairs. Kingship should be seen as an intermediate position between heaven and earth, the emperor, bearing the title 'Son of Heaven', being appointed to see to the people's welfare. It also came to seem logical that, while the head of government was the supreme intermediary between heaven and earth, if he neglected his duties or became corrupt, heaven would withdraw its mandate and confer it on someone else. When heaven's goodwill seemed to be withdrawn – drought or famine might be evidence for it – the ruler had evidently lost his supernatural qualities and therefore heaven's 'mandate' to rule. If an attempt to overthrow the emperor succeeded, it was evidence that the mandate had been properly transferred. If the move against the emperor failed, the mover had clearly been a mere rebel and deserved to die. It was a theory of government, based on the ruler's moral behaviour and on rule for the benefit of the whole population, that continued for centuries to influence politics. It also helped to shape foreign relations and, with it, a powerful sense of China's superiority.

These principles of social governance, politics and foreign relations, including the notion of the Mandate of Heaven and of the ruler as the link between heaven and earth, were only a kind of foundation on which others could build; especially two of China's – and the world's – seminal thinkers, Confucius (551–479 BC) and his disciple Mencius (372–289 BC), whose lives coincided with those of some of the greatest philosophers humanity has seen, like the Buddha, around 500 BC, and Socrates, Plato and Aristotle a century later in the Athens of Pericles.

Arguably the greatest of these, in China and perhaps beyond, was Confucius. It is he who developed the most influential of three more or less rival schools of Chinese thought. He was the educated son of a minor aristocratic family, and spent his life travelling widely among warring rulers, offering advice without having executive responsibilities anywhere. Only after his death did his disciples collect his ideas, many of which included thoughts not necessarily original to him, and set them down in the *Analects*, which have had lasting moral, political and philosophical influence. Their principles, dealing with the proper organisation of the family, of society and the state, with domestic order and relations with the outside world, were to underlie Chinese politics, and even foreign relations, for over twenty centuries. They have coloured many unspoken Chinese assumptions to this day. Even during Mao Zedong's Cultural Revolution of the 1960s, two and a half thousand years after Confucius, these ideas of family unity, deference to established authority and subordination of the individual to society shone through the general madness.

Coexisting uneasily with these views were the Daoists, students of a philosophy derived from Laozi, a sage traditionally assumed to have lived at much the same time as Confucius, in the sixth century BC.[3] These people argued that no centralised system was needed. The only thing that mattered was a focus on, and an understanding of, the mysterious force known as the *Dao*, or 'the Way'. While admittedly indefinable, it was nevertheless the source of all active power in the universe.[4] Politically, the Daoists wanted a return to primitive agricultural communities with a non-intrusive government that would make room for the people's spontaneous response to nature.

The third school of thought were the 'Legalists'. They held that individuals only respond to the fear of pain or, on the contrary, the desire for pleasure. Consequently, social organisation had to be built on strong laws providing for a clear system of rewards or punishments. Only the ruler and his responsible official – the Chancellor, who would draft laws – were the guides of society. Below them, the common people had just one duty: to live and work for the ruler and follow orders. To fail in a duty assigned by the emperor, for instance, meant punishment irrespective of the circumstances. It was quite meaningless to speak of anyone's 'rights' outside the scope of the ruler's demands. Only the present and not an irrelevant past, should be the guide for action. The ruler's authority should stem from the fact of his office, not from any moral example. Once his laws were in place, they would make the personal actions of the ruler himself much less relevant to the prosperity of the empire. Society could be managed simply by applying the rules set down. Capital should be socialised. The economy should enrich the state and strengthen its military power. It was a view with intriguing similarities to those of twentieth-century socialism in both China and the USSR. It was also certain to lead to arbitrary government, suspicion of, or even hostility to, intellectuals, and distrust of merchants and markets.

A Confucian Way of Life

What the Confucian analects provide – at least as interpreted by his followers and later generations – is a set of organisational but especially moral principles of family, social and political life, with special emphasis on the moral character of a ruler, whether of a family or a state.

Confucius emphasised order and hierarchy, with the common people entirely subordinate to the just ruler. Heaven remains the key, not as a divine tyrant but as the provider and embodiment of a system of law based on universal norms. Given that, the Confucian system was based on the idea of harmony as the basic principle of cosmic and human order. The ruler should not interfere in day-to-day affairs. Instead, he should rule by right conduct and by example. Right conduct was the basis not only of moral status but of power, and the ruler ought to be a father to his people. 'He who rules by moral force is like the pole star . . . When a prince's personal conduct is correct, his government is effective without issuing orders. If his personal conduct is not correct, he may issue orders but they will not be obeyed.' The ethical behaviour of the ruler would determine the moral and spiritual health of the whole of society. It followed, equally, that social reforms would come from the benevolent ruler, not from the common people (an assumption that might help to explain the Tiananmen massacre of 1989). Naturally, heaven might withdraw its mandate from the ruler if he ceased to carry out heaven's will, which obviously had to do with good government and moral conduct. While the mandate held, however, Confucius wanted rulers to preside over neatly subdivided domains where every individual was sensitive to his proper station in life. The individual should be subordinate to the community, and the kernel of social organisation should be the family, the state being merely an extension of the family concept.

For Confucians, the proper ordering of community and family life therefore depended on sincere ethical behaviour and the correct observance of traditional rules and public and private ceremonies. Harmony would be displayed in the behaviour of the superior man. It should have to do with self-respect, sincerity, benevolence and magnanimity; and, of course, good manners. Such qualities should be displayed in all facets of human behaviour. Family unity, obedience to the head of the household, and mutual love were high priorities. The family should be governed by its patriarch. The father should have authority over the son, the husband over the wife, and the elder over the younger brother. The same principle should govern the subject's loyalty to the ruler. Needless to say, it was equally the duty of the father, or the ruler, to repay such devotion with care and benevolence. Commercial values and profit motives, by contrast, were frowned upon.

Furthermore, since the ruler was the link between heaven and earth, and since heaven was, by definition, universal, the ruler who possessed its mandate was, also by definition, a universal monarch and all peoples, Chinese or others, ought to defer to him.

The Zhou dynasty lasted until around 400 BC, but was not a period of peace and quiet. As the political order of the land continued to become less unitary, with a complicated hierarchy of social ranks and land tenure, local lords became more absolute sovereigns in their own lands and there were major breaks. Moreover, the emperor's position became contradictory. On the one hand, since he was the 'Son of Heaven', he was the universal ruler. On the other, and in practice, the ruler's actual authority diminished sharply the closer one got to the periphery of the empire. For many purposes he was little more than a figurehead.

Meanwhile, too, iron-working and agriculture had greatly increased wealth and population numbers, though exact figures are not known. After 400 BC came a period of 'warring states', with disorder and social fragmentation which lasted until the middle 250s. Yet cities grew, became centres of culture and luxury, and attracted migrants. It was a period of major unrest, yet of increasing trade. The wars stimulated market exchanges, and commercial taxes did much for state revenues. At the same time, within states authority became more centralised. A professional governing class developed, too, partly because administrative competence was needed for the state to survive; and more attention was paid to recruiting able officials. Private ownership of land developed, also, as former noblemen and former serfs moved in to use the land of local natives. As families acquired land, the family head asserted a right to dispose of it or, at his death, to have it divided among his surviving sons.[5]

In time, these warring states lost all sense of allegiance to the central ruler, while wars also became much bigger affairs. Mercenaries were hired, and in the fifth century BC cavalry appeared, with rulers and commanders copying Mongol and Turkic neighbours. That made wars still bloodier affairs. In the north, some of the statelets continued to fight with the tribal groups outside the empire. By 300 BC or so, some of these Mongol and Turkic tribes, who had long mastered the art of fighting from horseback, formed a Xiongnu federation. As the empire's population grew, Chinese peasants migrated northwards and needed protection from the tribal raiders. So rulers set about building walls to keep the Xiongnu out. It was the start of a practice that would eventually produce the 'Great Wall'. The other development was the gradual amalgamation of these dozens, even hundreds, of tiny statelets. At one point there may have been a thousand of them. They gradually absorbed each other, and eventually only one was left.

The statelet that was left was the principality of the Qin, whose duke started to adopt the title of *Wang* or king. A great part of its population was not Chinese at all but partly Tibetan and Turkic. The rulers were, however, able to recruit almost the entire population to serve in war. In time, the Qin supplanted the Zhou ruling house.

By 221 BC they began the classical period of Chinese unification and the elaboration of Chinese culture. The central figure in this consolidation, the greatest Qin ruler and the first actually to call himself emperor, who ruled 'all under heaven', was Qin Shi Huangdi. He was born in 259 and came to the Qin throne at the age of thirteen. At first he ruled merely as king and only after escaping several assassination attempts[6] and eliminating lesser states, governed as emperor of what was becoming 'China' from 221 to 210 BC. His memory is still fresh in the Chinese imagination across the centuries. The very name of 'China' is probably derived from that of the Qin.

In the Qin unification, central government was strengthened at the expense of local barons. The process rested on very un-Confucian principles. Qin Shi Huangdi was in no doubt that he should govern the empire with legalist ideas and an iron fist. He was personally the apex of government and the great executioner of wrongdoers. Everyone else's power was held solely at the emperor's whim. The landed aristocracy was replaced by appointed regional officials. Aristocratic protest and rebelliousness were blunted by forcibly moving perhaps 120,000 of the leading families to new palaces at the capital at Xian, where they lived on stipends and the emperor could keep an eye on them. At the same time, the presence of this large aristocratic group attracted merchants and craftsmen so that the capital became a centre of culture and the arts.

Huangdi also ordered that city walls throughout the empire be torn down and private or clan weapons be collected and melted down. He fostered centralised bureaucratic power and a new official élite dependent on the ruler. There were novel principles of group responsibility, so that every member of a family or group was answerable for wrongs done by any other member. Which meant that an offender's entire family could be punished, even executed, for what he had done. All that brought a form of government that politicised every aspect of Chinese life, from commerce to manners, ideas and art. It extended to the elaboration of the distinctive Chinese systems of writing, art and literature, the development of a standardised script, and the first lexicon.

There were other practical improvements. By the time Huangdi came to the throne, much had already been done to codify laws and standardise weights and measurements, but he took these things further. He introduced a legal code uniform throughout the empire. He brought in a standard metal currency. He introduced great improvements in agriculture and irrigation.

At the same time, Qin Shi Huangdi was ready to employ talent from anywhere as he reorganised and centralised public administration. It was an early version of what the French, many centuries later, would christen the *carrière ouverte aux talents*. But there were harsh laws and tough punishments, too. Treason or rebellion could get you boiled alive in a cauldron, or torn apart by chariots or perhaps cut in two at the waist. Lesser offences merely incurred mutilation. At the same time, communications were enormously improved, not just by a great network of canals but by a huge 6,800-kilometre network of imperial highways. They held the empire together and could transport people, goods and food for the growing population. There was even a standard gauge for vehicles, so that wheels could fit into the deep ruts the traffic created in the roads. There was also the business of defence. Military technology was modernised, with the introduction of iron swords instead of bronze. In particular, the emperor extended the early, compacted earth versions of the 'Great Wall' for northern defence. It was a vast human and logistic operation, employing maybe 300,000 men, inevitably with a huge death toll. But he also waged campaigns of conquest in areas that are now Guangdong and Guangxi. His armies even reached Yunnan, Szechwan and the Red River delta in what is now Vietnam, and he tried to colonise new territories, for instance by having convicts shipped to them.

There was ferocious thought control, too. He ordered books of which he disapproved to be burned – mostly Confucian works, though he kept useful material on medicine or agriculture – and is said, notoriously, to have ordered some 460 scholars, also mostly Confucians, to be buried alive. At the same time, he was not just a great organiser, but something of a mystic. He had his palace built according to astronomical principles. He arranged his travels round the empire so as to correspond with the course of the sun; and his tomb was meant to echo the organisation of the universe. Perhaps his most famous memorial is this very tomb, only discovered in 1974, filled with valuables, given a vaulted ceiling and with crossbows installed to shoot at any intruder. The emperor was also followed in death by large numbers of his concubines. Workers were buried, too, so as not to reveal the tomb's secrets. Most famous of all, buried to guard him were some 7,500 life-sized figures of soldiers, each designed and sculpted as a separate individual, with his own posture and looks. They have become a major modern tourist attraction.

Yet the energy, drive, and human and material costs of Qin Shi Huangdi's reign may have been too much for the empire to sustain. There was deep resentment of the growing burden of military service, taxation and forced labour. The literate classes were resentful of thought control. When Huangdi died, rebellion reared its head. There were nobles who wanted greater power, populists who appealed to forced labourers, generals who wanted more freedom of action. A mere four years after the great emperor's death the second emperor, driven to despair, committed suicide and the empire started to collapse. A few turbulent decades later a rebel leader, Liu Pang, marched on the capital, dethroned the new young ruler, and proclaimed himself emperor in 206 BC. It was the start of the next dynasty, the Han.

2

FROM THE HAN TO THE SUI

206 BC to AD 581

H E   T O O K   T H E   throne with the name Gao Su around 200 BC, and began a time when the effects of Huangdi's conquests, the increase in China's wealth and population, and imperial unification made external relations much more important. It was more than 'foreign relations' in a modern sense. What began, and would continue for some twenty-two centuries, was not so much a process of continuing relations with foreigners as one of expansion and absorption of more peoples and territories into an increasingly large empire. The state the Han inherited from the Qin covered only a fraction of modern China, but in the two millennia from the time of Christ its population multiplied by twenty or more. Expansion was fitful and erratic; but the historical trajectory was one of growth and expansion. Nor was it solely a 'march of conquest', though a good deal of military conquest there certainly was. Instead, much of China's expansion resulted from two other factors. One was that almost imperceptible process of absorption and consolidation by which the Chinese had themselves developed from an aggregation of tribes into a single people. The other had to do with the attraction of China's growing power and wealth, and the dynamism of China and its culture, that made others, whether tribesmen from

Turkestan or Manchurian potentates willing to become part of a culture richer and more attractive than their own. Even foreigners who conquered China, like the Mongols and after them the Manchus, found they had to adapt to the peoples they were governing and became, over time, sinified. Most of all, one suspects, there was the sheer demographic weight of China's human mass, stimulating the ancient tendency of landless peasants to wander into fresh territory or Beijing's late-twentieth-century-AD policy of swamping the peoples and cultures of Tibet and Xinjiang by importing Chinese migrants.

In sum, the people who started to call themselves 'Han' expanded from the central Chinese plains in all directions, by population growth, by migration and by the conquest and assimilation of local tribes. China has always had more political and ethnic groups and states along its borders than almost any other state; and although the Chinese were ultimately driven out of Korea and Vietnam they did, over the centuries, expand where there was room to expand.

Chinese principles of government helped. For all the confusion and disruptions of the later Han times, not to mention the four confused centuries that followed, the great principles of China's unity, which the Han consolidated, were never again entirely lost. No less important, the emperor, responsible only to 'Heaven', remained a symbol of continuity and permanence, the paramount authority, the focus of service. He was expected to set a moral example, for, if he fell short, heaven would be angered. As not only the upholder of morality but the sole source of laws, his subordinates had a duty to warn him if his conduct became questionable or his policies looked like doing harm.

The Han ruled from 206 BC until AD 221, a period that is normally divided into two roughly equal halves. The dynasty began well. Emperors promoted economic recovery, reduced taxes, repealed unpopular laws and centralised controls. Over these four centuries they expanded their rule and trade in all directions. The most important of these rulers was the emperor Wudi, who came to the throne in 141 BC, at the age of sixteen, and ruled for half a century until 87 BC. Engravings show him with pronounced jowls and an ample girth and, like Qin Shi Huangdi, he became one of the greatest of China's emperors. He was even keener than his Qin predecessors on territorial expansion and military conquest, became known as the 'Martial Emperor' and spent huge sums, producing some imperial overstretch. He also created not just a state bureaucracy but, even more important, an ideal of empire and imperial administration that persisted. By the end of the Han period, and for all the 'times of trouble' that followed, centralised imperial government, resting on a loyal official class, its members appointed on merit and the recommendation of ministers, had become the unquestioned norm for organising human society.

What the Han rulers, and especially Wudi, did not stick to was Huangdi's legalism. Instead, the Han revived, endorsed and embedded Confucian principles.[1] So Wudi repealed the Qin edict ordering book-burning and revived the idea that imperial authority came from heaven, not merely from whatever laws had been decreed.[2] He strengthened the bureaucracy further and saw to the selection of candidates for his civil service. The way in which students trained in this way were appointed to government posts was the start of the famous Chinese system of civil-service appointments by examination that later became a model for the civil services of the modern Western world.[3] The later Han emperors themselves were given a proper Confucian education and most high officials came to be educated in the same tradition. The emperor was personally responsible for carrying out seasonal rituals to ensure good harvests and the people's welfare. Even the conduct of external conflict had its ceremonial structures and war itself became a religious activity, surrounded with rituals, divination, prayers and even the presentation of prisoners and booty before the ancestral altars of the victors. Beyond that, life for everyone was organised around public and private rituals, like those that appealed or paid homage to one's ancestors.

Peasant life began to be organised into a pattern that became the staple arrangement of Chinese rural life. People, perhaps as many as seventy family households, would form a village, with each family comprising five or so people. A group of villages would form a single market area, clustered within no more than a day's journey of a single market town. That tended to make the cluster self-sufficient not only as an economic arrangement but with a central township that functioned as a social centre, too.

Together with firm imperial guidance, and a growing population, came the elaboration of Chinese culture, including art, literature and rituals. A new genre of poetry developed, as in the poetical essays of Xi Kang, born sometime between AD 220 and 260. So did new forms of history-writing. The first dictionary was compiled. Tombs began to be carved into mountains and decorated with wall paintings and ceramics, many with intimations of immortality. Lacquer work and painting reached high levels. Astronomy and magic were developed and textbooks on arithmetic and medicine were produced. It was this common culture, and the common rituals, that established, even more so than bureaucratic or even military power, the unity that marked the empire. Furthermore, the Han fostered the spread of the Chinese language and written Chinese was widely adopted, or at least understood, by literate folk across large regions of East Asia.[4]

China's sense of superiority was further strengthened by a spate of Chinese inventions. By the time of Christ, the Chinese had already invented the decimal system, paper,[5] silk production (including rag paper made of silk), the horse collar and the plough-share. They had detected the circulation of the blood, and a brilliant scientist and mathematician named Chang Heng had devised the seismograph and – fifteen centuries before Galileo – even conceived of the world as a globe that could be looked at with a kind of grid. A few centuries later the Chinese would go on to invent gunpowder, matches and even the principle of helicopter rotors and blades. All that made China culturally dominant and disinclined to value the cultures of others.

Not surprisingly, many of the classics produced in this period continued to stress culture and virtue, rather than force, as the basis for successful rule. As that mysterious sage Laozi put it, for example, 'one who is good at being a warrior does not make a show of his might. One who is good in battle does not get angry. One who is good at defeating the enemy doesn't engage him.' This kind of thing affected not only China's domestic views and structures, but dealings with outsiders. Nowhere around the periphery of this growing civilisation could the Chinese have contact with any polity or group as civilised as they were. All of which was sure to make Chinese society even more strongly inward-looking and self-contained. It was also bound to produce a good deal of hubris, complacency and ethnocentrism.

PRIVATE LIVES

Han emperors promoted an austere Confucianism, but their private lives, and those of their friends and relations, were colourful. The first three Han emperors were bi-sexual, their sons and nephews engaged in incest and nameless cruelties, while many imperial relatives debauched every married woman that took their fancy. Wudi himself had a boyhood friend who remained his companion for many years. (Chinese society was indulgent about homosexuality.) He also had two other young men as constant companions until one of them killed the other for having transgressed with some of the ladies of the harem. Another favourite of Wudi's was an actor with a lovely voice, who shared the monarch with the Lady Li, the actor's own sister. When she died, Wudi wrote the famous poem:

No more is the swishing of silken sleeves,
Dust gathers on the smooth step of her court.
Her empty rooms are cold and lonely,
Yellow leaves pile up against the double-barred doors.
How do I long for that beautiful lady!
How shall my troubled heart find rest?

The major strategic imperatives that this empire had to address were its dangerous borders, especially in the north and west. The Central and Northern Asia regions, in the entire arc from Afghanistan to Manchuria, were after all highly unstable. Warlike peoples, like the Scythians, loomed just beyond the borders. Many others could be tempted by the empire's long, ill-defined and vulnerable borders, including Tibetans, Tubo and, later, Manchus. There were many others. Well before 300 BC one finds references to people as distant as those on the Amur river in the north. Han records mention the 'hairy people' of Yilou who washed themselves with urine.[6] The eastern coasts, too, were occasionally harried by piratical barbarians.

Around the middle of that first millennium an even more formidable threat had developed, this time from the nomadic horsemen of the northern steppes. These mounted nomads, riding bareback on horses, were highly mobile, with novel and superior military technologies, including the use of bow and arrow from horseback. In the Mongol tribes, especially, planning was careful and they could move at great speed, with fierce discipline. It is said that one Mongol chieftain, having trained his soldiers to shoot at whatever target he shot at, set them a test. He aimed successively at his best horse, his favourite wife, and his father's best horse. Each time, any soldiers who failed to follow his example were killed. Finally he took aim at his own father and took the throne himself.[7] These cavalry armies could select different points of attack and concentrate superior forces there quickly, while the slow-moving, defending Chinese infantry were thinly spread along the borders. So these attackers were apt to be much more effective in the frequent and difficult border wars.

The most important of these raiders were the Xiongnu, the nomadic people who roamed the steppes north and north-west of China and were ancestors of the Huns, who later became a legendary scourge of Europe. Most of the information about them comes from Chinese sources, so is predictably hostile. The reasons for conflict were not far to seek. The Chinese – especially landless peasants wandering northwards – wanted land. The Xiongnu needed food. The steppes were not fruitful, especially in winter, and the Northern people needed the food that more southerly Chinese peasants grew. The result was some four centuries of sporadic wars between the Xiongnu and the Chinese empire.

In time, this Xiongnu confederation managed to destroy some other tribes to the west and east and to absorb their people. They also had relations with the people of northern China, some of whom migrated to Xiongnu territory, whether as artisans and craftsmen or as trained administrators for the new Xiongnu state administration. The second head of the confederation, which he organised into an empire, was a remarkably able leader named Mao-tun. He murdered his father and, from 209 BC, forged Xiongnu unity and set about expanding his empire in every direction. He especially wanted to solve his people's food problem, and pushed into China's Yellow River region. But he could also see that if parts of China were to be not just conquered but absorbed, he would need a proper and equivalent framework of state authority, with a ruler who was also a Son of Heaven and due state ceremonial. The Xiongnu empire therefore developed a central administrative and religious organisation that threatened China not just by incursions but by actually attracting yet more frontier Chinese.

By 140 BC or so the Xiongnu had become a positive threat to the Han capital and its surrounding region. So Wudi began to take serious action to push them back and divide them from other tribal menaces, like the Tibetans. He also wanted to protect the caravan routes to the West, for by now the Han capital had become a centre of lively commerce from which the empire made handsome profits. It was decided to stop sending gifts to the Xiongnu to keep them quiet, and to look for allies. The Chinese heard from some Xiongnu prisoners of a nation that they had defeated and had fled westwards. Two years after assuming the throne, in 138 BC, Wudi decided to try to find them and persuade them to make common cause against the Xiongnu. He sent an enterprising and daring young man, the commander of the guards at the palace gates, Zhang Qian, on that diplomatic and information mission. Zhang set out across the fearsome Taklamakan desert, was captured by the Xiongnu but escaped. It took him thirteen years to return home, without promises of alliance but with a Xiongnu wife and a wealth of information about the peoples, territories and conditions he had found, including the formerly unknown realms of Ferghana, Bokhara, Samarkand and others. That intelligence whetted the imperial appetite for westward expansion, especially along the caravan routes leading through chains of oases through Central Asia to the modern Persia, Iraq and Syria. The two routes, north and south of the main deserts, became the famous 'Silk Road'. Wudi also learned of the existence in what is now Uzbekistan of a new breed of horse, a fast and powerful animal known as the 'Celestial Horse'.[8] It was just what Wudi needed for his cavalry.

THE HORSE IN CHINA

Domesticating horses probably began in northern China around 5,000 years ago. As early as the Shang dynasty (1600–1100 BC) horses were so valuable that they were buried with their owners, to be available in the next world. By the time of the Zhou, military might was measured by the number of chariots available to a ruler: much as, in the middle of the twentieth century, military power was largely measured in numbers of tanks or aircraft. As the Chinese empire grew, horses became more essential still for controlling land and people, communication and transport.

From the fourth century BC, the greatest threats to China came from the nomadic horsemen of the northern and north-western steppes. The Xiongnu, after them the Mongols and later still the Manchus created the finest cavalry armies in the world. So, by the time of the Han, around 200 BC, the Chinese had abandoned the war chariot in favour of cavalry. The wish to improve these forces led to campaigns like that of Wudi to acquire a superior breed of horse from Ferghana.

The history of the horse in China includes three major inventions and three periods of major change. The inventions were the horse collar and the breast strap as part of the harness – probably around 300 BC – and the stirrup. They made possible the full use of horsepower for horse-drawn vehicles without restricting the animal's breathing. (It was another millennium before breast-strap harnessing arrived in Europe.) The stirrup, which may have existed in India in the late second century AD, seems to have existed in China, probably independently, from the early fourth century. It was an invention of special importance, giving horse-men for the first time a secure platform from which to fight and making possible the use of shock weapons from horseback, such as the lance. That made it feasible to create heavy cavalry.

As early as the Han dynasty, horses were also used for display. Dressage was in use at the court and the performance of these 'dancing horses' became even more elaborate under the Tang, when hunting from horseback and polo became fashionable for both sexes.

As for the major changes, one was in the Han period (206 BC to AD 220) when, especially under the emperor Wudi, China went to great lengths, and expense, to acquire better breeds of horse from kingdoms further west. The next came during the Tang dynasty (AD 618–907) when horse breeding was improved by importing Turkish and Arab horses as well as by better breeding methods at home. The third change came during the Yuan (Mongol) dynasty (AD 1279–1368) when horse quality declined together with the Tang breeding programmes.

In spite of the horse's strategic importance, the empire's breed-ing methods were not often successful. Almost throughout the imperial period, therefore, China had to spend vast sums on acquiring horses from outside. Although the Tang tried hard, the effort declined under the Song, who had little equestrian tradition. Until the arrival of those marvellous horse soldiers, the Mongols, the empire had to rely on its ability to acquire horses from the north and recruit nomadic tribesmen or even tribes.

Campaigns to deal with the nomad dangers continued, at times with massive casualties on both sides. In 104 BC General Li Guang-li, brother of a favourite imperial concubine, was sent west across the Tarim basin but was repelled after many battles. Eventually peace was agreed with the Ferghana king, who agreed to come into the Chinese tribute system. So did other small states, including ones from Western Turkestan. Most particularly, General Li got some of those famously fast and powerful Ferghana horses, which became status symbols in China.

Inconclusive conflict with the Xiongnu continued after Wudi's death in 87 BC, with the Chinese suffering defeat from time to time but continuing to form alliances with various Xiongnu enemies and engaging in campaigns of sabotage and intrigue to create disorder and disunity among them. Not until 51 BC did the Xiongnu finally come to terms, classifying themselves as protectors of China's borders, and receiving generous rewards. Even then it took a further century for most of them to be persuaded to surrender and become a full tributary state.

Campaigns like these have consequences. Keeping the 'Silk Roads' open naturally meant securing them. That involved cultivating the small tribes that controlled one or other oasis, and denying their friendship to the Xiongnu. The Chinese therefore agreed to their independence – often as tributaries – in return for their toleration of, even support for, Han merchants and travellers. Some of these local chiefs might even be given some real or alleged Chinese princesses as brides, while the children of the chiefs were brought to live as comfortable hostages in civilised surroundings in China. Even then, the route might need to be policed. There had to be strongpoints, garrisons, and rest and supply stations for travellers.

Such concerns must have contributed to the strength of other probes. There was, for instance, the thirty-year career in the west of Pan Chao (Ban Zhao), perhaps the most famous Chinese general and administrator ever sent to Turkestan. He reconquered Xinjiang and even took an army of 70,000 men across the Tien Shan mountains and as far as the Caspian Sea. Never before had a Chinese force got so far westwards. One or two of Pan Chao's envoys may even have reached the Black Sea and modern Mesopotamia. These themes of nomadic challenges and the problems of Central and North Asia were important factors in Chinese politics and strategy for the next two millennia, and have strong echoes in modern Central Asia's wary relations with twenty-first-century China.

Not that the peoples to China's north and west were the only ones concerned about China's power – or magnetism. The 'Martial Emperor' spent huge sums on his wars and there were other campaigns in the south as well. The emperors extended China not only into the modern Guangdong and Guangxi, but into Fujian. Wudi himself brought Canton (Guangzhou), Guangdong, and most of China's south-eastern coast, under his control. Which gave him control of the seaborne trade of these regions, of the foreign merchants living and trading in their cities, and of their taxes. The Chinese got as far as Hainan Island as well as moving more fully into northern areas of Vietnam. There may have been efforts to set up a trade route to Burma (now Myanmar) and even efforts to establish contacts, by sea, with what is now Malaysia. The Chinese already had relatively advanced coastal seafaring skills, and were able to use the monsoon winds to carry vessels to islands off the coast. Power projection in the eastern and southern regions necessarily rested on these seafaring skills. A ship of the Han period has been discovered at Guangzhou with a centred stern-post rudder: possibly the first such steering mechanism anywhere. There was also Chinese penetration of Korea. Around the fourth century BC the Chinese had trouble with some warring tribes around the Yalu River – the modern Sino-Korean border – but it was the Qin who began real efforts to subdue Korea, and the Han who established colonies. In 108 BC Wudi conquered the several small states of western Korea which, among other things, gave the empire control of trade with the Japanese islands. Yet as soon as the Han faltered, the Koreans spread northward again;

though they also in time adopted Chinese models for Confucian training and administrative law.

In the west, too, especially in Yunnan, the tale is one of wars and rebellions, great loss of life, and eventual absorption. One reason for sending Chinese armies into south and south-west China, into Vietnam, Manchuria and Korea, was to dominate farming regions and their food supplies. But there were population movements, too, as Han migrants simply moved to Yunnan or even Annam and Tonkin. At the very time when the Roman consuls Marius and Sulla were battling their way in the Mediterranean world, Wudi was establishing an empire that stretched from Central Asia eastwards all the way to northern Korea.

Beyond conquest there was, of course, trade. Evidence about the earliest stages of such contacts is tantalisingly sparse. It seems likely that spices from the Indonesian archipelago became highly valued in Southern China quite early on. Similarly, Chinese silk production began very early and trade in it must have begun very early, too. Silk fabrics seem to have reached the Egypt of the pharaohs via ancient Syria or Phoenicia, for strands of silk have been found in the Nile region, probably dating back to around 1000 BC. There were other contacts across Central Asia. For a century after the death of Alexander the Great in 323 BC, Greek merchant groups seem to have flourished in ancient Baktria, in what is now Afghanistan. Here the Greek world met, for a short time, the nomads of the Siberian steppe and the world of the Indus River. In 1979 Soviet archaeologists discovered a vast and extraordinary golden treasure in a burial mound there – the locals had always called it Tillya Tepen or Hill of Gold – including Indian and Roman coins, Greek objects and a Chinese mirror.

What were the basic ideas behind all this? After all, no Confucian state, purporting to live by universal principles and responsible to 'Heaven', could reasonably create, let alone sustain, an empire without some coherent set of ideas and principles to explain and justify that. Principles might sometimes take second place to the

pragmatisms of time, place and occasion, as principles often do, but
what was the governing framework of ideas? How did these diplomatic theories and forms link into the practical problems of relations
with the outside world? For throughout the imperial Chinese system
the civil and military classes remained focused on the rituals of
keeping the life of Chinese society in tune with the universal order. It
was seen as a process in which influences and forces operated in
mutual harmony, in a scheme of complementary balance rather than
in opposition to each other.

In this context, people and officials continued to assume as self-
evident that the Chinese state, headed by the Son of Heaven, could
not be merely one state among many. Instead, it was the society of
the civilised world, with 'China' and 'Civilisation' two sides of the
same conceptual coin. China's ruler, being a figure of universal
significance and the embodiment of virtue, ought to be kind and
indulgent to those beyond his borders. They were, by definition,
'barbarians', in the obvious sense that they were not part of the
central civilisation.

The Chinese therefore thought of the world as roughly divided
into five hierarchic and concentric zones, with the imperial domain at
the centre. The outer circles were the barbarians, themselves divided
into inner and outer groupings. The outer barbarians were beyond
the empire's borders, but the inner barbarians were still within its
ambit, guarding the frontiers. Barbarians who gave tribute were given
the status of a dependent state, with a Chinese official in overall
charge, but with its local customs and way of life left unchanged. Like
the Romans at much the same time, and the British long afterwards,
the Han found it highly convenient to rely on the rich and powerful
local grandees. They were expected to pay tribute to the emperor and
that payment produced generous material rewards from the monarch.
Though the tribute system of the Chinese empire had its own
particularities, the custom of paying tribute to the central ruler
was in fairly general use in most parts of Asia and beyond as well
as, centuries later, in Europe.

*   *   *

The concept of the tribute system was reinforced by China's sheer size, power and sophistication. By the end of the millenium the empire's population had grown to perhaps 60 millions, and the tribute system was one in which China laid down the rules and controlled the forms and means by which foreign tribes and kingdoms could conduct their relations with China. It stressed ritual and ethical behaviour. In this system, outlying peoples sending missions to the empire were required not only to bring tribute but to behave in ways that reinforced both China's regional hegemony and Chinese views of themselves and their empire as the centre of human civilisation. That had to do not only with policies but with 'face', which had for centuries been a central element in personal, social and foreign relations. Not only was China the natural Middle Kingdom, set between heaven and the rest of the earth but the emperor, as the 'Son of Heaven', was the patriarch of a family of peoples centred on that China. So, in return for their tribute and their good behaviour, the foreigners were granted recognition and special trading rights. For the Chinese, such a system obviously gave constant reaffirmation of their view of the world. It demonstrated that beyond China there were indeed barbarians who were attracted by the brilliance of China's superior civilisation, its art, literature, theatre, porcelain and silks, and anxious to benefit from it. Many of these views continue to resonate strongly in the twenty-first century, among foreign admirers as well as Chinese.

Naturally, the foreigners' access would be subject to conditions. They would be granted permission to establish contact, and trade with China, provided that the local ruler, or his emissaries, demonstrated subservience to the Chinese emperor by bringing tribute. That tribute might be no more than a token offering of native products, but in presenting it, the tribute-bearer also had to perform, in the emperor's presence, the ritual acts of obeisance: the kowtow of three kneelings and nine bowings of the head to the floor. In return, the emperor would formally grant to the foreign ruler the status of vassal. An imperial letter of patent would be given to him, as well as a seal of rank and a Chinese calendar: all as symbols of acceptance into the Chinese world order. The new vassal would also receive generous gifts of gold or precious things. The tributary's legal trading privileges then continued for as long as the overall relationship was maintained. It was obviously a huge incentive to the foreigners to behave themselves.

There is also the tantalising question of early contacts between China and Europe. There do not seem to have been direct early contacts between Rome and China, though Rome did obtain, via various middlemen, not only Chinese silks but Indian pepper and Indonesian spices, which Rome may have paid for with glass or iron goods. There are also Chinese records that mention Western merchants claiming to have come from Rome. Certainly by the fourth century BC the Romans and Greeks began to speak of the 'Seres', the silk people, even though information about China, or any Chinese information about Rome, must have been, at best, fitful and garbled.

On the other hand, the Silk Road, and its goods, do seem to have brought some of the first indirect contacts between the Roman empire and China. In 53 BC Marcus Licinius Crassus and his legions were pursuing Parthians across the Euphrates – in modern Iraq – when the Parthians wheeled, stopped the legions in their tracks with a shower of arrows and unfurled great banners of silk. Their sheen, in that blazing sunshine, completed the demoralisation of the Romans. But the Romans also discovered that this wonderful stuff – much too wonderful to have been produced by the Parthians themselves – had come from the far side of Central Asia. The Romans at once sought more of this material, and Parthians and Arabs were quite happy to get rich as middlemen for East–West trade. Silk garments quickly became highly fashionable in Rome, so much so that in AD 14 the emperor Tiberius banned men from wearing it, lest Romans should become too decadent. By AD 166 the Romans sent envoys to the Han capital at Loyang and trading routes opened between south China and the Persian Gulf and Red Sea ports. Trading continued, with Rome and its empire sending to China glass, textiles, dyes, precious stones, metal, coral and amber; also gold, for the silk had to be paid for in precious metal. In return China sold not only silk but ceramics, lacquer, weapons and furs – and rhubarb, which many Chinese came to think was so essential to Westerners' digestions that threats to withdraw supply might be a useful diplomatic weapon. Trade profits grew, especially the profits going to the Parthian middlemen. So, by the second century AD merchants were using the alternative route: via India and by sea – very much the sea link that Alexander the Great had once thought of developing further.

But trade also started to illustrate a great imbalance. From the beginning the Westerners – traders and others – were highly interested in China and its ways. The Chinese, by contrast, showed no interest in exploration or travel to the far West, as distinct from some trade. Pliny the Elder, for example, noted that 'like savages, the Seres shun the company of others and wait for traders to seek them out'.[9] That contrast between the Europeans' desire for distant exploration and adventure, and the altogether more narrow and domestic focus of China, would continue.

SILK

Legend has it that sometime in 2640 BC the Lady Hsi Ling-shi, wife of the mythical Yellow Emperor, was having a cup of tea. A silk cocoon fell by accident into her cup. When she tried to fish it out, it came out as a long, single strand. The world had discovered silk. Later she introduced the loom as well. Whether that charming story is true is another matter. A small ivory cup with a silkworm design has been found, probably dating from 7000–6000 BC. And a silkworm cocoon has been found in northern China that can be dated to around 3000–2600 BC. Fragments and threads dating from the same period have been found elsewhere.

Other things are more certain. Silk was, at first, allowed only to the emperor, his close relatives and some of the empire's highest officials. The emperor himself probably wore a robe of white silk within the palace. Outside, he, his chief wife and his heir wore robes the colour of the earth, yellow. In time, silk came into wider and, later still, industrial use. It came to be used for musical instruments, bow strings and even rag paper as well as clothing. It was also used very early in the economy and in trade. For instance, a female Egyptian mummy, with strands of silk in her hair, has been discovered at Deir el Medina, near Thebes, and dated to the twenty-first dynasty, which ruled from 1070 to 945 BC.*

By the fifth century BC, at least six Chinese provinces were producing silk and each spring it was the empress herself who opened the silk-raising season. It was hard work, reserved for the women. The daughters, mothers and grandmothers of each household would devote much of each day to feeding and tending the silkworms, to unravelling the cocoons and to weaving, dying and embroidering the silk material. At the same time, the techniques and processes of its production were a state secret. To reveal the secrets or to try to smuggle silkworm eggs or cocoons out of China meant death.

As the use of silk became more widespread, the secret grew more difficult to keep. During the fourth century BC the Greeks and even Romans began to talk about the men of the kingdom of silk, and in the reign of the emperor Wudi, ambassadors travelled as far as Persia and Mesopotamia, carrying various gifts, including silk. Also during the Han dynasty, farmers might pay their taxes in silk and the material came to be used to pay officials. Indeed, it was used as a form of money: values were calculated in lengths of silk, as others might use gold or silver. In the meantime, around 200 BC, knowledge of how to cultivate silk reached Korea with groups of Chinese migrants. Soon afterwards, knowledge about silkworm cultivation reached India. Another Han embassy bearing silken gifts reached Baghdad in AD 97.

* Letter of 4 March 1993 in the science journal *Nature*.

Silk became popular in Rome. One report from AD 380 said that 'the use of silk, which was once confined to the nobility, has now spread to all classes without distinction, even to the lowest'. And less than thirty years later, when Alaric, king of the Goths, was besieging Rome, he demanded as his price for sparing the city not just gold, silver and pepper but 4,000 silken tunics. It is said that later, around AD 440 a Chinese princess married a prince of Khotan, a kingdom near the western desert, and smuggled silkworm eggs out, taking them in her hair. A century later, around AD 550, two Nestorian monks turned up at the court of the Byzantine emperor Justinian with silkworms hidden in their hollow bamboo staves. The Byzantines promptly created imperial workshops and from there, as well as by China's own exports, knowledge about silk continued to spread.

It is from these beginnings that silk has spread to become a favourite luxury textile around the world.

Still, no empire lasts for ever and the Han empire was no exception. From the start there were problems. Wudi's campaigns were very costly and used up savings that earlier administrations had made. His conquests meant sending out large armies of occupation which were a permanent drain on the imperial exchequer. These campaigns produced shortages of costly horses and too many peasants had to be conscripted. Foreign tribute missions had to be kept and expensively looked after in the capital. The hardships of the peasants became worse as the population grew, so that individual land holdings had to be reduced. Taxes went up even further but much of the revenue stuck to the pockets of officials and never reached the centre. Even the coinage started to be debased.

Inefficiencies and administrative weakness plagued the Han from the turn of the millennium onwards, as new emperors found it necessary to rely on court eunuchs, who promptly quarrelled with the bureaucrats. Gentry families started to form alliances among themselves, intermarried and became more powerful. If they could gain imperial favour by giving the emperor a lovely girl, she might become a favourite, even bear the emperor a son. Either way, she would be expected to bring members of her family into high office. Things became worse when the throne was inherited by infants, with the result that the infants' mothers often appointed people not on merit, but because they were family members. The resulting faction-alism and incompetence at the centre weakened the whole admin-istration. Popular discontent produced banditry and agrarian uprisings, with hordes of peasants eventually marching on the capital, murdering officials and in the end even an emperor.

By the middle of the second century AD the Han dynasty was bankrupt, socially and politically as well as economically. What remained was half a century of confusion, weak emperors, army rebellions, plots, murder and counter-plots. Local power grew further at the expense of the centre. Confucianism declined, too. The great landed families became too powerful for the central government to enforce controls over their local activities. They even started to raise private armies, while local gentry took control of recruitment to office in the imperial bureaucracy. As time went by, the gentry even became strong enough to stop enforcement of a new survey of land tenure, the basis of taxation.

Tribal groups caused more trouble, strong states emerged beyond the borders and there were further incursions of northern nomads into China. By AD 184, in addition to factionalism, corruption and treachery at the centre, two rebellions led by Daoist religious groups broke out, new kinds of nomads and raiders had appeared in the north and some nineteen Xiongnu tribes had to be settled in Chinese Shansi in return for their armed help. The fall of the Han really began with a conjunction of such rebellions at home with the continuing inability of the authorities to protect the northern borders.

Then came a Tartar conquest of northern Chinese lands. As the Chinese grip on the north and Central Asia relaxed, more nomads began to arrive, often adopting Chinese customs, tending to inter-marry with the Chinese and even setting up Chinese-type rule. For instance, there were the Tubo Turks who captured the capital and former Han centre of Loyang in 311, and took the then emperor prisoner. Then, around the middle of the fourth century the Tibetans started to organise themselves on military rather than tribal lines. Where the Xiongnu had just had cavalry armies, these Tibetans created infantry as well, even enlisting Chinese recruits. They quickly came to dominate some of the rich agricultural regions of northern China and went on, in the 380s, to campaign in the south, too.

As Chinese resistance in the north collapsed, the court fled south to Nanjing. Before the end of the Han, the heartlands of the empire's civilisation had been in China's north and north-west. By comparison, the lands of the Yangzi River basin, and the south, had been little better than colonies. But driven by these new pressures from northern barbarians, many people moved from north China down to the central and southern regions. So that after the Tartar invasions, the whole focus and hub of China moved further south, leaving northern China to be governed by non-Chinese for several centuries. By the time the Sui and Tang dynasties brought all these Chinese lands together again, areas like the (modern) Jiangxi and Zhejiang had become part of central China.

The final collapse of the Han dynasty was triggered in AD 189 by revolts in the army and the sacking of the capital and the imperial palace. The empire dissolved into anarchy. It limped on for a while, but the end came with a revolt by some great families in the north. In December AD 220 the last Han emperor abdicated and retired with appropriate privileges and a generous income. By the following year the dynasty was finished as an effective political body.

There followed three and a half centuries of unrest and short-lived administrations that coincided, as it happened, with the breakdown of the Roman empire and the resulting shambles in Europe. There were several centuries of confusion and disunion in China during which what had been a balance of power within the empire became a balance of weakness. Southern China, around and below the Yangzi, saw half a dozen dynasties in this disturbed period, while the north saw a number of other kingdoms. The period between the Han fall and the restoration of some unity under the Sui and the Tang is often regarded as China's 'dark ages'. It was a time of blood, not only in disputes between major groups but among ruling families. The population of the great Chinese cities declined and the population geography of China underwent permanent change. It was all very well to believe in the Confucian idea that the best government is when the people think they are doing everything for themselves, but it was more difficult to hold to that when one was living amid chaos and with, or next to, incoming barbarians.

The confusion of these centuries was somewhat limited by the arrival of Buddhism, with its quietist and other-worldly focus. Buddhism had been born in the sixth century BC in north-east India, and became the official religion of India three centuries later, after the conversion of the emperor Ashoka. It reached China, according to legend, following a dream by the Han emperor Mingdi in the first century BC but certainly filtered into China along the silk route or by sea. An envoy to India returned with sacred Buddhist texts and pictures but also with some Indian priests who explained their beliefs to the Chinese emperor. They introduced a mysticism wholly foreign to Confucian ways of thinking, so that for many Chinese it was not only foreign but gave little practical guidance. On the other hand, Mahayana Buddhism did have its charitable and humanitarian sides and could offer comfort in an age of turmoil. It did not, at first, attract large numbers, but as the post-Han turmoil went on and various rulers came to its support, it became much more widespread.

By the second half of the sixth century, though, the distempers of Chinese affairs had gone on long enough. It was another tough, hard-fisted general who created order, after usurping the throne of the non-Chinese Northern Zhou in 581.

3

HIGH CULTURE AND COLLAPSE

The Sui, Tang and Song
AD 581 to 1276

H E T O O K T H E name of Sui Wendi, re-established the centra-lised Han system and ideal of Chinese unity, and started conquering the south. At the same time he, his regime and the successor states that followed demonstrated what a multi-ethnic and even, to some extent, multi-cultural enterprise the empire was. Sui Wendi himself came from a partly nomad family and, as an old soldier, had served under the Turkic Tubo. His principal wife came from a noble family that had repeatedly produced tribal leaders. Both the Sui and the Tang intermarried with tribal families who became sinified, while the nomad rulers in northern China also adopted Chinese ways.

So, many of the successor states of the Han also had rulers and senior officials who intermarried with groups of non-Chinese no-mads. A number of these new dynasties were actually of barbarian origin, like the 'Northern Wei' dynasty that lasted from AD 386 to 534. The Tang were followed by the Liao dynasty of Khitan Mongols in China's north-east, that lasted from 907 to 1127. These connec-tions had their uses as, throughout the post-Han centuries, the Chinese borderlands went on needing careful management, and occasional raids from the Mongol regions continued. They also fostered the assumption in the Chinese bureaucratic, gentry and scholarly classes that whatever the political fluctuations of Chinese rule, sooner or later all incoming 'barbarians' would come to their senses and become sinified. At the same time, the more the warriors from the north became softened into Chinese civil society – a society whose Confucian principles, with their emphasis on rule by virtue, not force, produced contempt for things military – the less was the empire capable of serious defence. Conversely, the presence of the horsemen, as long as they remained horsemen, was all too likely to disrupt the Confucian ideal of stable social order.

Sui Wendi himself – his official portraits show a portly figure with full cheeks and a thin moustache – was a man of furious energy. He simplified administration and imposed a series of large-scale legal and other reforms. He unified the bureaucracy and demanded from his officials a military-style obedience. He was thrifty to the point of miserliness; though he did have to deal with an inherited financial crisis. He ordered land redistribution, and lowered taxes on both farmers and merchants, yet the increasingly efficient bureaucracy brought in adequate revenues. There was price control, especially on grain. He was also indulgent to both Buddhism and Daoism, even having a group of Buddhist advisers involved in his programme for the country's unification.

However, sections of dissatisfied gentry incited Wendi's son and successor to rebel. The emperor was killed and the prince succeeded as Emperor Sui Yangdi. He reorganised the Confucian examination system and undertook major projects, including the extension of the Grand Canal across the Yangzi to the Beijing region. It wholly changed food-supply patterns from the south to northern China by greatly improving transport facilities. It therefore improved northern defences into the bargain.

By this time, the dominant political force to China's north were the Turks, whom the Tubo tried to persuade to reconquer north China. The empire responded by setting various Turkic groups against one another and all of them against the Tubo. There were other campaigns against Tibetans. In fact, the emperor seriously overextended himself and became highly unpopular. He meddled dangerously in the politics of the northern tribes and fought wars in Korea, partly to forestall a Korean-Turkic alliance – and was defeated. The Grand Canal project, however beneficial in the longer term, cost far too many lives. Furthermore, and by no means least, he spent far too much on visible extravagance, leaving his government bankrupt. Rebellions flared in 613 and, while the emperor was once again absent, Liyuan, a general from Jiangsu province, occupied the capital. Five years later Yangdi was assassinated, and Liyuan took the throne with the imperial name of Gaozu and founded the Tang dynasty. So the throne was once again occupied by the scion of a non-Chinese family, this time one of Turkic origins.

The Tang lasted until 907 and became one of the most famous dynasties in the entire history of the empire. Tang China may well have become the richest and most sophisticated state in the world of its time. The dynasty presided over a period of cultural exuberance, and the brilliance of its poetry and ceramics has never been surpassed. Here, for instance, is Weng Tingyun's 'She Sighs on Her Jade Lute':[1]

A cool-matted silvery bed; but no dreams . . .
An evening sky as green as water, shadowed with tender clouds,
But far-off over the southern rivers the calling of a wildgoose,
And here a twelve-storey building, lonely under the moon.

Tang influence spread far and wide, into many parts of Asia and even as far as Europe and Africa. In the heyday of the Tang the imperial capital, Xian (Chang-an), was a great and splendid international metropolis, and something of a focal point for the entire Eurasian world. With its million or so inhabitants, it may have been the richest and most populous city in the world.

The Tang also set about further expanding the empire's borders. They continued the Sui practice of having a professional standing army. With additional support from auxiliaries provided by minority and border peoples, they resumed the steady expansion of the areas claimed to be Chinese, and of China's influence, not least in the vast lands to the west. A number of the western or north-western tribes and principalities made their peace with China, or were defeated as the Tang absorbed much of modern Xinjiang. At one point Chinese prefectures could be found as far afield as Samarkand. They defeated the Koreans, and moved south again to the region of modern Vietnam. At the peak of its power the dynasty controlled large parts of Central Asia all the way to Iran, as well as Manchuria and much of Korea. It also became quite good at using one set of barbarians to fight another.

Not everything, of course, was done by war. There were, for example, the Tubo, the ancestors of the modern Tibetans, who lived on the Tibet-Qinghai plateau. Early in the seventh century a strong man, Songtsan Gampo, united the tribes into the Tubo Khan kingdom, proclaimed himself king and made a point of seeking an alliance with the Tang. In AD 634 he twice sent envoys to the Tang court, suggesting that the emperor send one of his daughters to marry him. In 641 one of the princesses duly did. A century later another imperial princess was betrothed to yet another Tubo king. Later there were formal treaties to define borders.[2] Others, too, made agreements with China. For instance, there was a nomadic tribe living in the Altai mountains, the Tujue, who had formed the Tujue Khan kingdom and whose armies often harassed and plundered the central China plains. The Tang emperor Daizong (756–61) finally gathered an army, defeated them and they became a Tang tributary.

Or again, the north-western region of Xinjiang – larger than modern Germany, France and Italy combined – had come under vague Chinese control in the first century BC, but after AD 220 it was dominated by Huns and Turkic tribes who continued to own it for roughly another ten centuries. By the middle of the eighth century the ancestors of the modern Uighurs, the Huihe, united to form a powerful kingdom that maintained friendly relations with the Tang and three Tang princesses married Huihe khans. The Huihe twice even sent troops to help the Tang quell rebellions.

China did more than put pressure, or even state influence, on peoples scattered around its frontiers, in regions often well beyond its effective political power. There was nothing resembling the later Western notion of an international society of states which were legally equal, and the empire went on refining the 'tribute system'. Other societies continued to make formal obeisance to the emperor and in return gained stature and received concessions and help. That extended to Korea and parts of Vietnam. Envoys came from distant regions, even from Japan. It was indeed a multi-ethnic and cosmopolitan empire.

The larger world around China was also changing. One of the most important shifts came just after the Tang came to the throne, when the tidal wave of Islam altered political patterns throughout Asia. Here was a militant religion, whose armies carried its mission with fire and sword across from its beginnings in the Arabian peninsula to the entire Middle East, North Africa and deep into both Europe and Asia. Moslem expansion began in the seventh century. Persia fell to the Moslems in AD 642 and Byzantium was hard pressed by the Moslem onrush. There were major effects in China, too. Persian refugees were made welcome and the son of the last Persian king even became a general in the Chinese imperial guard. More importantly, ambassadors from the Moslem caliph appeared at the Tang court. Yet by the 750s the Tang had become overly ambitious, especially in the west. In 751 some Central Asian states allied with an Arab army to defeat Tang forces at Talas, near Samarkand. That ended Chinese rule in Turkestan, but not friendly relations with the caliph. By 756 Arab mercenaries even marched east to help the emperor. Some settled in China, intermarried there, and were the first set of Mohammedans to come into China.

Islam continued to spread as the Moslems took over Afghanistan, north-west India and important parts of Central Asia. In the two centuries after AD 1000 it was the Turks who rose to political dominance in this new Islamic world and spearheaded further Islamic advances against Christendom and Hindustan. Moslem expansion continued further, also producing a remarkable level of high civilisation, in poetry, arts and the sciences.[3] At the latest by the twelfth century, there were Moslem states and influences all round China's periphery. There were Moslem dynasties and states in India and the East Indies, as well as through Central Asia as far as Chinese Turkestan (now Xinjiang).

This Islamic explosion had multiple effects. It promoted two-way East–West trade across Asia, whether by sea or by caravan, or across the Mediterranean. Christian merchants, especially the Italians, could trade with Egypt. Cities like Naples and Amalfi, not to mention Venice, were often on good terms with the Saracens, from whom they imported goods like Chinese silks. However, the assault on the Christian world would also produce, as these things usually do, a profoundly important strategic reaction. In Europe, that had far-reaching effects by no means confined to the crusades to free the Holy Land. More importantly, there also came efforts to find the vulnerable flanks of the new Moslem imperium, and allies in the fight against Islam. That meant probes into East Africa to search for the legendary figure of the Christian king, Prester John. At Jerusalem, where pilgrims and travellers congregated, there were repeated rumours about this fabulous figure. The same drives encouraged approaches to Persian or Mongol princes and, together with the search for gold and slaves, would come to give a further impetus to exploration and conquest that would bring Europeans to the shores of China.

For states, external effort always depends on getting things right at home. In the case of the Tang, after dealing with some early local insurrections, and difficulties with powerful provincial governors, they set about once again confirming strong, unified government. Not only was the civil-service examination system tightened up, but officials began gradually to replace the old aristocracy. Around the mid-seventh century the entire population – by then some 50 millions or more – was governed by no more than some 13,500 officials. The Tang legal code was put together in 642 and proved influential far beyond China's borders, in Vietnam, Japan and Korea. Early Tang emperors saw to food and welfare. Agriculture was fostered and waste land brought under cultivation. At the same time, the centre of gravity of the empire continued its shift to the south, where rice-planting started to be organised for double harvesting while in the north, triple harvesting of sorghum became usual in the Yellow River valley. Taxes were adjusted so that every person owning land would pay three kinds of tax: tax in grain, tax in the form of materials like textiles, and tax in the form of labour or military service. Manufacturing was encouraged, too, in the form of iron-smelting, weaving, pottery and other things. Porcelain, in particular, achieved an excellence rarely equalled anywhere, for instance with the blue-green celadon ware from what is now Zhejiang province. Tang multi-colour ware, with its blues, browns, whites, yellows and greens became justly famous. The textile industry was also fostered, with silk from Henan and Anhui becoming especially noted for its high quality. Cotton, too, was grown in half a dozen provinces. Manufacturing and commerce needed transport, too. So the Grand Canal was further extended and roads were improved, while ships from all over South-East Asia and as far away as Africa came to China with spices and jewellery to exchange for Chinese silks and porcelain.

Above all, Tang rule was remarkable for refinements in scholarship and the arts, notably in poetry and literature. Society came to admire the Tang ideal of the universal man, who might be a statesman but also a poet or painter. Here were ideas that continued to resonate; even Mao Zedong saw himself as a poet as much as a statesman. Historical writing was promoted. There were major achievements in astronomy and medicine, and China published the world's first pharmacopoeia. Block printing was introduced, music and dance were refined. So was painting and, not least, that famous Chinese art form, calligraphy.

The Tang became notable for tolerance and intellectual curiosity. They re-emphasised Confucianism but also welcomed Buddhism, which made considerable gains, in spite of language difficulties.[4] There were pioneers, like the monk Xuanzang, who in the early seventh century made a seventeen-year pilgrimage to India to bring back a large volume of Buddhist scriptures, then spent another dozen years translating them. Interest in Confucian classics revived, too, and

Religious Toleration

The Nestorians were only the first of a long line of Christian visitors and missionaries to reach China. By the middle of the first millennium AD, there were Nestorian Christian bishoprics at Samarkand. The Chinese emperor Taizong granted the first Nestorian missionary permission to preach in 635; but the first proper attempt at conversion in China itself came when a certain Olopen built the first Nestorian church at Xian in 638. Later, the emperor Gaozhong even awarded him the title 'National Priest'. The effort was reinforced a century later, after the Nestorian patriarch appointed the first metropolitan for China and energetic new missionaries arrived from the West. Chinese records say there were at least four Byzantine embassies between 640 and 750; and by 790 the metropolitan at Siangfu (on the River Wei in modern Shaanxi), had a staff of six bishops and nine monks. Although most foreign religions were banned from China in the later days of the Tang, Nestorian beliefs and a priesthood survived, especially on the fringes of the empire, for instance at Kashgar. Indeed, by the 870s an Arab traveller is said to have reported that there were a lot of Nazarenes in China and the emperor seemed well informed about Christianity. By the eleventh century there seem to have been no less than four of these metropolitans in China and Mongolia.

Manichaeanism also found its way to China. It was an offshoot of Christianity born in Persia in the third century AD. In its Albigensian form it was fiercely persecuted in Europe as a wicked heresy, but it found refuge in Central Asia and China, where it became established under the Sui and Tang dynasties.

the Tang period saw some of history's greatest Confucian scholars, as did the later Song. The most influential of them in that later period was Zhu Xi, who in the twelfth century produced a synthesis of Confucian thought with Buddhist and Daoist ideas that became the official ideology from late Song times until the later nineteenth century. In particular, it gave fresh stress to the obligation of obedience of a child to the father, of the wife to the husband and, of course, of the subject to the ruler.

The Tang also cultivated diplomatic relations with the states of western Asia and welcomed visits from their priests and merchants. In fact, the world of the Tang and, after them, the Song became a magnet for all sorts of foreigners, not only religious missions or traders. Most of the emperors were remarkably open, even welcoming, to foreigners and foreign influences. People from Japan,[5] Korea, Vietnam, Persia and western Asia came to China's cities and the Tang empire was hospitable to communities of Nestorians, Zoroastrians, Hindus, Jews, Arabs, Persians, Mongolians and others. Nestorian Christianity, founded by Bishop Nestorius of Constantinople, may have been outlawed in the West, by the Council of Ephesus in 432,[6] but many believers fled east to the modern Persia and beyond.

Naturally Islam, too, made its appearance. A few years after the death of the Prophet Muhammad a mission, led by the Prophet's own uncle, left Baghdad to bring Islam to China, where the emperor allowed the establishment of China's first mosque – the 'memorial mosque' at Canton (modern Guangzhou). A small group of Jews also arrived, from India and bearing tribute, and built a synagogue at Kaifeng. All these groups were free to pursue their own religions even if they challenged Confucian verities; and all were tolerated, apart from brief bouts of oppression.

Chinese trade links also flourished in the Tang period. China's own shipping seems for long to have concentrated on coastal traffic and domestic waterways, with ocean shipping being left to the barbarians. Some of the Chinese vessels were large, said – almost certainly with great exaggeration – to be up to 700 tons with up to five decks. They were alleged to have crews of dozens, even a few hundred. Many of those crew members were born, lived, married and died on board. Such vessels were used to carry cargoes of grain from the south to the northern provinces threatened by the nomads, raiders and Koreans. But between the fifth and eighth centuries various Arab, Persian and Singhalese merchants began to extend the ancient shipping routes between Mesopotamia and India into southern China, using medium-sized ships of up to 500 tons. The Chinese noted that, when these ships went to sea, they took homing pigeons with them so that, in case of distress, messages could be sent.

Through such exchanges Chinese influence on others became quite profound, and considerably more important than the outsiders' influence within China. To be sure, Japanese dance and music became popular among the Chinese, as did delicious foreign fruit, like dates from Persia, not to mention spices from the East Indies. But it was much more usual for others, like the Koreans, to adopt Chinese ways and examples. Indeed, Korea also became China's greatest trading partner, while Korean students came in some numbers to China to study. Tibet came under still greater Chinese influence. Japan, loosely unified by AD 300 or so, was also deeply influenced by China, with Japanese monks coming to China to study Buddhism and Chinese students travelling to Japan in turn. In fact, the very word 'Japan' may stem from the Chinese pronunciation of the Chinese characters for 'Nihon' (Nippon).

Yet the Tang dynasty began to weaken as early as the eighth century. Expenditure on the military and foreign effort became too heavy. Court politics became more volatile and dangerous, emperors more arbitrary, often self-indulgent but also more insulated and remote from everyday affairs. Court factionalism increased. China's only female monarch, Wu Zetian (684–705) proved to be a skilful if murderous politician who ruled China with machiavellian ruthlessness and an iron hand. Oval-faced, with a tiny mouth, she began as the favourite concubine of the emperor Gaozong (650–83), had her competitors tortured and killed and started to govern the country herself after Gaozong had a stroke. (She also, rather like Catherine the Great of Russia, kept youthful lovers into her later sixties.) Soon after that, the imperial house became less ruthless but more ineffective. By mid-century the emperor Xuanzong (712–55), who had started by ruling wisely, caused vast offence by his extravagance. Even worse was his obsession with his concubine, the Lady Yang, to the point of quite neglecting his duties.

The Lady Yang was a famous beauty and the emperor loved to admire her naked body and generous curves as she played in the bath, granted her every wish and even took her sisters into the imperial harem. In a system in which everything depended on the person of the emperor, the imperial government decayed. There was a particularly important rebellion from 755 to 763, led by an adopted son of Lady Yang herself, in which the emperor's own troops blamed the imperial decline on Lady Yang and demanded her head. The emperor, in tears, had to comply. But the revolt militarised China, destabilised imperial rule and the dynasty never fully recovered. After it, government supervision and taxation of trade broke down, and the later Tang ceased altogether to be in control of economic affairs. Things got worse as wars broke out once more on the frontiers, while weakness at the centre necessarily brought a revival of power in the hands of local lords and potentates. In time, these people had to be allowed to raise their own troops or collect taxes. There were peasant uprisings over reviving problems of taxes and land. In other words, the empire dissolved into something like anarchy. Corruption reigned. Peasants were oppressed. Banditry increased. Turkic and other non-Chinese occupied much of northern China. After much turmoil the end came in AD 906 with a fresh army rebellion, and the last Tang emperor had to abdicate.

CONCUBINES, FAMILIES AND POWER

Concubinage is a very ancient practice, extending far beyond China and throughout much of Asia. It rests on some rather simple ideas. Many men, in most societies, find more than one woman desirable in their adult lives. The possession of many women has often been a sign of success and status.

In China, from ancient times families sought to have a large number of children. Having children implied divine protection while the childless family had obviously been punished by supernatural forces. Having sons was of special importance, for it was sons who would look after the family and fulfil its duties to the ancestors. That was true at all levels of society, with one important exception. Inheritance laws said that property, including land, must be divided among all sons, not just inherited by the eldest. For a peasant's land to be subdivided among several sons might just mean that none would have enough and all would be poor. It was an important limitation on family size.

On the other hand, it was natural for senior or rich Chinese to have concubines, most especially so for the emperor, for whom many children — in a period when by no means all children survived to adulthood — were essential. Having many sons not only gave assurance of legitimate succession but also provided a choice of successors.

Accordingly, rich and powerful men had several concubines. Emperors might have dozens, even hundreds. So much so that the emperors' advisers and minders often encouraged monarchs in sexual practices that involved conserving energies by seminal retention. That would mean that the man could absorb the woman's inner life force — thereby improving his health and life expectancy — without losing his own. It limited the amount of sperm allocated to any single wife or concubine. And it enabled the head of the house to deal with many of the women in his household. That was sometimes very large. One emperor of the Tang dynasty was said to have had 40,000 women in the palace; and even by the end of the Ming Period, around 1640, there were still some 9,000 of them.

Young women might become concubines for a number of reasons. At one end of the social scale it was a great honour to have a daughter selected as an imperial concubine. In any family, to be a concubine could be the start of years of misery under the tyranny of the senior wife. But it could also be the path to security, standing and the possibility of great political power as the consort of a governor or a prince. An imperial concubine might even hope to be the mother of the next emperor. A favourite concubine could also have considerable influence over the emperor and therefore over the court and the empire. Even at the bottom of the social scale, to be the mother of the head of the family could confer great and arbitrary power over the entire extended household.

It would therefore be quite wrong to think of concubines as invariably victimised and oppressed. Concubines could in principle be repudiated; but as long as they were members of the household, their position was protected by law. They were fully entitled to the protection and support of the master, and their children were entitled to a full share of the family fortune. The head of the house had to respect his concubines' rights and to fulfil his many duties to both wives and concubines. That meant not just economic support, but regular sexual satisfaction. It was also up to the husband to establish and maintain a balance between his duties and affection for his wife or wives and their acceptance, in turn, of his affection and duties to his concubines.

Not only that, but the head of the family might suffer if he failed to cater for individual preferences of his womenfolk, and the relations between them. If a man failed to maintain harmony in the household, he might even suffer professional or financial ruin, for the authorities usually kept in mind the ancient rule that a man who cannot keep his own house in order is not fit to hold a responsible position. Creditors, too, knew very well that a badly managed household is often one that gets into financial trouble.

In modern times concubinage is supposed to have been banned. But there is much evidence that it none the less continues, unofficially, in some parts of China.

There was an interval of almost half a century of chaos and warlordism before the next firm dynasty could take hold. It was once again a strong man who brought an end to turmoil. In 960 the commander of the palace guard was made emperor when his men forced him to take the throne. It was all done quite peacefully, founding the Song dynasties, which lasted until 1279. If court portraits can be trusted the founding emperor, Taizu, was a stocky man with a handsome, round face. He began with much broad consent to the peaceful reunification of an empire sick of confusion. Moreover, not only did the Song reunify much of core China and try to rule in peace, they renounced expansion into other lands. Generals were pensioned off and replaced with civilian officials. The best troops were brought back to the centre and the bureaucracy strengthened with more graduates. The north-east was left to the Khitans, who governed Manchuria. The north-west was left to the Tibetans. The westward land routes through Turkestan were neglected. A delicate diplomatic balance developed between the Song and the northern Jin empire, in which the Jin did not try to conquer the rest of China but the Song paid tribute to them on the grounds that it would cost less to pay than to create an army good enough to fight them. Instead, the Song quickly absorbed some of the smaller states in southern China and set about extending their influence as far as Vietnam and even Indonesia. The military arts were largely neglected. They were anyway difficult to accommodate in a newly Confucian period of civil and artistic creativity. These first and 'Northern' Song, whose rule lasted until 1126, presided over another uncommonly productive and civilised period when peace encouraged higher food production that fed into considerable population growth. It was a creative age, too, with inventions and high achievements in the arts, making the Song period another high point in China's cultural history. Its standards, whether in literature, theatre or most especially in ceramics and painting, have seldom been surpassed. Printed books appeared, and had an immediate impact on education and literacy. Civil-service examinations were tightened once more after the previous turmoil. The capital, Kaifeng, at the junction of the

Yellow River and the Grand Canal, and now supplied by cheap canal transport, became a sparkling centre of city life, whose population grew to possibly one million. It even housed some industry, like ironworks and the production of armour and weapons of iron, even early steel, not to mention gunpowder and early bombards.

However, military weakness always has a price. In 1126 the nomad cavalry of the Jin rode south to capture Kaifeng. Shortly afterwards they crossed the Yangzi to sack Hangzhou and Ningbo. Soon the Song were forced to abandon northern China entirely, and to move south. Within sixteen years these now 'Southern' Song had to agree to become vassals to the Jin. By now considerable numbers of Chinese in northern China found themselves ruled by non-Chinese. So the rule of the Jin produced a kind of dual polity. The new rulers of what had been the Northern Song had to govern Chinese by accustomed Chinese methods and rely on Chinese officials to do it. However, in their own still more northerly areas, government continued to be by men on horseback administering their own people in the old tribal ways. That eroded the old sense of clear distinction between Chinese and barbarians.

At home, though, the Northern and later the Southern Song built up efficient centralised government. Once again there was an effective bureaucracy manned by civilian scholar-officials. Civilian regional governors were appointed by the centre. Power was more concentrated in the hands of the emperor and his palace bureaucracy that it had ever been. By the twelfth century the population of the Southern Song, perhaps 40–50 million souls, were still administered by a mere 13,000 or so officials, 8,000 of them serving in the capital. Beyond, there was a mere handful of officials running each of China's 170 districts. But printing and education continued to spread, more and more people took the examinations so that the scholar class became much larger than the growth of state posts to employ them. So scholars who did not enter the bureaucracy tended to become local authority figures and a separate gentry class, able to deal with local problems like floods or food shortages, even some criminal cases.[7]

Growing wealth brought a new mercantile class of wealthy com-
moners. They promoted private trading, so that government office or
landholding were no longer the only ways to prestige and wealth.
Cities grew and by 1200, for example, the southern city of Hangzhou
was the economic centre of the empire and probably the world's
largest city, covering maybe seven square miles, with at least a million
(possibly 2 million) people. That was at least forty times as large as
London, then with 25,000 inhabitants. That growth was at least
partly fuelled by trade that imported foreigners and highly desirable
goods. Merchants came from many parts of Eurasia and the Middle
East, and Persian and Arab traders and shops could be found in many
parts of the empire. Foreigners were even given tax concessions to
encourage trade, and were allowed to settle and marry Chinese
citizens. Some were recruited into the Chinese bureaucracy. A couple
more Persian princes even settled.

Population growth increased yet further the importance of the
family as society's central building block. In the upper classes,
especially, the extended family was still the basic social unit, with
several generations living together. Absolute respect was given to
the family's moral and legal code in all matters. Moreover, since the
family line could only be carried on by boys, great weight attached
to the bearing of sons – a view that has continued into the twenty-
first century. While these folk, and the new middle class, lived in
larger homes, the working classes had tenements. If they were
lucky, they could live in buildings of eight or more storeys, rent
being paid to the landlord or the state. Instead of modern bathrooms there were buckets, emptied each day to fertilise the fields.[8]
Lower classes lived in still more hand-to-mouth fashion as labourers, pedlars, prostitutes or even criminals. In the countryside,
most people were tenant farmers or agricultural labourers, or even
serfs cultivating the Yangzi manors of the rich. In a good year,
ordinary men might make ends meet. In a bad year there would be
debt and famine, with small farmers being forced to sell their land
and sometimes their children, to become bandits – or to commit
suicide.

In any case, more commercial activities needed greater reach. A variety of contacts in travel and trade therefore continued throughout these centuries. China could, of course, continue to trade through the Arabs who had, by the tenth century, not only revived the ancient trade links between the Mediterranean, the Middle East and the Indian Ocean but extended it into a trading system from Alexandria to the East Indies and the China coast. That was especially valuable for the East Indies spices, like pepper or nutmeg, cardamom, balsam and myrrh, some of them used to disguise the taste of foods before the days of refrigeration but all of them a rich man's delight not only for cooking but for medicines, fumigants, scents and soaps. Foreign trade became a major business, especially under the Southern Song, with the exchange of spices for Chinese silks between the East Indies and south China.

At the latest by the tenth century, Chinese merchant junks were trading at South-East Asian ports and Ceylon, Vietnam, the East Indies and even India saw Chinese visitors. So, while Moslem traders came to south China, Chinese trading junks sailed to the East Indies and South-East Asia. They established local agents and some Chinese even stayed there. Indeed, so valued were the spices that the normal Chinese exports of silks, porcelain and copper cash were not enough to pay for them. The Chinese therefore resorted to inventions like paper money and even promissory notes. The government carefully controlled and taxed this trade, which was chiefly centred in places where, since the Tang, Arabs had been allowed to reside. Not the least important feature of all this was that trade naturally also brought information about far-away places, including not only Africa and Zanzibar but Egypt and the countries of the Mediterranean, including for example Sicily. The first Song emperor made a practice of visiting his shipyards. And the Southern Song even created a real navy, at first to operate on inland waterways and to protect their new river border against the northern invaders. They developed armoured vessels driven by treadmills and paddle wheels, manned them with crossbowmen and used them for fighting on rivers and canals. In time, there were hundreds of such ships and perhaps as many as 50,000 men manning them.[9]

Towards the end of the twelfth century, however, the Mandate of Heaven began to shift once more. The Song empire was undermined by the very peace and prosperity it had created and the population growth which that peace and prosperity had made possible. In its time population numbers grew, possibly to 100 million around AD 1000 and 120 millions 200 years later – considerably more than populations in Europe. That growth brought bureaucratic problems, including increased power to eunuch groups around the court. The government's willingness to coin more money to meet public expenses inevitably led to inflation, with resulting hardship, especially for the poor. Worse still, in the great estates of the south tax evasion became rife, producing constant central-budget deficits.

Most important of all in weakening the Song was the declining sense of ethnic particularism, certainly of patriotism and loyalty to the state. That came together with the notion, at the very core of the Confucian state, that government must be rule by virtue, not force. Governance was still run by an élite of degree-holding scholar-officials who thought that violence would merely beget more violence. While the Song, like every other dynasty, had originally gained the throne by military force, once securely in power deeply Confucian ideas soon dominated. In other words, this Confucian state not only lacked respect for martial virtues, but was chronically disposed to temper audacity with discretion.

The loss of patriotism also made people more relaxed about foreign intrusion. As more and more Chinese came under non-Chinese rule, the notion took hold: if invaders promptly adopted Chinese customs and promised to rule China in Chinese fashion, why worry? The old Chinese view of the world, and the 'tribute system', had for time out of mind been based on the notion that the civilised 'Middle Kingdom' would inevitably come to dominate the mere military violence of the tribes. But comfortable assumptions and moral authority can be trumped by power politics and force. Indeed,

Confucian pragmatism itself said that the unavoidable must be accommodated and rationalised. By 1165 the northern state of the Jurchen/Jins and the Southern Song agreed to regard each other as having equal rights, as 'brothers', albeit with Song China as the senior brother. That might have settled things, but behind the Jurchen appeared the increasing power of the Mongols. In 1233 the Song thought they would be clever and form an alliance with the Mongols to attack the Jurchen. The trouble was that the elimination of Jurchen power left the Song alone to face a growing Mongol menace; by 1276 the Mongols seized the Song capital and shortly afterwards the Song dynasty entirely collapsed.

In sum, neither the growing population of China, nor the wealth and comfort that its great cities had created, were likely to take easily – let alone effectively – to the need to defend by force what had been built up.

Least of all were they up to dealing with one of the greatest conquerors in the history of the world. His name was Ghengis Khan.

4

The Coming of the Mongols

AD 1210 to 1368

H E WAS BORN Temujin, probably in 1167, a scion of the minor Mongol aristocracy. He had a harsh beginning: his father was murdered when he was a child, the family became destitute and he had to fight from his late teens to win back position, and then to unite the Mongol tribes and create a nation in arms. From the start he was ambitious, careful, perceptive, self-disciplined and vengeful; but as a leader of men he also earned the reputation of being just and generous, and someone who knew how to reward the loyalty of followers. His fight to the top was hard – after one defeat, some of his men were put into vats and boiled alive – but he became khan in 1185 and by 1206 an assembly of leaders and princes gave him the title of Ghengis Khan (Universal Ruler). He went on to become the un-disputed leader of the Turco-Mongol tribes. By the time he died in 1227, he left a realm already large and under military rule, that his sons continued to expand into the greatest land empire the world has ever seen. At its greatest extent, under Ghengis's grandsons, the Mongol empire came to be organised in four divisions. The Great Khan himself ruled East Asia. There was also the khanate of Persia, which included Baghdad; and the khanate of Chagadai, which governed Turkestan. Finally, there was the khanate of Kipchak, or the Golden Horde, which, centred on the Volga, dominated Russia for two centuries. Though that total Mongol empire was not united for long, and not all parts of it flourished, Ghengis's grandsons governed two glittering and splendid empire-states that have remained great civilisations: Persia and China.

Ghengis was not the first Mongol leader to lead, or inherit, a military people but his military leadership was uncommonly forceful. War was the natural state for Mongols. All males between the ages of 14 and 60 were soldiers; but he also reformed military organisation. The army was organised into troops of 10 men, companies of 100, regiments of 1,000 and divisions of 10,000 (a pattern imitated by most armies since). Members of different tribes served together. Their deployment was prefaced and guided by Ghengis's use of an excellent network of spies.

Unquestioning discipline was the norm, and treachery or cowardice were the ultimate sins.[1] Although they had some small cannon for siege work, the core units, created and refined under Ghengis's leadership, were the culmination of a thousand-year development of mounted archers, doing battle in their bright-coloured robes, high boots and fur caps. These flying cavalry columns, equipped with armour of metal scales sewn on to hides, compound (multi-layered) bows and armour-piercing arrows, and fighting with disciplined ferocity for loot and killing, became the terror of Asia and the Middle East. Even in peacetime, hunting was not just fun but training for war. Mongol soldiers would form cordons, sometimes hundreds of kilometers in circumference, around an area of steppe or forest and gradually draw the circle tighter, driving the hunted animals – or, in battle, foes – into the centre, where they could be conveniently massacred. In battle, discipline was ruthless. Anyone who held back, let alone anyone who deserted, was killed. If any Mongol was taken prisoner and his fellows failed to rescue him, those fellows were killed, too. To save Mongol casualties, commanders would take the men from a region or province they were not attacking, to put into the front line against their current victims. Here, too, anyone who did not fight hard was liable to be killed.

Visiting Western monks like William Rubruck or John de Carpini have left detailed descriptions of these Mongol armies and rules of war. The men were often drunk, custom forbade washing their clothes and they stank of their favourite diet of mares' milk. Soldiers were accompanied on campaign by their families. They were allowed a polygamy that was, in principle, unlimited. Ghengis himself is said to have had over 500 consorts of one kind or another. A Mongol son had to marry his father's widows, except his own mother, as well as the widows of his brothers.[2] On the basis that this gave everyone ample room for manoeuvre, real adultery was often punishable by death. Each soldier had several remounts and the supply train – sometimes including whole houses – made use of ox-drawn carts, surrounded by a cacophony of cattle and camels. Apart from mares' milk, the soldiers would eat almost anything. If a soldier was hungry on the march, he would make a nick in his horses neck and drink the blood. If the horse became weak, it was apt to become dinner. One Mongol army besieging a Chinese city, a monk reported, found itself short of food – and ate one in ten of its own soldiers. On the other hand, loot was held in common.

Modern estimates suggest that between 1211 and 1223 the Mongol armies may have wiped out some 18 million people in and around Central Asia. But one reason for Mongol ferocity was that commanders, to avoid losing men, tried to frighten opponents into surrender: winning by terror. If they did have to fight, they were pitiless. There were no heroics, just a quick and brutal determination to win quickly, completely and without needless losses. If a group or army surrendered, many of their soldiers would be enrolled into the Mongol forces, which came to include all kinds of men from other tribes and ethnic groups. Similarly, if a city was devastated, other towns were likely to surrender. Ghengis's rule – which, fortunately, his successors did not always stick to – was that if any town, having been summoned to surrender, loosed a single arrow or stone in its own defence, and even if it later tried to yield, every man, woman and child there should be slaughtered. Together with that, though, went cunning. A seventeenth-century Mongol chronicle tells how Ghengis dealt with his first solidly walled Chinese city, which was obviously difficult to assault with a cavalry army. He offered to raise the siege if he were given 1,000 cats and 10,000 swallows. When they were delivered, he ordered strips of cloth to be tied to their tails and set alight. The birds and cats fled home – and set their largely wooden city on fire. In the confusion the Mongols stormed the town.[3] Ghengis himself defined his ideal of happiness as 'The greatest joy is to conquer one's enemies, to pursue them, to seize their property, to see their families in tears, to ride their horses, and to possess their daughters and wives'.[4] He and his family apparently practised what they preached. Not only did Ghengis Khan have hundreds of consorts, but his eldest son seems to have had forty sons and his grandson Kublai, who established the Yuan dynasty in China, had twenty-two legitimate sons and is said to have added thirty virgins to his harem each year.[5]

Ghengis began his wars almost immediately after his accession, acquiring not just riches in gold, silver and luxuries, but captive engineers, scribes, doctors and translators. His civil and support services recruited Persians, Iraqis, Indians, Georgians, Koreans, Chinese and even a few Europeans. In 1207 Tibet submitted to him and for the next twenty years, until Ghengis's death, paid tribute. Bokhara and Samarkand surrendered as soon as the Mongols appeared and Ghengis preached a sermon in Bokhara's chief mosque calling himself the 'flail of God'. In 1210 he rode into northern China itself, beginning a twenty-year campaign to rule the empire. By this time the Chinese military establishment was inefficient, overmanned and short of horses. It was also short of barbarian auxiliaries, whom it could not adequately pay. Old Beijing fell in 1215, the city was burned and the population massacred. Ghengis then turned west and destroyed other powers of north and Central Asia, like the Khitans in the north and the Khwarezmian empire centred on Samarkand. Many of these regions never recovered and became a semi-desert. The area that now covers Gansu and Shansi, part of the ancient heartland of China, had its population drastically diminished, the irrigation works could not be maintained and sand drifted over land and even towns.

One of Ghengis's grandsons, Batu Khan, led a grouping of

Mongols, known as the Golden Horde,[6] westwards into Russia and Ukraine to form the khanate of Kipchak, and stormed into Eastern Europe. En route his army and state absorbed the Kipchak Turks. By 1240 the Mongols had ridden to the Volga, destroyed Kiev and most of the Russian principalities. They are said to have started by totally devastating Russia: much of the land was empty, carpeted with the bones of men, women and children and strewn with ruined cities. Between 1237 and 1241 the Mongol armies went on to ravage Poland, Hungary, Bohemia and rode into Austria. By this time, these armies were largely composed of Tartars, Uighurs and Turks and others who had joined the Mongols as auxiliaries. What stopped further advances was not armed opposition but the death of Ghengis's son and heir, the Great Khan Ogodai. Mongol princes and leaders throughout the empire had to return to the capital, Karakorum, for the election of a new Great Khan. In the meantime, as a by-product of their iron-fisted governance of most of Eurasia, the Mongols had also created the post routes across Asia that made European contact with 'Cathay' – or China – possible.

Other Mongol armies moved into Persia and then Mesopotamia. Under Ghengis they had started with an orgy of bloodletting in Persia, partly to make sure that everyone would be properly terrified by Mongol ruthlessness, but also in revenge for the unpardonable murder of some Mongol ambassadors. By the time his grandson, Hulagu Khan, marched into these Moslem regions, things had calmed down and, with everyone hoping for stability, the Persian rulers had asked him to take the throne. The arrival of this cultured and talented prince did, indeed, herald a Persian revival, especially after he had eliminated the famously feared sect of the Ismailis – the assassins.[7] The next problem was the caliph of Islam, in his capital Baghdad. By then, Baghdad was a brilliantly civilised city of gardens, bath houses, libraries, music, flourishing sciences including mathematics and astronomy, a city where almost everyone could read.[8] In 1258 Hulagu brought a huge army, including Christian cavalry and other allies, to its walls. The prince – whose mother was a Nestorian Christian, as was his favourite wife, a Kerait princess named Dokuz

Khatun, who had previously been the wife of Ghengis's youngest son – called on the thirty-seventh and last Abbasid caliph, Al Mustasim, to submit. The caliph refused, there was a siege and the city was forced to submit anyway. Al Mustasim offered to order his men to lay down their arms, provided only that their lives were spared and he alone would have to die. But once the caliph's soldiers were disarmed, the Mongols killed them all, as well as slaughtering some 80,000 people in the destruction of this jewel of a city. Al Mustasim was killed a few days later, probably when the Mongols, to avoid heaven's wrath by spilling the blood of princes into the earth, put him into a sack and had him either kicked or else trampled to death by horses. All the males of his family followed him into death.

There remained Ghengis's first target, the Chinese empire. A good deal of the enormous wealth of northern China must have been destroyed in the initial campaigns, or else carried off as booty, by armies which now contained numbers of Chinese. Other Chinese submitted, as did the king of Korea. Then the Mongols moved further into China. They formed an alliance with the Southern Song and in 1233 Kaifeng, now the capital of the Jin, fell after a heroic defence, to Ghengis's successor Ogodai, who by then had the assistance of some 20,000 Song troops. Kaifeng may have held up to a million refugees from the surrounding countryside. Under the rules, all their lives were forfeit, but a Chinese adviser persuaded Ogodai to spare much of the city because of the great wealth and services it could furnish for the victors. All male members of the Jin dynasty were, however, killed and the women sent to the Mongol court.

Naturally none of this guaranteed the security of the Song. By the start of the 1250s, once another grandson of Ghengis, Mongke, had become Great Khan, the campaign against the Southern Song began. Mongke was assisted by his younger brother Kublai, who turned out to be much the ablest and most gifted of Ghengis's grandsons, and who had been carefully and even liberally educated by his mother, the Lady Sorghaghtani Beki. Mongke appointed him viceroy of China.

MONGOL WOMEN

Kublai Khan's mother, the Lady Sorghaghtani Beki, was a remarkable and hugely influential woman. She was Ghengis Khan's daughter-in-law and all four of her sons became khans of various kinds of seniority, two of them successive Great Khans. Her name is mentioned in many sources as, quite simply, one of the great figures of the thirteenth century. European missionaries said she was the most renowned of all the Mongols. Persians wrote about her. One Syrian historian quoted a poet who said, 'If I were to see among the race of women another who is so remarkable a woman as this, I would say that the race of women is superior to the race of men.'

She was herself illiterate, but recognised that if her sons, Mongke, Hulagu, Kublai and Arik Boka, were to achieve greatness, they would have to be educated. She saw to it that each one learned a different one of the languages of the enormous Mongol empire. Herself a Nestorian Christian, she recognised that the Mongols had to come to terms with the churches of the empire's various religions. So she and her sons provided support for each of these religions: Muslims, Buddhists, Confucianists, Nestorian Christians and others. She introduced her son Kublai to the ideas of Confucian scholars to help him understand China. More remarkably still, she could see that crude exploitation of subject peoples would make no economic sense and simple plunder would be self-defeating. Instead, she saw the need to support the Chinese peasantry and understood that if the local economy was supported, there would be increased production and more taxes. Each of her sons, especially Kublai, absorbed these lessons about religious toleration and economic good sense, and applied them with conspicuous success.

Sorghaghtani was not the only highly influential Mongol lady. Kublai was also greatly helped by his wife Chabi, whose role may have been almost as important as that of his mother. Chabi patronised Tibetan monks, who began to convert the Mongol élite to Tibetan Buddhism. When Kublai conquered southern China, she was influential in preventing revenge; and even took measures to look after the remnants of the Song imperial family, rather than allowing them all to be killed or enslaved.

Equally influential and politically powerful was the Kerait princess, Dokuz Khatun, who was married to Kublai's cousin, Hulagu Khan, the Il-Khan of Persia. She was said to be descended from one of the wise men who visited the new-born Jesus in his manger, and strongly influenced her husband in an anti-Moslem direction.

Nanjing itself was carried by Bayan, one of the greatest soldiers of the age, and the inhabitants, over a million of them, were slaughtered. Hangzhou, though, surrendered in time. By 1247 Tibet made even fuller submission and a leading lama became the Mongols' vice-regent.[9] Kublai conquered the modern Yunnan and marched into Vietnam, with Hanoi falling in 1257. The conquest of southern China continued until, in 1279, the last Song prince was trapped with his small fleet in a bay off the coast of Guangdong, and threw himself into the sea, together with his family and his ministers, to avoid capture.[10]

In the meantime, Mongke suddenly died of dysentery. It took another two years for Kublai to win a civil war and establish himself as the next Great Khan. He went on to rule the Chinese world for almost thirty-five years, from 1260 to 1294, and made himself the first emperor of the new Mongol dynasty of China, the Yuan. Their rule was to last until 1368: the first aliens to rule all of China, instead of merely segments of it, but by no means the last. For most of the next seven centuries China would be ruled by non-Chinese.

Kublai spent the next few years in making administrative and political reforms. He understood that in order to rule China he would have to make concessions to the Chinese. There were too many millions of them to be effectively governed by a few tens of thousands of Mongols. If he wanted Chinese support, he had to behave like a regular Chinese emperor. The Mongols generally found that one can conquer from horseback but not govern a large and diverse society like China in that way. It should not have been a total surprise. Eleven centuries earlier the scholar Lu had told the emperor Han Gauzu: 'you have conquered the empire on horseback; but can you rule it on horseback?' So the Mongols, too, had to rule through mostly traditional institutions.

Kublai also abandoned the old Outer Mongolian centre of Karakorum, and instead chose the site of Beijing as his capital, although he kept a summer residence north of the Great Wall at Shangdu, the site of the fabled Xanadu. He called the new capital Khanbaliq (City of the Khan) and began to rebuild it from the ground up, a process that the next dynasty strongly completed. There was the, by then usual, Mongol insistence on magnificence, ranging from the Mongols' addiction to glorious silks, brocades and gold-threaded fabrics to Kublai's policy of establishing not only palaces but new palace grounds with artificial lakes, hills and lovely parks.

The shift of the Mongol political centre into China had unforeseen consequences. For old-fashioned Mongols, the move from the steppes into the corrupt and effete urban environment of China was a sad betrayal of the Mongol heritage. Yet it also reinforced the Chinese notion that non-Chinese invaders would in the end conform, as such people always had, to the economic and cultural ways that the empire had developed over fifteen centuries. On the other hand, many important posts, at the centre and locally, were monopolised by the Mongols. For one thing, there were quite a lot of them: adding hangers-on and allies, like the Turks, there may have been a million or so of them in China, many more than any previous invader had brought in. For another, they wanted to avoid employing Han Chinese as far as possible, preferring non-Chinese from elsewhere: Central Asia, the Middle East, even Europe. That policy was not effective. After all, the people with Chinese administrative and clerical experience, who could read and write Chinese, were usually the Han. For sheer utility, and in an attempt to keep order among them, the

Mongols did reinstate Confucian governmental usages and, in later years, even examinations based on the classics.

They also, somewhat like the Manchus centuries later, tried to maintain the ethnic and cultural separation between the Han on one hand and the Mongols and their Central and west Asian auxiliaries on the other. The Mongols, with their garrisons scattered through large towns, were clearly the ruling class, with the Chinese getting lower status. Chinese relations with Mongol authority seem to have been properly submissive, without overt challenges, but with a fair admixture of stealth and trickery all the same, while Persian remained very largely the common language of all the governing classes

For all its initial ferocities, therefore, Mongol power brought long decades of peace to China, especially after Kublai ascended the throne. They brought unity, especially the unity of north and south. They also brought Yunnan and even Tibet into the Chinese realm. Kublai himself patronised painting and painters in the Chinese tradition and supported Chinese drama. Indeed, Chinese theatre went through a tremendous cultural efflorescence, especially musical drama. Economic developments were oddly contradictory. The rebuilding of Beijing itself caused a variety of difficulties. The capital had to house, feed and supply a very large imperial bureaucracy. That meant bringing in food, especially rice, from the south. That needed rivers and canal systems, including the Grand Canal, to be refurbished, which involved not just building and maintaining a fleet but impressing peasant labour. Furthermore, granaries had to be built throughout the empire to guard against famines.

On the other hand trade, and especially foreign trade, flourished with Italian merchants and Islamic traders alike made welcome. China arguably became the centre – though not the manager – of the world's largest trade network, extending from Japan to the Middle East. The power of the Mongols also brought much security to the caravan routes across Asia.[11] The new rulers regulated trade and made loans to traders. Foreign merchants were again allowed to live tax-free and permitted to travel freely through the empire. Many became wealthy, and commercial growth was supervised by Moslem financiers at the Mongol court.

Almost inevitably, the Mongols also went on trying to expand their realm in other directions. They sent missions into South-East Asia in search of fresh vassals. They moved at various points into Cambodia, and Cochin-China and Annam, in modern Vietnam. They invaded Burma and tried to conquer Java. Here, though, they overreached. In the tropical regions they, and more importantly their horses, were defeated by the heat and the fevers. Further north they had fewer difficulties. Having reduced the Tibetan empire to subjection they even tried to conquer Japan. Between 1268 and 1272 Kublai sent three embassies to the Japanese. They were ignored. Such a rebuff could not be tolerated, so he began to organise a punitive expedition. A force of 15,000 Mongol, Jurchen and Chinese soldiers was organised together with some 8,000 soldiers and 7,000 sailors from Korea. These forces carried the island of Tsushima and landed on the east coast of Kyushu, but when a major storm blew up, they put to sea and, after losing 13,000 men and a few hundred ships, the rest went home. In 1275 Kublai sent yet another embassy but the Japanese simply cut off their heads. So Kublai staged another invasion, this time with 100,000 troops, 15,000 Korean sailors and 900 boats of various kinds. There were two months of inconclusive fighting in Japan, but another typhoon came along the coast, much of the fleet was destroyed and up to half of Kublai's force died, if not by drowning then because the Japanese *samurai* warriors made short work of any survivors who reached the shore. The Japanese reverently called that storm a 'kamikaze', or 'divine wind' – a name of which much more would be heard 600 years later, in the Second World War. The disaster cast other long shadows, not so much because of the loss of men but because the affair shattered the aura of invincibility of the Mongol armies.

Religion went on posing major problems. Mongolia and Turkestan were the meeting places for several world religions, and the very scale of their conquests made the Mongols, who practised toleration, acquainted with Islam, Hinduism, Christianity and Manichaeanism. Buddhism gained a lot of ground and new temples and monasteries were founded and given tax-free status. In fact, the emperor himself was somewhat distracted by having to cater, at one and the same time, to his Moslem constituency, to be a devout Buddhist for Tibetan lamaists and to take an interest in the Christians and others.

By the 1250s the power of Islam had become a serious threat to the Mongols, as well as to Christian Europe and its precarious foothold in the Holy Land. That, and the fact that so many leading Mongol ladies, as well as senior officials, were Nestorian Christians,[12] led to various missions and envoys moving between Europe and the Mongol Great Khans, with the Europeans seeking not only Christian converts but co-operative action against the Moslems. The Mongols sought military and political leverage against Islam and particularly wanted co-operation over Palestine and Syria, where Christian crusaders were already operating. Toleration paid other dividends, When, in the thirteenth century, the Orthodox Christian principalities of Russia found themselves squeezed between the Mongols from the East and the Teutonic Knights in the West, they preferred to submit to the Mongols. At least the Mongols, unlike the intolerant Knights, gave religious liberty to Orthodox Christians. By the 1330s the Yuan empire had large numbers of Russian and Western troops; and as late as 1332 a detachment of Russians was even on duty at the Mongol court in Beijing.

A number of odd and adventurous European (usually Italian) merchants travelled to China. So did several European friars, even papal missions, while the Mongols several times sent emissaries to the West. One Christian embassy taking the northern route through Poland and Russia, was entrusted to the Franciscan, John de Plano Carpini, provincial of his order at Cologne. He set out in mid-April 1245, a mere eighteen years after Ghengis Khan's death, carrying a letter from Pope Innocent IV. Carpini, to whom we owe a detailed report on his journey, must have been a very brave man. He set out in his sixties, unfit, without knowledge of Asian languages and with no idea what his reception might be. Perhaps he would just have his head cut off by the first Mongol patrol he met? In the event he was hustled through Asia for weeks on horseback, to his total exhaustion, and arrived at the Mongol centre of Karakorum in time to witness the coronation of the new Great Khan, Guyuk, another of Ghengis's grandsons. He delivered his letter and returned in later 1247 with the Mongol response. Guyuk simply said:

'. . . Thou, who art the great Pope, together with all the princes, come in person to serve us. At that time I shall make known all (our) commands . . . Now you should say with a sincere heart: "I will submit and serve you." . . . If you do not observe God's command, and if you ignore my command, I shall know you as my enemy. Likewise I shall make you understand . . .'[13]

It was not encouraging. Carpini did, though, bring back a great deal of information, including some of the detailed reports on Mongol ways of war. A year later he was appointed archbishop. Shortly afterwards King Louis IX of France (St Louis), also heard that the Great Khan's mother was a Christian and the Mongols were eager for an alliance against Islam. His first mission came to nothing but he sent another Franciscan friar, William de Rubrouck (or Rubruck) equipped with a letter of credence already translated into Persian. William, also hustled by horse relay, reached the Mongol court just after Christmas 1253,[14] once again seeking a combined crusade against the Moslems. On his arrival, Rubruck found a number of French and other Europeans who had been captured in the Mongols' European campaigns. Not that Rubruck got to China proper, but he made detailed notes for his private report to King Louis. Incidentally, within two decades Kublai Khan, who naturally rather liked the Nestorians, since his mother had been one, allowed some Franciscan friars to become bishops of Beijing and there was soon even a new archbishopric of Khanbaliq.

A few other Westerners reached the Mongols, too, including craftsmen like the French silversmith Guillaume Boucher[15] and a Paris jeweller. No doubt there were others, many of them captives from the West: after all, craftsmen were useful. There must also, from quite early days, have been a trickle of Western traders whose names are not recorded.

Much the most famous of the early travellers, though, and the first to reach China proper, were the Polo family: the brothers Niccolo and Maffeo Polo, who were traders, and Niccolo's son, Marco. Niccolo and Maffeo travelled first. Equipped with a stock of jewels, they took a ship across the Black Sea to the port of Sudak on the Crimea, and the main centre for trade with the Mongols. From there, they travelled to the Volga River and the court of Berkhe, the ruler of the Golden Horde, and from there, much later, to Bokhara (now Bukhara in modern Uzbekistan), the capital of the (Central Asian) khanate of Chagatai. There they met a certain Sandaq, an ambassador from the new Great Khan, who told the Polos that Kublai would certainly be delighted to meet them, for he had never met any Latin people (i.e. Westerners). So instead of going west, the brothers went east. It took them a year, and a crossing of the Gobi desert, to find their way to Kublai Khan's court in 1266.

They found that the new emperor was a man of intelligent, broad and eclectic views, extremely hospitable, who welcomed these strangers from the far West, made much of them and interrogated them about Europe, the Roman Church and the pope. He even thought of attracting foreign Christians and their skills to bolster his empire. A year later he sent them on their return journey, equipped with a letter to Pope Clement IV, asking that 100 learned men be dispatched to teach the Mongols about Western science and Christianity. He also asked the pope to get him some oil from the lamp at the Holy Sepulchre at Jerusalem. To make sure that the Polos reached Italy safely, Kublai apparently gave them a special passport, in the form of a golden tablet a foot long and inscribed 'By the strength of the eternal Heaven, holy be the Khan's name. Let him that pays him not reverence be killed'. The tablet guaranteed the Polos help anywhere in the Mongol realm. It took them three years to get back to Venice.

All three Polos, the two uncles and young Marco, now fifteen, stayed in Venice for another two years before setting out again for 'Cathay' (China) and the Great Khan in 1271. This time they carried with them letters and gifts from Pope Gregory X to Kublai as well as some of that oil from the Holy Sepulchre that Kublai had asked for. They made their way to the mouth of the Persian Gulf, to Afghanistan, and across the Gobi desert to the Yellow River region. In 1275 they arrived in the capital, Khanbaliq. When Kublai was told they had come back, he sent a royal escort to bring them to his presence.

The Polos were hugely impressed by the magnificence of the court, the wealth of the country and the sophistication of its social arrangements; by the imperial postal system, the proliferation of bathrooms and bath houses with heated water for the city, the use of coal and especially the use of paper money. The Polos' stay at Kublai's court – with Niccolo and Maffeo probably trading in various parts of China and Central Asia – certainly made them very rich. But as the great Khan became older and reached his late seventies, they were anxious to be gone, together with their wealth. With great regret Kublai agreed to let them go provided that, on their way, they would escort a seventeen-year-old princess, 'a lady named Kukachin, of great beauty and charm' (as Marco wrote later), who was promised in marriage to Arghun, the recently bereaved Mongol khan of Persia. The Polos, together with the princess and some ambassadors, set sail from the Fujian coast in a flotilla of fourteen ships. By the time they arrived in Persia, of the 600 people who had set out with the flotilla (not counting the ships' crews), apparently only the Polos, the princess, and some 14 others had survived the journey. Moreover, the intended bridegroom turned out to have died, so the princess was married to his son, Gaikhatu, who had succeeded his father to become Il-Khan of the region. Meanwhile the Polos travelled back home from the Black Sea coast through Turkey and arrived back in Venice in 1295. Marco wrote the famous work on his travels and seems to have lived on until sometime in 1324/5.

MARCO POLO

By the time that Marco, much the most famous of the Polos, set out for China with his father and uncle, he was well educated, with an interest in strange peoples, animals and plants. He had a command of French and some Latin, and was to become fluent in four languages.

In China, he became a favourite of the Great Khan. He learned the language of the court and Persian, the lingua franca of foreigners. By his own account, he worked for the Great Khan from 1274 to 1291, was given high posts in his entourage and sent on various missions, within the empire as well as to Burma (now Myanmar), India and elsewhere. In 1277, Marco says, Kublai appointed him as governor at Yangzhou on the Grand Canal, north of the Yangzi, while his father and uncle designed siege engines for a Mongol assault on some Chinese town. It was also Marco who, after his return to Europe, wrote the book on his travels, *The Description of the World*, that became famous and contained, for the next couple of centuries, almost the only information about China that anyone in Europe had. (It is worth remembering that two centuries later Christopher Columbus hoped, by sailing across the Atlantic, to reach the realm of the Great Khan, not realising that Mongol rule in China had actually ended some 120 years before he set sail.) Marco's book was enthusiastic. The empire, he wrote, was vast, highly urbanised, rich, inventive and not given to matters military. In fact 'it is a veritable paradise on earth'. Powerful, too. 'If you put together all the Christians in the world, with their emperors and their kings, the whole of these Christians – yes, and throw in Saracens to boot – would not have such power, or be able to do so much as this Kublai, who is lord of all the Tartars [i.e. Mongols] in the world.' Sadly, though, the book's accuracy is another matter entirely. Although there is obviously much that rests on fact, there also seems to be a fair admixture of exaggeration, hearsay and sometimes sheer invention(*). For instance, it seems that at

* From the beginning, many Venetians refused to believe Marco's stories and the doubts have continued ever since. See for instance Frances Wood, *Did Marco Polo Go to China?*, Secker & Warburg, 1995. On the other hand, some of his tales seem verifiable. For instance, one of the gold '*laissez-passer*' tablets that Kublai gave to the Polos seems to have existed in Marco Polo's household as late as 1324.

Yangzhou, far from being a governor or even a senior tax inspector, Marco was a middle-ranking official in the salt administration. Not only that but he saw only cities, Beijing in particular, and therefore the centres of Chinese wealth and sophistication. He saw virtually nothing of the bulk of the population in its myriad villages.

Interestingly, the Venetians saw through him immediately and christened his work 'the book of a million lies'.

Not long after Marco Polo's arrival in Beijing came much the most important of the early Eastern missions to Europe. It was by no means the first but little had come of the earlier contacts. It was in 1286 that Ghengis Khan's great-great-grandson, Arghun, sent the important mission of Rabban Sauma, a Nestorian monk. Sauma was a Mongolian Turk, born in Beijing and with excellent connections to the Mongol court. In 1280 or so, Sauma and his companion, Rabban Macos, while on their way to Jerusalem, reached the Mongol khanate of Persia, but became embroiled in religious and political affairs there. Their onward journey to Jerusalem had to be postponed. Soon afterwards Rabban Marcos was named patriarch of the Nestorian Church, with its headquarters in the more or less revived Baghdad. He naturally enjoyed much influence at the Persian court. So when Persia's ruler needed an emissary for a diplomatic mission to Western Europe, to get European and Byzantine leaders to join in an effort against the Muslims in the Holy Land, Sauma seemed the right man to send. He was a close friend of the new patriarch and an educated Christian with experience of diplomacy and travel. He travelled via the Black Sea to Constantinople and from there to Rome. He arrived there in 1287 and stayed in Europe for about a year. During that time he saw not only the new pope, Nicholas IV, but Edward I of England and King Philip IV of France. He celebrated the Syrian liturgy in the presence of the pope, from whom Sauma also received

Communion. At Bordeaux, Sauma himself administered Communion to Edward I.

Sauma returned to Persia in 1288, carrying a number of sacred relics but without firm commitments for some unified crusade to liberate Jerusalem from the heirs of Saladin. On his return, Arghun made Sauma his chaplain, baptised his own son Nicholas, and built a chapel for Sauma that connected directly with the royal tent. However, Arghun died and the Mongols, instead of becoming allies of the Europeans, became gradually absorbed into Islam. Sauma did, however, leave behind journals of his life and travels. They were mostly written in Persian and dealt with his life in China and travels across Asia and Europe.[16]

The first Europeans to follow the Polos, so far as we know, seem to have been yet more Franciscan and Dominican friars; notably the Franciscan John of Montecorvino, with long experience of the East, by whom the pope tried to send more letters to Kublai. He set out from Rome in 1289 but only reached Beijing after Kublai had died. He stayed and worked under Kublai's successors, creating a small centre of Catholicism and converting one or two important people. Eventually, the pope got to hear of his efforts, appointed John as archbishop of Khanbaliq in 1307 and sent some helpers. There were a few other travellers, such as Odoric of Pordenone, who went to China in 1321, and reported back that there was now a Franciscan cathedral together with two Franciscan houses in the great port city of Zaytun (Quangzhou) in 1322. Ten or twenty years after that, there may also have been a small Italian commercial community there. In 1338 a mission from one of Kublai's successors as Great Khan came the other way, arriving in Avignon, in France, at the court of Pope Benedict XII. It carried a personal letter from the Great Khan, and messages from some Christian nobles in his service. They wanted, among other things, a new spiritual adviser. The pope appointed four legates to the khan's court, one of whom was John (Marignolli) of Florence, who arrived back in Avignon in 1353 and delivered a letter from the Great Khan to the pope, who was by then Innocent VI. He became bishop of Bisignano, but he does not seem to have left a very coherent account of his travels.

Such slender and erratic contacts, and embryonic Western influences, did not last. In 1362 the last bishop of Zaytun was killed by Chinese who were angry about foreigners and seven years later all Christians were expelled from Beijing. Indeed, in the second half of the century another great conqueror, Tamerlane, laid the whole of Central Asia waste, in the process not only undoing what the Mongols had built, but once more cutting off almost all communications between China and Europe.

In any case, neither in China nor in the larger Mongol empire that reached westwards to the borders of the Latin world did Mongol rule last very long. Even Kublai's own east Asian realm declined fairly rapidly after his death. In forty years there were seven emperors, some of them murdered. Within eighty years of Kublai's death the Mongol empire in China was played out, well before the last Great Khan fled.

There were several problems. The Mongols were mainly interested in power, and thought in military terms. Yet they themselves deteriorated. Once the major wars were over, the soldiery found itself sitting around in peacetime city garrisons, with nothing to do. There were other difficulties. Some of the most important were not always obvious when seen from the centre. The strategies of conquest the Mongols had employed, especially the massacres, had laid waste much of the empire: the population of the Song regions may have been as much as halved. Not only that, but the very nature of the new government seemed dubious to the Chinese. They deeply resented government by aliens. They expected hierarchy and hereditary succession, while the Mongols chose successive leaders by election through a collective of chiefs. Chinese laws were uniform, while Mongols applied to every individual his own tribal law. Altogether, the Yuan did not, perhaps could not, fully adapt to Chinese culture, and their moral and legal codes were too incompatible with Chinese traditions. There was also the problem of the Chinese gentry around the country, among whom the personal and family loyalties of the modern Mafia would have seemed fairly natural. In any case, the

Chinese despised the uncouth Mongols: they used to say that the Mongols stank so much that you could smell them downwind.

Within the court, intrigue and dissension became rife. Weak rulers failed to deal with inflation, floods, and quarrels among clans. Not only that but the peasantry became more impoverished by government tax policies and exactions. By 1325 there may have been several million peasants on or beyond the brink of starvation, and revolts began against 'the rich'. The Mongols, their own army severely weakened, coped poorly. In 1351 the Yellow River dykes burst and the need to impress labour for repairs made things worse in the countryside. There were more revolts, sometimes sectarian.

In 1368 the chief rebel leader captured Beijing and the last Great Khan fled without a fight, returning to his ancestral steppes. His successors were the Ming, starting with the ferociously energetic and ruthless ex-peasant, Zhu Yuanzhang, who made himself the founding Ming emperor.

5

THE MING, SOUTH SEA
BARBARIANS AND MISSIONARIES

AD 1368 to 1644

T HE MAN WHO became the emperor Hongwu (meaning 'immensely martial') was born to a dirt-poor peasant family,
orphaned at sixteen and became, variously, a beggar, a Buddhist
monk and a rebel. As late as 1340 he was an insignificant figure in a
minor rebel band in some plague-ridden village. But as bandit and
rebel he had found his true vocation. He grew quickly in rank and
reputation and soon commanded his own large and independent
band. Now he showed real strategic vision. Other bandit chiefs
concentrated on sacking cities and amassing loot, while Zhu set about
capturing places of real strategic importance. In 1356 he took
Nanjing, which became his capital and, indeed, that of Ming China.
Furthermore, instead of fighting the Mongols, Zhu concentrated first
on eliminating his rivals in the south-east. Within ten years he had
destroyed them and become the single dominant rebel leader. In
1368 his army, after conquering the whole of eastern China from
Shandong down to Canton, advanced on Beijing, the last Mongol
emperor fled, Beijing surrendered and Zhu established his new
dynasty.

The new emperor was a burly fellow, strongly built, heavily
pockmarked, with a determined chin and fierce energy. He combined

a passion for traditional Chinese verities and legalities with one for relief of the poor, of whom he had so recently been one, and with a determination to impose sweeping reforms, not least on the central administration. Once he occupied the throne, power was once again exercised by the ruler in person, or else by direct delegation. Government was a response to the will of one man. Policy was what the emperor laid down and it reflected his will. Authority and power operated by imperial decision and the struggle for it was a struggle for imperial favour and confidence. Advancement and honours, or else punishments, were also at his pleasure. Opposition, or failure to carry out a command, brought disgrace or death. Under Hongwu and his dynasty, which was to last for 276 years, the empire became great and rich, with long periods of deep and largely unbroken domestic peace. It once more achieved remarkable things in art and literature, theatre, lacquer work and ceramics. In porcelain, its achievements are probably also unsurpassed. Some Inner Asian tribes even came to think that Chinese porcelain had supernatural powers. Yet taking the Ming period as a whole, it is hard to avoid two striking impressions. First, that in broad outline, and for all the differences of detail, the chief factors that produced the rise, and then the decline and fall, of the Ming dynasty, are remarkably similar to those that had once affected the Tang and would, in time, similarly affect the successors of the Ming, the Manchus. Second, that in each case, the cycle had to do with three overlapping difficulties which these empires never really resolved and which eventually led to each dynasty's collapse. They were the problems of the volatile rim-lands and their peoples, especially in the north, of population growth with its problems of economic and political control, and of the inadequacies of the imperial core, centred on the emperor's person and his attendants.

For the Ming, the first of these began as not much more than a continuation of Zhu's march to power. He had to defend the empire against the Mongols who wanted to recover their lost dominance. Indeed, military policy and what to do about the Mongols probably remained Hongwu's chief concern throughout his reign. After he had dislodged them from Beijing and established his rule, his field armies continued to march north, burned down Ghengis Khan's old capital at Karakorum, and crossed into Siberia. Under his successors, the Ming remained fixated on the Mongol danger, especially around 1400 with a revival of Mongol power. A huge, and similar threat – which fortunately never fully developed – came in the reign of the conqueror Tamerlane – Timur the Lame – who was born in 1336 south of Samarkand and emerged as a great general twenty years later. By 1369 he sat on Samarkand's throne and sent expeditions to the Volga, to Persia, Baghdad and India. He then planned an invasion of China, but in 1405 died on the way there. Apart from specific campaigns, Hongwu copied the Yuan military system by stationing garrisons of professional soldiers around the country. The men could farm for themselves rather than rely on some central commissariat, while their commanders could be organised as a military aristocracy.

TAMERLANE

Tamerlane – or the Amir Temur – was one of those great conquerors whose name became a byword for death and destruction. Born in 1336, by the time he was thirty-three he sat on the throne of Samarkand. As his power grew, he styled himself 'Lord of the Fortunate Conjunction and Conqueror of the World'. Indeed, the scale of his conquests rivals those of Napoleon. He defeated the army of the Ottoman empire, captured Sultan Bayazid I and in 1398 invaded India, entering Delhi in triumph and massacring the inhabitants. He conquered the Persians, too, and in 1401 his armies sacked Damascus, where his soldiers, seeking loot, visited unheard-of cruelties on the inhabitants. Resisting cities and citizens were simply killed: we are told of mounds of 70,000 or more skulls. In modern Uzbekistan he has become a national symbol.

His word was law and his power absolute. He was ruthless, highly intelligent and energetic, and a great builder of monumental structures. As he himself said: 'Let him who doubts our power look upon our buildings.' But he was also responsible for parks and palaces, for mosques and madrassahs (schools), and encouraged artistic skills. Not surprisingly, and like other emperors of his era, he had, in the words of one modern commentator, 'a voracious appetite for wives and concubines' even into his seventies.

His army was carefully organised. Each conscript to the cavalry had to report with a shield, enough grain to feed a horse for a year, a bow and a quiver with thirty arrows. Every infantryman also carried a bow, plus an axe, a sword or sabre, a dagger and a small wooden shield.

As a soldier he understood the value of intelligence work and deception. He employed an army of spies, including wandering teachers and dervishes, to feed him information. A Persian historian recounts how, in one battle with the Moguls, Tamerlane ordered his soldiers to light hundreds of camp fires on the hills around the enemy, to convince them that they were surrounded. The enemy duly fled.

There is no doubt that the early Ming empire was exceedingly fortunate that Tamerlane did not live to carry out his China campaign.

Not that Mongols were the only problem. Other Ming forces reasserted Chinese power in Central Asia, but usually did not try to establish comprehensive Chinese rule. Instead, even in Turkestan (Xinjiang), they were content to hold the major cities. In the southwest, the Ming pursued a policy of sinification of minority groups, while establishing tributary relations with Tibet. From the later sixteenth century China even became involved in the politics of relations between competing sects of Tibetan lamas (monks) and various groups of Mongols. The Ming also had to keep soldiers in the south, where the earlier Mongol invasions of Thailand and Burma had made trouble with the local tribes. There, too, soldiers were stationed in military colonies that, over time, tended to make these areas more solidly Chinese. It is hardly surprising that, with these multiple military requirements, the Ming not only expanded the empire but militarised China and created a hereditary military class.

Hongwu's son, Yongle,[1] was an able and experienced soldier with long service against the Mongols, and tried to continue anti-Mongol campaigns with unreliable Mongol allies of his own; but also to use the Mongol dependence on Chinese goods to promote markets in which the empire could continue to buy from the north the herds of horses it never managed to produce at home. Yongle also moved the capital back to Beijing. He sent many expeditions into Mongolia and beyond and not always for war. For instance, he sent an expedition into Central Asia in 1413, much as Wudi had sent Zhang Qian fifteen centuries earlier. The expedition's chief, Chen Cheng, performed the due sacrifices to the gods of the western region and set out, at the start of February 1414 on the 4,000-mile trek to Herat, in modern Afghanistan. It was the capital of Sharuk Bahadur, son of the great Tamerlane. The expedition was laden with gifts for the rulers of the seventeen states whose lands it would have to cross. By now the Silk Road was a necklace of Chinese strong points, communicating quickly with one another by smoke, flag signals and excellent imperial relays. The expedition crossed part of the Gobi desert, skirted the even more fearful Taklamakan, and travelled through snow, drinking melted ice and building its own bridges across streams. It passed through Tashkent and the rich trading centre of Samarkand – now ruled by Tamerlane's grandson – and arrived at Herat some ten months after setting out.

Missions were also sent into Siberia. The tribute system was revived in parts of the north, on the Amur and Ussuri rivers, where tribal chiefs were invited to Beijing. In 1412 the emperor ordered a court eunuch to lead another expedition to the Amur. It travelled with twenty-five vessels and 1,000 soldiers, architects, masons and carpenters. It distributed cloth and figurines to local headmen and left temples as well as inscriptions in Tibetan, Mongol and Chinese, celebrating Ming benevolence. The emperor cultivated good relations in these regions, and made it clear that he was willing to forget all about Tamerlane's proposed invasion of China back in 1404–5. Five years after Chen Cheng's journey, in November 1419, Sharuk Bahadur sent a return embassy that stayed on, learning once more which was the great 'Middle Kingdom'.

Even more interesting enterprises were under way in the south and at sea. By the start of the fifteenth century the Chinese were not only the most advanced civilisation in various industrial skills, but their naval architecture had reached the point where they could construct hundreds of ships of various sizes. Chinese ships had reached India as early as the fifth century AD, and by the 750s there were those large groups of Arab traders at Canton. The shipyards at Nanjing alone are said to have been able to build some 2,000 seagoing ships in the fifteen years up to 1419. The story goes that they included almost 100 of the 'treasure ships' that were said to have been far larger and more commodious than anything then available in Europe. Some treasure ships, it is said, might have displaced up to 3,000 tons, and been over 400 feet long, the size of a modern football field. She might have four decks and a dozen sails, masts up to ninety feet high and maybe fifty cabins. Such ships used stern rudders, compasses and marine charts and could carry up to 500 people. Yet modern marine engineers have expressed serious doubts whether, with the timbers and other materials available at that time, ships of anything like that size could possibly have been successfully built, let alone sailed across the open sea. Since the Chinese authorities later destroyed the records and drawings, presumably as part of the effort to suppress seagoing, the issue may never be finally settled.

In any case, the Chinese achieved a brief dominance over some of the key commercial centres of the Indian Ocean, Ceylon (Sri Lanka), Calicut and, most particularly, the Straits of Malacca. These seaborne links also helped to bring the old tribute system to its peak: Ming records speak of over 100 different tributaries. These efforts culminated in orders from the emperor Yongle to the greatest of the Chinese admirals, the Grand Eunuch Zheng He, to lead great naval flag-showing expeditions along China's maritime trade routes. Himself a Moslem, Zheng He led seven such voyages between 1405 and 1433. The first of them, in 1405–7, may have had no less than 62 of the great treasure ships in a fleet of over 300 vessels. He visited Sumatra, Colombo, the mouth of the Ganges, and travelled as far as the mouth of the Persian Gulf and East Africa, which had long since acquired Chinese porcelain and coins via the caravan trails. No wonder that, with the system at its height, embassies arrived regularly from South and South-East Asia and from as far away as Ormuz at the head of the Persian Gulf. One king of Malacca paid no less than four visits to the Chinese court. Some embassies and presents came from as far away as East Africa, bringing zebras, and even giraffes from Malindi, on the coast of modern Kenya.[2] At one point, in 1411, Zheng He even seized a recalcitrant ruler from Ceylon and took him back to China to have the court deal with him.

After 1433 these probes, and with them all Chinese naval and shipbuilding skills, came to an abrupt end. There were many reasons. In a court always full of intrigue, there were plots against Zheng He, who was not there to defend himself. As the French say: *'les absents ont toujours tort'*.[3] Perhaps of greater weight were the views of Confucian officials who disliked foreign contacts and influences on principle. Moreover, expeditions like that of 1407 to Vietnam, for instance, led by the navy, produced twenty years later a series of setbacks that could only reinforce the view that China's business was China. Most important of all was the cost.

Naval power is very expensive and the Zheng He expeditions had no aims that seemed worth it. He did not try to explore, merely following trade routes already established, especially by the Arabs. Nowhere did the Chinese attempt to colonise. They did not even have a serious commercial purpose. The journeys were no more than diplomatic and flag-showing exercises, in areas where the Chinese empire had no serious political or strategic interests and from which it could foresee no threats. Moreover, the government was in a fiscal and budgetary crisis after its expensively failed attempts to conquer

Vietnam. Most important of all, what resources were available were needed to counter new and serious dangers in the north, most particularly the need to deal with that revival of Mongol power and morale. In fact, the Chinese government had to send several expeditionary campaigns into Mongolia to prevent the formation of some new Mongol confederacy. Worse still, in late 1449 the then emperor staged a totally mismanaged campaign against Mongol forces. His huge army was destroyed. The young emperor even managed to get himself captured. His younger brother had to be enthroned in Beijing, to continue the dynasty's mandate to rule and to keep up public morale. To support the dynasty, the captured ex-emperor renounced his claims to the throne; he only returned to it after the brother was killed in 1457. Small wonder that the Ming remained focused on the Mongol danger.

One result of all this was that the Ming abandoned forward campaigning into the north and set about strengthening, rebuilding and completing the empire's defensive works. Most particularly, they completed perhaps the most remarkable defence system in the world: the full, final and fantastically expensive version of the Great Wall of China. It was an effort that lasted until the end of the dynasty and its costs were astronomical in lives as well as money. Fortunately for China, there was that lucrative trade with and through Spanish Manila, which brought large quantities of silver home to China. It came from Japanese and Philippine merchants as well as from Westerners buying Chinese silks, tea and porcelain. The silver might originate from Japan or, later, from Mexico and Peru in the Spanish Americas. In any case, rivers of it became available for the imperial treasury – and building the Great Wall.

Given that focus, the very memory of China's more remarkable seagoing efforts was suppressed. By 1480 the war ministry, with relentless bureaucratic logic, destroyed even the records of Zheng He's voyages. Well before 1500 the emperor banned the construction of seagoing ships and forbade his subjects, on pain of death, to go to sea. That rule was honoured in the breach only slightly less than in the observance, but Chinese overseas trade remained tightly restricted until around 1560 and foreigners were confined to a few ports closely controlled by the bureaucracy, to avoid infecting China's peaceful domestic order.

These decisions turned out to be extremely costly. The seaboard had long been vulnerable to the Japanese, who were busy plundering Korean and Chinese coasts. When the Ming came to the throne, they saw that it was hardly possible to garrison the entire south-eastern shore. When the Japanese established official relations, Beijing demanded that they create an anti-pirate coastguard. Instead, Japan began organised raiding, while the Chinese coast remained unde-fended and open to pirates from anywhere. Not least to flotillas of robbers from China itself. The official suppression of Chinese sea-going know-how could only make matters much worse, with the pirates flourishing, killing, looting and seizing hostages for ransom. There were hundreds of pirate groups, including a motley assortment of ruffians: Chinese fugitives, Japanese, even black slaves who had escaped from the Portuguese at Macao. Yet the coast remained a minor concern to Beijing which, focusing on the north, could still see no serious strategic threat from the south. Neglect did, however, have long-term implications for sea defence. It became China's strategic Achilles heel until the twenty-first century.

Somewhere among these pirate flea-bites there arrived a new set of rough foreign sailors, this time from Europe. At first they were hardly visible to the imperial government, and certainly of no importance, yet they were the outriders of a European revolution whose effects were to shake Asia, and the Chinese empire, to their foundations. For Western Europe was finding itself in one of the most brilliant periods of religious, intellectual, artistic and scientific turmoil it has experi-enced in the last 2,000 years: the Renaissance, shortly followed by the political and religious earthquake of the Reformation. Among Eur-opean preoccupations at such a time, China ranked low indeed. The Renaissance meant a revival of classical learning, a disposition to naturalism in sculpture and painting and the secular in poetry, a focus on vernacular languages and some ideas of nationalism. Artistically, the period boasted some of the greatest sculptors, poets and artists in the history of the world. It was the age of Leonardo da Vinci and Michelangelo, of Raphael, Titian, Correggio, of Dante's *Divine Comedy*, of Petrarch and Ariosto's poetry. There were scientific advances, like the replacement of Ptolemy's astronomy with Copernican insights, and a general reaction against the theological despotism of the Middle Ages. At the same time Constantinople fell to the Turks in 1453, when Mohammed the Conqueror used Christian artillerists to cast the guns he needed to batter down its walls. There was turmoil in the heart of the old European system, too, with the sack of Rome in 1527 and the pacification of Italy under Spanish dominance. Then came the Reformation with its emancipation of reason and the human conscience in interpreting the Bible, and philosophers like Niccolo Machiavelli. Universities like Bologna and Padua blossomed. The period was therefore a social solvent, easing the transition from status to contract, from gift to market, from miracles to science and, not least, from a world of familiar rural neighbours to a world of mobile – and especially, given the growth of cities, urban – strangers.

Together with all that came the growth of commerce and wealth, especially in the cities: the new humanists and artists were urban folk, and their patrons were the wealthy bourgeois of the Italian and German cities. Their enterprise and curiosity promoted enquiry and exploration. That dovetailed with Europe's defence and security needs and strategies to meet the fresh threat from the Ottomans who, having conquered Byzantium, now threatened Southern and Eastern Europe.

Europe's overseas expansion, which was to have such profound long-term effects everywhere, including in China, therefore stemmed from a combination of strategic need, religious fervour, a search for wealth and a sense of adventure. The expulsion of the Moors from Spain in 1492,[4] and the rise of a Spanish monarchy destined to dominate Europe, came in the same year as that monarchy's dispatch of Christopher Columbus to the New World. At the other end of Europe, the Turks were beaten back from the gates of Vienna, at least temporarily, in 1529; and on 7 October 1571, in the great sea battle of Lepanto, the combined Christian fleets under Don John of Austria destroyed Turkish command of the Mediterranean seaways.

But the defence of Christendom also involved the start of Christian expansion around Islam's flanks, in search of possible allies. In addition to strategic need, that was, of course, driven by religion and by the need for spices, which became increasingly difficult to get past or through the newly Islamic regions and Turkish principalities of the Middle East. Even before the start of the sixteenth century religious devotion came together with a drive for defence, wealth and conquest. None of these drives could be pursued along the overland, trans-Eurasian routes that the earliest explorers had used to get to Cathay because, as the Mongol empires weakened, the stable Mongol governance of Central Asia fell apart, too. With the disintegration of that Pax Tartarica, travel and trade by land became unsafe again. Fortunately for the Portuguese and Spaniards, novel technologies gave them new and much more seaworthy ships than the old galleons: long, sleek caravels and larger carracks. They were much faster, stouter, more manoeuvrable and better armed than Arab ships. They could even carry artillery. Their navigators had quadrants, astrolabes and even magnetic compasses. Furthermore, Prince Henry of Portugal (later nicknamed the Navigator), not only promoted voyages of exploration but employed Arab and Jewish astronomers, organised many other aspects of navigation, and financed huge advances in cartography.

Even so, exploration needed more: it needed what the twenty-first century would call a multinational effort. It might be Castile and Portugal that began to send out men on tiny craft over long and dangerous voyages where disease, hunger and scurvy loomed. But neither had the capital or the organisational know-how that the new journeys needed. For that you needed to bring in Genoa, the Florentines and the great German merchant houses like the Fuggers.

The result was a series of travels and conquests in northern and western Africa. By 1471 the Portuguese held Tangier. Nine years later they built forts on the Gold Coast and were sending 700 kilos of gold and 10,000 slaves each year to Lisbon. The first intimations of a seaborne approach by Western Europeans to East Asia came when Bartolomeo Diaz rounded Africa and sailed, past a cape that his king named the Cape of Good Hope, into the Indian Ocean. A few years later again, in 1492, came Christopher Columbus's voyage to the 'The Indies', the fabulous East, by a westabout route that led him to the new world of the Americas. When he set sail, he carried a letter from the Spanish sovereigns, Ferdinand and Isabella, to the 'Great Khan of Cathay'. To avoid undue competition between Spain and Portugal, Pope Alexander VI used his authority to set the ground rules of exploration in a papal bull of 1493, whose details the two kingdoms set down a year later in the Treaty of Tordesillas. It divided the unexplored world between them, Portugal being allocated Brazil and most of the non-Christian world of the East, and Spain taking the Americas, the Pacific, the Philippines and the Moluccas. By 1498 Vasco da Gama, following Diaz, had reached India via the cape.[5] Other Portuguese found the way westwards, round South America, into the Pacific. The road to Asia was now open, not only for the Portuguese and Spaniards, but for the Dutch and English as well.

In that period the distinction between trade, robbery and empire was often blurred. Alfonso d'Albuquerque captured Goa for Portugal in 1510 and Malacca a year later. Its sultan, as a loyal Chinese vassal, appealed to the emperor for help, but none was forthcoming. Malacca not only gave d'Albuquerque control of the gateway to the spice islands but introduced the Portuguese to Chinese traders, who had long been in the habit of bringing their silks, satins, pearls and chinaware there, to exchange them for spices, incense and gold thread. So d'Albuquerque created the basis not only for the Portuguese empire in the East but for the world's first global trading network, from Portugal eastabout to Japan.

In 1513 the first boatload of Portuguese set foot on Chinese soil. Still driven by a combination of evangelism and trade, they came to the mouth of the Pearl River, near what is now Macao. Three years later, Rafael Perestrello sailed into China in a European ship and made a

MING CERAMICS

Ceramics in general, and porcelain in particular, was an area of formidable Chinese artistic achievement long before the Ming dynasty came to the throne. Ceramics were needed not just for the daily use of the imperial household but for the performance of the rituals, including sacred ones, that were essential for social cohesion and stability. Vessels were also needed after death so that the deceased could be provided with food, as well as houses and servants in the afterlife. Inscribed vessels were given to Buddhist and Confucian temples and very much used as diplomatic gifts.

The exceptionalism of Chinese ceramics in general, and porcelain in particular, probably began (apart from a brief period of excellence under the Tang) with the Song dynasty, which doted on refinement in the arts and crafts. Under that dynasty, lovely white ware was produced, in elegant shapes. These artistic achievements progressed under the Mongol Yuan dynasty when Jiangxi province became the centre of porcelain production for the entire empire. When the Ming followed the Yuan, their artistic achievement inevitably rested on the skills and traditions of their forerunners. So that, for instance, Mongol rule had brought together the styles of different regions that had previously been politically and socially separate. Not only that, but Chinese art began to feel the influences of other parts of the larger Mongol empire, brought into China along the trade routes, and the movement of people and religions. That certainly included the settlement of groups of Moslem merchants along the south coast and, at the other end of the empire, into China's north-west. One way or another, painted decoration and glazes became a notable feature of Chinese porcelain in the Mongol (Yuan) period, with the finest wares coming from Jiangxi. Porcelain production there was close to the sources of raw materials, and could draw on spare labour and good transport facilities. It was there, too, that important technical innovations in porcelain manufacture were made. These included the introduction of blue and red glazes.

At the start of the Ming period an imperial porcelain factory was established and successive emperors took special care with the appointment of the officials who would supervise it. In the early years of the Ming, the most important class of porcelain was plain white. It was this which, for a while, was the preferred variety used in the imperial household. But then a variety of innovations came along, including, variously, black-and-white porcelain, a further development of blues and reds, and one that achieved special fame – a light green. That was followed by the growth of multi-colour work. But the single greatest innovation of the Ming period, which was to become famous far and wide, was the production of blue-and-white porcelain, later so strongly imitated by the Dutch. It may first have been produced for the overseas market, especially in the Middle East, where Persian work with blue decoration had been known for a couple of centuries. Nor was porcelain the only kind of ceramic or carved work produced. In the late Ming period, for instance, rhinoceros horn imported from East Africa was often made into drinking cups or similar objects.

In any event, Ming porcelain became famous all over Eurasia. In Europe, too, Ming ceramics came to be highly prized. Before the sixteenth century, when there was little traffic between China and Europe, only a few porcelain pieces appeared, usually as gifts from Middle Eastern rulers or aristocrats. But in the sixteenth century, King Philip II of Spain created the largest collection of Chinese porcelain in Europe – some 3,000 pieces. It has been estimated that by AD 1600 about one-third of all the silver mined in Peru and Mexico went to East Asia to pay for spices, silks – and ceramics.

very handsome profit on his trade. It was the first of many sporadic visits to the ports of southern China by people whom the Chinese saw as just another lot of 'South Sea Barbarians'. The trade was so attractive that in 1517 King Manuel I of Portugal sent Tomé Pires, as the first Portuguese ambassador to the Ming court, to talk about expanding it, while Fernão de Andrade, the mayor of Goa, was sent to lead an exploratory mission along the Chinese coast. The two men arrived at Canton in September of 1517 in a squadron of eight ships. On arrival their guns fired a salute, much to the alarm of the local Chinese. Pires carried a letter from his king, but the Canton mandarins, knowing nothing about Europe, saw them as just another group of pirates and the governor sought permission to drive them away. Officials in Beijing, equally ignorant, also refused to receive the Pires embassy. But someone bribed officialdom at Canton and permission was eventually obtained for the embassy to move to the capital. Pires arrived in Beijing, but there his mission stalled. An envoy from the powerful Sultan of Bantam, in Java, arrived with news of some Portuguese kidnappings and enslavements of local people. There was also news from Canton that more ships under de Andrade were building fortifications and kidnapping women, maybe even attacking Chinese officials on the coast, not just verbally but physically. The emperor promptly sent the Portuguese back to Canton, where they were not only forbidden to trade, but imprisoned and tortured. The Chinese treated Portuguese prisoners as pirates and executed some of them, while other Portuguese only escaped execution because of court intrigues against the new Chinese governor in the south.

For a time there was clandestine Portuguese smuggling on the Fujian coast, but that produced further official Chinese reprisals in 1549, including the seizure of two Portuguese-owned junks. By 1553 one of the captured Portuguese, Galeote Pereira, managed to bribe his way to freedom and set down an account of his experiences and of Chinese government and customs, that reached the Jesuit College at Goa in 1561, was transcribed in the seminary there, and promptly translated into English and Italian. Here was the first report since

Marco Polo by a Westerner who was not a churchman. It was, in spite of Pereira's experiences, an admiring report. He commented favourably even on the Chinese justice system.

The Portuguese hoped to set up a permanent trading base at Macao, but the Chinese were none too keen on the idea. Not until 1535 did the Portuguese bribe their way to official permission to live and trade there. They agreed to pay rent, and customs dues on ships and commodities, with Chinese sovereignty remaining unaffected. Not until 1557 could the Portuguese rent the Macao peninsula, and only on condition that they rid the area of pirates. Within twenty years the Chinese had tacitly accepted the Portuguese presence, and the growing Portuguese monopoly of foreign trade in the area. By then, the Chinese had also lifted the old post-Zheng He prohibitions on sea trade, which had never been very effective, and designated a port close by the modern Amoy as the centre for it.

These approaches to China were, of course, part of a much broader Portuguese drive to bring the cross to the heathen and to get rich by trade. In 1592 they reached Japan. Or again, in the 1570s the conqueror of northern India, the Mogul emperor Akbar, met the Portuguese on the coast and pronounced himself most impressed by their ships, their artillery and their merchandise. An altogether remarkable man, he had a passion for theology, welcomed Jesuits at his court and even attended mass.

Other Europeans were quick to challenge the Portuguese. The Spaniards, in particular, looked with growing envy at the wealth the Portuguese amassed from the spice trade. Columbus's discoveries seemed to show that one could indeed reach the East by sailing westwards. In 1519 Ferdinand Magellan, a Portuguese in the service of Charles V of Spain, led an expedition of five ships around South America and, via Cape Horn, into the Pacific. More than two and a half years after setting out, he reached the Luzon islands. Though he and many of his crew were killed by natives, the survivors returned to Spain in 1522, going westabout round the Cape of Good Hope. Balboa the Spaniard crossed the South American continent and promptly claimed the South Seas and all its lands for the king of Castile.

There were other and shorter ways to China. Once Hernan Cortes had conquered the Aztec empire in Mexico, Spain commanded the west coast of the Americas. By 1526 Cortes himself had begun to build ships on the Pacific and to found ports, especially the good harbour of Acapulco. In 1564 Miguel Lopez de Legazpi sailed from Mexico to the Luzon islands, which were renamed the Philippines, in honour of king Philip II, with Manila as their capital. A year later Legazpi sent a sailor-priest, Father Andres de Urdaneta, to find a better return route. Urdaneta set off in July 1565 and found he had to sail north as far as the 36th parallel to get winds able to carry him eastwards across the Pacific to California. Sixteen of his forty-four crew died, mostly from scurvy, and when he reached Acapulco, only he and Legazpi's nephew had enough strength left to cast their anchor. No one had made that eastward Pacific crossing before and Urdaneta's notes and charts remained standard among navigators until the days of Captain James Cook, two centuries later.

By the time the Spaniards reached the Philippines, Chinese merchants had long been trading there. Here, too, as well as on the China coast, the problem of piracy was very serious. In 1574 a Chinese pirate leader, Lin Feng, with a fleet of 62 ships and some 2,000 men, women, and arms and implements, arrived at Manila intending to settle. They built a fort but in March 1575 the Spaniards burned the pirate fleet. That earned the thanks of the commander of an imperial Chinese fleet from Fukien (Fujian), who had been sent to deal with the pirates himself. The Spaniards seized the opportunity of opening relations with China, and entertained the Chinese commander at Manila. He agreed to take back to China a Spanish embassy consisting of a couple of Augustinian friars, the senior being the missionary Father Martín de Rada, who wanted to open up China to both trade and Christian missions. He was duly brought to China and given a friendly reception. However, in the meantime Lin Feng had managed to escape with some 30 ships and to return to the Formosa Straits, which deflated Chinese enthusiasm for the Spaniards, and de Rada was turned away.[6] But larger numbers of Chinese now arrived at Manila and, in time, a reasonably lively trade did emerge between Spain, Mexico and the Spanish settlement at Manila on the one hand, and some Chinese ports, like Amoy and Foochow (Fuzhou), on the other.

Other Europeans were pressing, too. As the Portuguese and Spaniards grew rich from trade, others wanted a piece of the action. First came the Dutch, moved by money, the sentiments of the Protestant Reformation, strategy and the new national passions flowing from their own successful revolt against Spain in 1581. They also had to respond to economic pressure as Philip II of Spain, in punishment for their revolt, barred them from the port of Lisbon, which was the centre of the Eastern spice trade. Some Dutch merchant groups responded by forming the East India Company at Amsterdam in 1595, and a year later Cornelius Houtman was making the first Dutch voyage to the Indies. By 1602 the Netherlands East Indies Company was officially set up, with authority from its government to maintain troops, colonise territories, and make war or peace agreements with countries in the East. The company seized the Moluccas, Java and Sumatra from the Portuguese and even won the right to trade in Japan. By 1604 the Dutch arrived in China proper.

Other Europeans came, too, including the French, the Russians and even Hanseatic traders and Prussians. Spices from the Indies were too important, and the English followed hot on the heels of the Dutch. In 1596 that excellent Latinist, Queen Elizabeth I of England, wrote a letter in Latin to the Chinese emperor. If it was delivered, there was no response. Four years later, she granted a fifteen-year charter to 'The Governor and merchants trading into the East Indies', a body that evolved into the East India Company. James Lancaster and John Davis seem to have been the first to sail there when they took five ships to Java and Sumatra. However, after such efforts were given a bloody nose by the Dutch in Java, the British concentrated their efforts on India.

The French were even more ineffective for the time being. Four years after Elizabeth's charter, in 1604, the French king, Henri IV, authorised the first trading company, formed by merchants on France's Atlantic coast, with a fifteen-year monopoly of the Indies trade. Nothing came of it, and the first larger effort dates from 1664, when Jean-Baptiste Colbert, Louis XIV's finance minister, created the Compagnie des Indes Orientales. The capital was 15 million livres, in shares of 1,000 livres. The king himself subscribed the first 3 million. The company was granted a fifty-year monopoly of French trade in the Indian and Pacific Oceans, from the Cape of Good Hope to the Straits of Magellan. Nothing much came of this, either. The company struggled on until 1719, when it was formally dissolved. The Germans were equally unsuccessful. The German ports had worked with Amsterdam, Bruges, Antwerp and London since the twelfth century and were all founding members of the Hansa organisation that had a hand in the Eastern trade quite early on. But it was not until 1670 that the Prussian royal house endorsed the founding of the Brandenburgische-Preussen ostindische Handelskompanie, a joint venture between a group of non-German traders and the king of Prussia. Though this effort also failed, it did not entirely stop Prussian commercial efforts in the East.

Much the most significant of the early European contacts, and the ones with the greatest long-term impact on the Chinese empire, were once more made not by traders but by Christian missionaries. To be sure, China continued to be relaxed about differing religious beliefs. But in the West, agitation about opening China to Christ increased. It was answered, most particularly, by the Jesuit order, founded in 1540 by the soldier-saint, St Ignatius Loyola. It immediately became much more important in China than the first few visitors to the Mongols had been. The Jesuits were fired with missionary zeal and St Francis Xavier himself, fresh from bringing Catholicism to Japan, came to China, though he died in 1552 before actually entering the empire. In 1573 came the appointment of a superior of all Jesuit missions in the East Indies, Alessandro Valignano. He sailed with forty-one Jesuits, arriving at Macao in 1577. He was clever enough to adapt the mission to China instead of trying to adapt the Chinese to Catholic practices. He demanded from his missionaries cultural accommodation to things Chinese. At the same time, these highly educated and learned Jesuits were able to deal with Chinese scholar-officials on equal intellectual terms. Valignano's rule was carefully followed by Michele Ruggieri and Matteo Ricci, who established a small church west of Canton. Both of them changed into Chinese dress, learned Chinese language and manners, and studied Confucianism. They were keen to cultivate influence through their skills in mathematics, astronomy and geography and so made friends with officials and scholars.

Ricci became especially notable and famous for his scientific work. He also wrote two large manuscripts on Chinese culture and society, and the history of Jesuit missions to China, both of which were found after his death and published in Europe in 1616. Like other observers, he greatly admired much that he saw in China. Here was a very large and unified realm, well ordered and with a central orthodoxy, namely Confucianism. Social life was regulated by rituals and manners that produced a harmony only too likely to be disturbed by foreigners. Administration was through a professional bureaucracy, selected on merit. It was all a stark contrast to the fragmented and embattled state of Europe after the Reformation.

The Jesuits did a great deal for China's progress in mathematics, astronomy, map-making and geography, and in other technical and scientific fields. Ricci himself was able to show that the existing calendar was out of date and inaccurate, a matter of huge importance in Chinese rituals and affairs, and therefore for the position of the monarch himself. As early as 1611 the Ming emperor asked Sabatin de Ursis to correct the official calendar. Soon afterwards, in 1622, arrived the most famous of all the seventeenth-century China Jesuits, the German Father Adam Schall von Bell. Between them, the Jesuits not only demonstrated that their forms of calculation were much more accurate than the existing Chinese ones, but they made new astronomical instruments. In effect, Ricci and his successors were the first Western technical experts in the empire; and for all the earlier progress of the Chinese in technical inventions, they had been and remained oddly slow to exploit and develop them further. The missionaries published, in classical Chinese, introductions to much Western learning and science. They also understood that the Chinese, for whom it was after all the emperor who was the link to the divine, were hardly likely to be much concerned with Christian dogma. So they presented Christianity as a system of wisdom and ethics that Confucians could accept. Perhaps that was wise, in a society where fear of punishment was often greater than the prospect of reward for innovation. As another Jesuit missionary, Louis Le Conte, wrote with some irritation, the Chinese 'are more fond of the most defective piece of antiquity than of the most perfect of the modern . . .'[7] Nowhere was that more true than in the many decisions to reject technology and modernisation.

For instance, gunpowder had long since been a Chinese invention, but the Ming showed comparatively little interest in its military applications. After all, using crossbows from behind walls was quite effective against nomad cavalry. The Mongols had already used cannon in their sieges and even the Ming had some early muskets and bombs, but it was not until the Japanese invaders of Korea had used cannon successfully in the 1590s that the Chinese condescended to learn much about them. In 1621, when the Portuguese offered four

---

JESUITS IN CHINA

The Jesuits in China were, by and large, an extraordinary group: learned, sophisticated, energetic. The two most famous among them were Matteo Ricci and the German Adam Schall von Bell.

Ricci was a man of vast patience and great charm, born in Italy in 1552 and educated at the Jesuit College of Rome. After joining the order he served in Goa and was sent to Macao in 1582. He learned the language and entered China in 1583, settling down near Canton. He did not reach Beijing until 1598 but by 1601 was given permission to stay, even receiving an imperial stipend until his death in 1610.

His willingness to dress, eat and live as a Chinese, willingness to learn, together with his scientific knowledge and quiet Christianity, made him very acceptable to the Chinese élite. He became famous and received dozens of visitors each day. But he also saw that he had something to prove about Western culture and especially science. He produced a global map for people who still thought the world was flat. He translated chapters of Euclid's *Geometry*. He interested Chinese scholars with his astronomy and European clockwork.

His own theology was broad-minded enough to let him accept early (though not later) Confucianism as an ancient system of ethics, and the ancestor worship of his converts as just another civil rite.

The German Adam Schall von Bell was born some forty years after Ricci, in 1591, and reached Macao in 1619 but could not enter China because of general anti-foreigner sentiment and especially a recent decree against foreign teachers. Some years later he and other Jesuits helped the Portuguese soldiery fight off an attack on Macao by the Dutch. Jesuits manned guns on the walls and a lucky shot hit a Dutch ammunition dump. The Dutch withdrew.

When the emperor heard the story he asked the Macao Portuguese, and especially the Jesuits, for help to fend off the Tartars (Manchus) in the north. Some Jesuits, including Adam Schall, travelled to Beijing.

Like Ricci, Schall was a man of charm, energy and intelligence, and soon became friendly with Chinese scientists. The astronomical knowledge that he and other Jesuits displayed was critical in strengthening their influence at court; most importantly, making sure that the calendar was very precisely calculated, which was extremely important in Confucian culture, and very much a field in which the Jesuits could display special expertise. After Schall had managed to predict, more accurately than the Chinese themselves, the 1629 solar eclipse, he was put in charge of the imperial astronomy office. He also led the way in calendar reform. Furthermore, the Jesuits were able to produce scientific instruments and maps to the point where they were invited to set up an observatory in the royal palace itself. In January 1639 a procession of court nobles came to the Jesuit residence and gave Schall, as a gift and high award from the emperor, a tablet recording special imperial praise.

As the turmoil of the final Ming years gathered pace, the emperor once more asked the Jesuits for help. In the end, Schall supervised the manufacture of some small cannon, but then went back to his missionary work.

The Ming dynasty duly fell, but the Jesuits continued to prosper under the new Qing rulers. Schall himself was appointed director of the imperial 'Board of Astronomers', and in spite of the jealousies of Chinese scientists, had a good relationship with the court.

When the new emperor, the regent's nephew, ascended the throne himself as the emperor Shunzhi, aged thirteen, he made Schall a mandarin. But the emperor died in 1661, to be succeeded by his six-year-old son Kangxi. By this time the Jesuit position at court was being undermined by rumours and innuendo from the royal scientists. Eventually Schall and some brother Jesuits were accused of false astronomy, high treason, and teaching a superstitious religion. Four of the Jesuits, and some of their followers, were sentenced to death. But on the day of their proposed execution came a great storm, followed by a fire, both of which were taken as omens. The sentences were suspended, and in time the accused were set free. Soon after that, in August 1666, Father Schall died, having spent forty-seven years in China. Not long after his death the emperor appointed Father Verbiest as Schall's successor and, to give Schall posthumous honours, erected a monument at his grave with an inscription reading: 'You leave us undying fame and the glory of your name.'

In the late twentieth century, after the Great Proletarian Cultural Revolution in Communist China, the graves of Schall, Ricci and Verbiest were restored and relocated and visitors can see them today.

cannon to the emperor, they found they had to send cannoneers with them. The following year the court asked Jesuits from Macao to cast cannon for China and twenty years later another of them, Adam Schall himself, was asked to cast more and teach the Chinese how to make them. In fact, some of the old Jesuit cannon were still being used in the nineteenth century.

To this point, then, dangers in the north and north-west were containable and it was possible to buy off some of the Mongols more cheaply than to fight them. In the south, by contrast, there were still no serious dangers. There remained, however, the other two major problems besetting the empire: population growth and administrative failures. The first had many causes, as population growth always does. It should have been a blessing; a result of peace, prosperity and domestic progress. It was certainly based in part on an unprecedented abundance of China's main food, rice. That stemmed from the renewed attention to irrigation and its machinery that Hongwu had begun, but it also came from new varieties of rice. They had begun to find their way into the empire some centuries earlier, even in the time of the Song, coming from Indo-China. The new rice turned out to be drought-resistant, more productive and could be sown earlier than the old varieties. The most useful new forms of rice were so quick-growing that peasants could get two harvests instead of one, so at a stroke doubling their production. At much the same time they began to put fish into their paddy fields, both because they were good to eat and because they would fertilise the rice plants. There was a further advantage, though no one could yet understand the links of cause and effect. The fish fed on the mosquito larvae in the water-logged paddy fields, which reduced the incidence of the malaria that had traditionally haunted southern rice-growing.

The reasons why population growth led to problems the Ming could not solve had very largely to do with the shortcomings of imperial administration. Hongwu himself insisted on consolidating a highly personal control of the state. It was not that his policies were malign. In domestic affairs he took care to hold down land tax to help the poor, to worry about erosion and flood prevention, to curb banditry and to ensure grain supplies. But centralisation of administration of a great empire in the hands of a single man was bound to produce bureaucratic constipation and sclerosis. Most particularly when, as was sure to happen, there were later emperors who lacked Hongwu's own thirst for hard work. Ming administration became huge and centred on the person of the emperor, who was supported by a large imperial staff, and six central ministries. Confucian scholars were once again brought in as senior officials and the use of eunuchs in high office was expanded by Hongwu's successors. Indeed, the eunuchs and Confucians tended to be at odds throughout the Ming period. The third emperor, Yongle, made a point of handing a large share of government business to the eunuchs. He also insisted on moving the capital to Beijing, even though the site was strategically vulnerable and rather distant from the main, and now southern, centres of population and industry.

Matters were not made easier by the fact that the early emperors were especially pitiless with anything smacking of dissent. Hongwu himself had a violent temper, was murderously paranoid and behaved with special cruelty to those higher up the social scale. In 1380 he suspected that his chief minister was plotting against him. He not only had the man's head cut off, but the heads of his entire family and even of persons vaguely connected with him. It is said that the total toll may have been as many as 40,000 people. There were other purges and he went on having high officials beheaded.[8] Not that his successors were much gentler. Around 1520 the emperor of the day had some 130-odd men flogged simply for advising him to stay in the south rather than return to the capital. Eleven of them died.

The Ming record is much less impressive in financial and economic matters. Hongwu himself was rather opposed to commerce, thought that trade was ignoble and that the country's source of wealth should be in agriculture. Indeed, both under him and, as Confucianism became more absolute, later Ming rulers, the view held that profit was evil and commercial enterprise inherently at odds with the interests of society and the state. Still, principle was one thing, practice another. The Ming might be officially scornful of trade, but all the same they nurtured the trade of tea for the horses from the north and the trade that brought in silver. Yet keeping taxes low came to mean a shortage of central revenues. Worse still, the revenue system was confused, with inefficient collection systems, a huge collecting staff and all the openings in such a system for corruption. The government tried to solve some of its problems again by printing paper money, but that produced inflation, there were coin shortages and, in time, much counterfeiting. Neither Hongwu nor his successors established any kind of monetary system of control or, more importantly, any single unit of account. In some places there could even be different exchange rates between copper coins and silver within the same city. From the point of view of the emperor, the entire fiscal system anyway existed for purposes of political control rather than for wealth management.

However, that is not the whole story. Hongwu, in particular, understood peasants, which is why he held down land tax and paid attention to dykes, curbing banditry and encouraging the local gentry to care for the poor. The empire also introduced crop rotation, so that fields no longer had to be left fallow. Peasants even started to experiment with cash crops and were encouraged to plant fruit trees. Relations between landlords and tenants were more often based on contract. Under Hongwu China also began massive re-afforestation, with large effects on the supply of timber. At the same time, the early Ming paid much attention to repairs of roads and canals. Bridges, shrines, walled cities, and of course defences, received similar attention. Naturally, these improvements also fed back into population growth. Modern estimates say that China's population around 1400 may have been some 80 millions. By 1600 or shortly afterwards, that had almost doubled to perhaps 150–160 millions.

Moreover, after 1500 or so, restrictions on commerce were relaxed and there was something of a boom, especially in small businesses producing paper, silk or cotton. Trade crossed borders as foreigners became even keener to buy quantities of Chinese silks and porcelain. But the Chinese found much less worth buying from outside, except perhaps South-East Asian spices. They therefore sought payment for their goods in silver. That further promoted those substantial flows of silver to China from both the Spanish Americas and Japan.

By the end of the 1500s, the Ming empire was at the peak of its power and glory. It was great and rich. It had remarkable achievements to its credit in education and culture. It had given China periods of long domestic peace. It had expanded and secured China's borders and achieved remarkable things in the arts, especially in ceramics or the poetry of Gao Qi, who paid with his life for poems that satirised the Ming court. Yet for all its power, the empire was showing signs of weakness and stress; and within two or three decades the dynasty was in terminal crisis. At bottom, the empire had just become too big, both in land and people, too diverse, too ungovernable by the existing structures of government. So when it came to face a fresh threat from the north, this time from a highly organised and well-led group calling itself Manchu, the danger eventually overwhelmed the dynasty. And the Manchus were able to take over largely because the Ming failed to cope with decline and disruption at home.

Some fundamental difficulties stemmed from the very successes of the Ming in producing peace and well-being. Population growth itself had helped to make peasant life, always precarious, even harder. The dangers of droughts or floods were not new. But with population growth, job prospects grew worse. More men became homeless, sold their wives and children, and roamed desperately around. Taxes rose in a period when more revenue was corruptly diverted into private pockets. They were increased even further by war, like that in Korea in the 1590s. In the two decades to 1636 the land taxes on peasants actually doubled. In 1601 there were riots in Jiangxi province and the Yangzi delta, with houses burned down and local tyrants lynched. There was hunger, banditry and rebellion in several regions. In the mid-1630s there was repeated drought, famine and rebellion in north and central China, where dreadful conditions gave rebel leaders a steady flow of recruits.

Yet defence costs, not only on the Great Wall but in sporadic fighting with Mongols, wars in Indo-China, Thailand, Burma, and dealing with rebels, accentuated inflation and budget problems. These costs grew so large that they disrupted China's internal market system and elementary banking arrangements. In 1639–44 things became even worse. That began with floods and locusts helping to produce further hordes of beggars. Parts of China were swept by epidemics and in places the population is said to have halved. As the inflow of silver dwindled, largely because of changed Japanese trade regulations, its domestic price in China rose, producing deflation, and shortages of silver for government spending.

Matters were made much worse by the loose grip of later emperors themselves, not all of whom were famous for sagacity. Centralised administration, in the hands of one man, of a great empire with poor communications produced, as such things almost always do, an impossible dilemma. On the one hand, the problems of time and distance in controlling far-flung provinces gave much local power to local officials and gentry. On the other, central efforts at supervision and control strengthened bureaucratic sclerosis. Wanli, who came to the throne in 1572, found himself unable to cope and withdrew altogether from public affairs. He and his successors left matters in the hands of the court eunuchs,[9] the most important of whom became overbearing and tyrannical. The court continued to be riven by plots and counter-plots among various factions, and riddled with corruption. The last few decades of the dynasty were too often a tale of factions, suicides and executions of people newly disgraced, or simply too powerful.

The problems of rebellion became worse as distress across the country grew. One rebel leader was Li Zicheng, in the north-western province of Shaanxi, who later called himself the 'Dashing King'. He emerged as a natural leader of rootless and unhappy rebels, and one with sound tactical instincts. By 1635 he was the leader of a large group in Henan province and contemplating attacks into the Beijing region itself. Over the next few years Li and another rebel leader, Zhang Xianzhong, roamed around central China, competing with each other for land and recruits, while the emperor, by now Wanli's grandson Chongzhen, proved impotent. By early 1640 the rebels were firmly established in central regions of China. By this time, although many generals remained loyal to the Ming dynasty, some rich locals began to recruit their own militias as a protection force.

In the meantime, foreign problems became more serious. There was again fighting along the southern borders, there were pirates on the coast, difficulties on the Central Asian frontiers or problems with raiding tribes. There were a few more approaches by European merchant ships, but they were insignificant. Mongol horsemen from the steppes once again threatened the west and the north.

The real trouble was that, by now, the Ming military response was no more effective against northern tribes than it was against powerful rebels at home. Indeed, since the dynasty needed not just frontier protection but the ability to fight domestic rebellion, it had to seek the co-operation of many of the non-Chinese tribes of Inner Asia. That was bound to produce ambiguous and complicated frontier relations. Part of the trouble was that there was still no competent professional military force. Not only that, but Chinese troops were still often commanded by Confucian-trained territorial administrators, or mere scholars who had studied military affairs. In any case, the imperial troops became unruly when, for long periods, they were not paid; many deserted.

In these conditions even Great Walls could not keep China insulated, especially from organised opponents just beyond the border, in Manchuria. China's dangers were increased even further by the consequences of those 1590s campaigns against the Japanese in Korea. The huge cost of the campaigns was bad enough, but worse still was the resulting crisis in Manchuria. The Jurchen tribesmen who lived there were a mixed nomadic lot, mainly descended from the semi-nomadic tribesmen who had once founded the Jin empire in north China. These Jurchen had long had an uneasy tributary relationship with the Chinese empire, though they adopted Chinese technologies and styles of living. But in the mid-sixteenth century they began to confederate and by the 1590s they acquired a remarkable new leader.

*　　*　　*

His name was Nurhaci. Born in 1559, he began his career as a minor chieftain, starting with only a handful of followers and, he claimed, thirteen sets of inherited armour. At first he lived in the household of a Ming general, where he learned to read Chinese and something of Chinese history and strategy. Then he began the task of creating an organisation that could unify the Jurchen. He created a tribal league of Manchus by making a point of good relations with the four major Jurchen tribal groupings. He went on to exchange wives and concubines with several neighbouring Mongol groups, and acquired the title of khan. He accumulated riches through a monopoly of furs and ginseng, and made sure that in exchange for his 'tribute' to the Ming he got silks and silver. He built his tribal groups into a nation in arms that in 1635 began to call itself 'Manchu'. He also started off with good relations with the Ming. In 1589 the emperor conferred title and rank on him and the following year Nurhaci headed a tribute mission to Beijing. In 1595 Beijing even appointed him as 'General of the Dragon and Tiger'.

He also established a highly efficient military and administrative system, organising his forces in the fashion that would later become standard for the 'Tartar' troops of the whole Manchu empire. In an idea copied from Ghengis Khan, the men were divided into companies, with groups of companies forming four 'banners'. Each banner had its own different colour: blue, red, yellow and white. Four more were added later. At first, the banner arrangement built on traditional tribal and clan divisions, but later, as the disciplined 'banner' units became increasingly mixed and non-tribal, former tribal leaders were simply enrolled in ad hoc fashion. Until 1619 Nurhaci waged successful campaigns against other tribes in and around Manchuria. He also offered posts to educated Chinese who might be willing to work for him. In 1616 he declared himself emperor of a new dynasty. Helped by various Mongols, he routed a large Chinese force two years later and in the years that followed captured all of southern Manchuria, moving his capital to Mukden (the modern Shenyang). There he created governmental and administrative structures leaning strongly on Chinese practice. Finally, after a twenty-year tributary relationship with the Ming, Nurhaci proclaimed his independence and in 1619 declared war against the emperor, and won over time a series of brilliant victories.

After he died in 1626 his eighth son and successor, Abahai, formed fresh alliances with the tribes of Inner Mongolia, subdued Korea in alliance with the Mongols and routed more Ming forces, bringing the entire region of the Amur River under his rule. In 1629/30 the Manchus even penetrated the Great Wall, marched into China and threatened Beijing before returning home to Shenyang, laden with booty. By now the Ming court panicked and struck out in all directions. Wicked tongues even falsely accused the ablest of the Ming generals of colluding with the Manchus, so he was condemned to the most humiliating and painful possible death: being cut to pieces in Beijing's market-place. In the meantime Abahai set up his own new state, proclaimed the Qing dynasty (meaning 'clarity') – making it entirely clear that he intended to overthrow the Ming. Ominously, Ming troops soon started to stage mutinies when ordered to march against the Manchus. In mid-1642, Abahai sent more troops on a seven-month rampage into China, capturing hundreds of thousands of prisoners and more mounds of booty. By now some Ming generals simply surrendered to the Manchus or even joined the invaders, while numbers of local Chinese officials were killed or committed suicide. The empire's affairs had become so disorganised that even army pay was badly in arrears, imperial granaries were empty, and morale plummeted. But Abahai died in 1643. Since his son and chosen successor was a mere five years old, the child's uncle, Prince Dorgon, became the Manchu regent.

The military and political collapse of the Ming, and of Chinese resistance, continued. Within the empire, things got worse. Various rebel movements threw up increasingly able leaders, especially but not only in the north-west. 'Dashing King' Li, by now the greatest of the Chinese rebel lords, purged potential rivals and started to appoint officials as alternatives to the Ming bureaucracy. He overran more areas in the west and got as far as the Yangzi valley, while other rebel commanders joined him. He prepared to strike at Beijing itself, at a time when the Ming capacity for resistance was gravely weakened by the desperate need to divert troops to guard against the Manchus in the north. By early 1644 Li announced the establishment of his own new dynasty, the 'Shun', and moved on Beijing with several hundred thousand troops, promising the people peace and prosperity in place of Ming cruelties. On 24 April 1644 he reached the outskirts of the capital. The next day the emperor, having failed to escape, gave his advisers permission to kill themselves, which thirteen of them did. He cut down his own concubine and the appalled empress committed suicide as well. Then, accompanied by just one loyal eunuch, the last Ming emperor walked up a little hill in the palace grounds, went to a small pavilion, and hanged himself.

Li's soldiers duly occupied Beijing. At first there was restraint. There was no violence against citizens, some looters were executed and Ming officials who had joined Li began to organise an orderly transition. Thousands more were called in to make use of their expertise. But within a week there were problems. The imperial treasury was empty, so how could Li's soldiers be paid? Soldiers began to use torture on people suspected of hiding money. Soon there was looting and even killing in broad daylight. Discipline collapsed. Li might have secured the help of remaining Ming troops, but the imperial commanders in the north, facing Manchu striking forces outside the Great Wall, had become thoroughly disenchanted with imperial officialdom. It seems that the senior Ming general, Wu Sangui, was particularly displeased when Li, back in Beijing, acquired Wu's most delicious concubine and refused to give her back. So Wu joined the Manchus, fought off Li's army, and invited the Manchus to join him in recapturing Beijing. Li retaliated by killing Wu's father and putting his head up on Beijing's city walls. There was a final frenzy of looting in Beijing before Li fled the city and started on his way back to his western strongholds. Meanwhile the Manchus careered down to Beijing and, two days after Li left, Prince Dorgon reached the imperial palace.

6

MANCHUS AND RUSSIANS

AD 1644 to 1727

FOR ALL ITS distinctions then, the Ming period was a mere interval of Chinese governance, separating long periods of rule by foreigners: first the Mongols and now the Manchus, who faced very much the same three fundamental problems as those that had afflicted the Ming – and who proved, over the long term and in spite of many successes, equally unable to master all of them. The first task was to establish and maintain the rule of the new dynasty throughout the realm. The second was dealing with the social, economic but also external security consequences of the alarming fertility of the Chinese people. The third was still external security when the borderlands were imprecise regions inhabited not by stable states but by fractious or marauding tribes who resented Chinese people but envied China's wealth. The result was frequently a Qing takeover of border regions, in wars of conquest that were also wars for security. So, for example, Tibet had to be controlled to make Xinjiang and Mongolia more secure; and to ensure that any attacker from the west or north would have to cross wide and unproductive regions, creating huge supply difficulties.[1] At the same time, it was an expansion of imperial power that, however impressive, had to make problems of central administration worse.

The conquering Manchu army was actually quite small – probably no more than 150,000 bannermen – and much smaller than Li's rebel Chinese force, but Beijing greeted these disciplined troops as liberators; and their commanders formally claimed the Mandate of Heaven for the new Qing dynasty. They understood that consolidating their power would be neither quick nor easy. For one thing, as non-Chinese rulers they would have to adapt to established Han Chinese ways of doing things. They took a good deal of trouble to make themselves acceptable to Chinese society, rather than simply holding down the Chinese people.[2] Their leaders honoured the dead emperor, his empress and the dead officials, and buried them in due ceremonial form. They maintained the rituals, carried out the appropriate ceremonies, promoted the classics, continued the custom of venerating ancestors and generally understood that proper conduct would reflect proper values. Of course, by the time they took Beijing, the Manchus were quite familiar with Confucian methods of government. It was not difficult to accept the traditional Confucian order, or to use it for their own ends.

Taking over Beijing was just the start. The Qing could destroy the Chinese rebels in the north in short order, but they had to consolidate their rule everywhere. They began by moving south almost immediately to capture Nanjing, the old cultural and economic centre of China. The behaviour of Ming generals and troops was not predictable. In May 1646 some 138,000 Ming soldiers simply surrendered and joined Manchu forces on their march to Yangzhou. The defenders of that city, on the other hand, fought to the death, and the Manchus conducted a ten-day massacre of Ming remnants – probably, as the saying has it, *pour encourager les autres* (to encourage the others).[3] They then left their new Chinese troops to complete their own programme of murder, rape and pillage.[4] The example was clearly impressive: the following month Nanjing simply surrendered, as did a further 100,000 Ming troops. Once the new dynasty had captured Nanjing and the economic heartland, the Ming cause became hopeless. Also, especially when the Manchus made clear that they would not tamper with land holdings, the gentry class accepted them. All in all, however, the pacification of the Yangzi valley and delta was a bloody business.

There were naturally holdouts. One of the most colourful Ming supporters, the pirate chief Coxinga, maintained himself for years on the south coast, in Amoy. In 1658 he even led an army north into the Yangzi valley to threaten Nanjing. Later he captured Formosa from the Dutch, only to die there in 1662. The island fell to the Qing twenty-one years later. The last major challenge to the Manchus came in 1673 when some south and south-western grandees rebelled. They included the very General Wu who had let the Manchus enter China thirty years earlier; and it took the great Qing emperor Kangxi eight years to reassert control. The Manchus also had to cut off foreign support for these Ming remnants. It was the final defeat of ethnically Chinese government in China, all earlier attempts at Ming reassertion having failed.

There were other and more private forms of resistance. During and after the military campaigns there were hundreds of suicides of men, and their families, who thought it shameful to support the new foreign rulers. Former imperial functionaries, in particular, faced a stark choice: loyalty to the new rulers, or death. Not just for themselves but often for their wives, children and concubines.

In general, though, the Qing welcomed experienced Ming officials who agreed to serve the new regime, and in many cases that created no difficulties. After all, the Chinese mandarinate had usually succeeded in letting non-Chinese occupy the throne, while at street level the empire went on being run by Chinese bureaucrats in familiar ways. On the military side, Manchu controls were further strengthened by enrolling Chinese into the increasing number of banner units which formed the strike force. In fact, in later years a majority of these professional soldiers, kept on imperial stipends, were Chinese, while Manchu garrisons were stationed at important points. Alongside them there was the army of the Green Standard, organised in small units as a kind of constabulary to keep local order in garrisons at various points. These local and more purely Chinese forces were long confined to provincial units used in police and anti-bandit roles.

So the Qing ran the empire largely on traditional principles, including the examination system for official appointments. It was a relief to many people to have a reputable government, no longer encrusted by court cliques and hundreds, even thousands, of eunuchs around the emperor. Some less useful elements of the old order persisted, too, including the governing classes' dislike of economics and commerce, and the inadequate tax structure. Nevertheless, the new rulers tried to strengthen imperial loyalties by spreading growing wealth. The imperial motto ran: 'wealth should be amassed in the hands of the people.'[5] In time the Chinese peasant became free, in practice and in law, to buy or sell his land. But the Qing also preserved racial separation, banning intermarriage between Manchus and Chinese as well as forbidding Chinese migration into the Manchu homeland. They wanted to avoid contaminating the martial virtues of the Manchus with more decadent Han habits, and to protect differences of customs, while carefully keeping authority in Manchu hands. In time, capable Chinese were left to do much administrative work, with loyal Manchus checking on them. Not that such arrangements settled everything. As early as 1650 or so the Manchus, like some of their predecessors, found it necessary to try to root out the endemic corruption of the governmental and judicial systems.

EUNUCHS

A eunuch is a male, part or all of whose external genitalia have been removed, whether by force or choice, and who is therefore incapable of reproducing. The practice is very ancient, recorded as early as the twenty-first century BC in Sumeria. It was known later in Assyria, pharaonic Egypt and Persia.

In ancient China, castration could be a punishment, but might also be used to gain employment in the imperial service. Chinese kings started to keep eunuchs at the latest by the eighth century BC. At the end of the Ming dynasty there were tens of thousands of such people serving the emperor. Although they were often employed for simple domestic and personal functions, like bathing the ruler or cutting his hair, such personal services also gave the eunuch direct access to the emperor, the source of all authority. No wonder that some of them gained official positions, sometimes of immense power, greater than that of the emperor's ministers. Qin Shi Huangdi's favourite Zhao Gao, the great early-fifteenth-century admiral Zheng He and the empress dowager Cixi's favourite An Dehai in the later nineteenth century were all eunuchs. Unsurprisingly, there was often bureaucratic warfare between the palace eunuchs and the mandarinate.

Eunuchs are probably best known for looking after the ladies of the royal harem. If the emperor's queens did not bear a living heir, sons of the highest-ranking concubines could succeed to the throne. Strict chastity among the women was therefore of huge importance, unquestionable paternity being essential for the ruler and his dynasty. After all, ancestor worship decreed that the ruler must perform the official sacrifices to his ancestors not only for his own sake but to maintain the harmonious balance between heaven and the Chinese people. Clearly the ancestors would not be pleased if an interloper appeared.

Consequently hordes of eunuchs were in charge of the harem, whose ladies could hardly move without being observed. On the other hand, some eunuchs might be very welcome there as lovers. If a man had his testicles removed after puberty he could still, in many cases, achieve an erection and maintain it with no danger of an ejaculation that could impregnate the lady involved.

Eunuchs have been known in modern times, too. In the eighteenth and nineteenth centuries some eunuchs, known as castrati, were highly valued, especially but not only in Italy, for their childlike voices. By the start of the twenty-first century there certainly remain millions of eunuchs in various parts of the world, not least the Indian sub-continent.

The second Manchu emperor, Kangxi, reigned for no less than sixty years, from 1662 to 1722. He proved to be a remarkable ruler. Indeed, the 133-year governance of Kangxi, his son Yongzheng, followed in turn by his grandson Qianlong, was very much the high-water mark of Qing civilisation. Kangxi himself – his pictures show a sharp, thin face and watchful eyes – was frugal, practical and extremely hard-working. He took a personal interest in many things: flood controls, conservancy, canal repairs. He pursued scientific interests with the Jesuits, was intensely interested in culture and learning, personally practising calligraphy, commissioning maps, academic collections, a major dictionary, an anthology of poetry and a huge encyclopaedia. But he was also a military leader in many campaigns.

There was no great change to the principles of foreign affairs. The empire continued to see itself as the centre of the civilised world, to which properly brought-up foreigners should pay tribute. The reception ceremonies which lay at the core of Chinese diplomacy, with everyone kow-towing in the presence of the emperor, remained more or less unchanged until the mid-nineteenth century. What, though, of foreigners within the empire? In particular, there were the Jesuits. They continued to operate in China throughout the turmoil of the decline and fall of the Ming, and the Manchus made use of them, especially in matters of science and mathematics. Kangxi continued to favour Adam Schall and actually made him a mandarin. Other able Jesuits came along, too. One of them, who became almost equally famous and important, was Ferdinand Verbiest. Inevitably, Jesuit influence fluctuated. But Kangxi had no hesitation in using the Jesuits as advisers on mapping and engineering, and put them in charge of the astronomy office. In 1687 five French fathers arrived and one of them managed to cure Kangxi of malarial fever by using quinine. In 1692 came an edict of toleration that allowed the Jesuits to build churches. A year later year one of the French fathers returned to France for fresh recruits and in 1697 Joachim Bouvet wrote a report for the French king, Louis XIV, with enthusiastic references to Kangxi's moral and military achievements.

When the Jesuits ran into trouble, it was not with the Chinese but with other Christian missionaries. The Jesuits presented Europe with a hugely flattering account of Chinese ethics, arguing that Confucianism was a civic morality and that the principles of Chinese civilisation could well be fitted into Christianity. Father Louis Le Conte, for instance, claimed that it was entirely justifiable for missionaries in China to adopt any prudent adaptation to Chinese customs in order to advanced the faith.[6] That aroused strong opposition from Dominicans and Franciscans as well as groups in France itself. Once the mendicant friars began to preach to the common people, they complained that Jesuits were just talking to Chinese élites, even getting involved in palace politics. More importantly, the Dominicans and Franciscans worried about Jesuit permissiveness towards Chinese customs, ethics, and Confucian morals. The Jesuits, they said, were quite wrong to say that China's system of rites was almost entirely secular, and that the principles of Chinese civilisation could be fitted into Christianity. In their concentration on the Chinese élites the Jesuits were giving away central Christian principles.

That created serious trouble, for the emperor insisted, as he was bound to do, on respect for the traditional Chinese homage to Confucius and the rites of ancestor worship. He demanded that the missionaries regard these as civil and not religious ceremonies, and that Christian converts should continue to practise them. The Jesuits were willing to accept that, but the Dominicans and Franciscans were not. The disputation had to be referred to Rome. Pope Clement XI sent out Bishop Maillard de Tournon, to investigate. He arrived in 1705 and was granted several meetings with Kangxi which ended in total disagreement. The issue, as the Church saw it, had ultimately to do with papal supremacy in matters of religion. From that point of view, the Jesuit willingness to accept Kangxi's opinions amounted to a critical weakening of the fundamental claims of Catholic Christianity. In 1715 came a papal bull banning the strategy of accommodation and Maillard forbade Catholic missionaries, on pain of excommunication, to obey the emperor in the matter. But there was no possibility that the emperor could tolerate that. After all, missionaries seeking to make converts were, by clear implication, attacking China's claims to moral superiority; and the papal claim to supreme religious authority would, if accepted, undermine central elements of the emperor's own position. Kangxi's response was therefore to expel anyone who did not sign a paper accepting his view. The emperor had Maillard imprisoned at Macao, where he died in 1707.[7] Most of the Jesuits duly signed. A number of Franciscans, Dominicans and others refused, and were sent away. The entire basis of the Western missionary effort in China was seriously weakened.

Kangxi did, though, want to reopen China to Western science and to restore trade. Which meant admitting foreign caravans in the north and foreign, especially European, ships in the south and east. Of course, Portuguese merchants had arrived in China long before the Qing took over. The Spaniards also came to Formosa in 1626 and set up a trade and missionary base. The Dutch failed to take Portuguese Macao, but managed to establish themselves on Formosa. British ships appeared on the coast from sometime around 1635 and within two years there was a small British merchant fleet at Macao. Later, and informally, the British were allowed to trade at Amoy (Xiamen), and then at Canton (Guangzhou). The British East India Company, having established itself in Bombay in 1662, opened a trading centre at Calcutta in 1690. Nine years after that, it came to Canton, where British trading quickly became a monopoly under the company's aegis. It used its monopoly to buy porcelains, silks and, not least, tea to cater for the growing demand back home in England.

There was also the Dutch trading centre on Formosa, which Coxinga seized. The Dutch East Indies headquarters at Batavia sent a fleet to help the imperial forces recapture the island. As reward, Beijing allowed the Dutch to trade in Fujian and Chekiang (Zhejiang), after which Dutch vessels regularly called at south China ports. Other Europeans came, too, the first French ship arriving at Canton in 1660. For the Qing empire, this European trade, while useful, had clearly very little political importance before the late eighteenth century; and the traders themselves were often a nuisance, if a minor one.

However, as Western pressures increased, the Qing, unlike their Ming predecessors, allowed some official foreign embassies to visit Beijing. There were several Dutch envoys between 1656 and 1687 and two Portuguese ones between 1667 and 1678. They all accepted Chinese ways of doing things, including the formalities under which tribute-bearing envoys brought gifts and performed the full kow-tow before the emperor. None of them achieved much, except to confirm the Chinese in their sense of ineffable superiority. Western merchants might have to accept Chinese ways of doing things, but for official groups the clash between Chinese and Western cultures was becoming irritating.

Still, dealing with missions like these required rather more Chinese circumspection than dealing with mere merchants. That could lead to an occasionally subtle shifting of Chinese diplomatic gears. The senior mandarins had begun to observe that the Europeans were not just ordinary tribute-bringers but represented major cultures. What the emperor could not see, and would have had no sympathy for if he had seen, was that the Europeans did not want to come to Beijing just to be impressed with its marvels and go away again. They wanted negotiations, on more or less equal terms, on trade and relations. But if the Europeans were blind to Chinese views, the Chinese were no less blind to the way in which their diplomatic forms, bureaucratic routines and delays irritated the Europeans. Still less were official European missions amused to find themselves in Chinese bureaucratic categories devised for Asian tribute-bearing tribes.

In fact, by the early or mid-seventeenth century the Chinese and the Europeans had vastly different impressions of each other. The Westerners were far more interested in China than the Chinese were in the West. They were also much more respectful. European views of China tended to be admiring. That stemmed not only from the writings of Marco Polo, the Jesuits and other travellers but the general impression of China's size and riches. Ricci himself had translated Confucius, and the pope was presented with Jesuit translations of some 400 Chinese works. All this literature promoted intellectual and religious turmoil in Europe. Some people argued that the Chinese were a survival from a period before Adam and Eve or that the Chinese language stemmed from the end of Noah's flood. There was also the Jesuit view that China could easily be fitted into Christian views about history, the universe and God.[8] That was particularly unsettling at a time when Galileo's idea that the world moved round the sun, not the other way round, or the discoveries of explorers, were anyway undermining established views of the world and much Christian teaching.

Chinese views were quite different. It was true that the Jesuit missionaries were highly educated and could deal with Chinese scholar-officials on equal intellectual terms. It was also true that their knowledge of mathematics, cartography and astronomy interested Chinese scholars; and that tens of thousands of Chinese had been converted to Christianity. But there is no evidence that European thought or practice had any influence on the beliefs of the Chinese governing and literary classes. As for the European traders to the China coast, they were apt to be adventurous, raucous and uncouth, and many of them, the Dutch especially, were a violent lot. Anyway, the Chinese found it hard to distinguish among them, for they were all 'red-haired barbarians'. The empire therefore tried to maintain the general policy of imperial kindness to strangers, and to tolerate their trading efforts. Official customs houses were established at four ports. Canton on the Pearl River quickly became the most important of them.

Dealing with Western Europeans remained of very minor importance compared with the empire's perennial problems in the west and north. The Qing were preoccupied, perhaps even more than their predecessors, with border raiders, especially the Mongols, and with Tibet. They invited the Dalai Lama to visit Beijing. He came in the 1650s and was received with marked respect and courtesy. Then all these problems with Tibet, the Mongols, and tribes from Turkestan to Manchuria, were complicated by the appearance of yet another, and much more formidable, set of foreigners on China's northern and north-western borders. They posed, potentially, at least as great a danger to the empire as the Mongols had done. They were the Russians.

The origins of the Russian push eastwards towards China stemmed from the slow collapse of the greater Mongol empire, starting in the 1300s. The Mongol rulers of the lands that would become Russia were not interested in settlement or government, merely in money and loot. They wanted taxes but were content to have them collected by Russian princes. By 1325 Ivan I of Moscow made a deal with the Mongols: he would be their tax agent for all Russian principalities. That focused the attention of colonists and traders on Moscow, which became an important regional centre. By 1478 Ivan III managed to bring most of Russia under his rule. He took the title of czar – from the Latin caesar – and claimed to be the true successor to the Roman and Byzantine emperors. This notion of Russia as the 'Third Rome' has been a thread running through Russian history ever since. These ideas, together with the needs of war, confirmed the absolutism which also became a permanent feature of Russian affairs.

The programme of welding Muscovy into a single state relied heavily on technical developments, especially in weapons. Ivan could see that as recently as 1452 Constantinople had fallen, not so much because Mohammed the Conqueror promised his assault troops free use of 'the women and boys of the city' but because he used cannon cast for him by Christian artillerists to batter down its walls. So Ivan acquired some cannon of his own and used them to conquer other Russian principalities, whose walls suddenly became useless, and began to expand his rule into the eastern plains. No one there had cannon. There were no mountains to block their movement. Instead, there were navigable rivers that could carry barges with troops and guns. So the czarist state began to expand rapidly across the vast eastern plains. There were few natural boundaries between Moscow and the Urals and even fewer on the plains beyond.

Expansion was encouraged by Ivan's successor, Ivan IV, known to history as 'the Terrible'. Endlessly suspicious, violently depraved, deeply cruel, he was also a devout churchman and one of the most literate of Russian rulers. He found problems not only in the east but in the south, from Tartars who kept raiding, and supplying Russian peasants to the slave markets of Constantinople. In the 1550s Ivan responded by conquering the Tartar principalities along the Volga River. But these dangers were only really checked in the seventeenth century, when the Russians started to build elaborate frontier defences. Ivan also began to take the area between Moscow and the Urals, which was the heartland of the Russian fur trade. One of his instruments was the commercial family of Stroganov. It received land and salt concessions in 1575 and was allowed to go and colonise. Small forts were built in the Urals and probes went further. Polish, German and Swedish war veterans were recruited, men who were willing to go on freebooting expeditions with a group of Cossacks. Their leader, a former river pirate named Timofeyevich Yermak, was engaged to remove the Mongol khan of Sibir from the eastern slopes of the Urals. These Cossacks – the word stems from the Turkic 'kazak' – were wild horsemen, originally descended from ancient Scythians but by now including Turks, Greeks, Tartars, hunters, peasants, exiles and others. Originally from the Ukraine, they were democratic groups of farmer-soldiers, adventurers, runaway peasants and convicts. Yermak started off in 1579 with almost 550 Cossacks, 300 Stroganov recruits and three cannon. A year later he crossed the Ural mountains and captured Sibir. He reported his success to a delighted czar. Yermak went on raiding eastwards, but a lot of men died of starvation during the winter of 1583/4, Yermak drowned and Sibir was abandoned.

That was merely the start of the eastwards push for here there was no other state in the Russians' way. Such steppe states as there were had anyway never recovered from the devastation inflicted by Tamerlane in the 1390s. Once across the Urals, the Russians could move into Siberia virtually without resistance. Expansion was astonishingly quick. Families arrived. Soldiers settled. By the end of the 1580s the town of Tobolsk was established. The new settlements were often formed from ex-soldiers or peasants seeking fresh land. They were joined by motley bands of Tartars, river pirates, deserters from various armies, Poles, Ukrainians, Germans, escaped galley slaves from the Turkish empire, freebooters and ruffians of all kinds. The government even used convicts and prisoners of war as settlers. Whatever their origins, these new Siberians faced a cruel life that hardened them to human suffering. Siberia itself, and especially its north-east, was very much a land that God forgot. It had some of the bitterest cold to be found anywhere; many travellers and settlers froze to death. Agriculture was impossible. Three hundred years later the mosquitoes of Yakutia were still locally known as 'fascists' and said to be able to suffocate reindeer by swarming up their nostrils. New Russian arrivals might, amid snowstorms and avalanches, be reduced to eating grass or roots, and sometimes each other. They also had a ruthless dedication to plunder. Everywhere, their expansion was helped by germs even more than by guns: the newcomers spread sicknesses of which the isolated native groups had no experience, like smallpox – much as other Europeans were doing in the Americas.

By the time Ivan the Terrible died in 1584, he had expanded his rule to the Ural mountains and the Caspian Sea. The mechanisms for Siberian expansion were by now well established. Siberia was divided into intendancies, each centred on a major fort (*ostrog*) and commanded by a military officer. Some small Russian landowners who acquired royal favour became *voevoda* (governors) in the east, and native chiefs could also hold official Russian posts. It was a rough and brutal regime, hard and dangerous, though civil troubles in Russian pushed more people to cross the Urals. More soldiers were sent and new *ostrogi* founded. These and other forts were typically sited at the junction of rivers, which were the highways for the eastwards drive. Each fort was a wooden stockade that served as a military and trading post, granary and customs office to assess and tax all goods. By 1590 Moscow had settled some 3,000 peasant families in western Siberia. It was only twenty years later, in 1613, that Mikhail Romanov, a distant relation of Ivan IV's wife, founded the new Romanov dynasty, which would last until 1918, when the Bolsheviks murdered Czar Nicholas II and his entire family.

The seventeenth century therefore saw the unfolding of a major imperial drama, acted out by tiny groups of men. They might be, more often than not, roughnecks and ruffians, but they achieved extraordinary things. Their entire march from the Urals to the Pacific across northern Asia, perhaps the most difficult and inhospitable terrain in the world, took a mere seventy years. By 1619 they had marched as far as the Yenisei River, beyond which lay China's Siberian borders, in 1632 Vassili Poyarkov founded Yakutsk and by 1639 a party of Cossacks under Ivan Moskvitin reached the Pacific. Okhotsk was founded and, ten years later, the Russians reached Kamchatka and the Bering Straits. By the end of the 1650s some 50,000 Russians had surged into Siberia and the number probably doubled by 1700.

The motives for all this eastward expansion are not far to seek. For the peasants, there was the lure of fresh land. For the Russian state, as well as the settlers and hunters, there were stories of the vast resources of gold, silver and other mineral resources of Siberia. There were also the riches of animal furs, known as 'soft gold'. Russia's own forests had become denuded by relentless hunting. So the hunters moved further east to get more, whipped on by tough *voevodas*. The Russians going east regarded both land and people as belonging to the czar and took over the old Mongol practice of taking tribute, paid in furs, from each Siberian tribesman. Refusal of tribute meant burned villages. Between 1638 and 1642 the *voevoda* of Yakutsk, Pyotr Golovin, collected as many as 100,000 sable pelts after he started to hang refuseniks from meathooks. He was almost equally hard on his own men, using pliers, hot coals and whipping on them and even their wives. When the tribes rebelled, the Russians replied with terror, so much so that in some places the natives, finding themselves slaughtered whenever they revolted, started to kill themselves and Moscow had to order local officials to stop natives from committing suicide.

However, as early as 1585 the czar received a total of 200,000 sables from Siberia, and by 1660 furs were providing one-third of all Russian treasury receipts. In fact, fur from Siberia began to play a role for Moscow not unlike that which gold and silver from the Americas had played for Portugal and Spain shortly before. The result was an even more frenetic search for more and more furs. As wildlife was killed off, the hunters pushed ever further into the east. Meanwhile that prospect of land and furs kept bringing more and more peasants and others to seek a new life in the east, rather as English and Scots emigrants started to seek a new life in North America at more or less the same time.

The Russian state had even larger motives. There was strategic pressure to seek defensible borders. There was a wish for direct relations with China, tales of whose fantastic wealth had long been promoted by Mongol traders and Jesuit accounts. Anyway, the Mongols had introduced Russians to Chinese goods. There was also Siberian gold and silver that Russia badly needed to pay for its wars in Poland, against Sweden and in the Crimea. Not to mention the modernisation drives of Peter the Great. He ruled from 1689 to 1725, spent time exploring Western Europe and, remarkably, himself worked there as a shipbuilder and, in disguise, as seaman, barber and even dentist. Perhaps more importantly, his drive for military modernisation allowed Russia to catch up, at last, with West European levels of military equipment and organisation, in addition to creating a brand-new navy. The result was, among other things, a sharp increase in Russian power relative to that of other European states.

In any event, the new Siberian settlements created major issues both for Russia and for China. In some ways the positions of emperor and czar were not dissimilar. Both monarchs were re-garded by their subjects with almost religious awe. Both restricted foreign missions. Both sought control of trade with Central Asia. Neither had remotely adequate information about the other. For the Chinese the central fact was that armed Russians were sitting just beyond China's north. There was as yet little appreciation of the fact that they were representatives of a Europe growing rapidly in might, curiosity and greed. As for the Russians, they did not even have remotely adequate maps of China or Asia. But there was the simple and irresistible demand for food. Siberia was cold – even frozen – dry and unproductive. Shortages of vegetables and fruit brought scurvy and beri-beri. There was hunger and starvation. People were forced to eat grass and roots and here, too, there was cannibalism. Clearly, the place to find food was further south: in China itself.

The first region to try was the Amur River basin. In 1643 the *voevoda* of Yakutsk sent Vassili Poyarkov with 150 men to go and have a look, to extract tribute from the locals and get information about China. He started out by camping at the Amur for two winters. His men plundered local villages for supplies and women, killing some of the men. The locals ran away or refused supply. In the hard winter of 1643/4 the Russians starved, or ate each other. Half of Poyarkov's force died before the rest could move on. Eventually he and the 20 or so men he had left made their way back to Yakutsk. But Poyarkov did bring back the first eyewitness information about the Amur region. It was, he reported, ideal for settlement. He was enthusiastic about the moderate climate, the good soil, a potential breadbasket, with a huge river, the Amur, sparkling with fish. Of course, while the expedition alienated the locals, its presence also warned the Chinese of the Russian approach.

In 1650 the *voevoda* sent Yerofei Khabarov and another band of Cossacks on an even more aggressive campaign to grab the riches of the Amur region. It was the start of attempts at settlement. Khabarov spent three years killing locals and exacting tribute, and told Yakutsk that the Amur contained even more fish than the Volga. The region could very easily support agriculture. He added that conquering the Amur region would be difficult, but numbers of Russian traders, peasants, deserters and vagabonds moved south anyway. A year after his first inspection, Khabarov launched a more sustained effort to force the locals to submit. With his 150 men he stormed a strategic village and its small fort, which had been garrisoned by some fifty Manchus, installed his own garrison, and called it Albazin. He spent three years exacting tribute, planting fields, building a couple of *ostrogi* forts, and raiding the surrounding areas for goods and women.

He then massacred, burned and pillaged his way to the junction of the Amur and Ussuri rivers and by 1654 was building the town of Khabarov.

In fact, the local people were Chinese tributaries. Qing officials, without interfering with either Poyarkov or Khabarov, reported to Beijing that 'man-devouring demons' had appeared in the north. However, Russian barbarism and lust for profit appalled the Daur tribes of the region, who appealed for help to the Chinese emperor. After all, the Manchus thought that the lands on both banks of the Amur were part of the Chinese empire, the natives imperial subjects and the Russians were intruders and freebooters. The Qing dynasty had from the beginning extended its reach to the Amur, partly to help safeguard the cultural and tribal purity of Manchuria. Now, the entire Chinese position in the north, perhaps even in Manchuria, was threatened. Imperial troops were sent and there were skirmishes. At first the Manchu general tried to take the barbarians alive, but he was defeated and lost several hundred men. News of the Russian victory quickly spread and hundreds of other fortune-hunters and ruffians came down to the Amur from all over Siberia. The Manchus adopted sterner tactics. They began by encouraging local people to leave their homes, so that Russian grain supplies and foraging dried up. Then, in 1658, and after more skirmishes, came a full-scale land and naval assault on the Russians. Their leader   Khabarov's successor, Onofri Stepanov – was killed, together with more than half of his troops, and the Chinese destroyed the Albazin fort. That Chinese victory drove the Russians out of the Amur.

But Emperor Kangxi withdrew his troops. For one thing, they were needed elsewhere, to help cope with rebellions. More importantly, Beijing still had only the vaguest idea of what it was facing in the north: it still thought here was just another group of barbarian raiders. After all, China did not send ambassadors abroad nor, by now, did Chinese merchants travel far to northern markets. Not that the Russians were much better informed. The first Russian to reach Beijing seems to have been Ivan Petlin, who was sent there in 1617 to gather information. Though he had no official position, the Chinese treated him as another tribute-bearer. He brought no gifts from the czar, but was allowed to return home with a Chinese letter inviting the Russians to send a mission and to trade. It took another thirty-five years for the czar to send Fedor Baikov as ambassador to the Manchu rulers. His task was to discover routes, distances, especially trading possibilities – and information about Chinese military power. He was also told not to perform the ceremonial kowtow. Baikov reached Beijing in 1656 and got nowhere. From Beijing's point of view, the Russians were now being dealt with and the Mongols kept quiet; so why create precedents that might affect other areas of foreign relations? Since Baikov also refused the kowtow he was sent away within a few months with, as it were, a flea in his ear; but with considerable profits on his trading. In fact, it became clear that China, and especially Beijing, was a hugely profitable market for Siberian furs. The Russians also acknowledged that the Amur region was part of the Qing empire. Which did not stop more years of failed embassies and occasional massacres on the Amur.

Once Kangxi had withdrawn his troops from the Amur, the Russians returned. In 1665 fugitive Cossacks went back to Albazin, in defiance of their own Russian authorities. In the same year, Polish exiles in Siberia killed their guards and escaped to the Amur basin. By the end of the decade other Cossack bands and outlaws had settled at Albazin. Once again, locals were raided, creating such hostility that, in sheer self-protection, they made their peace with Moscow and started to cultivate the land. In fact, forty Daur tribesmen, headed by Prince Gantimur, walked into the Nerchinsk *ostrog*, paid tribute to the czar and were baptised. Now Beijing became seriously alarmed. This could not be allowed to stand, or it would become a highly dangerous example to other border peoples, endangering the whole system of Chinese relations in these regions. So the Chinese protested forcibly, and tried to win Gantimur's allegiance back. They achieved nothing. The local *voevoda* made matters worse by sending a message demanding that the emperor of China should himself swear allegiance to the czar.

Fortunately for the Russians, their delegates in Beijing seem to have had more sense than to present that kind of demand to Kangxi.

In the meantime, around 1660 a new and charismatic leader of the Zunghar Mongols, Prince Galdan, began the attempt to found a new, independent Mongol state. He wanted to unite the Mongols and to promote manufacturing and agriculture. With the support of the Dalai Lama he succeeded in welding many tribes on China's Inner Asian frontier into a united fighting machine that swept through Moslem Central Asia. By the 1670s he controlled Xinjiang and swept on into Mongolia proper.

His successes posed several strategic threats to the Chinese empire. These Mongols threatened the Manchu heartland in neighbouring Manchuria, where Beijing already had problems maintaining Manchu ethnic purity and keeping out the Han Chinese. Galdan's advance to the Russo-Mongol border, and victories over other Mongols, pushed several tens of thousands of these people into the arms of the Chinese state, causing serious administrative and other problems on the border. Most important of all: what if Galdan's new Mongol state were to achieve an alliance with the Russians and threaten China's north and north-west? Beijing now had several objectives. It persuaded the Khalka Mongols to come to terms with the Qing empire with promises of peace and food. The Manchus tried to bring several such groupings into China's ambit and sinify them in administration, habits, language and culture. Some Mongols were even enticed to become Chinese military auxiliaries. The empire also wanted to avoid war with Galdan and safeguard the imperial borders. It wanted to avoid driving Galdan into alliance with the Russians, whom the Qing wanted to leave the Amur basin as well as to remain neutral in the Central Asian regions of greatest strategic concern to China. The Chinese also very much wanted to protect Manchuria and to promote trade. However, Galdan wanted unrestricted trade across the Chinese border, which the Chinese refused, trying, instead, to establish a buffer between themselves and Galdan. Various embassies travelled to and fro and it seemed that both wanted good relations with each other.

*   *   *

GALDAN KHAN AND THE ZUNGHARS

Galdan Khan was the last of the great Mongol raiders and led armies from the north-western grasslands that were for years the greatest foreign threat to the Chinese empire. If his attempt to create a unified Mongol state based on the Zunghar Mongols had succeeded, he would have created the strongest power in Central Asia. Instead, he paved the way for the extermination of his people.

The Mongols, who had almost always been a group of many disunited tribes, began to talk about confederation in the 1640s, but that failed and in 1653 one of the major Mongol tribal leaders, Batur, died, to be succeeded by one of his nine sons, Sengge. However, in 1670 Sengge's brothers killed him, at which point another brother, Galdan, then aged twenty-six, returned from a Tibetan lamasery (monastery) and took charge. Other Mongols said he was 'violent, evil and addicted to wine and sex' and the Chinese agreed, saying he was 'rough and crafty and likes fighting'. Still, he managed to rally his Zunghar Mongols and rose to become a major prince. The Manchu emperor Kangxi thought he needed Galdan to help resolve other border troubles and in 1677 accepted Galdan's offer of tribute. Two years later he sent gifts to Kangxi and announced that he had taken the title of khan.

For some time both sides, Mongol and Manchu, went on wanting good relations; at one point the Manchus even wanted Galdan to have more control over other Mongols, so as to keep the borders quiet. Instead, there was a major Mongol split. The emperor sent a message: 'You are all descendants of the same ancestors. If you continue fighting you will be eliminated. There is no profit in peace for me. There is gain in war for me.' So in 1686 the various Mongol princes swore to keep the peace.

It did not work. There were more disputes among the Mongols, for instance over Mongol custom and law. In any case, thousands of various Mongol groups fled from Galdan into China, where the authorities found themselves having to feed some 20,000 starving refugees. It was all too much. Galdan was not only not keeping the peace, but his manoeuvres were causing more trouble. There were other issues. His missions to Bejing had been too big and its members had committed crimes on their way. So, in 1690, Kangxi personally led a military campaign – it even included cannon carried on camels – to put down Galdan. Although the campaign failed, Galdan sought forgiveness for his crimes and Kangxi accepted Galdan's oath to withdraw from the frontiers of the empire.

It was a mere interval. A year after the Chinese and Russians had signed the Treaty of Nerchinsk, in 1690, Galdan sent envoys to Fyodor Golovin seeking a Russian alliance for an attack on rival Mongols; but Golovin no longer had any interest in a Zunghar alliance. Kangxi went further in isolating Galdan and insisted that the Tibetan leader, the Dalai Lama, must not support him. The emperor also managed to deceive Galdan, who had no inkling until it was much too late that Kangxi was now determined to wipe him out.

In the war that followed, Galdan was decisively defeated in 1696 by one of Kangxi's generals whose troops had, in forced marches, well outrun their supplies. They went into the fight knowing that either they would win and capture Galdan's sizeable herds, or else be left to starve to death. Now Galdan Khan's followers began to desert while Kangxi offered Galdan wealth and honours in return for submission. But Galdan continued to retreat, and more of his followers trickled away. In April 1697 he died, either by suicide or, more likely, when someone poisoned him.

Kangxi celebrated. His officers were promoted, other Mongol khans were impressed with the emperor's 'godlike mystery' and, perhaps even more, by his cannon. As for Galdan, Kangxi had determined that his body, and that of his young son whom the

Qing had captured, should after the boy's execution be burned. The bones should then be displayed on the execution ground in Beijing, and ground to dust. The dust would be thrown into the streets, while the heads would be put up on the city walls. It was a punishment, and a degree of of obliteration, far beyond anything laid down in the imperial penal code. It meant not just making sure that the victim's body and soul would not survive, but that the entire after-life would be rid of him as well.

However, by the time Kangxi's wishes were made known, the Mongols had already burned the body, though keeping the head and the ashes. In late 1698, in a grand ceremony in Beijing, Manchus, Chinese and Mongols watched as Galdan's bones were crushed and the dust was scattered. However, Galdan's wife and children were pardoned. His son, Sebteng, was even given high rank in the imperial bodyguard, as well as a wife, while the Zunghar troops who had surrendered were simply enrolled into the Manchu banner units.

Russian diplomacy was cautious. Moscow wanted to protect Siberia and to prevent any Mongol interference there, but also to establish proper relations with China. As early as the 1660s the Russians sent missions to Beijing that sought trade and conformed to the Qing system of managing foreigners. They declined Galdan's proposals for joint action against the Qing, who saw that these Russians were indeed only interested in trade, not in acquiring parts of China. The Qing court also, at long last, understood that it was faced by men who were not just some robber band but state-backed Europeans who had marched to them right across the Asian land mass. So, by the 1670s the Chinese responded with gifts for the czar. They requested that the great Russian ruler should note that his subjects had the bad manners to raid other people on the frontier. There were also hints that the Chinese would grant commercial privileges in return for a Russian evacuation of the Cossack settlements, including Albazin.

The czar responded by sending as his new envoy a famous Moldavian scholar, Nicolai Gavrilovich Milescu. Nicknamed 'spathary' (from his time as an official of the Moldovan ruler; the name can be found to this day, from Albania and parts of former Yugoslavia across to Moldova), he was widely travelled in Europe, had excellent connections and enormous conceit. He entered Russian service after being introduced to the czar by the Greek Orthodox patriarch of Jerusalem and was selected in 1674 for his mission to Beijing. He was to regularise trade links and establish diplomatic relations along European lines, including the dispatch of a Chinese envoy to Moscow. Unfortunately the Russians knew so little about China that the letter to the Chinese emperor was merely addressed 'To the most noble Bogdykhan of the city of Kanbulak and of all the Chinese Kingdom Ruler'. Moreover, Milescu was much too arrogant and contemptuous of the Chinese to endear himself at Beijing. As one of his biographers put it, he was 'at once haughty and cunning [with] a love of intrigue and an absence of scruple'. Although he led an unusually well-prepared embassy, and the czar sent generous gifts for the emperor and money for bribes, the intelligence Milescu received en route convinced him that the Chinese were frightened of the Cossacks, and in any case had their hands full with domestic problems. They were therefore weak. So when he arrived at Beijing, although his brief was to establish diplomatic relations along European lines, he decided not to give way either on substance or on matters of protocol. The Qing bureaucrat who met him was Mala, a well-born Manchu appointed as a leading 'barbarian expert'. He wanted Milescu to behave not as a scholar representing a Christian monarch, but simply as a visiting barbarian. Given these contrasting expectations, it took Milescu some seven weeks even to be allowed to enter Beijing. There were disputes about whether the presents he had brought were gifts or tribute. Not only that but, from Milescu's point of view, Mala kept harping on side issues. What the Russians were after was a commercial treaty and here was Mala complaining about minor irrelevancies like Cossack raids and the Gantimur business.

Some of the Jesuits at the Qing court, especially Ferdinand

Verbiest, tried to explain to Milescu that the Chinese were furious about the raids and especially about the threat the Gantimur affair posed to the loyalty of the northern tribes, and therefore to the Chinese state. Milescu ignored him, and repeated his demands about trade. The Chinese responded with three demands of their own: peace on the Amur, the return of Gantimur to the Chinese, and the replacement of Milescu himself by someone who would be more reasonable. That should also mean – Milescu having refused the obligatory kowtow to the emperor – someone willing to stick to Chinese usages. The upshot was that neither side would give way on the central issues of protocol, commercial relations, boundary disputes, the return of defectors or, of course, control of the Amur region.

Given his many preoccupations, it was not until the 1680s that Kangxi could start fresh preparations to drive the Russians from Albazin. Once the Russians understood Chinese intentions, and after minor Chinese attacks on Cossack detachments, they set about strengthening their position; but saw that there were too few men for a determined defence, while the difficulties of command, communication and supply over the huge distances to eastern Siberia were almost insuperable. In October 1683 the emperor wrote to the czar that the Russians had invaded China's frontiers, 'disturbed and injured our hunters, boldly engaged in robbery, and repeatedly harboured our fugitives . . .'. There were several other such letters demanding that the Russians withdraw from the Amur and stop harassment of the frontier Manchus. At the same time, the Qing gave sanctuary to Russian rebels and treated captured Russians well. Nor was trade interrupted. Chinese tea, silks and porcelains continued to get to Russia and Russian furs reached China; all via the old caravan routes through Central Asia.

In the end, when the Russians showed no signs of withdrawing, the emperor decided to attack Albazin. This time the Chinese were well prepared. They recruited troops from the frontier Manchus, created military colonies in Manchuria, and set up strong points, supply bases and other facilities on the approach routes to the Amur. They improved transport and supply. They even built warships for use on the Amur River. In 1685 three thousand Chinese soldiers surrounded the Albazin fort and were about to attack when the Russians surrendered. The Chinese allowed most of the Russians to leave for the town of Nerchinsk. The Albazin settlement was burned down and some Russians were brought back to Beijing, where they remained under Qing 'protection'.

Yet by September 1686 the Nerchinsk *voevoda* allowed 669 men to return to Albazin, re-establish their fort, and harvest the crops they had sown. He even gave them guns and supplies and they went so far as to kill members of Chinese patrols. This time the Chinese reacted immediately. Kangxi ordered another attack. His commander was told to accept a peaceful Russian surrender, failing which he could take Albazin, and march on to Nerchinsk to put an end to this northern nuisance once and for all. The Chinese siege of Albazin lasted six months but was lifted when the Russians announced that an ambassador would come to negotiate a settlement.

Indeed, the Russians had decided to abandon the whole drive to the Amur. For one thing there was the 1685 fall of Albazin and the evidence of Qing power. For another, the fresh Chinese attack confirmed Russian worries about trying to hold such vast and distant regions. There also remained, on both sides, major strategic concerns. Russians worried that if the Chinese were driven into alliance with the Mongol and tribes, the entire Russian position in the east would be at risk. The Chinese did not want a full-scale war either, since they had the opposite worry: a war might propel the Russians into an alliance with the growing power of Galdan's Mongols, which could produce really major dangers for China itself. In any case, both sides were strongly interested in trade. So, after Moscow received letters from Kangxi requesting the evacuation of Albazin, it was decided to send an envoy to seek a peaceful solution.

The man sent out was Fedor Alekseyevich Golovin, the 35-year-old son of the *voevoda* of Tobolsk. He would later be created a count, promoted to admiral-general, and be effectively prime minister, entrusted with the conduct of the czar's entire external relations. His instructions now were to get a trade agreement, even if that meant sacrificing territory. When he came to the Amur, escorted by 1,500 troops, he saw the local military and political realities and concluded that Russia could, indeed, not seriously defend these far-flung lands. So Russian and Chinese delegations met at that crude frontier town of Nerchinsk, while thousands of Chinese soldiers camped outside. It was the first time in modern history that there were serious negotiations between China and a major foreign power. The Chinese side even included Kangxi's uncle and was accompanied by two Jesuit interpreters in the persons of the Frenchman Jean-François Gerbillon, and the Portuguese Tomás Pereira (each with the temporary Chinese rank of colonel). Although both the Russian and Manchu sides could use Mongolian, it was the Latin of the official Jesuit interpreters that became the language of negotiations and even of the treaty. That had time-consuming and sometimes amusing results. Every step of the talks had to be translated into Mongolian for the Chinese and into Russian for Golovin's people.[9] The result was the Treaty of Nerchinsk of 27 August 1689, which largely regulated Russo-Chinese relations for the next century and a half and whose equal signatures by both sides strongly implied an unprecedented acknowledgement by the Qing that another state could be equally sovereign. There were Russian, Chinese, Manchu and Mongol versions of the document, but it was agreed that the Latin version would be authoritative.[10]

When the two delegations met, Golovin's opening bid suggested the Amur River as boundary. The chief Manchu negotiator, Prince Songota, suggested Lake Baikal, a few hundred miles further west. The two Jesuits eventually suggested a compromise: a line half-way between Albazin and Nerchinsk. The final agreement laid down fairly precisely just where the frontier should be. In effect, Golovin surrendered the entire Amur basin except Nerchinsk itself, which would now become a mere trading post. Albazin and other Russian forts in the valley would be destroyed. Russian residents would be sent back to Russian territory and Russian travellers and hunters would find the valley closed to them. To prevent any repetition of the

Gantimur affair, it was agreed that all current fugitives could stay where they were, but future defectors had to be sent back whence they had come. Indeed, all future deserters and fugitives would be returned and anyone who had in the meantime committed theft or murder would be duly punished.

The treaty cast a long shadow. It, and the follow-up Treaty of Kiakhta, settled the borders and dictated that all persons, settlers, refugees or traders had to be subjects of one side or the other. From China's point of view, that settlement, with its trade provisions, fulfilled two strategic aims. It confirmed China's dominant position on the Amur, and made it altogether less likely that there could be a Russo-Mongol alliance. In addition, both sides accepted something like free trade, and the Chinese agreed that trading caravans could come regularly to Beijing. These trade arrangements turned out to satisfy both sides once another Russian mission, headed by a Danish merchant named Eberhard Isbrand Ides, had gone to China to settle details. Among other things, the new arrangements specified controlled trading centres that were to be a model for future Chinese trading arrangements with the West, in dealing with Europeans and Americans on the south and east coasts.

Kangxi was now in a much better position to deal with Galdan and the Mongols. He had suppressed rebellion in the south-west by 1678, seized Formosa in 1683 and now done a deal with the Russians which, among other things, isolated Galdan. In fact, Galdan repeatedly sent futile embassies to the Russians, seeking support. He tried, equally without success, to detach Mongols who had made their peace with China. Kangxi also made sure that Galdan would get no support from Tibet and began work on a better logistic system to support an army moving into the Mongol regions. The final battle came in 1696 and a year later Galdan was dead.

There remained the business of Sino-Russian trade. Frameworks like the Nerchinsk treaty are just that. There are always difficulties and details that remain to be settled. Here, too, it turned out that the Nerchinsk treaty was not enough. From 1698 to 1718 ten official Russian caravans travelled to China, and although Kangxi became friendlier to the Russians and even noted that 'the people of Russia are loyal and respectful', there were irritations. The Russians wanted an increase in the number of people allowed to travel with each caravan. They wanted higher prices for their goods. They wanted permanent consuls in Beijing. Some unofficial caravans travelled with forged papers. There was smuggling, and so much illegal selling that it depressed the prices for official trades. All of which deprived the Russian government of income and taxes. The Chinese also became unhappy with the caravan trade. There were too many caravans, and too many Russians stayed too long in Beijing.

There were other difficulties. By the early 1700s – yet another period of rapid population increase at home – the empire found itself again fighting against minorities in the south-west and not long afterwards with Mongols, Kazakhs and Kalmuks on the borders. In 1718 the Mongols invaded Tibet, and the Chinese responded by driving them away and stationing troops in the capital, Lhasa. There were fresh problems with the Zunghars, too. As for Sino-Russian trade, in 1719 the czar sent Lev Izmailov to China to try yet again to resolve things. Moscow wanted Russian merchants to be allowed to travel freely throughout China, and without customs duties. There should also be Russian consuls in Beijing with jurisdiction over Russian subjects. (That foreshadowed China's difficulties with the Western powers, especially with Britain, a century later.) The Russian mission was received pleasantly enough but Izmailov achieved little except to find out that Kangxi was by now quite well informed about Russia. Once again the two sides talked, as it were, past each other. The Russians wanted commercial concessions, the establishment of more Russian Orthodox facilities in Beijing and a Chinese language school for Russian students. But the Chinese wanted the territorial issue resolved before anything else.

There matters rested to await a change of monarch on both sides: the death of Kangxi in 1722 and that of Peter the Great of Russia three years later. Both sides saw that 'normalisation' was needed and in 1725 Moscow decided on yet another embassy. This time it included a number of people, including geographers and military

秦始皇

姓嬴名政始自稱皇乙卯即王江庚辰併天下稱皇帝

在位三十七年居王位二十五年即帝位十二年壽五十

Founding emperor Qin Shi Huangdi.

Wine vessel bronze, *c.*800 BC.

Wine vessel bronze, 10–11th century BC.

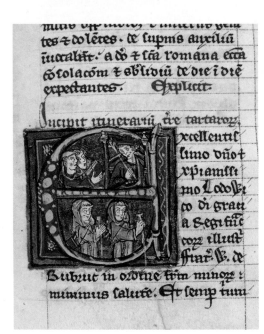

Illuminated letter from William Rubruck's (1220–1293) manuscript of his journey to Karakorum.

Possible portrait of Marco Polo (1254–1324).

Kublai Khan, the first Yuan emperor, on horseback, 1280.

Founding Ming emperor Hongwu (1328–1398).

Covered bowl with dragon design, early to mid-1400s (Ming dynasty).

Dish with three immortals, c.1600 (Ming dynasty).

Vase with floral scrolls, Hongwu reign, 1368–98 (Ming dynasty).

Floral globe vase, Yongle reign, 1403–24 (Ming dynasty).

Ming emperor Xiao Zong (1488–1505).

The first Western atlas map of China (with an East–West orientation),
from the *Ortelius Theatrum* atlas, 1584.

A senior civil servant collecting taxes, 1690.

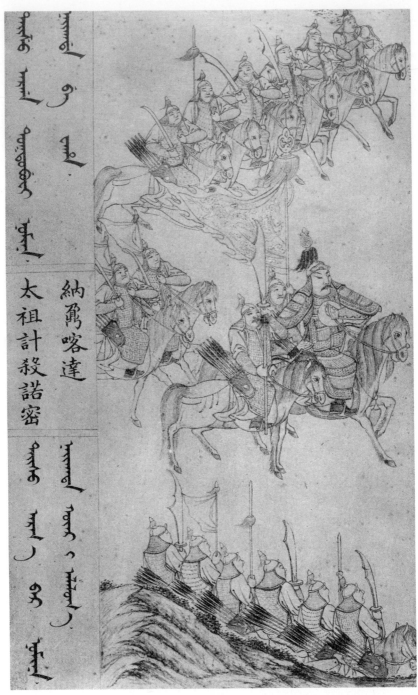

The first great leader of the united Manchus, Nurhaci (1558–1626), looks
on as two Mongol leaders are put to death outside a city wall.

P.MATTHEVS RICCIVS MACERATENSIS QVI PRIMVS E SOCIETAE
IESV EVANGELIVM IN SINAS INVEXIT OBIIT ANNO SALVTIS
1610 ÆTATIS 60.

Portrait of the first major Jesuit figure in China, Matteo Ricci (1552–1626).

Ferdinand Verbiest (1623–1688).

The German Jesuit, Adam Schall von Bell (1591–1666).

Qing
emperor
Kangxi
(1654–1722).

Passport from the
Qing dynasty.

Count Fyodor Golovin
(1650–1706), Russian
negotiator of the 1689
Treaty of Nerchinsk.

View of the summer palace, Peking (Chinese artist, date unknown).

Lord George Macartney, Britain's first ambassador to China, kneeling before the emperor (cartoon by James Gillray), 1794.

The Great Wall of China, by William Simpson, 1886.

Canton, *c.*1850.

officers, who had some experience of China and Central Asia. The 1,500-man mission reached Beijing equipped with generous presents for the Chinese emperor. An agreement to flesh out gaps left by Nerchinsk was concluded in 1727. It was the Treaty of Kiakhta, which regularised border arrangements further and accepted Chinese dominance in the nomadic regions. The caravan system was retained and yet more closely regulated. There were fresh arrangements for markets on the Sino-Russian frontier. China agreed to create trading centres in two towns, including Kiakhta itself.

There were also new arrangements for Russians living in Beijing. This was not a huge innovation; after all, for centuries, barbarian missions had been given homes in Beijing while they waited for the emperor to see them. Permission was often also given for envoys to bring a few merchants. Decades before Kiakhta, when the Chinese brought back Russian prisoners from the Amur, they were allowed to maintain their own Russian Orthodox church. Some even took Chinese wives and the group became part of a small Russian community, and a kind of commercial and diplomatic listening post. Now, as part of the Kiakhta arrangements, the Chinese granted a special hostel – a kind of consulate plus commercial agency – for Russian envoys in Beijing, and allowed the building of a proper Russian Orthodox church. Four students at any one time would also be allowed to come to Beijing and learn to read and write Chinese, while some Chinese students would be selected to study Russian.

On the other hand, the Chinese court conceded that the Russians were not just another tributary state. In fact, Russia gained something like a recognised place in the Chinese system, and even the Chinese capital, well over a century before other Western powers were granted anything similar. Kangxi himself noted that, while receiving tribute from the Russians would be splendid, 'I am afraid that when it is carried on into later generations it may become a source of trouble'. He even referred to Peter the Great, as his 'equal'. Indeed, soon after Kiakhta the Chinese sent a mission to Moscow: the first time the Chinese had sent an embassy to a major Western power. Not only that, but these envoys actually kowtowed to the czarina. On the other hand, it was only later in the eighteenth century that the Russians formed a more comprehensive view of China.

Were these arrangements, though, likely to be enough? In the longer term the Russians were most unlikely to be satisfied with recognition and trade. To be sure, for a century after Nerchinsk the Russians ignored the Amur and concentrated on the Pacific seaboard, Kamtchatka and the Kurile Islands. There was much exploration, too, as far as Alaska and beyond, and cartography. But the essential Russian drive was nothing less than an imperial push for the control of Siberia as far as the Pacific Ocean. That was all too likely to continue, depending on reliable supplies of food. It was also sure to depend on the local tribes: either they would be loyal to Russia or they would be exterminated.

7

EUROPEANS, MISSIONS AND TRADE

AD 1719 to 1816

FOR CHINA FRESH difficulties cropped up all round the empire's periphery. Of all the foreign pressures, the ones of greatest long-term importance came once again from Europe. Just as the unobtrusive arrival of the Portuguese and Spaniards on the shores of Ming China had had its origins in revolutionary political and economic changes deep within Europe, so European demands on the Qing would in time, and even more forcibly, undermine China's desire for social stability through insulation. In fact, there were almost eerie similarities between the frontier difficulties, as well as the problems of population and central control that had undone the Ming and those that would, in time, do the same to the Qing dynasty (1644–1911).

Once again it was European revolutions that brought wider change, in particular the seventeenth- and eighteenth-century upheavals of the Enlightenment in ideas, and the Industrial Revolution in power and reach. Structural problems were also dealt with. For instance, at much the same time as the Qing takeover of the Chinese empire came the 1648 Treaty of Westphalia in Europe. It not only ended Europe's Thirty Years' War, but defined new standards for inter-state relations and the sovereign equality of rulers. Shortly afterwards, in 1683, came the final defeat of the Ottoman threat to Christian Europe, when John Sobies-ky's Polish lancers, with their black feather standards, tiger skins over their cuirasses and silk pennants on their lances, streamed into battle to relieve the last Turkish siege of Vienna. At much the same time – also in the time of Kiangxi – King Louis XIV of France launched an era of military and political, and especially cultural, French dominance that had long echoes in European and world affairs and made French the language of Europe's polite society. Dutch financial and even naval power peaked in the 1660s, while Britain started to emerge from the long traumas of the Stuart dynasty and entered upon commercial and industrial revolutions that would soon bring it to the forefront of world powers.

That same century that brought the Qing dynasty to power saw from the mid-1600s the beginnings, also in Europe, of the modern scientific revolution, shortly followed by the Enlightenment, which changed the very vocabulary of politics. With its stress on social perfectibility through reason, it promoted political ideas that, among other things, fuelled the drive for American independence. The arrival of steam in the eighteenth century, which revolutionised transport and manufacturing, brought factory systems, growing markets, increased productivity, a vast growth of capital and credit – and a good deal of social misery. Meanwhile growing production and technical innovation hugely in-creased the reach and ambitions of Europe's major states. Mixed up with that were two other notions which, in conjunction, were to prove remarkably powerful. One still had to do with converting the heathen; the other, with the virtues of free trade: not just its commercial benefits, important as they were, but its contribution to political and even spiritual liberalisation. Trade would be a harbinger of civilisation and Christianity, as well as profits. From the East, there would be an even freer flow to Europe of spices, silks or delicious cottons. In parts of seventeenth-century India, transparent cotton was romantically known as 'the web of the woven wind' and highly favoured for wives and concubines. London and Paris, too, fell in love with Indian chintzes. And, of course, there were always those Chinese silks, porcelain and tea.

*   *   *

TEA

There is a pleasing legend about how the Chinese discovered tea. It holds that around 2737 BC one early emperor, Shen Nung, who was not just a noted ruler but a scholar and creative scientist, fastened on to the idea that, to be healthy, water should be boiled before drinking. During a journey into his provinces, the emperor and his retinue stopped to rest; and the servants started to boil water. Some dried leaves from a bush accidentally fell into the water, and coloured it brown. It was, of course, a wild tea tree. The emperor was intrigued, decided to sample the liquid and was delighted. It quickly became famous for its healthy and refreshing qualities and, in fairly short order, the use of tea spread into every corner of Chinese society. By the third century AD its fame continued to spread by word of mouth and in writing.

Tea and tea-drinking seems to have spread to Japan when Buddhist priests started to move between China and the Japanese islands.

In India, the legend is different again. It says that the Buddha himself spent seven years without sleep and in concentrated contemplation. In the fifth year he did start to feel drowsy, so he took a few dried leaves from a nearby bush, chewed them to stay awake, and found them highly refreshing. It was, of course, once again a wild tea tree.

It seems likely that it was the Arab traders who first sailed the Indian Ocean, trading as far as the modern Indonesia and China, who brought tea to the Middle East from where the Italians – probably Venetians – brought it to Europe. But it may be the Dutch and Portuguese who made it the subject of regular trade. Tea-drinking and the tea trade seem to have reached Portugal in the early sixteenth century and by 1600 there were regular shipments to Holland, France and the Baltic coast, with the English following suit once the East India Company had been set up shortly afterwards. It was first sold in London coffee houses and by 1660 it was being advertised as 'making the body active and lusty' and 'preserving perfect health until extreme old age'. But it was very expensive, with the result that a smuggling trade in tea developed with ships from Holland and the Baltic bringing tea to the English coast.

For the moment, however, and before the middle 1700s, the Europeans remained a minor nuisance for the Chinese authorities. There were the Jesuits, of course. Or the papal legate, Apostolic Visitor Carlo Ambrogio Mezzabarba, who came in the footsteps of Maillard de Tournon in 1719, and left just as empty-handed. Then came more state missions. The Portuguese king sent another embassy, headed by Alexandre Metello de Sousa e Menezes, to persuade the emperor to modify his anti-Christian policies. By now the Chinese were starting to see that here was a group of states not only of great cultural brilliance, but of increasing economic, technical and political clout. At any rate Metello was more considerately received than some of his predecessors, being allowed to bring with him a suite of more than forty people, and even receiving from the Qing an advance of 1,000 *taels* for travelling expenses. He was allowed to present his credentials to the emperor in person and had no difficulty in kowtowing when required. However, he took the advice of the Beijing Jesuits and did not raise the problem of admitting missionaries directly with the emperor. In 1753 came another Portuguese ambassador, Francisco de Assis Pacheco de Sampaio, who was allowed to present his letters to the emperor in person and was even invited to the summer palace.

Now there was a pause. Not until around thirty years later did another flow of European embassies come to China. Then, in the 1770s and '80s three developments came together. One was dramatic changes in the politics and power relations of Europe itself. A second had to do with changes in China's control arrangements for foreign traders at Canton. A third was fresh European and notably British efforts to establish formal state-to-state relations with China, as the Europeans understood such things, in order to bypass the obstructionism of Canton officialdom and bring ideas about freer trade, and Western economic and scientific thought, straight to the court at Beijing.

The political changes stemmed from the Franco-British Seven Years' War that confirmed British primacy in India and the East and, very largely, command at sea. That was followed by the decisive Franco-American victories of the American War of Independence, followed in turn by the French Revolution and the Napoleonic Wars that confirmed Britain's industrial power and dominance on the high seas.

Throughout this period, as European contacts with China continued, they also brought fresh and more detailed information about that empire to the West. Some of the Jesuit missionaries continued to write commentaries on what they had seen, mostly sympathetic, even admiring. Russian and Dutch missions thought much the same. But Chinese and European reactions to the increasing flow of information were, once again, wholly different. It was not that Chinese views of Europeans were always dismissive. There were those Jesuit lessons in science and astronomy. Or, at the start of the 1770s, Qianlong, wanting to celebrate his conquest of Chinese Turkestan, had sixteen drawings by Catholic missionaries sent to Paris for copperplate engraving. The missionaries also brought some of the earliest Chinese visitors to Western Europe, some of whom returned home as priests. Yet even now, it hardly occurred to the Chinese ruling classes that – apart from such oddments – the Europeans might have anything to say that would be of great interest, still less anything that might cause China to amend its political or diplomatic habits. Yet some of the people who were now arriving were intellectually formidable, and all of them had considerable clout with their governments back home.

In Europe the reaction was quite the opposite: debate about what Europe might learn from China. Some of the leading lights of the European Enlightenment were greatly attracted to the riches of

Chinese culture, and saw China, with its rigorous examination system for officialdom, as a perfect meritocracy, where hereditary distinctions were ignored. One of Louis XIV's tutors wrote in one of his books 'On Confucius – the Socrates of China'. At the end of the seventeenth century Gottfried Wilhelm von Leibniz (1646–1716), the German philosopher and co-inventor of calculus, thought that Chinese civic morality had major lessons for Europe and, together with Western mechanical invention, might even help to found a progressive world civilisation. Germany's greatest poet, Johann Wolfgang von Goethe (1749–1832), was another admirer, as was the great French writer Voltaire (1694–1778), who thought that China was much more civilised than barbaric Europeans; in fact, Europe was only just catching up with some of the things China had long known, including rationalism and stable rule. He was particularly in favour of China's practical Confucian wisdom and recognition of the close connection between capacity to rule and the moral character of the ruler.[1] In China, religion and morality were 'wise, august, free from all super-stition and all barbarity'. Much of this penetrated into Russia, too. Peter the Great corresponded with Leibniz about China, and Cathe-rine the Great was in touch on the subject with Voltaire and others. Also, by the middle of the eighteenth century, Chinese art and design in rugs, porcelain and gardens suddenly became highly fashionable in Vienna, Paris and London, producing a wave of enthusiasm for Chinese-style artefacts and design that became known as chinoiserie. Indeed, by the later 1600s the Chinese imperial porcelain-making industry may have employed as many as 100,000 people and several million of their pieces were shipped to Europe each year. Europeans drank Chinese tea from China cups or decorated their houses and palaces with wallpapers with Chinese themes. (To this day, the visitors' shop at Buckingham Palace in London offers gentlemen's ties with a Chinese motif.) The Royal Botanical Gardens at Kew acquired Chinese styles, complete with a pagoda. Even in St Petersburg, Catherine the Great had Chinese rooms and a 'Chinese palace' built at her palace of Oranienburg. She also had a model Chinese village built and started a Chinese theatre.

These enthusiasms did not last. The most important reasons had to do with increasing on-the-spot reporting, not only from the Western traders, but from the reports of the first naval and diplomatic visits to China. Doubts had already been voiced. Montesquieu thought China was a despotic state 'whose principle is fear', and by the later 1600s Russian visitors, though impressed by some aspects of Chinese life, also noted the low moral qualities of the Chinese with whom they mixed every day. They found them crafty and unreliable in business. The Russian Orthodox mission in Beijing, which was responsible for translating foreign documents and training twenty-four students at any one time in Russian, was also able to send back first-hand reports from around 1715. These first official and semi-official Western missions were only the forerunners of much more powerful and practical difficulties. The Westerners wanted trade arrangements, and therefore some kind of official representation, but nothing was further from Chinese officials' minds than to have foreign diplomats resident in China – least of all in Beijing – claiming some kind of diplomatic equality.

Meanwhile, for China frontier difficulties continued and strong emperors still wanted to create stability in these regions. Which turned out to mean imposing control. In fact, the emperors convinced themselves that many of these areas, and their tribes and statelets, were really just part of the empire of the Son of Heaven. Which allowed some independent Moslem princes in Turkestan to be treated simply as 'rebels'.

It was Qianlong, in particular, who started in the late 1740s a forty-five-year series of no less than ten campaigns against Central and South-East Asian peoples. In the south, there were three Qing campaigns against Burma in the 1760s, all over the issue of control of frontier tribes, which incurred progressively heavier Chinese losses. It turned out that the Manchu cavalry arm was not useful in Burmese rainforests. In 1788/9, an invasion of Vietnam also failed at great cost. Matters became still more complicated as Han migrants began to move into South-East Asia. At the other end of the empire,

Chinese from drought-ridden regions migrated to northern rivers or Manchuria, which the Manchu rulers had been so careful to keep free of ethnic and cultural pollution. The Chinese also set up military strong points on the Amur, and officials who came to collect the fur pelts brought gifts to the locals. As early as 1720, the Qing also began to marry Manchu girls to Amur tribal chiefs. Soon after, local chiefs from as far afield as Sakhalin began to visit Beijing to be given brides and confirmed in Chinese ranks.

The biggest difficulties, though, concerned Tibet and the Mongols, especially the Zunghars. Even with Galdan's ashes scattered to the winds, it was not the end of the Zunghar problem. The trouble from the Qing point of view was that any military solution to the Mongol problem ran, as Kangxi found out, into enormous logistic difficulties. It was, after all, the Mongols themselves, with their steppe grasslands, on whom the empire relied for a supply of the horses its armies needed and China seemed unable to produce. Not only that but the food supply that Manchu soldiers needed had to be carted to the north-west with draught animals that also had to be fed and watered. Here were problems that the Chinese quartermasters had never been able to solve properly. So the Qing spent the first couple of decades of the eighteenth century greatly extending and strengthening the northern and north-western bases and supply arrangements.

Rival Mongol leaders in Tibet came to blows, though, and Zunghar troops occupied the Tibetan capital, Lhasa. Kangxi responded by sending troops and stationing a garrison there. The Zhungars rose again in the 1730s and inflicted a severe defeat on the Chinese. They achieved a truce in 1738, but grew weaker as both the Qing and Russian empires expanded in Central Asia. The end came when Qianglong, full of impatience with these difficulties, sent an army that scored a decisive Qing victory in 1756. On his explicit orders, it was followed by Chinese butchery of tens of thousands – probably half a million – Zunghars to settle the problem once and for all. Qianlong was delighted with this scheme of ethnic cleansing, proclaimed the end of the Zunghar campaigns in 1759 and tried, not always successfully, to promote economic revival in the lands ravaged by the Zunghar wars. He also declared, retrospectively, that all past Mongol lands had really belonged to the empire. But Chinese repression and corruption stirred up Moslem resentment in other areas, including Kokand and even, as late as 1815, a Kirghiz revolt.

By the later 1700s, these various efforts had extended the Qing grip over northern Manchuria, the whole of Mongolia, Chinese Turkestan (Xinjiang) and the north-western tribal areas as far as Lake Balkhash, Tibet and the grasslands north of the Tien Shan mountains. They also had serious influence over tributary states including Nepal, parts of Indo-China and Korea. There were lively Chinese merchant communities in South-East Asian ports which, while not under Beijing's administrative or political control, contributed mightily to the empire's wealth. In other words, within a few decades of Kiakhta, the empire expanded to its greatest extent ever – greater even than its successor, the People's Republic, in its 1960s–70s heyday.

However, size is not everything. It is not even necessarily the same as strength. By the middle of the eighteenth century the Qing empire was at the peak of its power and wealth; but also starting to exhibit signs of weakness. The power and wealth stemmed from the time of the great Manchu domestic peace in the early and middle parts of the century. The arts flourished, production grew and the art of central government achieved even greater perfection as Kangxi's fourth son and immediate successor, Yongzheng, stressed uniformity and centralisation and dealt with problems like land reclamation while keeping imperial revenues up but taxes down. Roads were built or repaired, and so was water transport from the south to northern regions. The economy flourished and banks began to develop. The next emperor, Qianlong, was an enthusiastic art collector, who put together an enormous collection of paintings, ceramics, antiquities and calligraphy.

As always, it was the land that set the conditions for China's fate. Society and the economy still depended on it and here conditions changed with increases in the cultivated area, improved irrigation, multiple cropping and the use of fertiliser, together with better varieties of rice. Most important of all was the rise in food production,[2] coming from increased productivity, growing land use and new varieties of produce. That again fed through into life expectancy and population growth; whose large, blind movements proved once again that demography is destiny. By the 1780s there were quite high population densities, especially in regions that had a surplus of grain. China's population grew from 150–180 millions in 1644, at the time of the Qing takeover,[3] to perhaps 330 millions by 1790 – compared with India's 180 millions, while Russia had 36 millions, France 28 millions and Britain (including Ireland) a mere 15 millions.[4]

Growth, however brought problems. More people meant a worsening ratio of people to land. It made more people more vulnerable to any food shortages. That, together with the cost of foreign wars, meant general impoverishment, though conspicuous imperial luxury continued. At the same time, the imperial structure, confronted with growing social complexities and tensions at home and a larger empire to govern, became less effective. It started to cope poorly with flood or famine relief, or even with the need for increased tax revenues. New territories had to be expensively administered and defended. Which was often difficult given the hostilities created by restrictive Chinese regulations, or locals cheated by Chinese merchants or exorbitant tax demands. The domination of Mongolia itself was a mixed blessing. The imperial armies were weakened by a decline in the quality of the Manchu troops, by corrupt supply systems, as well as miserable leadership. Once more, power devolved to the local gentry. By the last two decades of the eighteenth century, misery produced, yet again, a series of rebellions. The most important was the White Lotus, fed by a combination of religion and poverty, combined with a tax rebellion, impatience with administrative incompetence, corruption and even a wish to get rid of the Qing altogether and restore the Ming.

Western interests were still only in state-to-state relations and increased trade with the supposedly enormous and rich Chinese market. Although the Chinese economy had indeed done well during the Manchu peace, and domestic trade had grown and with it the power of the merchant class, China's trading system remained largely inter-provincial. China as a whole was largely self-sufficient, and China's own merchants remained subject to uncertain taxes and the arbitrary impositions of officialdom.

Nevertheless, from the mid-seventeenth century commerce on the coast had steadily increased, especially in regions like Guangdong. Between 1720 and 1806 the volume of trade between Canton and Europe is reckoned to have doubled every eighteen years. Even so, there were major obstacles to the kind of trading relationship the West wanted. In the Confucian hierarchy of values, and especially the values of Chinese officialdom, trade was still an inferior activity. Commercial growth remained within the established framework of imperial autocracy. The official world operated far above the world of commerce, let alone the life of China's myriad villages, which were still ruled by custom, local opinion and elders.

China's rulers distrusted foreign traders, especially perhaps Western ones, as liable to disturb the empire's domestic peace, however much China needed the flow of foreign earnings. Kangxi tried to think quite early about such dangers. In 1717, no doubt forewarned by his experiences with the Russians, he noted that 'there is cause for apprehension lest in centuries or millennia to come China may be endangered by collision with the nations of the West'.[5] Even so, long-term imperial worries did not mean immediate hostility to the foreigners. After all, the emperor was a universal monarch. The first charter of the Canton colony, in 1720, began 'Foreigners and Chinese are members of one family . . . and must be on an equal footing'.[6] Popular views were less accommodating. As Europe's presence became more visible, the populace was often sullenly hostile to the barbarian devils.[7]

In any case, foreign trade required detailed regulation. Accordingly, the empire set up a system that was controlled, stylised and with its own rituals. Up to the middle of the eighteenth century Amoy (Xiamen), in Fujian, was the major port for China's trade along the coasts and with South-East Asia. After that, foreign trade was concentrated at Canton (Guangzhou), which became the filter shielding the population in general, and the official world in particular, from foreign disturbance. Contact was maintained through a selected group of Chinese merchants, known as the Cohong, who operated both as brokers and as superintendents of the foreign traders. One or other Chinese firm had to take responsibility for every foreign ship. These merchants were, in turn, answerable to the imperial superintendent of commerce for the region, known as the Hoppo. This official, normally a Manchu from the imperial household department in Beijing, and the Cohong, between them taxed foreign imports and exports, particularly silks and tea. In addition, the Hoppo often put the squeeze on the Chinese merchants who, as a result, were apt to run into debt with the foreigners. Here was an export process by which China earned large quantities of money, in the form of silver. Which had, among other things, inflationary consequences. Modern estimates suggest Chinese imports averaged some $10 million worth of silver per annum for the seventeenth century.

Not that foreign merchants were actually allowed to live at Canton. They could reside in their 'factories' – a combination of living quarters, offices and warehouse – on the Canton waterfront only during the trading season from October to March, after which they had to withdraw, in most cases to Macao. They were not allowed to bring wives or children to Canton either,[8] or to communicate directly with imperial officials. Communications had to go through the Cohong. They had to be worded as 'petitions', and mostly went to the Hoppo, who might or might not choose to deal with the matters raised. The smallest details of the foreigners' lives and goods were subject to regulation. In practice, the system worked quite well. Yet Beijing had no coherent state-run system of control or even taxation of the foreign commerce. Much was left to local official initiative, even whim. The result was that the people who benefited most from the irrepressible entrepreneurialism of the coastal regions were local officials who could amass huge fortunes from licensing and the customary forms of bribery.

This Canton system was quite separate from the foreign-relations machinery in Beijing which dealt chiefly with things like getting reliable information on Russia and Central Asia and looking after their envoys during their long visits to the imperial capital. The chief agency here may have been founded as early as 1638, a kind of forerunner of the proto-foreign office, the Tsungli Yamen of 1861. It employed specialists, arranged for audiences with the emperor and saw to it that supplies and food were granted to envoys residing in Beijing according to their rank. Both Kangxi and after him Qianlong took a personal interest in these foreign matters.

For traders, there were other difficulties, notably the Chinese legal system, which created fundamental problems for Westerners. In China, justice rested not on codes of law but on social norms and universal principles of Confucian morality. These would be applied by a court to any particular case in a process which also invariably leaned towards state interests. The imperial code was strongly weighted towards social order, and law was – and in modern China largely remains – a tool of administration, without reference to any 'higher' notion of natural law or even any system akin either to Roman or to Anglo-Saxon common law. That naturally created much uncertainty not just for the accused, but for the judge himself. There was no commercial law in a modern Western sense, although written contracts, and even some oral agreements, could be enforced by magistrates. Westerners could and did resolve disputes through channels like the merchant guilds, or the webs of friendship, but they had difficulty with the absence of 'due process'. Nor, since Chinese firms were essentially family businesses, was there any sense of firms as legal individuals. There was no Chinese equivalent to Western notions of sanctity of a written and signed contract. In practice, commerce, and especially any major undertaking, needed official patronage. That created important links between officialdom and the merchant groups, and strong pressures to preserve the status quo. For European traders and sailors trying to operate in China, general regulation was therefore fine but Chinese legal procedures were not. By the start of the nineteenth century that was causing serious difficulties.

All the same, from the middle of the eighteenth century a lot of foreigners were trading in Canton: Dutch, Germans, French, Portuguese, Spaniards, Swedes, later Americans. In 1750 King Frederick II of Prussia tried again, for instance, establishing a royal trading company at the port of Emden that chartered four ships.[9] Though it failed to sell Prussian woollens in China it did bring back some tea, porcelain and Chinese medicines. But much the most important group of foreign traders at Canton in the eighteenth century, and for the first three decades of the nineteenth, remained the British and especially the Scots, with the East India Company as most important foreign trading organisation.

The company found that while buying tea and silk was fine, selling goods to China was more difficult. There was little demand for woollens or other British manufactures. What did exist was an insatiable demand for silver, and a growing demand for opium. That had been used for centuries in the entire arc from the Balkans to South and East Asia, and in China quite legally for medical purposes. Then the British eighteenth-century conquest of Bengal changed things at Canton. The East India Company acquired the Bengal opium monopoly and sold the product, again quite legally, at auction in Calcutta. What buyers did with it after that was their own business. As time went by and the Chinese tried to ban opium imports, the company ceased to trade in it at Canton, but continued to treat it as a normal commercial product in India.

The British also found that informal or private arrangements of any kind with the Chinese might not be enough. As the premier sea power they were particularly sensitive to shipping difficulties and found that without formal arrangements the odd British messenger, or even ship seeking refuge in a Chinese port – after a storm, say – was liable to be treated with obtuse rudeness by Qing provincial and port officials. A prime example was the visit of Commodore George Anson in 1743.

Perhaps imperial officials had been used for so long to dealing with 'lesser breeds without the law' – barbarians – that they quite failed to understand who Anson was and, more important, whom and what he represented. In fact, he was a very different personage from the missionaries or traders who had come to China before him. He came from a powerful family, was a sailor of conspicuous skill and a senior officer of the world's greatest navy, which he would later go on to head. He sailed around Cape Horn in command of six ships, losing three in the process. Only 335 of his original 961 men remained alive when, commanding a battered and unseaworthy HMS *Centurion*, he put into Canton, towing a prize: the annual Spanish 'Manila galleon', which had been carrying riches in bullion, spices, silk and cloth from the trading centre of Manila to Acapulco[10] in modern Mexico. When ship and contents were eventually sold off, Anson's share of the prize money was likely to be half a million pounds.[11] Now, given his position, he rashly concluded that since he was no merchantman, he should not pay Canton harbour dues, that the necessary supplies would be made available to him and that he and his crew would, as a matter of course, be received by the viceroy.

Nothing of the kind happened. He got no help, found himself cheated from start to finish by traders or interpreters, and had one of his officers mugged when strolling ashore. He concluded that 'in artifice, falsehood and an attachment to all kinds of lucre, many of the Chinese are difficult to be paralleled by any other people . . .' Chinese military preparations and defences he dismissed with contempt. Anson's account of his voyage, published in 1748, became popular and quite influential, even with philosophers like Montesquieu in France. His biting commentary on China, and his story of Chinese dishonesty and cupidity, caused surprise and shock. His indignation at China's treatment was widely shared. As one later American writer put it:

> It was contrary to the spirit of the age that a vessel in distress or requiring aid should be treated as an intruder in the ports of any people . . . the efforts of China to resist the progress of the world in shipping and commerce were destined to an early and humiliating failure . . . it was plain that a radical change could be accomplished only by force . . .'[12]

Experiences like Anson's were not likely to be the end of the story. Trade at Canton was increasing, especially with England's boom in tea consumption after the English tariff on tea was sharply lowered after the mid-1700s. Moreover, as early as the 1740s the East India Company could see that the Dutch had their convenient base at Batavia, the Portuguese theirs at Macao and that even the Spaniards had Manila. So they thought that a base of their own would be a good idea. In 1763 Lord Clive in India, apparently overcome by his own victories over the French and the Moguls, even suggested to the British government that he should be sent to conquer China. The prime minister, William Pitt (the elder), had the good sense to point out that it would be sheer lunacy to try. Still, to regularise things, in 1788 the British tried to send an ambassador, although company officials at Canton had already warned that 'The Chinese government looks with contempt on all foreign nations. Its ignorance of their force gives it confidence in its own strength. It does not look on Embassies in any other light than acknowledgements of inferiority.' Nevertheless, Lieutenant-Colonel Cathcart was sent out, but died at sea before reaching China.

Three years later the idea of an embassy surfaced again and this time produced a mission that carried altogether larger portents for the future. It was sent from a Britain that was not just the greatest sea power but, through its position in India, much the most important European influence in the East. It also had, by this time, the beginnings of the Industrial Revolution fermenting in its society and body politic. (As the inventors of the steam engine, Matthew Boulton and James Watt, explained to King George III in 1775, 'Sir, we sell what the world desires: power.') The mission was sent, like the ones before it, to look for more openings for trade. It was conveniently, and rather generously, financed not by government but by the East India Company. Behind all that, though, lay something altogether more far-reaching, for it also sought permission for a permanent British ambassador to settle in Beijing. Though London may not have realised it, for the Chinese emperor and a culturally conservative autocracy, that was almost sure to be an entirely unacceptable and revolutionary demand. It meant that this strange kingdom on the other side of the world would claim a kind of equality with the Celestial Empire. It would even, and quite intolerably, imply that the emperor was no longer a universal monarch. The mission was probably foredoomed to failure.

It was headed by Lord George Macartney, who sailed without illusions. Long before, a Russian friend had told him that, in China, Chinese superiority in all things was axiomatic. Everyone was either civilised or a barbarian. Among Chinese mandarins, a barbarian who pledged fealty to China was known as 'baked' and one who did not was 'raw'. Raw barbarians were simply unwilling or unable to play a role in the celestial order of China. In the imperial archives all foreign missions continued to be listed simply as 'vassal delegations'. So Macartney equipped himself with a copy of Anson's book and was carefully briefed by East India House. He was given a paper explaining China's xenophobia and fear of foreign traders, passion for stability, and avoidance of societal change. His instructions also pointed out that English traders in China had no support from their own country and were '. . . unavowed at a distance so remote as to admit of a misrepresentation of the national character and importance, and where too their occupation was not held in that esteem which ought to procure them safety and respect'.[13] Nevertheless, his chief mission was to get Chinese agreement to the opening of some additional ports, so that Britain (and others) could trade with the presumably vastly rich Chinese interior. In addition, and given the problems of Chinese jurisdiction, he was to acquire some piece of territory, or an island, close to the areas of silk and tea production. There, British merchants might live subject to British laws, and stay the whole year round instead of, as at Canton, only for the trading season. There was no secret about this. As the French explorer Jean-Antoine d'Entrecasteaux had explained in a letter to the missionaries in Beijing back in 1787, Britain's plan was simply to create a number of free and independent settlements on the China coast.[14]

The Chinese were not impressed. What, after all, could China have to learn from mere foreigners? The emperor Qianlong put his

MACARTNEY

The Macartney embassy was prepared and staffed with special care, and timed to coincide with Qianlong's eighty-third birthday. In 1791 Prime Minister William Pitt appointed to the post of home secretary his friend Henry Dundas, who understood the problems of the Canton market and its massive official corruption. A mission in the name of King George III himself might help. So Dundas chose Macartney, an old friend, to head it. An urbane and experienced Irishman, Macartney was a fellow of the Royal Society, a friend of Voltaire and Edmund Burke and acquainted with Rousseau. He was highly experienced, had an excellent memory, a talent for writing, a command of French, Italian and Latin, and great energy. He was married to a daughter of the former prime minister Lord Bute and had been chief secretary in Dublin. He had been knighted back in 1764 and served as envoy to the court of Catherine the Great of Russia, where there had even been rumours of some small scandal concerning a chambermaid. He had also served as governor of Madras, in India, where he had come to think that the China trade would help to meet the costs of British India and determine Britain's future in the subcontinent. He accepted the China mission on condition that on his return he be created an earl. He was.

He went to China in considerable style, heading a party of almost 100. It included not only officials but artists and scientists, scholars, soldiers, musicians, aristocrats and servants. Most of its members were intelligent and highly educated. Even Macartney's page, Thomas, the twelve-year-old son of his deputy Sir George Staunton, was a remarkable linguist. The boy was already fluent in French, German, Greek and Latin, and on the way to China learned Chinese well enough to be able to copy documents for the emperor. The party was accompanied by two Chinese monks, Li and Zhou, culled from the Collegium Sinicum at Naples to serve as interpreters, since there were none available in England. The mission was also equipped with a great array of presents for the emperor, including telescopes, clocks, fine swords and a carriage, all meant to impress the Chinese court.

thoughts into a poem, pleased with his own kindness and generosity to 'men from afar' who had come to pay homage. It was also clear that, as a matter of 'face', the Chinese would insist on homage to the emperor taking the normal form of the demonstrative kowtow, which was especially important for domestic consumption. China's highest officials, and even princes of the blood, performed it. The 1655 Dutch mission had kowtowed not just to the emperor, but to the empty throne and even to mere documents carrying the imperial seal. Several other foreign missions had since then had no difficulty complying with established Chinese ceremonial forms. Macartney was different. Before being received by the emperor at Jehol, the imperial summer residence north of Beijing, he spent some weeks carefully negotiating with court officials to explain his unwillingness to perform the kowtow. He would not do more than go on one knee and bow his head, the honour he would show his own king. While at Jehol, he was courteously received for informal talks and on such private occasions the issue of the kowtow did not arise.

Nevertheless, the Chinese had their own ways of responding to the ambassador's presumption. The mission was given endless verbal assurances and flatteries. The emperor was especially delighted with twelve-year-old Thomas Staunton and made much of him. Nevertheless, Macartney discovered that, behind the pretences, there was barely disguised suspicion. For all the coldly exquisite Chinese courtesy, for all the exchanges of presents, the way the mission was treated left it exhausted and wary. In the end, the emperor's official responses to Macartney and his king amounted to a monumental snub. The decisive edict from the emperor, addressed to King George III, was actually written some time before Macartney even arrived. It was handed to him before he left.[15] It began by putting the British in their place in the universal scheme of things: '. . . You, O King . . . impelled by your humble desire to partake of the benefits of our civilisation, you have dispatched a mission respectfully bearing your memorial . . .' On the two main British requests Qianlong was categorical. On the issue of a resident ambassador: '. . . this request is contrary to all usage of my dynasty and cannot possibly be entertained.' As for trade:

> Our dynasty's majestic virtue has penetrated into every country under Heaven, and Kings of all nations have offered their costly tribute by land and sea . . . I set no value on objects strange or ingenious, and have no use for your country's manufactures . . . It behoves you, O King, to respect my sentiments and to display even greater devotion and loyalty in future . . .

Chinese court records are equally dismissive, and even mention – rather improbably – a suggestion by Macartney about an Anglo-Chinese alliance against France. There is no other record that Macartney ever made such a proposal to the Chinese.

Macartney's mission was therefore a failure at all major points. He was ordered to leave after forty-seven days in Beijing. His valet remarked later, perhaps a little unfairly, that 'we entered Peking like paupers, we remained in it like prisoners and we quitted it like vagrants'. From a larger point of view it did serve important purposes. The mission brought back first-hand reports of the magnificence of China's culture, its palaces, the sophisticated splendour of its gardens. It collected new information on China's east coast and northern waters. More importantly, it brought the first official information on China's government apparatus, its official views, personalities and prejudices. It noted Beijing's lack of interest in, and ignorance of, the non-Chinese world, the role of Western industry, or the changing conditions of the balance of power or the conditions of trade. Even on lesser questions, the British encountered simple incredulity. For instance they found the Chinese simply refused to believe that in Europe firearms had long since superseded bows and arrows.[16] No less important, the mission returned home with strong views on China's large-scale misery, and the barbarity of many of its practices. It had also seen at first hand the xenophobia that lay just under the surface of official politeness and popular indifference. Macartney himself noted that the Chinese élite 'rather wonders at our curiosity than esteems us for our knowledge' and thought the 'British search for understanding China impertinent to them and useless to ourselves'. His secretary, George Staunton, noted that 'in this country they think that everything is excellent and that proposals for improvement would be superfluous, if not blameworthy'. Other travellers were highly critical of the contrasts between Chinese principles and practices, or about Chinese legal codes, or the Chinese contempt for anything new or foreign; indeed the general Chinese tendency to arrogance, authoritarianism and xenophobia. Macartney was also shrewd enough to note, on his cross-country return journey from Beijing to the south coast, that while the empire seemed huge and powerful, it was actually threatened by serious internal weaknesses.[17] For all his admiration of many aspects of Chinese culture he could detect important social fissures, like the continuing, underlying, Han-Manchu tensions. He noted that the entire imperial structure amounted to the 'tyranny of a handful of Tartars over more than 300 millions of Chinese' and thought that

the Empire of China is an old, crazy, first-rate Man of War which a fortunate succession of able and vigilant officers have contrived to keep afloat for these hundred and fifty years past, and to over-awe their neighbours merely by her bulk and appearance. But, whenever an inefficient man happens to have command on deck, adieu to the discipline and safety of the ship. She may, perhaps, not sink outright, she may drift some time as a wreck and will then be dashed to pieces on the shore; but she can never be rebuilt on the old bottom.

The Americans, too, joined the Canton trading system under their own brand-new flag. Before the War of Independence almost all

American trade with China had been done through the East India Company, with products shipped through England. Direct commerce seems to have started in 1784. The first US trading vessel to reach China was probably a former privateer, the *Empress of China*. She reached Canton with goods worth the then vast sum of $120,000, ranging from lead to ginseng – an alleged aphrodisiac much prized in China – harvested from New England forests. When the *Empress* returned to New York, she made a very handsome profit. Other ships claiming to be first or second into China were the *Harriet* and the *Hope* and their merchants. One of the first shipmasters on that route was Amasa Delano, a great-grandfather of President Franklin Delano Roosevelt. When he sailed to Canton he was vastly impressed. 'China is the first for greatness, riches and grandeur of any country ever known.' Together with his son Warren he founded the family fortune trading on the China coast. In time, Warren became a partner in the House of Russell, the chief American trading firm in China, selling seal skins and sea-otter pelts and buying Chinese luxuries.[18] The Americans also found that they could buy Turkish opium at Smyrna on the Mediterranean coast and ship it very profitably to China, even though Indian opium was held to be of better quality there. By the 1830s Russell and Co. was the third-largest opium dealer on the China coast (the Scots Jardine and Matheson being the first) and New England-built clippers were particularly successful in shipping it. Needless to say, after 1794 the Americans continued to condemn the British empire while happily using its trans-continental banking to promote their own businesses.

Within five years of the *Empress of China*'s journey, some fifteen US ships were trading with China, and establishing amicable relations with the British, French and Swedes there. The first of them were mere cockle-shells, almost never more than 100–200 tons and often much smaller than that. They had very crude navigation instruments and, more importantly, had to carry heavy armaments for protection against the pirates of the China coast. (Two hundred and fifty years later, at the beginning of the twenty-first century, gangs of armed and ruthless pirates continue to make the South China Sea one of the world's real danger spots.[19]) Even so, owners could reckon on making 100 or even 200 per cent profit on a China journey, laying the basis of many a New England fortune. There was, however, no American attempt to extend contacts from trade to diplomatic relations. Private trading was quite enough. Indeed, the first US 'Consul', Samuel Shaw, himself a trader, found the Chinese Hong merchants 'As respectable a set of men as are commonly found in other parts of the world . . . intelligent, exact accountants, punctual to their engagements . . .' But respect did not always imply close understanding. It has been said that the Americans traded at Canton for forty-five years before any one of them could understand, speak or read Chinese. In any event, respect was not much returned, at least at official levels. One Chinese edict spoke of 'foreigners . . . depraved by the education and customs of countries beyond the bounds of civilisation' and of their 'perverse obstinacy'.

Nevertheless, Macartney's conclusions had been shrewd. In the final decade of the eighteenth century the Chinese empire was indeed running into trouble. In London, its pretensions became seriously irritating, especially after the Macartney mission and others had brought back their highly unflattering reports of the empire's weakness and corruption, and the misery and ignorance of its masses. For all the learning of China's scholars and the magnificence of the court, the ordinary people, it was now seen, had no rights, no education and were sunk in deepest filth, misery and superstition. The revolutionary and Napoleonic wars ensured that Europe, and especially the British and French, had little attention and energy to spare for China during almost the whole of the reign of Qianlong's successor, the emperor Jiaqing (Chia-ching). Franco-British rivalry only affected China on two occasions. In 1802 and 1808 the British actually occupied Macao, for fear that the French would seize it and so achieve command of East and South-East Asian trade. In 1802 they withdrew after a (temporary) peace was concluded in Europe. But on the second occasion the British admiral refused to evacuate. The Chinese responded by stopping trade. The admiral sent some ships up the Pearl River towards Canton, there were Anglo-Chinese clashes and the British only withdrew from Macao after the Portuguese agreed to pay a ransom. There was another incident a few years later when the British, during the 1814 war with America, seized the American steamer *Hunter* off Canton and refused to give way in the face of Chinese protests.

The British were by no means alone in changing their views on China. Almost everywhere in Europe, in so far as Europeans thought about China at all, that mid-eighteenth-century enthusiasm for Chinese culture and mores continued to erode. The reports of Macartney and other members of his mission not so much created as reinforced the growing conviction, in many parts of Europe, of China's corruption and backwardness. Anson had proved not to be alone in arguing that Chinese morality was only a confidence trick. Protestant Jansenists on the Continent and Bishop Berkeley in Ireland thought Confucianism was nothing more than rules of experience; it rested on no principles. Even more important, there was the growing scepticism of leading Western thinkers about many aspects of Chinese life: about the absence of liberty there – anything that the twenty-first century might call 'human rights' – or of any notion of progress, or the backward-looking rigidities of Chinese education and culture. Montesquieu in France had already rejected the idea that Chinese moral systems rested on principles. In Germany, the two major philosophers who were producing new historical views, Fichte and Hegel, were critical, Hegel being especially cutting: 'The Chinese . . . empire is the realm of theocratic despotism . . . The individual has no moral selfhood . . .'[20] In Scotland, Adam Smith reflected on the abysmal poverty of masses of the Chinese population, the infanticide, and the isolation of the economy from the rest of the world. Other economists, like David Ricardo and Thomas Malthus, offered critiques of various kinds. John Stuart Mill wrote about 'oriental despotism'. Marx and Engels criticised the 'Asiatic mode of production'. Perhaps too much should not be made of this. As Catherine the Great of Russia once rather pointedly wrote to Diderot, the views of academics 'existe seulement sur le papier, qui souffre tout'.[21] Still, such views had their effects.

Even some of the Protestant missionaries who now arrived were far from starry-eyed. Robert Morrison, for instance, who published his dictionary of the Chinese language after many years in China, observed that 'the Chinese are generally selfish, cold-blooded and inhumane'. Other early nineteenth-century evidence produced even more enlightened European disdain, not only for many Asian views and customs but for the stagnation, poverty and underdevelopment of its regions.

Irritation grew at political levels, too. After Macartney, Chinese arrogance and assertiveness (or was it defensiveness?) actually increased, while the reach, power and self-confidence of the West, especially of Britain, grew further. Macartney himself had thought that stronger measures might be necessary to deal with the Chinese but later visits received even worse treatment. In 1803–6 the Russian admiral Adam von Krusenstern commanded the first Russian expedition to explore the Pacific and, among other things, tried to explore further trade with China. His account commented on the 'purely tyrannical' government of China.[22] The next diplomatic mission came from the Netherlands, headed by Isaak Titsing, a former head of the Dutch East India Company in Bengal and Japan. He and his group were hurried into a long and impossibly uncomfortable overland trip, in bitter cold, from Canton to Beijing. The group's members were expected to perform the kowtow before a large fish sent them as a 'present' from the emperor. They were kept in extreme cold and discomfort, treated without respect and another kowtow – with repetitions enforced by whips if the first movements were not deferential enough – was demanded in a final session before the emperor. A decade later, in 1805, the Russians sent another mission, headed by Count Golovkin. Before he got anywhere near Beijing, the local governor asked him – as a special honour – to join a ceremony including the kowtow before a pair of scented candles. Golovkin refused to believe that the candles had, by a kind of transsubstantiation, become the emperor. Argument continued about the rites the Chinese would require the Russians to perform. Finally, when Golovkin was asked to commit himself three times in writing to a willingness to kowtow in Beijing as often as required, he refused, arguing that one written undertaking was quite enough. The Chinese simply sent him back home.

THE KOWTOW

In the Chinese imperial court, every small detail of procedure was set by rituals and precedent. Here, the kowtow was an essential and visible assertion of the uniquely special and superior position of the emperor.

The custom can be traced back to the period before about 200 BC when there were no formal benches or chairs in China and people usually sat on mats of reed or bamboo during conversation or meals. The mats tended to be of increasing richness and quality according to rank. Sitting on such a mat meant going down on it with both knees, with the person's body resting back on his heels. It was the precursor of the later imperial kowtow.

Once chairs and benches appeared, the customs of the original sitting posture gradually changed. The forms of sitting and bowing came to be used as a symbol of class differences and a sign of reverence and respect when minor officals met ones of higher rank or when servants presented themselves to masters. The custom even spread to the common people during birthday and other celebrations for the elders.

The precise path by which these customs developed into the elaborate kowtow of imperial times is not clear. But by the time Macartney reached Beijing, the ceremony had become a major element in displaying and emphasising the authority of the emperor and of the deep respect and devotion owed to him by all Chinese, even of the highest rank. Nor, of course, was that authority confined to Chinese society itself but, perhaps even more importantly, was asserted in relation to the outer world of tributary states and 'barbarians' for whom China was properly the 'Middle Kingdom' with the emperor as the central link between heaven and earth. In that context the kowtow evolved into the full pattern of three separate prostrations, with the forehead touching the ground three times with each prostration.

Although the kowtow proper was peculiar to China, there were various forms of kneelings and prostrations, with very similar purposes, at other times and in other societies. For instance, when Alexander the Great arrived in Persia some two millennia before Macartney visited Beijing, he found that the highest princes and noblemen would elegantly perform the ceremony of prostration before the emperor, the king of kings. When Alexander, on assuming the imperial role himself, tried to press his Macedonian commanders to follow the same practice, they refused for reasons very similar to those that moved Macartney 2,000 years later: prostration (or kowtow) would be humiliating and incompatible with Macedonian or, later, British, pride. For the princes and nobles of both Persia and imperial China, the newcomers' refusal to perform the customary courtesies was merely a demonstration of what crude boors they were.

Another decade later, in 1816, the British tried again, with a mission led by Lord Amherst. It proved to be another a test of diplomatic strength. The emperor Jiaqing noted Amherst's arrival with the discouraging comment 'All in all, I am not glad of this event'. Amherst carried a letter to him from Britain's prince regent which was hastily returned when the Chinese saw that it began: 'Sir, my Brother . . .' On their way, the British were, like the Russians before them, brought to a table with scented candles. The Chinese kowtowed. Amherst refused. Outside Beijing Amherst was met by senior officials with whom he argued for some ten days about the kowtow, which he eventually refused to perform. He was only willing to kneel three times before the emperor. Along the journey the mission encountered driving rain, inadequate accommodation and constant, outright harassment. Even that was not enough. 'As there is only one sun,' Amherst was told by one very senior mandarin, 'there is only one Jiaqing emperor; he is the universal sovereign, and all must pay him homage.' Amherst's group arrived in Beijing, desperately tired, badly needing baths, around midnight. It was noticed that the officials present were in ceremonial dress. Suddenly he and three others were summoned to an audience with the emperor. When he prevaricated, a crowd of screaming and furious officials tried to manhandle him to the audience chamber. Amherst resisted, citing exhaustion, his dirty clothing, the hour of day. He also reaffirmed his refusal to kowtow. An angry emperor ordered his immediate expulsion from Beijing and recorded: 'China is Lord and Sovereign of the world; was it possible for Us to submit calmly to such a display of irreverent arrogance? . . .'[23] Amherst's return journey was made even more difficult, with an openly hostile escort, importunate beggars, stinks and dirt. Yet at local levels the Chinese were prudent enough to issue decrees favourable to European trade.

This was not at all the kind of treatment to which the victor of Trafalgar and Waterloo, the principal European industrial, financial and naval power, was by now accustomed. Britain was simply not going to put up with being treated as an inferior by some far-away, arrogant and ramshackle Chinese empire, a society that closed its eyes to all things new, that lacked any institutions for improvement or scientific progress. It became clear in London that there were only three possible ways to proceed: Britain could play by Chinese rules, or abandon the Canton trade, or move towards threats of force. Abandoning the China trade was clearly not an option. The use of force seemed excessive, not to mention expensive. So, for more than two decades, it was agreed to play by Chinese rules. While the emperor's blunt refusals might be annoying, the practical needs of trade remained. Foreign commerce, still confined to Canton, had multiplied by some two and a half in the two decades to 1800, and tea had become essential in Britain and the Chinese had a monopoly[24] of it. The British, who had bought two pounds (weight) of it in the early 1660s, were by the 1780s buying 15 million pounds and by the 1830s that would double to 30 million.

At the same time, Canton was becoming the financial hub of Britain's entire commerce in the East. Because the Chinese did not want to buy British goods, they demanded that silk and tea be paid for in silver. Paying the Chinese in silver for sharply growing quantities of tea and other goods meant trying to find more and more of it on the international market. But finding more silver – especially the Spanish silver coins of which the Chinese were particularly fond – became harder and harder. There was, though, one thing the Chinese did want to buy more of: opium from India. That produced problems for the Chinese government, not only because of opium's social effects but because it produced a drain from China's economy of the silver needed to pay for it. These overlapping problems of the Canton trade, financial operations, opium-smuggling, official corruption and Sino-foreign relations, came to a dramatic head in the time of Jiaqing's successor, the emperor Daoguang, who reigned from 1821 to 1850.

8

THE MANDATE OF HEAVEN DISSOLVES

AD 1816 to 1860

DAOGUANG CAME TO the throne in a period when world affairs changed once more, dramatically. By 1815 the chief concerns of the European powers focused almost entirely on the concert among them and on the simmering unrest in various parts of their own continent. The Napoleonic period had been a political earthquake and 1830 saw revolutions in Belgium, parts of Germany, Italy, Switzerland, Poland and once again in France. The French were also busy with the conquest of Algeria and growing worries about the rise of Prussia/Germany. There and in Italy, nationalist movements were stirring. By 1834 some seventeen German states with 26 million people had joined in a customs union. Belgium was about to separate from the Netherlands, which was also facing revolt in the East Indies. Even more important changes were coming with the march of industrialisation: Europe was at the dawn of the railway age that would once more transform its social and political patterns.

Britain led that industrialisation, and for the moment remained dominant in heavy industry, modern technologies, in sea power, sophisticated banking and finance. Even twenty years later Britain was producing 57 million tons of coal while all of Germany produced only 6 million and France, Britain's only serious industrial rival, was producing 4.5 million. Britain commanded over half the world's ocean-going shipping. It was developing more reliable public statistics, had widened the tax base, developed centralised fiscal systems and was able to meets its defence costs largely through loans. Its political attention was focused on getting rid of the Atlantic slave trade, on church affairs, as always on Ireland and, above all, on increasingly urgent questions of social and parliamentary reform. By 1832 these issues would lead to the great parliamentary reform bill about which the Duke of Wellington was duly sceptical. 'Beginning reform,' he told a friend, 'is beginning Revolution.' The US had begun to expand across the North American continent, for Thomas Jefferson's notion continued to linger: a 'North American road to India' across the Pacific, diverting the whole trade of East Asia from Europe to the US.

For the great powers, therefore, the most important thing about China was its relative unimportance; for balance-of-power politics, China was barely a sideshow. Seen from London, Paris, St Petersburg or even Washington, China was a far-away, rickety empire exhibiting an odd mixture of splendour and barbarism; huge, but militarily insignificant; proud, but decadent and quaint. Most nineteenth-century works on British or French or Dutch foreign policy, or even biographies of major statesmen like Palmerston or Wellington in England, or Talleyrand or Thiers in France, barely mention China.

At the same time, three principles of early-nineteenth-century European political philosophy dominated relations among the powers. If each was important in its own right, they were even more powerful in conjunction. The first concerned state sovereignty and equality. That was the basis of the post-1815 balance, certainly not to be denied by quaint views from China. The second emphasised the primacy of European civilisation and its duty to spread Christianity and Western values in the world. The third, strongly linked to the first two, was the importance of trade which, as only a Frenchman can put it, 'benefits both seller and buyer, who [are] like lovers, each depending on the other for satisfactions neither could provide singly'.[1] Also, trade meant the growing dominance of the free-trade views of Adam Smith and, later, David Ricardo. Belief in the ability of trade to benefit and transform societies became a kind of moral imperative. Here was a church beyond which there was no salvation: as John Maynard Keynes wrote a century later, in 1933, 'I was brought up like most Englishmen to respect free trade not only as an economic doctrine which a rational and instructed person could not doubt but almost as part of the moral law.'

Moreover, freer trade was not just moral and right in principle, it was necessary if Britain was to be able to buy things it needed; which, from China, certainly included tea and silk. In addition, it was clear to everyone in London who mattered that, as Macartney had foreseen, the China trade was extremely important to British India. Others followed quickly in Britain's wake. Russian naval and scientific expeditions in the Pacific came together with Siberian officials trying to open trade with Japan, the US, American colonies like the Philippines and California and with China. Or the American sailors who, in those tiny vessels, came to China almost as soon as the American War of Independence was over, and found themselves helped by the French.[2] Even the German Hansa cities started to try again and there were private merchants, from France, Denmark, Sweden.

Interest in China was not confined to merchants. Most particularly, there were still the missionaries, especially the Protestants. The London Missionary Society was founded in 1795. The Boston *Missionary Herald* began publication in 1805. American missions to China began with Robert Morrison in 1807. The American Board of Commissioners for Foreign Missions was set up in 1810 and soon began, from its base in Hawaii, to translate the Bible into local languages. By 1830 or so there was a whole group of Protestant missionaries at Canton. They included well-known figures like Elijah C. Bridgman and S. Wells Williams. By 1834 they were joined by an even more important figure, the enthusiastic young Yale divinity and medical graduate, Peter Parker.[3] When he left Yale he was aflame with passionate religious fervour. 'It is for the sake of Christ,' he wrote to his sister, 'that you part with your only brother; it is that he may bear

the tidings of your savior's love to the millions of China . . .'[4] By
1840 the numbers of Protestant missionaries had reached forty-four
Americans, nineteen British plus four Germans and Swiss. Even that
was merely a part of a much broader picture of European exploration
into new and so far unknown lands – for religion, for romance, for
curiosity, for science, for the country, king or czar.[5]

For the Chinese authorities, however, Canton and Macao were
simply about trade, under regulations that had become complex
but by 1830 were working perfectly well. Even a senior British official
commented that 'perhaps there is no place where a higher degree of
mutual commercial good faith subsists than at Canton, or where it is
more needful that such a feeling should be carefully fostered'. The
foreign traders operated in three places. There were their 'factories'
outside Canton's city walls. There was Macao, the old Portuguese
base, which was the place not just for normal trading but also for
smuggling operations by very many foreign merchants. It was also
where the Canton traders' families stayed, and most of the missionaries. Finally, there was the anchorage at Whampoa, some twelve
miles downstream from Canton, where foreign ships put in, the river
between there and Canton itself only being navigable by smaller boats.
Foreign ships had to come to Macao for Chinese permits to proceed
to Whampoa. Once there, the foreign trader was entirely in the hands
of the Chinese merchant who became responsible for him, even
paying the duties on his imports to and exports from China. The
foreign ship was not allowed to leave again until an official stamp had
been issued, certifying that all duties had been properly paid. In other
ways, too, foreign traders were in the hands of the Chinese. No official
schedule of duties existed, let alone one for the semi-official payments
to officials. All that was handled by the Hong merchants, so foreign
traders could never be sure what duties they were actually paying, or
what bribes were going to whom. On the other hand, the Hong
merchants, while suffering haphazard and unpredictable demands
from their own officials, were apt to do their own trading with Europe
or America through those same foreign merchants.

For the imperial mandarins, however, the situation was ideal. Whether at Canton or Macao, the foreigners ran themselves, in accordance with the traditional Chinese habit of letting foreigners look after themselves, subject only to the overriding authority of the empire. Officials still did not communicate directly with the foreigners, or even formally acknowledge their existence. Yet their practical control of the traders through the Hong merchants was effectively complete, since they wielded the sanction of cutting off communications, even trade itself.

Most of these Canton arrangements were not even exceptional. Quite similar things were happening on the China's north-western frontiers. Chinese Turkestan (Xinjiang), for example, was for long more important for trade and defence than Canton. As one senior Chinese official later remarked, 'Xinjiang was the first line of defence in the Northwest. It protected Mongolia, which in turn protected Beijing . . . If Xinjiang were lost, Mongolia would be indefensible and Beijing itself threatened . . .'[6] It was also a region where the government's authority was often undermined by the way in which its officers, and Han merchants, violated regulations and cheated locals. In the days before Qing rule, when Turkestan had been under Islamic rulers, there had been occasional cavalry raids into the (Chinese-controlled) Kashgar region. Later, Kokand, beyond the border, asked for special privileges in the Kashgar market. The Chinese authorities refused, and Kokand gave one of its younger Moslem leaders, Jehangir, his head. He started a holy war against the Manchus and invaded Xinjiang in 1826. The Qing reconquered Kashgar, Jehangir was betrayed and sent to Beijing, where the emperor had him cut into quarters.

But how could the Qing pacify the frontier and arrange trade? Once Jehangir was safely dead a settlement was worked out in 1835. It said that Kokand could station a political representative and commercial officers at Kashgar. They would have police powers and jurisdiction over foreigners there. They would levy customs dues on the foreigners' goods. From a Chinese point of view it was an eminently satisfactory exercise in managing barbarians. It echoed the arrangements made with the Russians after the 1727 Treaty of Kiakhta and created parallels with other border arrangements, including those with the British at Canton.

Nevertheless, tensions there grew since there was more at issue for the British than trade. The private or 'country' merchants – the non-East India Company people – became impatient with two things: pettifogging Chinese restrictions, and the power of the East India Company monopoly. In 1834 parliament in London abolished the monopoly, throwing the Canton trade open to all comers. The results were fateful. So far, the merchants had been supervised by an East India Company officer, but now London had to appoint a government official instead. That, as the Chinese soon realised, was a very different and undesired state of affairs. The first official 'superintendent', was William John, Lord Napier. The scion of an old Scottish family, he was a captain of the Royal Navy and a personal friend of the king, William IV, who had once been Napier's shipmate and helped him to get the Canton job. In China, Napier found that nobody does symbolism, or political one-upmanship, more artfully than the Chinese. He was immediately confronted by the fine details of official protocol. That included approaching the Chinese authorities solely by missives labelled 'petition' and channelled through the Hong merchants. Napier thought it absurd to expect a representative of the British crown to behave in this way.[7] London, and especially the foreign secretary, Lord Palmerston, agreed. So Napier refused to accept the Canton governor's bombastic declaration that 'the great ministers of the Celestial Empire are not permitted to have private intercourse by letter with outside barbarians', but insisted on direct official-to-official communication. He even threatened to use force. The Chinese responded with a variety of pressures on both trade and people. Napier fell seriously ill, and eventually had to withdraw in demeaning conditions to Macao, where he died and was buried in Macao's cemetery among the frangipani trees.

The Napier episode made it clear that there were two underlying issues. One, the more fundamental, had to do with national standing and relations among sovereign states. The key figure in London was the foreign secretary, Henry John Temple, Viscount Palmerston. One of the greatest of British nineteenth-century foreign secretaries, he flatly refused to allow official British representatives, officers of the crown, to adopt the 'petitioning' manner the Chinese expected, or to accept China's general presumptions. No man was more conscious of Britain's power and eminence among nations, more convinced of the benevolence of British purposes, or embodied more fully the views and attitudes of the Briton of his day. Several shrewd commentators thought he was much too undiplomatic. Charles Greville, for one, wrote that

> events have so befriended Palmerston that he is now in the right, and has got his colleagues with him; but where he is and always has been wrong is in his neglect of forms; the more *fortiter* he is *in re*, the more *suaviter* he ought to be *in modo* . . . that is the reason he is so detested by all the *Corps Diplomatique*, and has made such enemies all over Europe.[8]

François Guizot, the French conservative and historian who was to become prime minister in 1847, saw things quite similarly: 'l'orgueil ambitieux, la préoccupation constante et passionée de soi-même, le besoin ardent et exclusif de se faire partout sa part et sa place, la plus grande place possible, n'importe aux dépense de quoi et de qui'[9] (an ambitious pride, a constant and passionate preoccupation with himself, making it forcefully and exclusively his business to establish everywhere his own role and his own standing, making it as significant and grand as possible, no matter what, or to whom, the cost might be).

It took the Chinese some time to grasp what the fuss was about. From their point of view, the British were only one more lot of foreigners trading on the frontiers, under regulations that worked well. As the issues gradually became clear, though, they could see that what the British were asking for rested on Western notions of state sovereignty that could fundamentally challenge the position of the empire. For 3,000 years China had never, with only the minor exception of Russia, confronted a modern state in any sense its equal. Mongols and Manchus had been fierce but uncivilised barbarians who had in time been absorbed. Others had come to China to learn, to admire, to pay tribute. But not to negotiate, least of all as equals. The British, even the French and Americans, were therefore wholly new phenomena for the Chinese tradition of how to deal with foreigners: wholly novel in ideas, in power, in technology, in arms and in political demands; and not assimilable by China and its ways.

CONFLICT OF LAWS

Chinese concepts of law, and the imperial code, were fundamentally different from Western law. The standards and institutions of justice were not necessarily inferior to those of Western states, but they were strange, incomprehensible and unacceptable to many foreigners. There was an administrative and mainly penal code, essentially an instrument of government, designed to preserve the social order and the imperial system. There was no notion of a 'higher' law, stemming from divine will or from universal 'human rights'. Confucius himself had not reasoned from systematic and fundamental principles, still less from any idea of the rights and liberties of individuals, but rather from everyday and observable life, and what that might suggest for maintaining social order and harmony. Chinese officials were, after all Confucians, concerned with the rule of virtue, where Western and especially British officials were apt to be lawyers, concerned merely with the rule of law.

Much of Chinese law had to do with procedures, inheritance law and the like, and breaking the rules was something to be dealt with as a matter of practicalities, not of philosophical principles. Therefore offences against the social order attracted special severity. A child's disobedience to the father, for example, was a particularly dreadful crime: a son who actually struck his father might have his head cut off. Failure to obey an imperial order was certainly a capital crime, whatever the circumstances.

Beyond that, there were no legally effective rights of private property, no protection against a state which was quite unconcerned with private property and investment, and nothing resembling modern Western commerce and society and its networks of legal rules and sanctions.

There was no such thing as a legal profession, nor any idea of private lawyers. There was nothing resembling modern Western notions of protection for individuals through 'due process', no 'legal right' to a defence, least of all any notion of 'innocent until proven guilty'. In magistrates' courts the presumption was of the guilt rather than innocence of the accused. There could be forced confessions. Plaintiffs as well as defendants could be subjected during interrogation to torture, whose forms were carefully prescribed. Arrests could be arbitrary and detention or imprisonment indefinite. However, the system was tightly and precisely organised and administered. Cases were subject to review and appeal. Moreover, given China's system of collective responsibility, someone who might be personally innocent could be executed simply as the representative of a group, or a scapegoat. Family solidarity being such a powerful element of Chinese society, guilt by association was often assumed and punishment of relatives was a regular practice.

Europeans were bound to regard such principles with horror. That made the question of jurisdiction over foreigners in China, or in Chinese waters, highly sensitive and became increasingly acute as time went by. In 1773 the Portuguese acquitted an Englishman at Macao of killing a Chinese man, but the Chinese insisted on re-trying and executing him. In 1784 a salute fired by an English ship accidentally killed a Chinese onlooker. Some sailor, who probably had nothing to do with the affair, had eventually to be turned over and was unceremoniously strangled.

Similar things happened again in 1807. Then, in 1821 came the 'Terranova' incident that became a landmark in such matters. A Chinese woman died, allegedly struck by debris thrown overboard from an American ship, the *Emily*. The Chinese demanded that the culprit be handed over. It seemed as though it might have been an Italian sailor named Terranova. When the Americans refused, the Chinese threatened to stop all American trade. To preserve commerce, the Americans gave in, and allowed Terranova to be surrendered. He was tried in secret, with no American present, and promptly strangled. The Chinese piled insult on injury by praising the Americans at Canton for their properly submissive behaviour, which fitted in well with the arbitrary and somewhat contemptuous attitude of Chinese officials towards foreign merchants. There was no official American protest, but the affair rankled, and not only with the Americans. It greatly strengthened Western determination not to allow Western citizens to be subject to an 'arbitrary and corrupt' Chinese police and judicial system; and therefore strengthened the determination to find some spot, perhaps a small island just off the coast – like, eventually, Hong Kong – where Westerners could be dealt with by Western laws and not by the Chinese.

The other major issue at Canton was the opium trade and it became increasingly difficult as the 1830s wore on. From 1800 it had grown as part of China's foreign-trade patterns. The reasons remained what they had been for a century. Western demands for Chinese products, especially tea, soared further. Paying for it became still more difficult. China wanted to buy some things in return, like raw cotton, but nothing like enough to counterbalance Chinese exports of tea and porcelain. The answer, more urgently than ever, was opium from India. Not only the British but the Americans and other foreigners were selling it.

In China, opium had for centuries not only been used as a medicine but was a recognised import: it was, after all, the best

pain-killer anyone could get before the invention of modern syn-
thetics. As China's population grew, and domestic troubles wor-
sened, opium consumption also rose, in part surely to deal with social
stress. Eventually, the emperor tried to ban its import, whereupon the
East India Company stopped trading it into China,[10] although private
merchants could buy it in India and, together with hundreds of
Chinese, including hordes of corrupt officials, smuggle it into China
anyway. Profits and corruption grew. By the later 1820s the Chinese
patrol fleet, formed to stop the smuggling, routinely let smugglers
pass for a fee of 36,000 *taels* a month,[11] or around £12,000
(equivalent, according to the Bank of England, to half a million in
2002/3). The admiral in charge personally transported opium in
return for a cut of the profits.

Foreigners, or Chinese merchants, could sell opium in China for
silver that could be banked at Canton (in exchange, say, for drafts on
London). That silver could then pay, quite legally, for tea. Even the
British in India were apt to send their remittances home by buying
opium there, shipping it to Canton and selling it for silver which was
then used to buy tea to ship to London, making a profit at each stage
of these transactions. Merchants on the China coast could also settle
their accounts by drawing bills on London in the complex commission and banking arrangements developed at Canton and later Hong
Kong. Wealthy Chinese merchants themselves could trade on their
own account, or invest funds in places like America. These complex
money and credit operations, and the stockpiling of silks and other
goods in or near Canton, encouraged even more official corruption.
That helped to make trade at Canton even more complex, financially
and administratively. Canton merchants became agency houses for
firms in Calcutta and London, or operated sophisticated money-
exchange and credit operations with London and New York. In fact,
by 1830 the finances of British India itself depended critically on all
these opium and money-exchange operations.

For the Chinese authorities, the rising opium consumption created
not only social and health problems, but a growing drain of silver
from the Chinese economy. It was partly to pay for opium but partly

also because Chinese were hoarding and hiding it in times of trouble. Either way, it raised the domestic silver price, while leaving everyday copper coinage unchanged. That had powerful deflationary effects and, since imperial taxes had to be paid in silver, meant effective tax rises for ordinary Chinese.

As smuggling grew, the British had three comments to make. First, that the opium trade was China's problem, no one else's. Second, it was China's and not Britain's business to control Chinese coasts and trade, in any way that China's rulers might please. No British superintendent at Canton approved of opium-smuggling. But discouragement was all they could offer because, throughout the 1830s, London refused them legal powers to discipline British merchants, let alone non-British ones. The third comment dealt with the most obvious question that was forcing its way to the top of the Chinese agenda. Should the prohibitions against opium be rigidly enforced or should the trade, on the contrary, be legalised, regulated and taxed? All British advice was that, since the Chinese were unable to stop smuggling and use, the empire should stop trying. Here was an exact forerunner of the twenty-first-century 'drug wars' arguments in the Western world. Not that Chinese mandarins would have noted foreign advice on anything. In 1837, for example, the British super-intendent at Canton, Charles Elliot, in a note to the governor mentioned his hope for amity between the two nations. He found himself severely snubbed. The governor explained that foreigners were only allowed to trade through the goodness of the emperor. 'How can there be what the barbarian superintendent is impertinent enough to term "the bonds of peace and goodwill" between the occupant of the Dragon seat and the ministering servants to whom he distributes his bounty?'[12]

In any case, the emperor decided to make war on the laws of supply and demand. Imperial Commissioner Lin Zexu was sent to Canton to deal with the problem. A remarkably able, intelligent and cultured man, he made serious efforts to understand the British. The difficulty was that, like every other Chinese statesman, he stuck to traditional ideas about foreign relations. He came to Canton not to negotiate but to give orders based on a sense of Confucian right-eousness. He used gradually increasing forms of psychological, political and even physical coercion on the British, eventually compelling the surrender of the large and valuable opium stocks. But he showed scant respect for the Union Jack or Queen Victoria's representative, Superintendent Elliot. He was also infuriated by the death of a Chinese man after a sailors' brawl ashore, and Elliot's inability to identify and surrender a real or presumed killer. So he began to threaten not just men but, it seemed, women and children at Macao, effectively forcing them to seek refuge on board British ships. By the New Year of 1840 the entire British community of men, women and children was embarked on merchant ships off Hong Kong – and so outside China's reach – awaiting protecting troops from India and orders from London. There were repeated Chinese attempts to send fire-ships among these merchant vessels. At one point Lin even refused to let them buy food and water ashore and barred the British from trading in China.

None of that stopped all opium-smuggling, while American mer-chants – not being under the Chinese interdict – were happy to profit by transporting tea from Canton to British traders at sea. For British officials, opium was still not the issue. The cause of conflict lay elsewhere. London was outraged by reports of China's affront to the British crown, the denial of state equality, the seizure of property without due process and, above all, the danger to British women and children. When Thomas Babington Macaulay, the brilliant essayist and now secretary of state for war, told the House of Commons that he would make the 'name of Englishman as much respected as ever had been the name of Roman citizen', he was taken to be stating a simple truth. In any event, the British aboard ships off Canton called for armed protection and support. The Royal Navy sent ships. Shots were exchanged, partly by accident. War began.[13]

Not everyone in London was happy with this outcome. Why had things been allowed to come to this pass? The Chinese had not invited the British to come; surely they were entitled to set the terms on which other people could visit and trade? Was Britain really entitled to use force? How could this war be regarded as just? In April 1840 a three-day debate in the House of Commons pitted the leading lights of political London against each other. Palmerston and the government narrowly won their vote. A year later, after the government fell, the successor Peel administration continued with Palmerston's China plans.

Within four or five decades it came to be almost universally believed that the conflict had been an 'Opium War', fought by the British to force more opium into China, in search of profits and irrespective of the consequences for the Chinese. Yet that view is flatly contradicted by the evidence that British decisions to fight were taken for entirely different reasons.[14] That was was well understood at the time. In May 1841, while the war was under way, John Quincy Adams, a casually erudite man who had been sixth president of the United States, explained to the Massachusetts Historical Society that opium was

> a mere incident to the dispute, but no more the cause of the war than the throwing overboard of tea in Boston harbor was the cause of the American revolution . . . the cause of the war is the kowtow – the arrogant and insupportable pretensions of China that she will hold commercial intercourse with the rest of mankind not upon terms of equal reciprocity, but upon the insulting and degrading forms of the relation between lord and vassal.[15]

A year later he again echoed Western principles of sovereignty and independence that might have come from the mouth of Lord Palmerston himself. China's attitude to the British in 1839 had been plain wrong. It violated the principle of 'love thy neighbor', was anti-commerce and immoral, 'an enormous outrage upon the rights of human nature, and upon the first principles of the rights of nations'.[16]

The war itself was odd. During the first half, the British spent more time talking than fighting the Chinese. The local Chinese viceroy and Charles Elliot tried to make a deal, but London and the Chinese emperor promptly rejected it. Then came an interval; partly because there was a change of government in London; but especially because of the British military catastrophe in Afghanistan. Back in 1839 they had sent a grand expedition to put their candidate on the Afghan throne. The military as well as the political sides of the affair were appallingly mismanaged, as finally became clear when the sole survivor, Dr William Bryden of the Army Medical Corps, stumbled on his exhausted pony into British-held Jellalabad (a town of which London would hear much more in the post-2001 'War on Terror'). Clearly, the first priority had to be to deal with the effects of that disaster.

Later in 1842 the China war resumed, with fresh British commanders and much greater professionalism.[17] The Chinese forces, though sometimes suicidally brave, suffered from several decisive handicaps. They were no match for British discipline, training, tactics, arms or equipment. It was the British who had the guns – what the French king Louis XIV had once called the *ultima ratio regis* (the final argument of kings). Furthermore, many senior Chinese commanders displayed a genius for failure, and their command, staff, supply and intelligence arrangements were hopelessly, at times even ludicrously, corrupt. By the middle of 1842 Chinese forces had been humiliatingly defeated by relatively tiny British forces whose men had scant respect for most of the Chinese. In the final stages of the campaign, with British forces grown from 2,000 to 9,000, a thirty-mile-long British fleet train made its stately and irresistible way slowly along some 450 kilometres of the then-uncharted Yangzi River to the ancient imperial capital of Nanjing. With the British on the brink of storming it, the empire signed the 1842 Treaty of Nanjing.

It made no mention of opium, but conceded almost everything London had asked for, including the opening of more ports to trade: Shanghai, Fuzhou, Ningbo, Xiamen (Amoy). During 1842 and '43 came supplementary agreements. For instance, it was laid down that Britons would be tried by their own consular officials, in accordance with Western law. The British also acquired the island of Hong Kong, which immediately became a magnet not just for the British and other

Westerners, but for the Chinese, from fishermen to merchants, who welcomed the security and order of its British administration. By the middle of 1843 Hong Kong, which had been largely barren and almost empty not long before, had a population of 25,000. It also became a particular base for missionaries.

Hard on the heels of the British followed the French and, more especially, the Americans. Until 1842 American interests in China were almost entirely confined to private commerce. Merchants were on their own. In fact, Washington's involvement, and even visits by ships of the US Navy, was unwelcome. Trading conditions were as good and profitable as the merchants could imagine. What could the government do that they had not done already, except disturb a perfectly satisfactory and peaceful situation? But the Anglo-Chinese war changed things. Americans in China, and especially ones with official connections, were critical of the Chinese. Even missionaries often thought that a successful British war would make their task easier by breaking down China's entrenched conservatism. Nevertheless, for the time being the American role in the western Pacific region remained low-key; and in China it made sense to sail in Britain's wake. As one commentator unkindly said, the Americans played 'jackal diplomacy' – picking up, under most-favoured-nation arrangements, concessions that had already been won by the British. Chinese officials soon saw the point, too, and warned the emperor that the Americans just watched the British bringing the Chinese to terms and then moved in to share the spoils.

However, by the 1840s Americans began to see the Pacific more as an extension of the country's 'manifest destiny'. As the British were winning the war, it became clear that official positions would have to be established. There was also young Dr Parker at Canton. He had quickly found that his medical skills were in much greater demand there than his preaching. In November 1835 he opened an ophthalmic clinic in one of the factories and in the first three months found himself treating 900 patients. He became trusted and even, towards the end of the decade, treated Commissioner Lin for a hernia.[18] While the British blockaded Canton, Parker sailed back to the US, met the president and the secretary of state, Daniel Webster – a relative by marriage – and recommended that a proper US diplomatic mission be sent to China. He was co-opted into working for his government.

The administration selected a New England lawyer, Caleb Cushing, to be the first minister plenipotentiary and Cushing appointed Parker as secretary and interpreter to the mission at the handsome salary of $1,500 plus expenses. Cushing came to China, carrying a friendly letter from President Tyler. After the Treaty of Nanjing, his task was to negotiate a separate Sino-American treaty. The Chinese were not going to make difficulties. In November 1843 the emperor issued an edict to say: 'Now that the English barbarians have been allowed to trade, whatever other countries there are, the United States and others, should naturally be allowed to trade without discrimination, in order to show Our tranquilising purpose'.[19]

But Chinese views firmed. The emperor was told that the English, Americans and French interpreted the details of their treatment by the Chinese court as a measure of their national status.[20] It reinforced his determination not to let Cushing go to Beijing. The advice to him about how to respond to President Tyler said merely that of all Western countries the 'US is the most remote and the least civilised; solitary and ignorant'. The emperor should therefore confine himself to a simple response whose meanings were obvious.

So Cushing had to cool his heels on the south China coast and negotiate there with senior mandarins. Still, on 3 July 1844 he got his agreement, the Treaty of Wanghia. In it, the Chinese conceded the same privileges as those accorded to the British, including access to the treaty ports and the exemption of Americans from Chinese jurisdiction. It meant conceding to the US a status of equality that would have been inconceivable five years earlier. For the first time, American and Chinese officials dealt with one another as equals. In addition, the most-favoured-nation arrangements meant that, while the Americans would get the benefits, it was still the British who would have to bear the onus for creating the system that had made it possible. The French concluded a very similar treaty shortly afterwards.

However, it turned out in short order that for the Chinese signing treaties was one thing, doing what they said was quite another. They would soon insist, as they have done ever since, that here were just 'unequal treaties' whose very name implied that they were unfair and needed to be revised. In any case, Beijing could not always secure compliance from local authorities wanting to obstruct the foreigners. That resistance to treaty observance was by no means confined to officialdom, for the war and its outcome fuelled popular anti-foreign sentiment. As early as December 1842 there were riots with mobs looting and burning some foreign factories. The 1840s saw sporadic atrocities, including murder. Confucian mandarins focused on maintaining the imperial and social order, subject only to the need to avoid fresh Western attacks. One way was the traditional one of keeping foreigners away from the population. The British, having acquired Hong Kong in 1842, obtained another concession at Shanghai three years later that developed, by 1860, into the principal international settlement in China. The French got a similar Shanghai concession in 1849. Towards the end of the decade the emperor explained why the grievances of foreigners were not his chief concern: 'the only important thing is to appease the people's emotions. If the people's loyalties are not lost, then the foreign bandits can be handled. From now on, if there should be any incidents in Sino-barbarian relations, we must not be unduly lenient [i.e. to the foreigners] for fear of giving offence.'[21] Chinese appeasement of the Western powers remained, at best, fitful through the 1840s. By 1850 a new emperor abruptly ended even that.

The Europeans became indignant. Western countries, by no means only the British, were impatient with repeated Chinese failures to carry out the chief treaty provisions – in particular, access to Canton or sending embassies to Beijing. Perhaps nothing demonstrates more starkly the inadequacy of China's management of foreign relations than Beijing's inability to deal properly with the Europeans in the two decades after 1840.

The British and US treaties therefore had mixed effects. The American one had considerable benefits for US shipping: by 1850 or so, American clippers were carrying half the trade of Shanghai. There was even a lively trade, especially at Amoy, in Chinese coolies for cheap labour in California and Australia.[22] American as well as the British missionaries went on thinking that Christianity and free trade were the hallmarks of civilisation and that manufacturing, railways and the telegraph were its instruments. Given the immunity of American citizens from Chinese jurisdiction, American sailors became notorious, especially at Shanghai. Soon it was said that every blue-eyed whore in the East claimed to be American. By the later 1840s, after several anti-foreign riots and some atrocities, Peter Parker had become a strong supporter of British attempts to secure the rights and the safety of foreigners in China.

While friction continued, by the end of the 1840s both China and the Western powers found themselves acutely distracted. In 1848 a fresh wave of revolutionary fervour swept Europe. In France, soon afterwards, Napoleon Bonaparte's nephew became president and, four years later, came to the throne as Emperor Napoleon III. The Netherlands moved towards parliamentary government. There was nationalist revolution and unrest in Italy and several parts of Germany. Even Austria-Hungary was threatened with collapse by a rebellion in Hungary which had to be quelled with the help of Russian troops provided by a czar still mortally fearful of revolution. Russian nationalism also grew, under the surface of an official policy to preserve the old order and to resist European revolution.

Until the middle of the century, that helped to keep Russian attention and external policy focused on Europe and the Middle East. By the 1830s, though, the Russians had also become disillusioned with Chinese somnolence, complacency and corruption. Not only that, but the 1839–42 war focused Russian attention on the weakness of the whole of North-East Asia to British sea power. It was a worry that grew more acute as British, American and French naval activity in the Pacific increased. By 1843 St Petersburg decided that frontier issues needed to be clarified, though the foreign minister, Count Nesselrode, wanted no Russian land-grabs or damage to good relations with the Chinese; relations which, among other things, made possible a trade by which the Russian state was earning more and more money from tariff revenue at Kiakhta.

Nationalism also fuelled a sense of a pan-Slav mission. That focused mainly on the Ottomans in the Balkans and around the Black Sea. It raised concerns about increasing British moves into Central Asia, themselves undertaken largely to forestall suspected Russian ideas about moving south to the Himalayas and the frontiers of British India. The same combination of strategic need and pan-Slav sentiments strengthened a wish to bring Siberia out of its bottomless poverty and misery. The Russians could also see that the 1842 defeat and the Treaty of Nanjing had loosened China's grip even in the north. Its demoralised troops failed to stem a new wave of migration of Chinese peasants into Manchuria and even Siberia. In its need for cash to counter rebellion it even sold waste Manchurian land to Han settlers. In 1848 Czar Nicholas I appointed a mere stripling of thirty-eight years, Nikolai Nikolaevich Muraviev, as governor-general of eastern Siberia, and he set about strengthening Russia's position on the shores of the Pacific, and especially on the Amur boundary.

For Beijing, in 1850 even such problems with borders and foreigners faded into relative insignificance with the outbreak of a rebellion that would cost millions of lives and devastate some of China's richest lands. It was the so-called Taiping rebellion, which mixed ethnic anti-Manchu resentments, anti-tax fervour and elements of sometimes bowdlerised Christianity. It was started by an obscure member of the southern Hakka minority, Hong Xiuquan. In 1843 he failed his examinations at Canton for the fourth time and developed a growing rage at Manchu domination of Han China. He also learned something of Christianity from an American missionary, Issachar Roberts, convinced himself that he was the younger brother of Jesus Christ and in 1851 proclaimed himself the Heavenly King of a new dynasty, the Heavenly Kingdom of Great Peace. He attracted hordes of followers into a fiercely militant popular movement that briefly attracted Western interest as a possibly effective, even quasi-Christian, alternative to the weakening Qing regime, though these ideas were soon dropped. The Taiping armies quickly occupied much of central China and the Yangzi valley, and made Nanjing their capital. However, their attempts to spread further were defeated and they were eventually countered, less by the inadequate and often corrupt imperial

MURAVIEV

Muraviev was a colourful soldier, with a splendid moustache and a record of bravery in Turkey, Poland and the Caucasus, where he was wounded. Born in 1809 he was a general by the age of thirty-two, but transferred to service in civil government, becoming the first provincial governor to propose the abolition of serfdom to the czar. He was a liberal-minded autocrat and expansionist, impatient with court politics or business intrigues. He wanted freedom of the press, land for serfs, reward for talent, and promotion of commerce, but he also had strategic vision.

By the time he was thirty-eight he was appointed governor-general of eastern Siberia, where he could see the Amur as a way to project Russian power into the Pacific. His policies were largely based on balance-of-power notions. He saw several potential dangers for Russia flowing from the 1840–2 Anglo-Chinese war. The British were sure to try to expand their influence. They might even have designs on the mouth of the Amur River. The English and French might also revitalise China with their trade and technologies, or station fleets in the northern Pacific. In 1849 he wrote to the czar arguing that European incursions into China would lead to the Russians losing parts of Siberia as well as portions of their China commerce. The answer had to be to strengthen Russia's own hold on the mouth of the Amur River – then still, technically, Chinese territory – and on what would become the naval base of Petropavlovsk. In fact, it was necessary to think about a Russian warm-water supply route along the Amur and all the way across to the Kamtchatka peninsula.

In 1858 he concluded the Treaty of Aigun with the Chinese, whereupon the grateful czar gave Muraviev the title of Count Amursky. Ten years later he retired – to Paris, where he died in 1881.

forces than by the initiative of regional governors in creating new armies. The rebellion was finally crushed in 1864, having produced tens of millions of dead.

Rebellion or no, by the early 1850s the British, American and French governments were increasingly irritated with Chinese intransigence about observing the old treaties and tried to insist that the arrangements of 1842–4 needed to be revised. Nothing happened. That led to demands by the British, closely followed by the French and, soon, the Russians, for even broader Chinese reforms and concessions. It was not that the Europeans were unsympathetic to China's plight. In 1854 the British appointed a new governor of Hong Kong and plenipotentiary. He was Sir John Bowring, deeply Christian, experienced in commerce, a founder of the Peace Society and a friend of London radicals. He also believed, fervently, in the links between morality and trade. 'Jesus Christ is free trade,' he once said 'and free trade is Jesus Christ.' Palmerston, now back in office, told Bowring to try to get access to the entire China coast and, most especially, to have a British ambassador admitted to Beijing. In that same year the British also strongly backed the creation of a Chinese inspectorate of customs that, staffed very largely by foreigners and headed by a wise and incorruptible Irishman, (Sir) Robert Hart, was to play a critically helpful role in keeping the imperial finances afloat. Moreover, the Western powers began to worry about the very cohesion of the Chinese empire.

Yet the Chinese continued, throughout 1854 and '55, to treat Bowring, and a new American minister, Robert M. McLane, with studied contempt. By 1856, with the British, French and Americans all wanting greater access to the Chinese market, a French missionary was arrested for preaching the gospel, caged, beheaded and his head thrown to the dogs. The Americans, including Peter Parker, by now the US commissioner, began to think that force might have to be used. Parker wanted to see the US in a triple alliance with France and Britain to put pressure on the Chinese, and a US acquisition of Formosa to balance the British possession of Hong Kong. But the Chinese had grown to detest his arrogance and stubbornness and President Franklin Pierce was to recall him in 1857.

In the meantime, the European powers had once again become distracted. In 1853/4 Britain, France and Russia were embroiled in the Crimean War. While it lasted, few people in Paris, London or even St Petersburg had time or resources to spare for China. But as Anglo-French naval squadrons threatened Sakhalin and Kamtchatka, Governor-General Muraviev started to encroach on Chinese territory in the name of Russo-Chinese security.

Of altogether greater long-term importance were quite other events in the Pacific. For two centuries, since 1637, Japan had been kept in determined isolation under the governing Tokugawa shogunate. But by 1808 the presence of powerful British ships from the Indian Ocean and Russian ones from Kamtchatka were causing alarm. In 1825 the authorities ordered the destruction of foreign ships entering Japanese waters but worries increased with the easy British victories over the Chinese in 1840–2. The Japanese could see the growing power of the British and Russian Pacific squadrons against which Japan had no defence. The immediate reaction was some appeasement of the foreigners: in 1845, for instance, a British Royal Navy ship sailed into Nagasaki and was allowed to take food and water on board. The turning-point came in 1853, when the American commodore Matthew Galbraith Perry sailed his four armed 'Black Ships' into Edo Bay (near the modern Tokyo) and demanded in the name of President Millard Fillmore that Japan open six ports to US ships and allow foreigners to travel in Japan. The Americans thought that once Japan was open they would be able to fulfil that old dream of a direct North American road to Asia. Japan, said Secretary of State Daniel Webster, was 'the last link in that great chain, which unites all the world, by the early establishment of a line of steamers from California to China'. For the Japanese, the impact of American power was unavoidable, even though Perry's 'Black Ships' consisted of only one sloop of war, one supply ship and two coal-burning paddle steamers. The Japanese were confronted with the lose–lose proposition that they could either resist the American barbarians and be defeated, or else comply with Perry's demands and risk rebellion at home. The story of Japanese politics between 1853 and 1868 is largely that of a more and more agonised debate about how to resolve these dilemmas. When it came, the resolution would transform the strategy and politics of the whole of the western Pacific, and critically influence the fate of the Chinese empire.

There, at the end of 1856, and soon after the death of that French missionary, came the straw that broke the camel's back of Western patience. It was another of those faintly absurd Anglo-Chinese incidents: the *Arrow* affair. The *Arrow* was a Chinese-built and manned boat, but flying the British flag, that Chinese soldiers boarded in search of pirates, hauling down the flag while doing it. British impatience with China was by now enough to start another conflict. The Royal Navy was called in and shelled parts of Canton; and the Americans became involved when Chinese forts fired on a US Navy corvette conspicuously flying the American flag. Commodore James Armstrong, commanding on the China station, used his three ships to capture and dismantle the forts from which the shots had come, and captured some 167 cannon in the process. Seven Americans were killed as against 300 Chinese casualties.

To the Chinese, it seemed quite absurd that something as trivial as the *Arrow* business should trigger a conflict, while to the British it was no less absurd that the Chinese should refuse satisfaction for yet another insult to the British flag. In any case, discussion in London immediately concentrated on the broader issue of observing treaty provisions and getting proper diplomatic and trade arrangements. When debate about British actions reached the floor of parliament, the government lost by eighteen votes. Palmerston resigned, called a general election, fought it on the themes of patriotism and the honour of the flag, and won by a comfortable majority. So the China issued would be pursued – in spite of all the distractions of the 1857 Indian Mutiny. Beijing would be forced to come to terms, and this time the British and French would join forces. Palmerston sent the Earl of Elgin to take charge. Elgin, stout, white-haired and looking, as someone said, like a 'bewhiskered cherub', was not enthusiastic about fighting the Chinese. He thought privately that the *Arrow* business was 'a scandal to us' and that 'nothing could be more contemptible than the origin of our existing quarrel . . .' His instructions were to secure complete observance of the existing treaties, access to Beijing for a British envoy, and the opening of more ports to trade. He was also told that, just as in the Treaty of Nanjing fifteen years earlier, Britain did not want exclusive privileges but freer trade for everyone.[23]

The French appointed a high commissioner to accompany Elgin, while Washington and St Petersburg sent sympathetic observers. Canton was taken, after a slow and limited bombardment. Elgin, watching it, remarked, 'I am sad. I feel that I am earning for myself a place in the litany, immediately after Plague, pestilence and famine.'[24] By this time the old Chinese hold on Central Asia, as well as in the Ussuri river region, had also collapsed and been replaced by Russian influence. Muraviev had begun in 1854/5 by sailing Russian forces down the Amur, past Nerchinsk, accompanied by colonists wanting to settle on its banks. He went on through the 1850s taking soldiers and settlers down the river, to the confluence of the Amur and Ussuri rivers, and founded a new town that he named Khabarovsk. In 1857/8 Admiral Count Poutiatine tried to start discussions with the Qing on the Amur boundary issue but found himself snubbed. Instead, in May 1858 the Chinese governor of Manchuria started negotiations with Muraviev, who had created new outposts and strongly reinforced them with several thousand men from other parts of Siberia. The Russians now claimed exclusive rights on the river's left bank and invited the Chinese side to talk about the transfer to Russia of both banks of the Amur. The outcome was the 1858 Treaty of Aigun, which awarded the left bank of the river to Russia and the right bank, as far as the Ussuri, to China. That gave the Russians all the lands north of the Amur and guaranteed them free navigation on the major regional rivers. The Qing empire had signed away some 180,000 square miles of territory. Even more important, the treaty contained some ambiguities of which Muraviev took immediate advantage, claiming the territory between the Ussuri and the sea, as well as stretches down to the Korean frontier, appropriating a thousand miles of Chinese coast. No wonder that, when the terms of the treaty became known in Europe, Karl Marx's friend and collaborator, Friedrich Engels, sarcastically complimented the Russians for 'despoiling China of a country as large as France and Germany put together' and doing so without spilling a drop of blood.

In the meantime, the Anglo-French campaign kept moving, while the Chinese were still trying to cope with the Taiping rebels – but with Western help. By late May 1858 the allies had moved north to the Bei He River and moved on to Tianjin. The emperor accepted a Treaty of Tianjin under which foreign ambassadors should come to live in the capital, trade should be widened and toleration would be granted to Christian missionaries and their Chinese converts. The treaty also, finally and without fuss, legalised both growing and trading in opium. By July 1858 the new US consul, Townsend Harris, secured a commercial treaty very much on the pattern of Tianjin.

Shortly after Tianjin, Poutiatine negotiated a fresh Russo-Chinese agreement as well, under which the Qing removed many of the former restrictions on Russian trade and opened several ports to the Russians. But once again Beijing prevaricated about ratification. At that point an experienced Russian official, Count Nikolai Ignatiev, was sent to hurry treaty ratification along. He found that the Chinese were quite blind to the dangers they faced from the British and French. He therefore urged the British to march on Beijing, while telling the Chinese that if they met the czar's demands in the north, the Russians would make the sea barbarians go away.

The Chinese also tried to prevaricate about ratifying their treaty with the French and British. In 1859 a new British minister (Elgin's brother, Frederick Bruce) arrived at the Bei He, on his way to Beijing, escorted by a Royal Navy flotilla. The Chinese refused to let the foreigners land, the British and French tried to force a passage, and were repulsed with considerable loss.[25] In fact, the whole fight was probably caused by mere issues of prestige. The American minister, now John E. Ward, landed peacefully elsewhere on the coast, and was received and escorted to Beijing. He was not, though, received by the emperor when he refused the kowtow, explaining that, as a Southerner from Georgia, 'I kneel only to God and woman.'

For the British, though, there was still no sign that Beijing appreciated its changed international position, or the way in which new power relations had spread across the globe. In 1860 Elgin was sent back to China, to get the Treaty of Tianjin ratified and obtain an apology for the Chinese firing at British ships. The Russians were trying to persuade the Franco-British army not to force an occupation of the imperial capital, lest that should lead to the fall of the dynasty and to anarchy and chaos in the empire.[26] So Elgin was told not to press the Chinese authorities to the point where they lost command of a China whose cohesion was already threatened by the Taiping rebellion. The French had their own agenda. As their foreign minister said, France would demand a Chinese indemnity and the restitution of Catholic church property.[27]

The British mustered 10,000 British and Indian troops. The French sent Baron Gros, together with 5,800 troops under General de Montauban. It spoke volumes for the character and cohesion of Chinese society that the Anglo-French force advancing towards Beijing was loyally assisted – even in battle – by Chinese coolies from the south who seemed quite happy to have their northern cousins defeated. The French calculated that the allies had some 5,000 of these coolies and servants.

Allied tempers flared when the Chinese captured and tortured some envoys, officers and men sent to parley under a flag of truce. Some had their heads cut off, others died after being roped so tightly that circulation was cut off and limbs filled with maggots. When the remaining envoys were told by their captors to send messages back to Elgin, they managed to include notes in Hindustani to say that the Chinese had dictated what they said. Elgin was fiercely determined to exact revenge for their treatment.

The French and British agreed to march separately and meet at the imperial summer palace outside Beijing, which had been built at the start of the eighteenth century to Jesuit designs. The French got there first, to find marvels of gardens and lakes and of pavilions filled with elegantly magnificent jewellery and ornaments. By all accounts they went a little crazy as they took a lead in sacking that gorgeous palace with its unique treasures. One young French officer wrote home to say that nothing like it had been seen since the sack of Rome by the barbarians. An English interpreter found the French commander, General de Montauban, scrabbling about on the floor of the imperial throne room with a pile of choice curios, sorting out what to send to Napoleon III and what to Queen Victoria. One of the British Army's brightest young officers remembered later that French officers and men seemed to have been seized with a temporary insanity. Having arrived without transport, they apparently left with 300 piled-up wagons. When the British arrived, they more or less followed suit. Beyond that, Elgin wanted to exact revenge for the killing of the British and French envoys and to do it in a way that would hurt the emperor, not his people. So he had troops set fire to the already sacked ruins of the summer palace. A young English engineer officer, Charles George Gordon – the very man who would, much later, die a famous martyr's death in the Sudan – had to help direct the burning. He wrote home to his mother: 'You can scarcely imagine the beauty and magnificence of the places we burnt. In fact, these palaces were so large, and we were so pressed for time, that we could not plunder them carefully . . . It was wretchedly demoralising for an army. Everybody was wild for plunder.'[28] In Paris, Victor Hugo called the allies bandits. But in London, almost everyone approved. Unquestionably, then and later, Elgin was full of pity for the Chinese and saw himself as an honourable man, seeking to limit the sufferings of the Chinese people and acting at all times 'as China's friend'.

Nevertheless, Elgin was determined to see trading and political issues settled after years of Chinese prevarication, and determined to impose proper peace terms, including the provisions the Chinese had previously refused to honour. He did it with just the kind of formal political ceremonial at which the Chinese themselves were so adept. He had himself slowly carried in a red sedan chair through Beijing's central artery, carefully preserved from the time of Kublai Khan almost 600 years earlier. At the imperial Hall of Audience he was received by the emperor's brother, Prince Gong. There the new Convention of Beijing was duly signed in late October and the former Treaty of Tianjin finally ratified. The next day Baron Gros held the same ceremony for the French. In addition, the British and French also received 8 million *taels* of silver each. Here was the end of imperial China's attempts to maintain its sovereign power against the West by force of arms. A month later Elgin left China, not before annexing the Kowloon peninsula to Hong Kong. In London, he was given a triumphant reception.

In these concluding weeks and months Prince Gong, the senior Chinese negotiator, had actually sought Russian help in ridding Beijing of Lord Elgin and his Anglo-French armies. Once they left, Ignatiev and the Chinese did agree on a fresh treaty to ratify what had been agreed at Aigun and Tianjin, ceding to Russia all the lands between the Ussuri and the sea. So Russia managed, without fighting, to acquire not only hundreds of thousands of square miles of territory but the fertile soil of the entire Amur basin, which at last gave Russia the capacity to maintain a sizeable population in her new maritime provinces. In the summer of 1860, Muraviev's men began the construction of a new Pacific city: Vladivostok.

As for the Chinese, perhaps the most far-reaching result of these events was not so much the loss of territory or treasure as the opening of more ports and the greater freedom of foreign travel. The critical point turned out not to be trade, important as that was, but the removal of China's protection against foreign people, technology and, most importantly, ideas. These things were, indeed, to cast long shadows. The old emperors had not been wrong to worry about the connection between foreign influence and domestic instability.

9

COLLAPSE AND REVOLUTION

AD 1860 to 1911

T HE BEIJING CEREMONIES therefore did more than settle a war: they heralded the empire's final decline and collapse. What proved fatal to the dynasty was not merely the devastation of the Taiping rebellion and its countless deaths, or economic damage, or even China's humiliating defeats at the hands of Western forces. It was the uncertain and hesitant handling of the twenty-year crisis, at a time when the tectonic plates of global politics were shifting again, not to China's advantage.

There were further changes in the European balance as the idea spread like wildfire that 'unification into one great state represents the way to historical greatness'. Italy was united, largely at Austria-Hungary's expense. In Germany, the forces unleashed by the Napoleonic wars and industrialisation led to a German customs union and, after the Franco-Prussian War of 1870, the creation of Bismarck's new German Reich. That became Europe's foremost industrial and military power and the centrepiece of Europe's diplomatic alignments, as well as the home of some of the world's greatest centres of philosophy, science and technology. The rise of Germany as well as of America and Russia alarmed the British and the French. Each thought (in the face of strong domestic dissent) that the way to remain at 'the top table' of European and world affairs was to unify empire and home country into a single, powerful political entity. Both were destined to fail. In America, a civil war had by then headed off the danger of secession, with President Abraham Lincoln managing to preserve the Union. That war, and its huge industrial effects, further strengthened the drive for American expansion across the continent to the Pacific. Only a few years later, in 1867, the US bought Alaska from the Russians for $7.2 million, and no one asked the local Indians.

After 1860 change was everywhere fuelled by the rapid growth and spread of heavy industry, railways, the telegraph and chemicals, and expansion in Asia by the opening of the Suez Canal. In 1870 Britain had 32 per cent of global manufacturing capacity and was the largest industrial power in the world. By 1910, though Britain was still dominant in banking and insurance, that manufacturing figure had shrunk to 14.7 per cent with the Germans at 15.9 per cent and the United States at 35.3 per cent. In 1860 British coal production was 81 million tons, with Germany at 12 million tons and the United States at 3.4 million. By 1914 those figures had become 292, 277 and 455 million tons respectively. In 1880 British steel production was 1.3 million tons, with the German and American figures at 700,000 and 1.3 million tons respectively. By 1914 the British were only producing 6.5 million tons while German production had shot up to 14 and American to 32 million tons.

The social and economic energies of these major powers began to turn even more strongly to the world outside Europe. With France and Britain in the van, Europeans sought, or consolidated, imperial possessions, especially in Africa and Asia. The Dutch were concerned with the pacification and economic development of their restive holdings in the East Indies, while the newly independent Belgium played a major role in everyone's 'Scramble for Africa'. In the process its dreadful king, Leopold II, displayed a rarely equalled combination of greed and cruelty.

The world with which China had to deal was therefore becoming altogether more complex, more intrusive, and more insensitive to inherited Chinese ways. France had begun to send out missionaries already in the eighteenth century. The post-1815 colonial programme started with the conquest of Algeria in 1830. It was only two decades later, ten years after the 1848 Paris revolution, that the French began to extend into South-East Asia. They tried for a colonial base on China's borders and gained control over Annam and Tonkin (modern Vietnam), as well as Cambodia. There were efforts to create a sphere of influence over adjacent provinces of China, like Guangdong and Yunnan; and perhaps to extend the Tonkin railway into south-west China. It was part of a broad effort by France to spread her political and civilisational influence not only to South-East Asia but to Syria, to Mexico and elsewhere. Economic motives were largely secondary. The French, unlike the British, did not need colonies to sell goods or invest capital. Instead, before 1914 French money was invested in Southern and Eastern Europe, and especially in Russia and its railways. That seemed safer than to put money into the Far East. In any case, investment strategies supported more critical French aims: strengthening Russia, Serbia and the Ottoman empire would help to contain the rising power of France's most dangerous European rival, Germany.

In Britain, by 1857 earlier worries about the Atlantic slave trade were overshadowed by the bloody affair of the Indian Mutiny and sporadic campaigns in Burma. The British also acquired footholds around Africa – not least for coaling stations to allow the Royal Navy secure access to India – and promoted the building of the Suez Canal. They also moved into Central Asia – Tibet and Afghanistan – once more so as to protect India from the supposed threat of Russia. They even encouraged Chinese to migrate westwards into Central Asia. At the same time, they continued to administer their empire with maximum reliance on self-rule by local chiefs.

Germany also turned its energies to seeking a 'place in the sun' outside Europe. By 1860 Prussia suggested a customs-union-style agreement to the Chinese and a year later concluded a trade treaty with Japan, while a Prussian expeditionary squadron of four warships under Count Eulenburg sailed to have a look around East Asia. In

September of the same year, China accepted that the Prussian ambassador would represent all the still-independent German states while German consuls would be admitted in Chinese ports, with legal control of German merchants. By then German scientists, explorers and, of course, capitalists, could also be found in most parts of the world, including China. In 1863 the first Prussian minister travelled there,[1] fourteen years before a Chinese legation opened in Berlin. After 1871 the Germans sent China military goods and instructors, while the feeling grew further that Germany needed colonies, like everyone else. The result was that after the 1878 Congress of Berlin all six of the great powers – Austria, Britain, France, Germany, Russia and Turkey – were involved in a delicate system of alliances and in a series of overseas and colonial rivalries.

In Japan, there was a huge political earthquake, destined to change the strategic and political map of the entire Eastern hemisphere. Back in 1853 Commodore Perry had merely asked the Japanese for trade and treaties, not land, just as Lord Palmerston had done in China a decade earlier. But Perry, whether he knew it or not, started something altogether more fundamental. The years after his visit saw agonised and often violent Japanese debates about how the country could meet the evidently growing foreign dangers; and what domestic reforms might be needed. The immediate response was isolationist. In the early 1860s the Japanese fired on a British squadron at Kagoshima, which returned the shots. In 1864 an international squadron forced the Shimonoseki Straits. In Japan, chauvinistic hysteria grew and some officials were assassinated. There was more unrest as foreign goods entered post-Perry Japan, producing some economic hardship among local producers; and in 1863 the emperor called out soldiers to clear Kyoto streets. By 1867 the shogun's army was overwhelmed by revolutionaries, who seized the young emperor. The following year the Tokugawa shogun abdicated and his office was abolished.

What then began was nothing less than a transformation of society and the state that came to be called, after the emperor who took the name of 'Meiji', the 'Meiji restoration'. Bureaucracy was centralised.

The old domains became prefectures. The samurai became officers in the new army or were pensioned off. Reforms were issued as imperial decrees. The founding document of the Meiji era was the Charter Oath of 1868 which spoke of 'the seeking of knowledge throughout the world in order to strengthen the foundations of the Throne'. Hundreds of foreign experts were invited to advise on science, education, engineering, finance, and military and naval affairs. The Japanese learned from Prussia how to build an army, from the British how to build and organise a modern navy and from the Swiss how to make watches. From 1871 hundreds of students were sent to America, Britain, France and Germany to study. In short order, Japan became a major Pacific industrial and military power.

After 1860 all these changes led to more, and more varied, demands on China from everywhere. Only Russian priorities drifted away from the Pacific as Alaska was sold to the US and most of the Kuriles handed to the Japanese in exchange for Sakhalin. Eastern Siberia, on the other hand, needed strengthening, given its vulnerability to British naval power or Chinese incursion. During the Crimean War, for instance, some Russian settlements on the coast had had to rely for their supplies on Californians running the British blockade. The Russian navy could concentrate at ice-free Vladivostok, but as late as the 1870s Vladivostok had to import its drinking water from Japan or Korea. The Russian fleet had to buy ordnance in San Francisco and get repairs done in Nagasaki. There was also foreign incursion across the new free-trade zone along the Sino-Russian frontier. By the 1870s four-fifths of the people in the Russian Far East had migrated there, not just from Russia but from every corner of the world. In Vladivostok, 80 per cent were Koreans or Chinese; and soon people began to talk about foreigners dominating commerce, even about bandit raids from Manchuria across the border. From the 1880s the Russian authorities tried to reverse this 'Asianisation'. Thousands of Chinese were driven out of the Russian areas, while the migration of Russians themselves into the Far East was much encouraged. Between 1859 and 1917 some half a million newcomers arrived in what some called the 'New America'. Cross-border trade complicated matters. The social reformer Alexander Herzen might dismiss China as stagnant, but by the 1880s Chinese settlers were turning Manchuria's Sungari plain into a rich granary and Russian wheat farmers on the Amur wanted to limit the importation of Manchurian grain. Other Chinese farmers supplied fruit and vegetables to Vladivostok and Khabarovsk, and Chinese contractors leased coolies to Russian enterprises. By 1915 three-quarters of the workers in the Amur gold-fields were Chinese.

Russians also began to assert themselves in Mongolia and Central Asia. In Mongolia, the Qing tried to keep foreigners out, but after 1860 more and more Russians arrived to live and trade there and established consulates. Meanwhile, in Central Asia the Russians advanced into Samarkand and Bokhara, again in that competition with the British that Rudyard Kipling christened the 'Great Game'.

China faced other demands. The British wanted control of trade in the Yangzi valley. Their first attempts came in 1863, in the closing stages of the campaign against the Taiping rebellion in which that assertive English Christian, Charles Gordon, played a minor but celebrated role. A group of British and American firms at Shanghai asked for a railway concession from Shanghai to Suzhou, upstream on the lower Yangzi. The local governor said, sensibly enough, that the railway would only benefit China if it was run by the Chinese. However, it did not come into Chinese hands; and the authorities became increasingly worried about foreign activity in the empire. The Americans wanted open trade (later, the 'Open Door'). Russia wanted to dominate Manchuria and to have access to ice-free ports on the Pacific. Even the Germans wanted trade and diplomatic links.

Everyone had problems, though, as in Korea, where China was still the titular sovereign but for which Chinese ministers refused to be responsible. In fact, they declared that, although Korea was subordinate to China '. . . yet she is wholly independent in everything that relates to her government . . . in none of these things has China hitherto interfered'.[2] In 1866, nine French priests had their heads cut off by the Koreans. The French Asiatic Squadron under Rear-

Admiral Pierre Gustave Roze put a landing party ashore and proclaimed a blockade of the city of Seoul. The Koreans refused to take any notice of them, let alone negotiate. The baffled French withdrew to China, having accomplished nothing. In the same year the US ship *Surprise* was wrecked on the Korean coast and her crew treated kindly;[3] but a month later the crew of another American ship was attacked after bad behaviour by sailors a shore. Eight of the men were killed, the rest taken prisoner. There were other incidents. In 1869 the Germans tried to start negotiations but were snubbed. In May 1871 a US naval squadron under Admiral John Rodgers arrived in Korea, carrying the US envoy to China. Attempts to start negotiations with the Koreans failed and the squadron was fired on. The Americans retaliated, sent in landing parties, destroyed five Korean forts and killed some 250 Korean soldiers, but the Koreans still would not negotiate and the Americans had to withdraw. In China, Robert Hart commented gloomily that 'If America goes no further in the matter, Korea will ripen like a pear and drop into the jaws of Russia'.

The new Japan, too, had wishes. In September 1871 Tokyo and Beijing signed their first treaty, giving each other equal status and agreeing to consult if there should be threats from outside powers. Three years later 3,000 Japanese troops landed on Taiwan to exact punishment for the killing of fifty shipwrecked Okinawans. The Japanese also claimed the remainder of the Ryukyu Islands – a claim that China conceded in 1881. In 1876 came a Japanese naval demonstration off the Korean port of Pusan that led to a treaty of friendship and commerce with Korea. Even then, the position of Korea remained ambiguous. When some French priests were arrested in Korea at the end of the 1870s it was the Chinese who secured their release. Yet the Chinese also advised the Koreans to deal directly with the Western powers whereupon, in the early 1880s, the Koreans signed a raft of treaties with the Americans, British and French, as well as with Germany, Italy and Russia. The Americans and Japanese sent separate envoys to Seoul, while everyone else appointed their Beijing envoy to look after Korea as well. During this entire period, the Korean Chosun dynasty was decaying and, while refusing to reform, trying to insulate itself (as Japan had once done) and earn the title of the 'Hermit Kingdom'.

Crises usually offer opportunities, so a crisis can be a terrible thing to waste, as China did the interlocking crises of the 1850s and '60s. In Beijing, three forces were in play. First, and most obvious, there was the enormous shock and affront to deep-seated assumptions of Chinese superiority. Second, there was the evidence of Chinese inadequacies in the modern world, producing a sense that reform and modernisation were badly needed. Third, there was the position of the Qing court.

The burning of the summer palace and Elgin's honoured procession to the Hall of Audience symbolised the failures not merely of a government but of the Confucian principles that governed the imperial structure. A basic principle of Chinese affairs had, since time out of mind, been the assumption of morality and righteous conduct of rulers and officials. Whatever the behaviour of any one emperor, the imperial institution was sacrosanct and the moral standing of officials taken for granted. Failure or loss of office meant, *ipso facto*, that the man concerned must have been guilty of moral failure; and moral opinion clearly trumped law. In government and society a man's reputation was all. It was at least as important as life itself and a fall from office might be redeemed by suicide.

From this point of view, the failures of the empire were, by definition, moral failures as much as political or military ones. The lost wars against the British and French in 1842 and again in the 1850s were only part of the indictment. There was also the legalisation of opium in 1858, which was a denial of the previous, and morally based, posture of prohibition. There were the rebellions from the 1850s to the 1870s, of which the Taiping movement was only the most spectacular. After 1860 things became even worse. It was all profoundly at variance with inherited convictions of China's centrality and superiority. The Western impact was a huge psychological and political shock, creating intolerable tensions in Chinese society and the Chinese body politic.

The second strand was recognition, by no means in all quarters, that the West was simply far more advanced and that China needed to change, to import Western science, technology and industry, perhaps even Western ideas and advisers, as part of a huge modernisation effort at home. That produced a movement given the classical name: 'Self-strengthening'. But how and in what ways should China modernise? There was – if anyone in China had cared to look – a stunning example of rapid and effective modernisation just across the water in Japan. Would China follow such an example, even if it meant abandoning a 3,000-year-old view of the world, and of China's place in it?

That might have been the right thing to do but, thirdly, the person at the centre of imperial decision-making was the dowager empress Cixi, and she wanted none of that. She was a tiny woman, shrewd, ruthless, almost certainly murderous, and deeply ignorant of the world beyond court politics, which she played with consummate skill. Instead of adapting China to a changing world, her first and last aim was to preserve and strengthen Manchu rule and her own power. It is difficult to know, at this distance, exactly what she thought and what her calculations were. She certainly had no real grasp of, let alone interest in, the outside world. Perhaps, in her mind, the borders of the empire had always fluctuated, and been porous to boot. What mattered were not the peripheries but the centre, the core, the imperial heart of things. To protect that, she adopted twin policies. Beijing accepted the 1860 treaty system to appease the foreigners. She also put more Han into local and provincial posts, in order to dilute the anti-Manchu strain in the Taiping and other rebellions. But these were mere outer defences around a core of unrepentant maintenance of imperial customs. She did not even reduce imperial nepotism, corruption and extravagance. The first and last reaction in the court at Beijing remained the shoring up of the Qing imperial system.

*　　*　　*

CIXI, DOWAGER EMPRESS

Her given name was Yehonala and she was born on 29 November 1835. Her parents stood in the middle ranks of Manchu society, but by the time she turned seventeen, and although she was no outstanding beauty, she had become one of the concubines of the Emperor Xianfeng. 'Cixi', meaning kindly and virtuous, became her court name. Like others, she had to conform to humiliating rituals. For instance, whenever the emperor sent for her to come to his chambers, she would be escorted or carried to his room by eunuchs and left naked at the foot of the bed, a custom to ensure no weapons were brought into his room. The emperor, like all his predecessors, naturally had many wives and concubines, but it was Cixi who managed to give him a son. As soon as the child was born, she moved up in the court rankings. But her relations with the emperor were apparently not smooth. She was hungry for power, resented his sole exercise of it, and sought greater influence of her own. When her husband died in 1861, she became a dowager empress with the title of Empress of the Western Palace.

The new emperor was her own five-year-old son, Tongzhi; and she was only one of eight regents whom the old emperor had nominated to govern during Tongzhi's minority. The other seven could have removed her from power but she had powerful allies of her own. With the support of some military commanders, together with some of the more influential of the court eunuchs, Cixi seized control. She effectively became the sole ruler of China, although rule could still only be exercised through her son, and when he turned seventeen, his mother's reign ended. However, she selected a wife and four concubines for him, to keep him so busy that she could rule for him. A few years later, in 1875, the young man died of veneral disease. His young wife, Alute, died of poisoning soon afterwards in mysterious circumstances and Cixi took back sole power. Cixi had indeed become the 'Dragon Lady'.

It was not the end of plotting. From 1889 the new emperor was Cixi's nephew, Guangxu. For the next decade he had a merely nominal role while his aunt wielded real power. Then, in 1898, on hearing that China might be in serious danger of being partitioned by outside powers, he tried to assert himself. He issued a series of reform decrees on most aspects of government administration. However, he had no serious political base, so she was able to imprison him and to have his advisers killed. It is almost certain that she later saw to it that he died before she did.

She encouraged the Boxer Rebellion of 1900. That was started by the society of the 'Righteous and Harmonious Fists'. When the group first organised in 1898, it was secretly supported by Cixi's government since she feared growing foreign influence and thought that if the foreigners came to control Beijing, her own rule would be over. By 1901, after the Boxers failed, Cixi decided to favour China's modernisation. The empress also promised a constitution and representative government. None of it could rescue her beloved dynasty. In the four decades of her reign she had been clever and masterful but narrow minded and ultra-conservative. She had tried to keep the outside world at bay, and China mostly stable, but had entirely failed to bring modernisation to the empire.

In 1908 Cixi suffered a stroke. She died on 15 October 1908, at the hour of the goat. Her catafalque was kept waiting for the best part of a year before the court astrologers could decide on the year, the day and the hour most suitable for her burial. Eventually the marvellously elaborate funeral procession set off, with eunuchs, musicians, camels, cavalry escorts and even the Dalai Lama. It took four days to reach the Eastern Tombs and for her to be finally sealed into the vault where her husband, the late emperor, had been waiting for her for over four decades. Extravagant to the last, she was buried in splendour, covered in diamonds.

In 1928, revolutionaries dynamited her tomb, looted it and desecrated her body. A mere half a century later a British politician, who probably knew nothing about her, coined a phrase that might serve as her epitaph: 'All political careers end in failure.'

In spite of Cixi's lack of sympathy, the groups who saw that 'self-strengthening' was unavoidable gained ground. So did some European cultural and even artistic influences. Among the earliest changes was the build-up of new armies to fight the Taiping rebels. A series of rebellions from the 1850s to the 1870s – in the north because of famines and in western China by Moslems and others – was put down by provincial armies, using modern weapons and often led by gentry. Such men led in suppressing rebellion, looking after agriculture, education and taxation, and were also quite willing to use modern tools in building steamships, arsenals, producing modern arms and trying to use Western technology. The far-seeing scholar-official Li Hongzhang at Shanghai, for instance, set up an arsenal there in 1864, to build gunboats and guns. What with foreigners now living in the capital, Beijing also created a kind of foreign office in 1861, the Tsungli Yamen, which began to use Western law in defence of China's own interests. The missionary W.A.P. Martin helped with a translation of Wheaton's writings on international law,[4] and an interpreters' college was set up to prepare people for diplomatic tasks, though authority on policy remained with the Grand Council.

These reform efforts lost their way, both because of lack of support from the centre and because the dominant conservatism was incompatible with real modernisation. There was opposition from the established scholarly class, which saw threats to its influence, based on classical learning. The doctrine of 'Chinese learning as the fundamental structure, Western learning for practical use' simply embodied too many contradictions. It also became clear to conservatives that if China wanted to acquire the West's industry and technologies it would need the political, legal, and technical ideas that went with them. That would mean imitation of, and help from, the West, or at least some Western individuals. Industrialisation was therefore inherently dangerous. Modern industry would have to be based, not on Confucianism, but on its own ideas and on people trained to use and maintain the machinery. So there would be social disruption. Old skills would go, people be thrown out of work. Railways, mining, the telegraph would not only disturb the harmony of man and nature but create restive workers' groups and dependence on machinery and technicians.

Moreover, the connections between different elements of modernisation were not understood. In the mid-1870s, for instance, a Chinese steamboat company was subsidised to help carry rice from the Yangzi delta north to Tianjin. The boats needed coal, so coal mines were opened near the city. To ship the coal, China's first permanent railway was opened in 1881. But the scheme didn't work. The mines, indebted to foreigners, came into foreign hands in 1900, while the steamship company, robbed by its own employees, lost ground to the British. When a wave of railway-building did come, at the very end of the century, it was largely done by foreigners in their own regions of influence.

Much of this confusion troubled sophisticated Chinese. The dilemmas are illustrated by Beijing's first minister to London, Kuo Seng-tao, appointed in 1867. Another member of that immensely attractive Chinese class of scholars and gentlemen he was, Gladstone thought, the most urbane man he had ever met. Already while journeying to England he wrote in his diary, deploring the old Chinese policy of isolation: 'Western states have been established for two thousand years and their principles of government are entirely civilised and rational.' When he eventually returned to China, he commented that 'Confucius and Mencius have deceived us' – mean-

ing that he now understood there was more than one way of
governing a country. When he later sought to publish the diary, it
was officially banned.[5]

The Chinese welcome for Western industry was therefore at best
guarded, and failed to lead to real reforms. For example, by the 1880s
the empire tried to build a modern navy. But millions of public funds
were diverted to build a new summer palace for the empress; and in
the Sino-Japanese war of 1894–5 it was found that some of the navy's
shells were full of sand instead of gunpowder. In fact, there was much
more here than imperial incompetence or even local corruption; there
was active resistance to change. True, some enlightened officials saw
to it that Western business and even government involvement in trade
and investment grew. British businesses were expanded. Other
Westerners came too. After 1850 German firms could open branches
in Hong Kong. Hanseatic companies, especially from Hamburg and
Bremen, followed. Many Western individuals toiled for China; like
the American Horatio Lay, who worked to regularise procedures in
the customs service, one of the government's more important sources
of regular revenue; or, after him, the outstanding Irishman, Robert
Hart, who was by now in charge of Chinese customs, worked in
China and became a deeply respected adviser to the Chinese
government. Many of these people, officials, business people, missionaries, even soldiers who had fought in China, developed deep
feelings of love and respect for China and its people.

Not that everyone admired China. As Charles Gordon wrote in
October 1863, 'I am perfectly aware from nearly four years' service in
this country that both sides [i.e. Taipings and imperial troops] are
equally rotten.' Even Karl Marx commented acerbically that the
Chinese government operated only at three levels: regulating the
use of water, a fiscal policy of domestic plunder, and a foreign policy
of plunder abroad. Still less were all foreigners, let alone foreign
governments, selfless. States are not organisations for altruism and
business men are not always governed by disinterested benevolence.
Although the Western powers tried to keep each other from getting
undue advantages, advantages were indeed sought. There was open

French interference in south China, systematic bribery of officials, and local gentry often found it wise to appease the foreigners. As early as 1871 one finds memos to the throne from the governor of Guangxi saying that foreign residents, especially the French, were 'using the missions as a pretext to raise taxes, to occupy territories, to raise troops and to choose officials from among the people . . .'.[6] The British and Americans set up and expanded the foreign settlements – notably but not only in Shanghai – and, while promoting investment, growth and modernisation, also increased their assets in the empire. By the turn of the century these foreign settlements were in many ways rather similar. Each had a foreign section of town, on the fringe of the Chinese city. Each had its own non-Chinese institutions and its own laws. Each was likely to have its own post, transport and communications, was effectively governed by its own consuls and protected by foreign gunboats off the crowded commercial waterfront with its warehouses and swarms of Chinese coolies.

Yet the foreign efforts brought disruption to Chinese society. One reason for keeping foreigners apart from the population had always been to protect them from the perennial Chinese suspicion of outsiders, even from occasional attacks. Too often foreigners were the focus of public detestation and assumed to be responsible for oppression, humiliation and difficulties. Economic penetration created more resentment, especially the foreign ownership of new railways, or Chinese unemployment created by foreign imports or machines. In time, resentment led to condemnation of foreign activities generally and, yet more potently, reinforced China's sense of victimhood. That also helped to stall economic modernisation. Furthermore, the confused mixture of patriotism, anti-foreigner resentment, and impatience with China's impotence, began to boil over into nationalist and revolutionary movements, including a further upsurge of Han Chinese resistance to the foreign Manchus. All that created problems for Beijing. If popular anti-foreignism was not damped down, it could lead to even more foreign intervention. Yet seeming to take the foreigners' side would make the authorities deeply unpopular.

'CHINESE' GORDON

Charles Gordon was one of the more celebrated military heroes of Victorian England, and died a legendary 'martyr's' death in the Sudan in 1885. Born in 1833, he was commissioned into the Royal Engineers, fought in the Crimean War and, among other things, became a passionate Christian. He was another of those brave and devout men whose moral force, even more than their physical bravery, built much of the British empire.

In 1860, following the Chinese surrender, 3,000 allied soldiers were left at Tianjin to await the payment of the Chinese war indemnities. Gordon, an able but opinionated officer, was one of them. In 1862 he was ordered to Shanghai, where the British commander, Admiral James Hope, wanted to clear the Taiping rebels from the area around the city. Gordon was deeply shocked by the devastation the rebellion had caused: '. . . words would not depict the horrors these people suffer from the rebels or depict the utter desert they have made of this rich province,' he wrote.

He was not much impressed, either, by the 'Ever-Victorious Army' which the imperial commander in the region, Li Hongzhang, asked him to lead. It was a group of Western mercenaries and Chinese ragamuffins that had earlier been raised by an American, Frederick Townsend Ward, to fight on the imperial side. Ward himself was a freebooter with natural military talent, who became a Chinese general and trained Chinese troops for the first time to fight in the European manner. That made them a model for Chinese imperial forces. Gordon noted pessimistically that 'You never did see such a rabble as it was . . .', yet he soon led them to victories, not least by the moral effect of leading from the front, carrying nothing more than a walking-stick. He had other peculiarities. He refused to allow his men to loot captured cities. When they staged a mutiny, Gordon quashed it within the hour. He shot one of the ringleaders dead and threatened to shoot another of the mutineers every hour until the mutiny was over. Order was promptly restored. He made drunkenness in battle a capital offence, ended trading in opium and women, and insisted on drill and training. He was also happy to recruit Taiping prisoners, whom he found much more satisfactory soldiers. He developed marked respect for the Taipings, whose 'mandarins are without exception brave and gallant men', far superior to the imperial officers.

In December 1863 the city of Soochow (Suzhou), earlier occupied by the Taipings, fell to imperial forces, helped by Gordon's men. The Taiping leaders were executed, according to custom. But Gordon, who thought he had guaranteed their safety, felt deeply dishonoured. His temperamental outbursts made both the British and the imperial commanders increasingly impatient and in 1864 Li agreed that the Ever-Victorious-Army should be disbanded. By that time, and although Gordon's force had made only marginal contributions to the anti-Taiping campaign, the Shanghai merchants and the English daily press had made him into a heroic figure: 'Chinese Gordon', the man who had single-handedly put down the rebellion.

To the British public – and therefore in the arena of British politics – he became a Christian hero and an iconic figure. He was quickly promoted to general. When he died (quite needlessly, as it turned out) in the Sudan in 1885 as Islamist forces under the 'Mahdi' overran its capital, Khartoum, the British public poured blame on the prime minister, Gladstone, for not having rescued Gordon. In fact, Gladstone was promptly translated, in the public mind, from Grand Old Man (GOM) to Murderer of Gordon (MOG)* and his

---

* There was even a music-hall ditty:

> The MOG when his life ebbs out
> Will ride in a fiery chariot
> And sit in state
> On a red hot plate
> Between Pilate and Judas Iscariot.

government fell. The public insisted that an entire military expedition be sent to avenge Gordon's death. In the climactic battle of Omdurman the Mahdi's army was duly destroyed; and a certain very young and unknown officer took part in what was probably the last British cavalry charge in military history. His name was Winston Spencer Churchill.

Even the most disinterested and benevolent foreign efforts often made things worse. The presence of the missionaries could not help harming established ways of life or social well-being even further; and the Western, and especially the American and British, missionary effort in China grew strongly. The forty years from 1860 to 1900 saw mission stations, schools and clinics spreading into every province of China under the new treaty rights. Though many of the missionaries were loved in their immediate surroundings, the missionary presence often increased general resentment and hatred of foreigners. Missionaries and local gentry were natural and inevitable competitors for local authority. For the population at large, since foreign powers had forced China to let them come, they were clearly foreign agents trying to undermine Chinese ways. In any case, not only was Christianity the religion of British and French aggressors, but a bastard version of it, in the form of the Taiping movement, had already caused untold suffering. When a Roman Catholic cathedral was dedicated at Tianjin in 1869, it was built on the site of an ancient Chinese temple. Christian ceremonies, like baptism, smacked of magic. The missionaries' attention to waifs and orphans created more distrust, as did the notion of burial in consecrated ground.

In such an environment things were made worse by the grotesque allegations about Westerners that surfaced from time to time. Back in the days of the Ming dynasty there had been official documents explaining in detail the Portuguese practice of boiling and eating Chinese children. In the 1830s even Commissioner Lin had had to agree that the foreigners looked like animals or devils. In the 1860s and '70s suspicions grew further and there were rumours that mission orphanages acquired or sold Chinese children for immoral purposes; or made medicines out of their eyes and hearts. The *Beijing Gazette* and court reports gave detailed accounts of such alleged practices. There was a whole literature of baroque pornography describing the orgies of priests, nuns and converts. No wonder that Chinese mothers carefully shielded their babies from the unlucky glances of foreigners and particularly from the magic eye of Western cameras. No wonder, either, that missionaries were harried, or attacked and sometimes killed in the Chinese interior.

A notable example came in Tianjin in 1870, where the mission cemetery contained childrens' bodies. Some Chinese men were tried for kidnapping children and executed, but not before one of them said under torture that he had sold children to the mission orphanage. Though that was shown to be false, and the local imperial commissioner tried to calm the situation, the French consul rushed to the commissioner's office and apparently fired into the crowd outside. The result was that the consul, his secretary, ten Sisters of Mercy and two priests were killed, the consulate looted and burned and four Protestant chapels sacked. The Chinese apologised to Paris, paid reparations and took the heads off twenty coolies.[7]

In these tides of popular opinion, opium played no role, except as just one more instance of foreign aggression. Western liberals and missionaries argued with growing passion that the West was guilty of corrupting China. The Chinese said Western opium was deeply responsible for China's weakness and decline. None of it was true. What was keeping Chinese from Christianity was Christianity, which was deeply subversive of China's social order, while the people preaching it were of course foreign agents. The truth was that no one, Chinese or foreigners, knew how to persuade Chinese not to grow or use opium. Still less could anyone prevent foreign merchants from shipping it into a very willing market. In any case, the great majority of China's opium supply was by the 1860s and '70s being grown at home. One guesstimate is that by

1900 there were about 40 million consumers of opium in China, about 13.5–15 million of them addicts.[8]

What of China's position in the larger international balance? In the half-century after 1860 there was movement throughout the North Pacific region. British, German and American trade flourished and US power expanded with acquisitions from California in 1848 to the Philippines in 1898. Japan acquired the Ryukyu Islands in 1879, Formosa in 1895, and Korea in 1910; and the unreformed China quite quickly became a pawn in the manoeuvres of the major powers. For at least a decade after Elgin's stay in Beijing, the British tried in many ways to be supportive. They were content to dominate most of China's external trade from their eminence in the financial world and the economic control of China's Yangzi valley heartland. When the Taipings invaded the Yangzi delta and threatened Shanghai in 1862, the British and French took the lead in defending the city. As late as 1910–13 the British empire remained China's principal trading partner and foreign investor, while showing no sign of wanting to govern China's masses, or of allowing anyone else to do so, notably the Russians, who did now want to dominate much of China. So long as there were no good trans-Asia routes to China, British sea power could check any partition attempts. Together with the French and Americans, they could see that further diplomatic or military pressure on China could produce an imperial collapse. Propping up the empire was the alternative to chaos. The British also tried to help China in other ways, including by the promotion of industry and technologies.

America, once William Henry Seward became secretary of state, sent Anson Burlingame as representative to China, with instructions to co-operate with the other powers. A few years later Prince Gong – who had dealt with Lord Elgin – agreed to send an elderly mandarin to Europe; but the man was so appalled by European manners that he promptly turned round and came home again. However, the Americans remained determined that their role in China should be redemptive, and should liberate China from its fossilised ways and bring modernity. In 1867 Burlingame resigned from the American service, entered the Chinese one and became China's own envoy to the Western powers. He was sent to conduct talks in America and Europe. It was, in effect, China's first attempt to create ongoing modern international relationships. In 1868, Burlingame negotiated a Sino-American treaty in Washington. Seward signed an agreement on Chinese immigration rights into the US and there were promises of most-favoured-nation treatment. In Europe, the Chinese envoys were assured by Lord Clarendon in London and, more vaguely, by Prince Bismarck in Berlin,[9] that there would be moderate policies towards China.

Even these arrangements led to trouble. Chinese middlemen had long organised transport for thousands of Chinese workers to go abroad. They came from the poverty-stricken Pearl River delta and their arrival overseas was often valued. Rudyard Kipling, on his travels, was astonished to find how much of Singapore was effectively run by the Chinese. The coolie trade was now extended to California. Arriving mostly at San Francisco, the Chinese bound themselves to a 'broker', who sold their labour to mining and building enterprises. But they were not allowed to become citizens or to own property. Still, by 1852 Chinese immigrants formed 10 per cent of California's population. Fifteen years later there were over 100,000 Chinese in the US and many Americans wanted to see fewer. By the 1870s and '80s the protests grew louder. There were anti-Chinese riots in California in which some twenty people were killed. Just eighteen years later, in 1888, Benjamin Harrison, accepting the Republican nomination for president, spoke of his 'duty to defend our civilisation by excluding alien races whose ultimate assimilation with our people is neither possible nor desirable'.[10] By then the Chinese had been fully excluded from the US, as they were from Canada in 1885, from Hawaii in 1898, and from the Philippines in 1902.

In the czarist empire, the last two or three decades of the century were a period of turmoil. The Russians were conscious of being overtaken in technology and industry by Germany, America, Britain and France. But the more the czar tried to modernise, to root out corruption, to develop enterprise, education, technology, railways, above all urbanisation, the more he undermined social stability. Yet it was also a time of great cultural flowering. Russia's greatest romantic composer, Tchaikovsky, flourished, as did Russia's two greatest nineteenth-century novelists, Fyodor Dostoevsky, whose *Brothers Karamazov* came out in 1879/80, and Leo Tolstoy, who published *Anna Karenina* in 1877. But it was also the time of the founder of modern anarchism, Mikhail Bakunin, and of the growth of Marxist revolutionary cells. In 1881 Czar Alexander II was assassinated. Six years later the authorities hanged another obscure young man, Alexander Ulyanov, for plotting the death of the new czar. They were sounding the death knell of the entire Romanov dynasty: for Alexander's younger brother, Vladimir Ilyich, became the ruthless revolutionary known as Lenin. In the meantime, Alexander III was attracted by neo-mercantilist economics. The government brought in tariffs to protect infant industries, and became more entrepreneurial, stimulating naval construction and railway-building. It paid more attention to North-East Asia, and gave fresh official encouragement to having more Russians flood into Siberia. In the two decades from the early 1880s a quarter of a million new peasants duly arrived. Russia built the first railway eastwards across the Urals and expanded in Central Asia.

None of this, however, dealt with naval weaknesses on the Pacific coast; the Russian Pacific squadron still depended on imported coal and winter anchorage at Nagasaki, while the British took over some Korean islands, apparently, the Russians feared, to prepare for operations against Vladivostok itself. The idea therefore gained ground that there should be a railway line all across Siberia to Vladivostok – possibly even to Beijing. In 1890 the German emperor Wilhelm II, in the first and perhaps worst blunder of his reign, failed to renew Bismarck's old reinsurance treaty with Russia. The czar promptly agreed to make an alliance with republican France, even if he did have to stand to attention for that revolutionary hymn, 'The Marseillaise'. It was an understanding that Paris badly wanted. William tried hard to repair relations with Alexander's successor

Nicholas II, but it did no good. Count Sergei Yulyevich Witte, Russia's great interior minister, could now plan to build that Siberian railway, financed by French loans. It was one of the most ambitious engineering projects of the nineteenth century. It meant a drastic change in the strategic patterns of North-East Asia: supplies and reinforcements for Russia's Far East could in future arrive by land, immune to interference by the British at sea. The prize might be strategic domination of China.

The Qing responded to the Russian threat by further encouraging Chinese migration into Mongolia and Manchuria, to resist by demographic means any Russian attempts at absorption. They also intensified the sinification of local Mongols and Manchus. However, the turning-point in all these agonies of imperial maintenance came with even more catastrophic defeats in war. French inroads in northern Vietnam and southern China caused growing friction. In 1882/3 the two sides came to blows and China lost. By June 1885 China had to accept a treaty recognising French sovereignty over Tonkin. Much worse was to come.

In Japan, the new Meiji system was consolidated. In 1881 the emperor promised a new constitution and popular representation. The following year Prince Hirobumi Ito went abroad to get constitutional ideas. He was especially attracted by Germany, which had industrialised while maintaining its empire and its élites. In 1889 came the new Meiji constitution. But the Japanese also had to protect their strategic raw material sources from the growth of Russian power. They established Korea as a buffer state, independent of the Chinese empire, which still claimed Korea as a tributary. In 1894 Japan decided that, since Korea was now an area of primary interest, Chinese influence there could no longer be tolerated. The Korean king had for some time tried to assert his independence and lean on some outside power, Russia or Japan. Or even the US. Matters came to a head in 1894 when, threatened by local rebellion, the Korean government appealed to Beijing for help and Chinese troops entered the country. The Japanese sent troops, too. The Chinese told Japan their troops were merely being sent 'in harmony with our constant practice to protect our tributary state'. But, as Prince Ito made clear, 'Japan would have Korea always independent and under no foreign influence'. One Japanese diplomat in Europe explained: 'We are fighting in Korea for our own future – I might also say for our independence. Once let Korea fall into the hands of a European power, and our independence will be threatened.'[11] The armed forces agreed. General Aritomo Yamagata, the head of the army, argued that the first principle of Japanese strategy must be control of a 'line of advantage' beyond Japan's own coast, a line of which Korea was a principal element. Controlling Korea would render the Sea of Japan a Japanese lake, serve as a jumping-off point for Japan herself and be a way to keep threats at bay. Whereas Korea in hostile hands would be a 'dagger' pointed at Japan. The Russians were building that Trans-Siberian railway: if Japan did not control Korea, the Russians might seize it.

Sino-Japanese hostilities began in the final days of July 1894, and China started to pay the price for its neglect of modern military power and Cixi's diversion of funds. The Japanese advanced across Korea. The British failed to organise support for China by European powers. To universal astonishment, the newly reformed Japan destroyed China's fleets and armies.[12] General Yamagata routed the Chinese at Pyongyang, while the Japanese navy destroyed its Chinese opponent in the Yellow Sea. By October 1894 Yamagata crossed the Yalu River into Manchuria (as the American General Douglas MacArthur wished to do almost sixty years later) and captured Port Arthur. In January 1895 the Japanese landed on the Shandong coast, and took the forts and guns that sheltered the Chinese fleet. The Chinese squadron had to surrender.

Li Hongzhang, by now China's grand old man, asked the powers to intervene. The Russians, alarmed by the Japanese advance, pressed Tokyo to accept a mutual withdrawal, and the British worried even more about China's cohesion. Japan eventually accepted a cease-fire, but Prince Ito insisted on negotiating on the basis that the Chinese must acknowledge complete defeat. In April 1895, by the Treaty of Shimonoseki, China ceded Formosa, the Pescadores Islands, and the

Liaotung peninsula, including Port Arthur – the strategic keys to northern China. The Chinese also recognised the independence of Korea and agreed to pay an indemnity to Japan, which was given extraterritorial rights.

Japan had clearly become a first-class power. The Russians started to be deeply concerned, for Japanese gains posed a threat to Russia's own plans to link the maritime provinces and Vladivostok more securely with Siberia. Port Arthur was not only Manchuria's premier outlet to the sea but controlled access to Beijing iself. If Japan were allowed to hold it, Witte argued, the Japanese emperor might become ruler of China as well, and threaten the entire Russian Far East. So the Russians joined with Germany and France to curb Japan's ambitions. The Germans had no interest in Manchuria, but tying Russia down in the Far East would help to secure Germany's own frontiers with Eastern Europe. The French also had little interest in Manchuria, but wanted to demonstrate the effectiveness of the Franco-Russian alliance and obtained concessions in southern China as well. The outcome was that China agreed to recognise Korean independence and Japan agreed largely to return its mainland gains to China. China's post-war indemnity to Japan was financed largely by French loans.[13]

In Japan, opinion was infuriated by the Europeans' casual denial of gains that Japan had made at the expense of so much blood and treasure. The brilliance of their victories made the subsequent humiliation worse. That simmering resentment helped to produce, ten years later, an even more spectacular Japanese victory over Russia. A few years later the emperor decided that all navy and war ministers must be admirals and generals on active duty. That change gave the army and navy veto power over national policy: the commander-in-chief of either service could topple a Cabinet by simply ordering that service's minister to resign. This was to have vast consequences. In the meantime the Russians, once more with Sergei Witte in the lead, devised a plan to shorten the length of the Trans-Siberian railway by taking the line to Vladivostok through Manchuria, the project financed by a Russo-Chinese bank, established with Li's agreement and French money, and backed by a Russo-Chinese alliance. The

Russians also, at the insistence of their military people, got the Chinese to lease them the very Liaotung peninsula they had denied to Japan. That meant gaining their own naval base at Port Arthur, the key to the Yellow Sea.

There were other shifts as not just Japan and Russia but Britain, France and Germany all claimed spheres of influence or naval bases in China, and railways into the hinterland. The British, provoked by the Russian acquisition of Port Arthur, accepted China's offer to put a base into Weihaiwaei, on Shandong's northern coast.[14] They also took out a lease of Kowloon, and concluded a Russo-British agreement that Britain would not interfere in affairs north of China's Great Wall, while the Russians would leave the Yangzi basin alone.

In Germany, there was some enthusiasm for a role as China's friend; which dovetailed with the idea of showing Russia that Germany might be a better Far Eastern partner than France. That would help to divert Russian attention from the Balkans and from friction with Germany's ally, Austria-Hungary. At the same time, the Germans saw the strategic importance of the Shandong peninsula and decided on a naval base on its south coast, at Kiaochow Bay (Jiaozhou). In 1897 the murder of some missionaries provided the pretext for the acquisition of Qingdao,[15] as well as some pushy German behaviour over railway and mineral rights in Shandong province. It was all part of Germany's belated drive for a 'place in the sun',[16] in other words asserting Germany's growing power and acquiring a colonial empire overseas, like everyone else.

At much the same time the area of the former English and American settlements at Shanghai, which had already been merged into a self-governing international settlement, multiplied by four under French pressure. The British worked their way to an alliance with Japan in 1902 to contain the expansion of Russian influence, but also to balance that new German East Asiatic Squadron at Kiaochow Bay. There the Germans, with two armoured and three light cruisers, became qualitatively superior to the Royal Navy in the region and, by 1914, caused serious headaches to the London Admiralty.

On the other side of the world, the contrasting European alliance system – Germans and Austrians versus France, Russia and, probably, Britain – were beginning to congeal. In 1897 the German emperor, Kaiser Wilhelm II, had openly abandoned Bismarck's Continental policies in favour of a *Weltpolitik* (global policy) of naval construction and colonial power. A year later he declared himself 'protector' of the world's 300 million Moslems, which was followed by German economic and railway penetration of the Turkish empire. That challenged British and French positions in the Middle East and beyond. The result was that France and Britain drew closer, just as Bismarck had feared. By 1906 their general staffs began discussions about common problems. In the meantime, the pan-Slav policies of Russia implied support for Serbia in its growing frictions with the Austro-Hungarian empire, Germany's ally.

Most Americans, meanwhile, still wanted trade in China without involvement on the ground; business lobbies told the government the potential of the China market was 'simply incalculable'. So the secretary of state, John Hay, seized on an idea that had already been floated by Joseph Chamberlain in London. It reached Hay through an English official of the Chinese Imperial Maritime Customs Service, who happened to be visiting Washington. The idea was to ask the great powers for an 'Open Door' policy for trade, and respect for China's integrity. That echoed the old demand for most-favoured-nation treatment, and had arguably been implied in American China policies for almost a hundred years. It would also help relations with the British. Soon afterwards President Theodore Roosevelt emphasised American goodwill. His first State of the Union message went on to call for the expansion of US military and economic power so as to bring the American frontier right into the interior of China. It was clear that America, too, had become a major player in the Pacific.

In the eyes of most European chancelleries and of the US, Japan's victory over China changed more than the Pacific balance. There was growing irritation with China's reluctance to modernise its habits, procedures, economy and industry, and even disgust with the government's weakness, backwardness and corruption. The war and its outcome therefore finally transformed China from an inter-locutor into a mere object of policy. To be sure, an object that had to be kept out of the unfettered grasp of others, but not a serious partner in discussions among the powers. Even before the war, Lord Curzon commented on the Chinese 'sullen resistance of a national character self-confident and stolid . . . wrapped in the mantle of a superb and paralysing conceit'.[17] After it, many outsiders were so exasperated that they began to see the Japanese army as the very harbinger of Chinese modernisation, since so catastrophic a defeat could surely leave Beijing no alternative to fundamental reform.

Within China, defeat by Japan did produce changes. Nowhere had Chinese forces looked like winning. On land and at sea Chinese commanders had been at best incompetent, at worst cowardly. The shock of such a defeat by a people whom the Chinese contemptuously dismissed as the 'dwarf nation' was huge. In foreign affairs, Li Hongzhang now saw Japan as China's principal enemy and officials understood that China had better lean towards the very powers that had intervened to limit Japan's gains: France, Germany and Russia. The Chinese even invited the Russians into northern Manchuria in order to check Japan; and coldly calculated that, to pay the war indemnity, China would have to borrow from European bond holders. In June 1896 Li himself travelled to St Petersburg for the coronation of Czar Nicholas II;[18] he was paid 3 million roubles and negotiated with Witte a defensive alliance against Japan which meant that Russian troops would have to have access to Manchuria. Witte, though now quite worried about a possible Chinese collapse, con-cluded that he had acquired a dominant influence in China, since its finances were now largely controlled by his Russo-Chinese bank.

Under the Chinese surface the changes were larger. Though the court failed to plan for the now obviously essential reforms, in wider circles many old prejudices were abruptly revised. The drive for reform, national assertion, and 'national salvation', gathered steam. Indeed, for many people the nature and swiftness of the Japanese victory made Japan the very country to emulate. Qing reformers obtained help from

Japanese advisers, and whole generations of Chinese students started to go to Japan for education and training. By 1914 Japan had become China's biggest trading partner, and the largest contingent of foreign residents in China was Japanese.

One element in the reform drive was the 1898 movement for 'progressive reform', led by a scholar from Canton, Kang Yuwei, who came to the attention of the court for his attempts to bring Confucian traditions up to date. The movement developed the reforms of the final stages of the Qing empire, even trends towards constitutional change. Kang and his disciples were nationalists who wanted to assert China, under the leadership of the Qing dynasty, in the world of the Social Darwinism then so much in vogue. By 1898 the danger that China might be partitioned at the hands of Western powers seemed immediate and Kang caught the attention of the authorities but the Manchu princes began to patronise a peasant secret society, the Boxers. The movement probably had its roots in the old 'White Lotus' secret society. Shandong peasants, whose local magistrates would no longer protect them against the foreigners, began to organise secretly. Their society, which took the name of Boxers, combined martial arts – 'boxing' as in kung fu – and spirit possession in the form of trance. After such possession, their leaders persuaded them, they could be magically immune to swords or bullets. Their slogan was: 'Support the Qing, destroy the foreign.' The movement spread quickly across northern China. In 1899 the experienced soldier/administrator Yuan Shikai was appointed governor there in order to deal with them, but they fled to another region, where the local governor welcomed them. Their views and claims convinced Cixi and the court that they now had the backing of the people in getting rid of imperialist oppression. By May 1900 the Boxers advanced towards Beijing, seized railway lines, expelled foreign workers and burned down churches. By mid-June they broke into Tianjin and Beijing and started looting and killing Christians, often with great cruelty. It was not just allowed but encouraged by the empress. On 19 June Cixi even published a declaration of war against the powers and ordered all foreign missions to leave Beijing immediately. Next day the German minister, Klemens von Ketteler, was killed while on his way to the Tsungli Yamen; and a day later the entire legation quarter was besieged by Chinese troops and Boxers, to be cut off until 14 August. The 475 foreign civilians and 450 troops of eight nations, together with some 3,000 Chinese Christians, found themselves under fire and had to fend off assaults for some eight weeks before relief arrived. The Chinese governors in the south, including Li Hongzhang in Guangdong, refused to support Cixi in any of this. So did Chinese diplomats abroad, who declared that the whole thing was simply a 'Boxer rebellion'.

At one point the Boxers even seemed to threaten Russian lives and property in Manchuria. At least the Russians said so; protection may or may not have been the sole motive for claiming parts of Manchuria and for sending in some 175,000 Russian troops to protect the new railway. As for the legations in Beijing, Japan was ready to send troops at once, but neither Germany nor Russia wanted to have Beijing relieved by a mainly Japanese force, or to have European troops serve under a Japanese or American general. At the start of July Emperor William II learned of von Ketteler's death and flew into one of his rages. He was still feeling a painful need for respect and, unfortunately for Germany, tried to meet it by blustering about 'blood and iron' or Germany in 'shining armour'. The only result was to remind everyone of Napoleon's dictum that Prussia was 'hatched from a cannon ball'. Now William demanded 'exemplary punishment and revenge', and German command of any international relief force. He even told his soldiers, in a remark that became notorious, that they should get themselves a reputation like the Huns who had terrorised Europe a millennium earlier under King Attila.[19] The allies eventually agreed to the appointment of the German field marshal Alfred von Waldersee, but on 15 August, five days before Waldersee even set out for China, the siege of the legations was lifted by a small but quite adequately competent allied force, consisting of some 8,000 Japanese, 4,800 Russians, 3,000 British, 2,100 Americans, 800 French and a few Italians and Austrians.[20] The field marshal only arrived at Tianjin on 25 September – over six weeks after Beijing's relief. Meanwhile there

SOME BOXER KILLINGS

It may be useful to go behind historians' abstractions and general-isations and look at what could be seen by people who were there. Here are brief extracts of eyewitness reports.

First, the chief of the Russian ecclesiastical mission in Beijing: 'The day of reckoning for most Orthodox Chinese was June 11, 1900. On the eve of that day leaflets were posted in the street calling for massacres of Christians and threatening anyone who would dare to shelter them with certain death. In the middle of the night gangs of Boxers with flaming torches spread over Beijing, attacking Christian houses, seizing Christians . . . [and forcing them to deny their faith. For those who did not] . . . they were ripped open, beheaded, burned alive . . . [Others] were interrogated and burned at the stake . . .'*

Second is an eyewitness report of events on 9 June at the Shansi governor's palace in Taiyuan: 'The first to be led forth was Mr Farthing [an English Baptist missionary]. His wife clung to him, but he gently put her aside, and going in front of the soldiers knelt down without saying a word, and his head was struck off with one blow of the executioner's knife. He was quickly followed by Mr Hoddle and Mr Benyon, Drs Lovitt and Wilson, each of whom was beheaded by one blow of the executioner's knife. Then the Governor, Yu Hsien, grew impatient and told his bodyguard, all of whom carried heavy swords . . . to help kill the others. Mr Stokes, Mr Simpson and Mr Whitehouse were next killed, the last by one blow, the other two by several.

'When the men were finished the ladies were taken. Mrs. Farthing had hold of the hands of her children who clung to her, but the soldiers parted them, and with one blow beheaded their mother. The executioner beheaded all the children and did it skillfully, needing only one blow, but the soldiers were clumsy,

* Russian sources from the website 'New Martyrs of China' of the All Saints of North America organisation.

and some of the ladies suffered several cuts before death. Mrs Lovitt was wearing her spectacles and held the hand of her little boy, even when she was killed. She spoke to the people, saying, "We all came to China to bring you the good news of the salvation by Jesus Christ; we have done you no harm, only good. Why do you treat us so?" A soldier took off her spectacles before beheading her.

'When the Protestants had been killed, the Roman Catholics were led forward. The Bishop, an old man with a long white beard, asked the Governor why he was doing this wicked deed . . . [the Governor] drew his sword and cut the Bishop across the face with one heavy stroke; blood poured down his white beard and he was beheaded.

'The priests and nuns quickly followed him in death. Then Mr Piggott and his party were led from the district jail, which is close by. He was still handcuffed, and so was Mr Robinson. He preached to the people to the very last, when he was beheaded with one blow. Mr Robinson suffered death very calmly. Mrs Piggott held the hand of her son, even when she was beheaded, and he was killed immediately after her. The ladies and two girls were also killed.

'On that day forty-five foreigners were beheaded in all, thirty-three Protestants and twelve Roman Catholics. A number of the [other] Christians were also quickly killed. The bodies of all were left where they fell till next morning, as it was evening before the killing was finished. During the night they were stripped of their clothing, rings and watches. The next day they were removed to a place inside the South Gate, except some of the heads which were placed in cages on the city wall. All were surprised at the firmness and quietness of the foreigners, none of whom, except two or three of the children, cried or made any noise.'*

* Richard O'Connor, *The Spirit Soldiers: A historical narrative of the Boxer Rebellion*, New York, Putnam, 1973, pp. 341–2.

was much allied looting in the Chinese capital, including in the Forbidden City.

Beijing appointed Li Hongzhang as chief negotiator with the allies. At the start of September 1901 a protocol was finally signed. It included abject Chinese apologies, the promise of death penalties for the guilty, the creation of a larger and more secure mission quarter in Beijing, and huge compensation in the form of 450 million *taels* payable over thirty-nine years.[21] Meanwhile the allies feuded among themselves about getting 'concessions' on other matters. At the end of September the foreign forces withdrew – except for the Russians in the areas they wanted, most especially the ice-free Port Arthur. The Russians also asked for economic concessions in Korea. The Japanese, worrying about Russia's strategic acquisitions, concluded that 1902 alliance with the British.

The Boxer affair and its aftermath demonstrated – as if fresh demonstrations were necessary – how little regard the powers were now willing to pay to China and its interests, as compared to the management of relationships among themselves. For them, the settlement was just retribution on a Chinese empire that had broken all the rules of international dealings and even disregarded its own wisest statesmen. Beyond that, they were concerned with other matters. The British were deeply involved in the much more important business of the Boer War in South Africa; and worried about the frictions that was causing with Germany, given the kaiser's vocal support of the Boers. The French were only interested in northern Indo-China. Their chief focus remained very much on Europe and on strengthening their links with Russia to contain German power. As for the US, even before the end of the century casually expansionist Americans were flexing their new industrial muscle. They also took over, without much fuss, the remnants of the Spanish empire in the Pacific. In 1898 Commodore George Dewey took Manila and, by the Treaty of Paris, the US acquired the entire Philippines, earning in the process the advice – and the warning – in Rudyard Kipling's famous poem 'The White Man's Burden':

> Take up the White Man's burden –
> And reap his old reward:
> The blame of those ye better,
> The hate of those ye guard[22]

Blame or not, the US was now a major West Pacific as well as an Eastern Pacific power, and, fatefully for the future, created a new North Pacific strategic triangle of Japan, Russia and the USA. In passing, the US also acquired Cuba – with Theodore Roosevelt earning renown in a famous charge – saying it wanted to promote a safe environment for business. In 1900 the new American governor of Cuba, General Leonard Wood, reported to the president, 'When people ask me what I mean by stable government, I tell them, "Money at six per cent".'[23]

It was, perhaps, inevitable that there should be a clash between Russian assertiveness in the Far East and the rising power of Japan. For the Russians there was a mixture of bureaucratic ambition, racial prejudice, the pride of half a century of foreign-policy successes, and belief in Russia's mission as the standard bearer of Christianity and civilisation in Asia. They also thought the Japanese would not dare to fight a major European power. In any case, the czar decided to put the issue to the test, refused to compromise with Japan, dismissed the cautious Witte and promoted commercial expansion into Korea. The Russians also reinforced their Manchurian garrisons.

The Japanese felt trapped. The government had to cater to the country's new national pride, and deep resentment at being deprived of the fruits of its victory in China. There was Korea, that dagger pointed at Japan, not an area to be left in potentially hostile hands. There was also the critical question of food. Between 1875 and 1903 Japan's population rose from some 34 millions to over 46 millions. The country's own agriculture could not feed such numbers and any prospect of a Russian grab for the Manchurian breadbasket was intolerable.

Prime Minister Taro Katsura and Foreign Minister Jutaro Komura manoeuvered carefully. A demilitarised zone along the Yalu River was proposed and a clear division between Japanese rights in Korea and

Russian ones in Manchuria. The Russians ignored these suggestions. The Japanese staffs saw that time was not on Japan's side, for the Russians were bringing in more ships and troops. In January 1904 came the final Russian offer: a Russian promise to respect the 'Open Door' in return for Japanese recognition of Manchuria as a Russian sphere of influence. It said nothing about the key bone of contention, Korea. The Japanese Cabinet, though still far from sure that force would succeed, voted for the now unavoidable clash. Prince Ito put it sadly: 'We are bound to fight, even at the price of our national existence.' The navy said that, having fewer ships, it would have to strike first and without warning.

On 5 February 1904 the Japanese severed diplomatic relations with Russia and sent two fleets to sea. One headed for Inchon on the Korean coast (where America's General MacArthur would stage a famous surprise landing just half a century later, in the Korean War). It destroyed Russian ships and started to land troops. The other fleet went for Port Arthur, where it found the Russian squadron disorganised. Only after the Japanese attacked did the Russians discover that they had no ship-repair facilities; and that anyway their fleet was divided between Port Arthur and Vladivostok, with neither half able to reach the other without running a blockade by superior Japanese forces. All the Russians could do was to restore duty-free status to some of their ports as an incentive to neutrals – including President Roosevelt's daughter Alice – to run that wartime blockade. Nevertheless, from the outset the Japanese gained command of local waters needed to transport their troops safely and land half a million of them. They then attacked on the Yalu and opened the way to Mukden (modern Shenyang), the capital of Manchuria. By June the Japanese were besieging Port Arthur itself. The Russian naval squadron there was destroyed by superior Japanese arms and tactics. The land battle for the great port began in mid-August, the Japanese being led by a fierce old-fashioned warrior, General Maresuke Nogi, who invoked the aid of the souls of men who had fallen in the 1895 war against China. By 5 January 1905 the Russians gave in and surrendered Port Arthur.

Even then, neither side was ready for peace. The prizes that Prime Minister Katsura now had in mind were not just Japanese control of Korea, Port Arthur and the south Manchurian railways, but the expulsion of the Russians from Manchuria altogether. Czar Nicholas II, on the other hand, still saw Russian expansion in Asia as his personal mission. He had a special grudge against the *samurai* and promised to 'proceed with the war to the bitter end rather than negotiate with "little monkeys".' Moreover, his Baltic fleet had already begun an 18,000-mile journey to the Pacific theatre. It set off in October 1904, wretchedly serviced and supplied, but with some fifty ships and 12,000 men. Since Russia had no coaling stations on the way to Asia, fuelling and progress were very slow, ships and morale deteriorated and sickness spread. While the fleet was on its way, the Japanese defeated the Russian army again at Mukden and occupied the city. In Russia, there were army mutinies, peasant revolts and workers' strikes. When the fleet did finally arrive on the China coast, the result was disaster. Admiral Heihachiro Togo simply destroyed the Russians in the Straits of Tsushima, sinking thirty-five ships while the Japanese lost just three torpedo boats. It was a dramatic end to a conflict that aroused intense interest everywhere. Everyone sent experienced officers as observers to the battlefronts and their conclusions strongly affected planning for the next European war, that of 1914.[24]

President Theodore Roosevelt offered to mediate and Japan responded at once. Their terms included a free hand for Japan in Korea, control of Port Arthur, and Russian withdrawal from Manchuria. The Japanese army and public opinion wanted much more, and the Russians much less, but the czar, trying to deal with the 1905 revolution at home, had to accept Japan's terms. It was, however, Roosevelt who presided over the peace conference, held at Portsmouth, New Hampshire, where he held the balance between Foreign Minister Komura and Sergei Witte. The conference confirmed the transformation of the balance of the entire Eastern hemisphere. The first result was that Russia and Japan drew closer together; the Russians resented the way Washington had favoured Japan during the war and the Japanese could clearly see that the US would be their strongest counterweight in the Pacific. In 1907 the two went further and signed an agreement recognising Russian primacy in northern Manchuria and Outer Mongolia while the Russians accepted Japanese primacy in south Manchuria and Korea. Soon afterwards they agreed on mutual support if anyone interfered with their prerogatives. The Americans underlined their support for the 'Open Door' in China and strengthened discrimination against Japanese visitors or migrants. The Qing encouraged still further Chinese migration into Manchuria, whose population rose from 9 millions in 1900 to 20 millions a mere sixteen years later.

In Beijing, the Manchus and even the Dragon Lady herself finally started to see that reform was necessary. The attempts of the scholar Kang Yuwei to adapt Confucian traditions to the modern world had proved inadequate. Nationalist sentiment had grown, especially since the defeat by Japan. Now, after 1900, unrest and armed rebellion began to simmer in many places. There were riots and unrest along the borders. It also became clear by this time that the provinces were less and less under central Beijing control. More importantly, not just revolutionary but anti-Qing ideas were becoming louder. In an attempt to head off discontent, missions were sent abroad to study constitutionalism; though it was plain that modern notions of re-presentation contradicted Confucianism. Cixi agreed that Manchus and Chinese might marry and allowed the creation of some modern-style ministries. Even the old examination system was abolished – and with it perhaps an entire old moral order – and education was reformed to be more utilitarian.

For the Qing imperial structure it was all much too little and too late. Accepting change was now mere death-bed repentance for the dynasty. In 1908, in her seventy-third year, Cixi suffered slight strokes, even dysentery, and died. But not before she had seen to the death of her nephew and manipulated the succession for her great-nephew, Puyi, barely three years old. By now, though, much larger forces were in play than these remnants of empire, let alone a baby emperor, could cope with. There was a growing, reform-minded urban élite in China that wanted self-government and development. The relationship between China and the governments and nationals of other powers had also become extremely complicated and lent itself to Chinese misunderstanding and national-minded resentment. There was also the way in which the regional armies that had beaten the Taiping had developed into regular provincial forces, with new naval and military academies created for modern officer training. There were other groups wanting much more, not just the end of the dynasty but outright and far-reaching revolution; and it was just those foreign connections that the modernisers had sought for so long that played a large role in stimulating it. From the start, the self-help policies had included sending some of China's brightest young people for study abroad; and nothing was more inevitable than that they should soak up new, reformist and revolutionary ideas. Other young reformers had found places in the treaty ports and joined the movement to take control of mines and railways back from foreigners

In the south, there were now a number of rebellious-minded groups. Their leaders included a young man named Sun Yatsen. Born in Guangdong, always a centre of unrest and foreign connections, he sailed to Honolulu at the age of thirteen to stay with his older brother, and went to school there. He then studied medicine in Hong Kong and, in 1884, was baptised by a Congregationalist missionary. He grew up to admire Lenin and to think about liberating Asia from white imperialism. What reformers like Sun now wanted was radical change. He established contacts in Tokyo as well as with the French in Paris and Hanoi. He talked to the French about getting arms sent via Tonkin to southern China. He sought French loans. His entire approach to revolution in China started by travelling overseas to get help in various forms. He was in the US and Europe from 1903 to 1905 and then, for another two years, in Japan. What he at first had in mind was a secessionist Han state in southern China, which would offer him a base area far from Beijing's control, grown from a connection with Indo-China. The trouble from Sun's point of view was that, given France's primary focus on Europe, its policy on China gradually changed from expansion at China's expense to seeking an understanding with Beijing.

It was Japan that played the most critical role. Both reform and the actual 1911 revolution were largely nurtured there. After 1895 Japan, having modernised, began to feel it had a duty to help a still-backward China; and after 1900 there was a concentration of Chinese students in Tokyo. Some of them set up a 'Revolutionary League' with Sun as its leader and Japanese help. That help to China's reformers continued even after the fall of the empire.

In 1911 republicanism finally flared into open revolt in the south. It began in Wuhan, largely over the construction and control of railways, and spread like a forest fire. Sun's Revolutionary League set up a Chinese republic in Nanjing on 1 January 1912, with Sun himself as president. The trouble, of course, was that he had no substantive political base; support by students and from overseas could never be enough. Most people agreed that the one man to run the new government was the reform-minded, experienced and wily Yuan Shikai, the chief trainer (after Li Hongzhang) of China's new army. The upshot was that the child emperor, Cixi's great-nephew, abdicated,[25] Sun resigned, and on 12 March 1912 Yuan became president of the republic. A revolution, as Napoleon once warned, is an idea that has found bayonets. In China, it briefly seemed, revolution had come almost without bloodshed. It was an illusion: the bayonets were yet to come.

10

THE DRAGON AS PAWN

AD 1912 to 1941

I N THE AFFAIRS of states, incoherence is one of the luxuries of impotence; and for the next few decades China's affairs were indeed impotent and incoherent, both at home and abroad. At home, the decade after the fall of the empire saw a bewildering mixture of political confusion and economic and cultural development. It was an era of warlords but also of flowering ideas and of activities not under government control, like the press and education. Foreign ideas, goods and influence came in, from Japanese power politics to missionary zeal in education, health and famine relief, or the role of foreign merchants or the parliamentary-style reform ideas of the British and Americans. Meanwhile, foreign governments went about their business, treating China as an object or even ignoring it altogether. Chinese citizens and patriots were aghast, but helpless.

With the creation of the new Chinese republic came the beginnings of more fundamental changes. At first, the role of the provinces increased, with growing power for the new governors, usually from the military. The gentry class deteriorated and, in consequence, so did local administration. Mongolia developed a fully fledged independence movement, but even in a region like Xinjiang, for all the resentment of Chinese oppression by many Kazakhs, Uighurs and

Moslems, there was no move to sever ties with China. Things settled down there after the first governor reduced taxes, set limits to corruption and gave some powers to local chiefs. In the meantime the new Guomindang (GMD) Party organised a national parliament. Elected assemblies flourished at the expense of the old local élites. Yet it did not take long for the new president, Yuan Shikai, to reassert autocratic central rule, with parliament abolished and some of its leaders killed. However, his governance suffered from a fatal flaw: he did not have efficient tax-gathering or budgeting systems. He accepted a foreign loan, funded by a consortium of five powers, to enable him to pull the country together. Unfortunately, the GMD saw the loan as an insult of China and a new form of imperialism. Although the GMD leader, Sun Yatsen, visited Japan, where the prime minister, General Katsura Taro, made helpful noises and encouraged him to think about forming a pan-Asian community, it turned out that Japan had supported a variety of Chinese groups, not just the GMD. When Sun staged an uprising on July 1913, Yuan turned out to have enough money to ensure the loyalty of business and the army. Sun was defeated and went into exile in Japan, leaving the GMD disorganised.

Other problems loomed. One still had to do with people moving across the Sino-Russian borders. The Russian authorities had started to be concerned about 'Asianisation' in their eastern regions as early as 1880, but 300,000 additional Russian settlers arrived between 1908 and 1917, while thousands of Chinese, Japanese and Koreans came to join them. There was a real 'Chinatown' along the shores of Amur Bay. By 1910 some 10–12 per cent of the entire population of the Russian Far East were Chinese. In 1913 General Aleksei Kuropatkin, the minister of war, published a book that argued 'a yellow peril threatens Russia', but Chinese immigration increased further with the growing demand for labour after the outbreak of the 1914 war. In 1916 alone an additional 50,000 Chinese migrated to the region. So did numbers of Japanese contractors, merchants and others.[1]

Other countries were less concerned with China. The French by now had far more important issues to deal with than colonies, let alone East Asia. When Georges 'Tiger' Clemenceau became the prime minister in 1906, Paris concentrated even more on Continental strategies, and Germany. From the beginning of the Anglo-French *Entente Cordiale*, with King Edward VII driving amiably through the streets of Paris, it had been a beautifully loose arrangement that did not actually commit anyone to anything and left the French worried. It was not that London was uninterested so much as complacent and, like all British governments, deeply reluctant to accept any firm Continental commitments that were not immediately necessary. There were semi-private staff talks between the two sides about what might happen if France found itself at war with Germany and at one point, when General Sir Henry Wilson asked his French counterpart, General Foch, what would be the minimum British force the French would need in such a war, Foch famously replied: 'One soldier – and we will make sure he gets killed.'

As for China, in British eyes Yuan seemed to represent constitutionalism and government efficiency. After 1914, the British ambassador, Sir John Jackson, who shared Yuan's wariness of Japanese ambitions, strongly encouraged him to concentrate on maintaining the regional status quo. The Americans, too, saw the Chinese republic as the agent of democracy and Christianity; they and the Dutch agreed with Beijing that the entire region should be neutralised.

Within China, confusion was compounded by sharp division between regions governed by the new warlords and the foreign concessions and treaty ports. In warlord areas local administration got worse. It was in the foreign concessions that modern banking, business and professional life took hold. So did the growth of an independent press, even if it reached only a tiny percentage of China's population. The first green shoots of a new politics appeared there, too. John Fairbank, that great scholar, has commented that 'the unequal treaties, while humiliating in principle, were often of material help in fact'.[2] But help or not, the new politics included large-scale and, for the first time, united resentment of the foreign presence. It extended to Chinese modernisers who worked with Europeans and found themselves accused of coming under foreign influence. It was certainly fuelled by fierce resentment of the demands of Japan, which was faintly ironic since no one had done more than the Japanese to help China develop reformist or revolutionary ideas in the first place.

For most of the world, Chinese developments became all but invisible with the political earthquake of the First World War. That was in no way planned. European politics had got so far out of kilter that by mid-1914 no one seemed to know how *not* to go to war. Yet, in almost all the belligerents, populations greeted its outbreak with jubilation, flowers and parades. One ordinary young man, looking back ten years later, wrote that when it broke out 'I fell down on my knees and thanked heaven with an overflowing heart for granting me the good fortune to be alive at that time'. His name was Adolf Hitler. Only the old men, and more serious military thinkers, saw further. In England, the foreign secretary, Sir Edward Grey, famously remarked that the lamps were going out all over Europe; and the great Lord Kitchener, who had commanded the army to avenge Charles Gordon's death in the Sudan, told an appalled and disbelieving Cabinet that 'we must be prepared to put armies of millions in the field and maintain them for several years'. In Germany the fat, intelligent chief of the general staff, von Moltke, who read Nietzsche's philosophy in his spare time and translated French poetry, had already told his emperor what the next war would be like. It would not 'be settled by one decisive battle but will be a long wearisome struggle with an enemy who will not be overcome until his whole national force is broken . . . a war which will utterly exhaust our own people even if we are victorious'. Everywhere, military professionals who had studied the bloody lessons of the Franco-Prussian and more especially the 1905 Russo-Japanese War, understood that modern weapons would mean massive casualties with large and unpredictable social consequences. Even the gentle, white-haired old man who by now embodied Austria-Hungary, the emperor Francis Joseph, quietly told his chief of staff: 'If the monarchy goes under, let it go under with dignity.'

What followed was disastrous not just for the balance of power, but for European societies: four years of desperate but (except for Russia) inconclusive struggle, from East Prussia to France and the Bosphorus, with unprecedented casualties. When it was all over, the known dead, per head of population, were 1 in 28 for France, 1 in 32 for Germany, 1 in 57 for Britain and 1 in 107 for Russia. Amid these titanic struggles China was a possible prize but otherwise barely a footnote; though it had short-term benefits. The wartime drop in European exports to the Far East spurred growth in the region. The price of China's raw-materials exports rose. So did the world price of silver, increasing China's purchasing power. The crisis also encouraged the growth of Chinese banking and commercial organisations, especially in the foreign concession areas.

The war made Pacific transport routes vital for Russia. Once Germany and Austria blockaded the Baltic and the Black Sea, the only major port through which Russia could get foreign supplies was Vladivostok. Japan's position was hugely strengthened: for a Japanese statesman like Kauru Inoue, the European war was 'divine aid . . . for the development of the destiny of Japan'. The Chinese, though, could see what was coming. 'Japan is going to take advantage of this war,' said President Yuan Shikai, 'to gain control of China.' While the British, Americans and to a degree the Russians wanted an East Asian status quo, Japan was an expansionist power. In August 1914 they seized most of the German possessions in the Far East, including the island chains in the Pacific. That added to the conquest of Taiwan in 1895 and the acquisition of Korea as a dependency in 1905. (It became a full Japanese colony ten years later.) China itself became part of Japan's informal economic empire, absorbing some 20 per cent of Japan's exports, and advice on modernisation. Japan did even better once the war started, with rising investment in China to make use of cheap labour and raw materials. More fundamentally still, ideas of ethnic kinship encouraged help for China's modernisation and preservation. By 1914 Japan also had a new foreign minister, Takaaki Kato, a former ambassador to London. While he thought the 1902 Anglo-Japanese alliance was no longer especially useful, the war offered huge opportunities in China, and the British alliance might still be helpful in exploiting them. Japan benefited from the war in other ways. US–Japan trade boomed – Japanese exports to the US multiplied by five – and the trend continued afterwards. By the 1920s America was providing 40 per cent of Japan's foreign investment.

The British had their own concerns about the security of their empire and its seaborne lines of communication. Ever since 1905 the growth of the German High Seas fleet had become the greatest threat to Britain's mastery of the sea. In the Pacific, the London Admiralty had to worry about the threat the German base at Qingdao posed to British shipping. The German East Asiatic Squadron was numerically comparable to the Royal Navy's force on the China station, but superior in quality. What was to be done? The answer seemed to be to get the Japanese navy to track down German ships and protect Allied shipping lanes. So Sir Edward Grey sought Japanese help, and the Japanese told London that, since the Germans threatened peace in the region, they would declare war and get rid of German influence in China. They duly did. Sixty thousand Japanese (accompanied by a small British detachment) simply marched through Chinese territory and by November 1914 the Germans at Qingdao surrendered. It was the end of German naval bases in the Pacific. Grey's approach further encouraged the Japanese to consolidate their position with the acquisition of the North Pacific islands as a kind of down-payment on the general growth of their empire. The whole thing was a boon for the Japanese navy's shipbuilding programme, too. By 1910 their navy was twice as big as it had been in 1904.

Yuan tried hard not to involve China in any of this.

By January 1915 the Japanese were ready to move even further. On the 18th they put twenty-one demands to China that included a consolidation of Japan's hold on Manchuria and in Inner Mongolia, and even China's consent to accepting Japanese political and military advisers. It amounted to a kind of Japanese protectorate in China. These demands lost Japan, for good, the leadership of China's reform movement, but by 1916 the British, French and Russians had all accepted the revised Japanese gains. Only the Americans, quietly concerned about the expansion of Japanese power and the security of the Philippines, began a serious programme of naval construction. In the meantime, Yuan tried to get Allied support for his claim to become China's new emperor. He would even supply Chinese forces for service in Europe. Grey consulted the Japanese, who feared a new Chinese army might be used against them; anyway, what Japan wanted was a Chinese puppet, not a real emperor and besides Yuan died in 1916. In mid-August 1917 the Chinese declared war on Germany regardless and offered to find 300,000 men for service in Europe. They hoped, among other things, for a seat at the peace conference.

The outcome of the war brought much larger changes to the global scene than anyone had foreseen. The Austrian, German, Russian and Ottoman empires disappeared and, with them, the entire old balance of power. New nations and boundaries were created throughout Europe and the Middle East and maps had to be re-drawn over most of the globe. The changes in social and economic affairs were even more profound. The war had sapped the vital energies of the peoples of Europe, yet fierce resentments continued to flourish. A mere ten years after the war, Winston Churchill wrote prophetically about these effects. In the war

> Events passed very largely outside the scope of conscious choice. Governments and individuals conformed to the rhythm of the tragedy, and swayed and staggered forward in helpless violence, slaughtering and squandering on ever-increasing scales, till injuries were wrought to the structure of human society which a century will not efface, and which may conceivably prove fatal to the present civilisation . . .[3]

So they did. And produced a peace which, as someone said long afterwards, had the tragedies of the future written into it as by the devil's own hand. In Russia, Italy and Germany utopian, populist and violent revolutionary movements changed social outlooks and political organisations, though the wider impact of each was somewhat different. Italian Fascism, led by a strutting, boastful former journalist, Benito Mussolini, had little appeal beyond Italy itself and Italian groups elsewhere, though there were imitators in a few places. Communism in the new Soviet Union and National Socialism in Germany proved altogether more formidable, and between them dominated world affairs for most of the rest of the twentieth century. The German one was more immediately dangerous, not only because Germany was a more powerful state, but because National Socialism was able to ally itself with three deeper German trends. One was nationalism inflamed by a passionate belief that the post-war settlement had cheated Germany. In the middle of 1918 the German empire had been at its greatest extent ever. Its armies had been close to Paris. It had held the Ukraine and the Baltic states. The Russian collapse of 1917 had opened the way to the oilfields of the Caucasus. (There were to be striking parallels in Germany's Eastern conquests of 1940–1). How could Germany suddenly, by the end of that very same year, be called 'defeated' and labelled Europe's 'guilty man'? A second trend was a widespread German longing for social security after the traumas of the 1920s. The third, with wide appeal beyond Germany's own borders, was National Socialism's role as the 'defender of Europe against Jewish Bolshevism'. Adolf Hitler personified these resentments and longings and came to power in 1933.

But it was the Bolshevik revolution of October 1917 in Russia which had the most profound and lasting influence everywhere around the world, and would continue to have it for most of the rest of the century. Russian socialist revolutionaries had gained support since before the Russo-Japanese War. Disturbances and strikes spread and were met by machine guns and Cossacks, and followed by strong police suppression. By 1916 strong anti-war propaganda was coming out of St Petersburg and spread by the new railways and telephones. Wartime defeats and imperial incompetence brought matters to a head. In March 1917 revolution unceremoniously ended the czarist state. Nicholas II abruptly resigned and the imperial era was over. The provisional government that took over was led by a popular lawyer, Alexander Kerensky. It proclaimed social equality and civil liberties but proved ineffective and in October 1917 an entirely different person and a wholly new kind of political organisation took the reins in Russia. The younger brother of the Ulyanov whom the czarists had hanged decades earlier was by now the fierce and hardened revolutionary Vladimir Ilyich Lenin. His tough, centralised Bolshevik Party promised to revolutionise the international relations and social systems of the entire world; and to make Moscow not just the capital of a great power but the centre of a whole international revolutionary movement. This second 1917 revolution, and the civil war which followed, meant the total overthrow of all existing social and administrative structures, even the squalid murder of the last czar whose family, the Romanovs, had ruled for three centuries. It did much more. It was a fulfilment, a putting-into-practice, of many of the dreams that socialists, Marxists and other radicals had harboured for much of the previous century. And, possibly most important of all, it brought to power that entirely new kind of political organism, the Leninist party organisation.

At the same time, the European victors were greatly weakened. In 1900, Britain stood at the zenith of imperial grandeur. In 1920 both Britain and France were gravely weakened. In Britain, the war had also produced huge social shifts, with the country's old aristocratic class being largely wiped out as the flower of its younger generation died in Flanders, with new taxes ruining what remained. America's nineteenth-century industrial giants, like Andrew Carnegie and the railway magnate Cornelius Vanderbilt, had done their work well, so now it was America that stood on the brink of industrial pre-eminence and power and was in a key position to make the arrangements for peace. To that process, President Woodrow Wilson brought a language that dominates international relations to this day. It has to do with the importance of morality in international affairs, with faith in international law and multilateral solutions, and with the belief that liberal democracy is the true path for everyone. It was, of course, a collection of clichés, inexact and confusing in the impression they gave. At the same time it reflected the American tendency to transplant legal concepts into politics, and to believe that international society should operate on the basis of contractual obligations, even verbal undertakings, rather than concrete interests. But there is no doubt that, from the first, his approach fell on receptive ears. For the public, the lesson of the Great War was that national self-assertion could produce disaster while multilateral systems would secure peace.

In truth, the Wilsonian design was deeply contradictory. He had, from the beginning, seen America's role as that of impartial arbiter, but at the same time as an actor with grand objectives of his own. He said, with matchless arrogance, that he wanted America to stand 'ready to help the rest of the world' and to bring 'standards of righteousness and humanity' to these Old World discussions while reaping 'a great permanent glory out of doing it'. His twin organising principles for designing the post-war world were national self-determination and the need for a global organisation – the League of Nations – to order world affairs. On the one hand, as Wilson told the US Congress in 1918, 'Peoples may now be dominated or governed only by their own consent'; and in the peace settlement the interests of the subject peoples must weigh as heavily as those of the victor powers. That was politically magnetic. It was also profoundly subversive for all non-national or multinational structures, while entirely failing to cope with the fact that it would be quite impossible to design any neat and tidy territorial separation of ethnic and language groups from one another. In the event, the creation of new frontiers in pursuit of 'self-determination' left some 30 million people on the 'wrong' side of these lines. Which exacerbated inter-state disputes, directly contradicting Wilson's second great principle, embodied in the league as an organisation able to maintain peace. For how could self-determination be reconciled with disputed borders on the one hand and on the other a league that never looked like developing an enforcement mechanism and therefore had no power to act? Wilson had forgotten, or chosen to ignore, Thomas Hobbes's seventeenth-century wisdom: 'Covenants without swords are but words, and of no strength to secure a man at all.' Moreover, neither defeated Germany nor the newly revolutionary Soviet Union joined the league. Many, including the Japanese, were aggrieved by the fact that its covenant failed to include a clause on racial equality. Even the US Congress, determined not to get involved in Europe or Asia again, refused to allow America's own sovereign decisions to be fettered by joining the new Wilsonian league.

Many of these flaws were obvious from the start, especially to Wilson's own secretary of state, Robert Lansing, who was horrified by the implications of 'national self-determination'.[4] Even so, Wilson was shocked by divergent views. In 1918, for instance, he asked the Australian prime minister, little Billy Hughes, whether Australia was seriously proposing, by expanding into the former German colony of New Guinea, to flout the opinions of the civilised world? Was it really trying to profit from Germany's defeat and extend Australian sovereignty to the equator? Hughes baldly replied: 'That's about it, Mr President.'

In China, the Bolshevik revolution had ripple-effects almost immediately. Since 1900 there had been growing interest in anarchism and Marxism among students and intellectuals. After 1917, when ideas of social revolution through party organisations began to be urged by the Bolsheviks, they became particularly influential, both because of their demonstrable effectiveness in action and the way they could dovetail with traditional Confucian ideas about the duty of the individual to support the state. Leninism had a particular impact among young people studying in Tokyo and – like Zhou Enlai, later Mao Zedong's deputy and foreign minister – in Paris. China even played a marginal role in the post-revolution Russian civil war. As early as 1916 the Russian empire had begun to conscript Central Asians into the Russian army, with the result that some hundreds of thousands of Uzbeks and Kazakhs fled to Xinjiang. These regions became centres of anti-Red forces and the Chinese agreed to let a Bolshevik force cross the border to deal with remnants. By 1924 there were Soviet consulates at Kashgar and Chinese consulates in Soviet Central Asia. However, the first major impact of the Bolshevik revolution on a broader Chinese public only came in 1919 when the deputy People's Commissar for foreign affairs, Leo Karakhan, announced that the Soviets would annul all the existing unequal treaties with China. That became known around March 1920 and created a huge wave of enthusiasm and sympathy for the new USSR. In the same year, 1920, the new Communist International, the Comintern,[5] sent Grigor Voytinsky to China, where he was present at the foundation of the Chinese Communist Party (CCP) in Shanghai on 1 July 1921. That whole meeting was arranged with the help of the Comintern, which was convinced that once imperialism was denied the opportunity to exploit Asia, the whole of capitalism would collapse. There were now several levels of Soviet policy. Many of the special concessions that czarist Russia had won were now disowned. Envoys were sent to China. At the same time, Comintern agents were dispatched to help organise the fledgling CCP. Both Soviet diplomats and Comintern agents urged Sun Yatsen to accept Soviet aid and let Communists join his Nationalist Party, suggestions that Sun was happy to adopt. So the founding CCP congress decided – on Comintern insistence and rather against its own better judgement – on an alliance with Sun's GMD. Not only that but for the next eleven years, until 1932, the CCP had the closest possible ties with Moscow. Indeed, many decisions critical to the CCP's development were actually made in Moscow, its policies decided by Moscow agents and its leaders appointed or sacked by the Kremlin.

All this took place in the shadow of Chinese nationalist resentment of the West. That intensified when the peace conference at Versailles decided, without much argument, to leave the old German Shandong concessions in Japanese hands and to have the former German-held islands administered as Japanese mandates. That in spite of the principle of self-determination and in spite, too, of the fact that China was by now a member of the victorious alliance. That aroused helpless fury in China and led to a further upsurge of nationalism. There were mass student demonstrations in Tiananmen Square in Beijing on 4 May 1919 by some 5,000 students from several Beijing universities. Similar demonstrations came in other cities, including Tianjin and Shanghai. Some merchants went on strike and staged a boycott of Japanese goods.

Interesting longer-term consequences followed. The demonstrations launched an entire Marxist and anti-imperialist movement. Nationalism, a radical bent, and the fact that the Bolsheviks sympathised, turned not just the CCP but all nationalists towards Moscow, in policy as well as ideas. Chinese cadres began to be sent to Moscow for training, and study groups on radicalism were created in several Chinese counties and cities. One activist from Hunan province was called Mao Zedong. Born in December 1893, he was an odd candidate for later political genius. Coming from a not very well-to-do provincial family, incompletely educated, often coarse and with a lifelong yen for purposeful violence,[6] he was also enormously ambitious and manipulative. He graduated from the 4 May demonstrations to reading German philosophy and becoming active – in the language of a later age, 'thinking globally and acting locally' – in his province. In 1920 he organised a study group on Soviet affairs and in July of the following year took part in that founding meeting of the CCP in Shanghai.

The major powers took little notice of this, of course, having much larger and more important matters to deal with. The contradictions of trying to support both self-determination and ideas about international peace-keeping affected America's role in Europe as well as the Pacific. The rise of Japan, and its growing ambitions in Korea and China, confronted the US with a dilemma that could not be resolved until the Second World War. After 1918 it was obvious to everyone that it was the US and Japan which would dominate the Pacific region. However, Japan's wartime acquisitions in China and among the islands implied control of large areas of the Pacific and threatened the West's 'Open Door' approach in China. The Americans therefore confronted a dilemma. As Theodore Roosevelt had put it to State Secretary Knox some years earlier, America could either stop insisting on the importance of Chinese sovereignty, and equality of economic opportunity for outside powers, or else it could prepare to confront, and if necessary fight, an increasingly powerful Japan. Unsurprisingly, Washington had not the slightest wish to fight, and failed to insist on the 'Open Door'.

Even larger worries stemmed from Japan's burgeoning naval construction programme: between 1917 and 1921 it absorbed around one-third of the entire imperial budget. In response, the Americans transferred the bulk of their fleet from the Atlantic to the Pacific and opened a dry dock at Pearl Harbor. It looked like the start of a naval arms race at the very time when President Warren Harding, in the middle of the economic depression of the early 1920s, was trying to reduce international commitments, and the American public insisted on disarmament. Fortunately, the British urged the Americans to call a four-power conference to deal with Pacific problems. It became the Washington conference of 1921–2 at which a great secretary of state, Charles Evans Hughes, scored major successes. The British agreed to abandon the old 1902 Anglo-Japanese alliance, which the Americans disliked. The Americans, French, British and Japanese joined in a four-power non-aggression pact, although that did not seem to mean much more than talking. More substantive was a new five-power treaty (the four plus Italy) to limit the size of everyone's navy. The tonnage ratios of the British, American and Japanese fleets were set at 5:5:3, with France and Italy set at 1.75 each. In addition, limits on the type and size of ships were also agreed, forcing the British Royal Navy to scrap 651 ships, 26 of them battleships, a total of 1.5 million tons.

It was the end of two or three centuries of British dominance at sea, or Rule Britannia. It therefore also heralded the coming end of an empire whose lifeline that navy was. Since 1914 British power had precipitately declined anyway. One small example will make the point. As late as 1903/4, the Younghusband expedition from India to Tibet had forced the Tibetans to agree not to deal with any other power without British consent. Now, the war's losses in treasure, blood – and confidence – had made even quite minor assertions of such a sort almost inconceivable.[7] In the Far East especially, Britain had drastically declined by comparison with the United States, Japan and arguably even the Soviet Union. Indeed, London quickly understood that defending Britain's position in *both* Europe and the empire was beyond her strength. By the 1920s and, even more, the 1930s,

Britain's European problems had become virtually insoluble and in the Pacific the country was a second-rate player. After 1933, faced with German rearmament – especially the growth of the German air force – and with the US committed to neutrality, the only way to safety seemed to be to work for peace at almost any cost.

There was in any case much more to the Washington meeting than naval power. The old Anglo-Japanese alliance was dissolved because it ceased to have much utility for Japan, and the British were not about to annoy the Americans by keeping it. Instead, in addition to the non-aggression pact and the naval limitations there were two further treaties. One was a nine-power document to guarantee the integrity of China and the maintenance of the 'Open Door'. The other was a four-power treaty – Japan, the US, Britain and France – accepting each other's island possessions. The talks as a whole therefore reflected the new post-1918 Pacific balance and set up a framework for peace in the region. The Japanese gained little. The future foreign minister Kijuro Shidehara championed a policy of non-interference in Chinese internal politics. Under American pressure the Japanese also agreed to return Germany's old Shandong concessions to China. Their older holdings in Manchuria remained unaffected, though the Japanese were worried about American attitudes they found overbearing, even belligerent. China itself sent a team headed by the ambassadors to London and Washington, Wellington Koo and Alfred Sze. Their objective was to secure the abandonment of as many of the foreign privileges and concessions in China as possible.[8] The Americans were especially pleased with the conference results. Their diplomats, having seen Congress back away from the League of Nations, thought that in the Pacific, at least, they had fulfilled Wilsonian ambitions about collective security. Few were worried about the absence of enforcement mechanisms, yet there were important snags. The Japanese were left to pursue their special relationships in and with China. Many of the old systems of 'unequal treaties' about tariffs or extraterritoriality were left standing. And for all Russia's importance to East Asia, the Soviets were not asked to take any part. Instead, delegates from both Sun's GMD and the CCP could shortly be seen attending a Comintern-sponsored conference in Moscow meant to condemn the Washington arrangements.

In fact, the Soviets continued to play a subtle game, managing to help the CCP while simultaneously negotiating with the nationalist movement, so far two unequal entities. By 1922/3 the Nationalist Guomindang Party was a large national grouping and may have had some 50,000 members. By comparison the Communists were numerically insignificant with about 300 members; though the Leninist precedent showed what a determined and disciplined conspiratorial group could do. Still, the result was that for most of the 1920s the unification and independence of China was sought by two party dictatorship, each organised on Leninist lines. In their various discussions, internally or with each other, the Chinese politics of resentment echoed strongly. If China was lamentably weak, the most obvious and congenial explanations were two. Each resonated with traditional Chinese attitudes and each blamed barbarian wickedness. One of them, following Karl Marx and Lenin, focused on general anti-imperialism. The other emphasised the greed of particular Western powers. After all, Marx himself had ascribed the rise of the Taiping rebels to British guns and British opium, which had ruined Manchu authority and its mandarinate.

By 1922 Sun, now the pre-eminent Nationalist leader, agreed with Soviet diplomats to allow Communists into the GMD, and decided to learn more from the Soviets. Though he did not think Communism was appropriate for China, he began to reorganise the GMD along Soviet lines. The Comintern sent more agents to China and Sun had Soviet help in setting up his government at Canton. He agreed to joint Sino-Soviet management of the Chinese Eastern Railway through Manchuria and his deputy, Chiang Kai-shek (Jiang Jieshi) even went to Moscow in 1923 to study Red Army organisation. He followed that Russian example when, a year later, he founded China's new Whampoa Military Academy, with Zhou Enlai, destined to be the prime minister of Communist China, as its political director. Meanwhile, more Soviet advisers to the GMD arrived, including the professional revolutionary Mikhail Borodin, to help organise the party, train its cadres, teach it how to gain mass support and even to help draft its constitution. Borodin himself was a highly experienced man, having already seen much service for the Comintern in Europe and North America. There was a Soviet military mission, too, consisting of forty veterans headed by Vasili Blyukher, a 35-year-old general with a record of major victories in the Urals and Siberia during the Russian civil war. All these people agreed, at least officially, that China needed independence and unity. Unofficially, the Soviets continued to work for revolution. Their agents planned, from the start, to develop the infant Chinese Communist Party to infiltrate and eventually control the GMD itself. In fact, the Soviet Communists continued to see China as a major element in the whole global struggle against imperialism. As the head of Moscow's official mission to China, Adolf Joffe, wrote to Lenin, China was 'a great trump card in our world game'.

Meanwhile, civil unrest and confusion in China continued, and for foreign powers there remained, until the late 1920s, the problem that no Chinese government was seriously in control of the whole country. Northern China and Manchuria were in the hands of warlords. Sun's people were badly split between one side that supported his 'big tent' attitude to the Communists, and the alliance with the Soviets, which the other side feared and resisted. Though everyone agreed on the need for national revival and resistance to foreign aggression, even here there was confusion. Some of the anti-drug campaigns, for instance, were given legitimacy by linking resistance to drugs to the very survival of the Chinese nation beset by foreigners. Yet while Sun was being installed at Canton, two rival governors of Shanghai and 120,000 men were fighting over the control of that city's opium traffic. No wonder that the French Premier, Aristide Briand, had dismissively asked some years earlier: 'What is China?'

In 1925 Sun died and there was another outburst of anti-foreign nationalist emotion. (Not only in China. In Vietnam, too, nationalist resentment against both the French and Chinese merged into Communism and led to the formation of a party along Guomindang lines.)

Sun's place was taken by Chiang, who proclaimed the GMD as the national government of China and set about reunifying China and expelling foreign interests. In 1925 his forces, led by his own Whampoa graduates and equipped with Soviet rifles and guns, launched a 'Northern Expedition', winning a series of victories against the warlords and capturing guns. It was not a purely military operation: GMD and CCP people moved ahead of the army to try to organise workers and peasants. By mid-1926, moving north from Canton (Guangzhou), he extended GMD rule into the Yangzi valley, began to push towards Shanghai, and conquered half of China. His soldiers made themselves popular by paying for what they used, but further splits developed both within the GMD and between Chiang and the CCP. In March 1926 Chiang dismissed his Soviet advisers and began, in a small way, to cut the CCP down to size. The Communists moved out of Canton to Wuhan. The Americans remained hopeful about GMD authority and in January 1927 Secretary of State Frank Kellogg even said the US might further pare down American rights by handing tariff autonomy to a Chinese government, if it could command the loyalty of the Chinese people and protect American lives and property.

Two months later Chiang's troops seized Nanjing from local warlords. His troops looted British and Japanese consulates and killed some Europeans. Other foreigners were evacuated, often by British troops or American marines deployed on Chinese soil and under the guns of some of the forty Western warships anchored there. Numbers of missionaries left the Chinese interior in fear of the anti-foreign violence. The British, Americans and Japanese sent stiff notes to the Nationalist government, demanding apologies and reparations. Much of Chinese anger had focused on the British, as the leading imperialist power, who responded by restoring their old concessions on the Yangzi to China; while also leading other powers in assembling an international force to protect Shanghai. All of which left Chiang on the horns of an old dilemma. Conciliating the foreigners was liable to make him look like an imperialist lackey, while rejecting foreign complaints might provoke the powers into forceful intervention.

At much the same time Chiang's troops entered Shanghai, crowded, rich, bustling, the place where foreign trade produced riches, not least for the compradors who acted as go-betweens for the foreigners,[9] of whom there were far fewer than was later claimed. Of the half-million people living in the French concession area, for instance, only about 1,400 actually came from France. The rest were Chinese and others, enjoying the electricity, telephone services, cars, running water, commercial systems and law that the foreigners had introduced. Chiang was able to come into Shanghai largely because he was by now enjoying close links with the powerful local 'Green Gang'. Once there, he turned fully against his Communist allies, expelled the remaining Comintern people, suppressed the CCP and even denounced the Soviet Union as a 'red imperialist'. In fact, he set about destroying the entire CCP apparatus in Shanghai and beyond. Communist Party and labour leaders were hunted down and massacred as the 'White Terror' spread far and wide. He set up an anti-Communist government with Nanjing as its capital, and Nationalist China became a single-party state. At mid-year Mikhail Borodin left China. His own summing-up of his failed mission was calmly philosophic, but Mao later dismissed him as a 'blunderer'.

BORODIN

Mikhail Markovich Borodin was a professional revolutionary sent to China as an agent of the Comintern, the 3rd Communist International that Lenin founded to help hasten world revolution. Borodin came from a Russian Jewish family and by his late teens had become a Bolshevik. After the 1905 revolution in Russia failed, he went to America, returning in 1917 but the following year was sent abroad, to America again, to Spain, Scotland, the Netherlands and Mexico.

He was ordered to China in 1923 to help Sun Yatsen organise his Nationalist Party, at much the same time as Sun sent his chief of staff, Chiang Kai-shek to Moscow. Borodin, by then in his forties, was a strong, well-built man of considerable charm, with intense dark eyes, and a luxuriant moustache. He also had a razor-sharp mind and a memory – someone said – 'like a filing cabinet', not to mention a passion for chess and riding. He got on well with Sun, who liked his air of moderation. He not only became official adviser to the committee trying to reorganise the Nationalists – now named the Kuomintang (Guomindang or GMD) – but arranged for arms shipments from Vladivostok to Sun's people at Canton.

He was the leading member of the Soviet support groups in China. But in 1924 Moscow also sent a military mission of some forty veteran Soviet officers, headed by 35-year-old General Vasili Blyukher, who had famous victories in Siberia and the Urals under his belt. Blyukher operated under the pseudonym of Galin, but no one was deceived. By 1925 some GMD people were muttering that, between them, Borodin and Galin 'held the supreme military and political command'.

The trouble was that there were too many conflicting interests between the Soviets and the Chinese Nationalists, as Soviet advisers reported back, accurately enough. The conflict of views made Borodin's task impossible. Even worse were the tactics that Stalin's confused and confusing orders imposed on him, making him side with Chiang while also using his influence to restrain Chinese revolutionaries, even in 1926 and early 1927 when Chiang was actually arresting Chinese Communists.

This impossible dance ended when, in April 1927, Chiang had Communist and labour leaders in Shanghai rounded up and shot. At the end of July Borodin left China, his mission a failure. He accepted philosophically that he was one of those who 'struts and frets his hour upon the stage, and then is heard no more', for his own melancholy summing-up was:

'I came to China to fight for an idea. The dream of accomplish- ing world revolution by freeing the people of the East brought me here. But China itself, with its age-old history, its countless millions, its vast social problems, its infinite capacities, astounded and overwhelmed me, and my thoughts of world revolution gradually sank into the background. The revolution and the fight for freedom in China became an end in itself, and no longer a means to an end. My task was to grasp the situation, to start the great wheel moving, and as time has passed it has carried me along with it. I myself have become only a cog in the great machine.'*

* Aage Krarup Nielsen, 'Borodin's Swan Song', *Living Age*, July–December 1927, pp. 1002–3, cited Spence, *Helpers*, p. 202.

Shortly afterwards, in December 1927 and within sight of victory on the Yangzi, Chiang married again. He had become enamoured of Meiling Soong and married her after dumping his second wife. Meiling was more than attractive. She was the daughter of one of China's richest men, so the marriage offered Chiang a medieval alliance of power and wealth, giving him access to the vast Soong family fortune. Their personal relations may have been another matter. The distinguished American scholar Owen Lattimore, who became Chiang's American adviser, saw much of them at first hand and wrote later that 'the relation between Chiang Kai-shek and Madame Chiang was something like that of political allies who do not entirely trust each other'.[10] Nevertheless, her charm, and the fact that she had been educated in America, won her much admiration in the US, not least in Congress. She proved to be a considerable diplomatic asset for Chiang and, in fact if not in name, an influential ambassador for him and for China.

By 1928 Chiang completed the northern expedition and occupied Beijing. He was now in control of all of China south of the Great Wall. While Japan was unwilling to let China have control of any part of Manchuria, Chiang controlled most of China for the next decade. Though his rule may have been authoritarian and corrupt, his China was, at least, more or less at peace. It was not, though, the end of nationalist factionalism, for Chiang was, and remained, an uncertain leader with a brittle base. His power rested not on a united and disciplined group but on a network of alliances among shifting groups of regional bosses, as well as of links among the various wings of the GMD. At some points he only prospered because he had the support of criminal syndicates and bosses, like Du Yusheng, Shanghai's leading gangster. In reality, the Nationalists were not so much a coherent party as a loose federation of forces. At the same time, and rather incongruously, many of those who dealt with him found him unyielding and unreasonable. Certainly few foreigners understood him any more than he understood them. Some of his Soviet advisers thought that he 'acts entirely according to his individuality . . . in order to obtain glory, which is his goal, he sometimes wants to utilise the masses, the Chinese Communist Party, and ourselves'.[11] Stalin remarked that 'I know that he is playing a cunning game with us, but it is he that will be crushed. We shall squeeze him like a lemon and then be rid of him'.

The Americans, however, continued to see themselves as champions of Chinese rights and sovereignty – as long as the US was not directly involved on the other side of the Pacific. In spite of American dislike of Chinese revolutionary enthusiasms, they continued to press for modernisation; and looked forward to the consolidation, at long last, of a strong, unified, modernised and independent China. As so often in the USA, domestic debate about such things focused on abstract principles. Even criticism of President Woodrow Wilson for letting Shandong stay in Japanese hands was treated by the public less as a practical matter of international relations than as a defeat for the principle of self-determination in whose pursuit Wilson had already carved up much of Europe. But exactly whom or what should the US in practice support? President Calvin Coolidge was warned that the GMD would be a power to be reckoned with, but the administration continued to think that only once order was established in China could one usefully talk about political issues. Many Americans also thought that the Communists were just harmless social reformers while others pointed out that Bolshevism could anyway not take root in China's family-dominated social environment. The American secretary of state, Frank Kellogg, thought Chinese nationalism was likely to be the best bulwark against the expansion of Soviet power. It was therefore useful to support the Nationalists and in any case important to retain America's position as China's best friend, while the Soviet Union saw its influence almost entirely excluded from China.

Meanwhile there were political changes in Moscow of incomparably greater importance for the world, bringing shifts of power with geo-political implications. The question of Lenin's successor was finally resolved between Leon Trotsky, the brilliant theoretician, orator and charismatic commander of the Red Army, and Joseph Stalin, the cunning, pock-marked former seminarian from Georgia. In the end it was the Georgian who proved to be a master of party and administrative politics: Trotsky was ousted and banished into exile, to be murdered in Mexico thirteen years later by a Stalinist agent. There were Stalin/Trotsky differences on many issues, including China. Stalin wanted the Chinese Communists to remain allied with Chiang until they were strong enough to take over the GMD. Trotsky wanted to build up a separate system of Chinese Soviets. There were even more fundamental differences between the two men about the Soviet Union's place in the world. Trotsky wanted to move immediately towards European and world revolution. Stalin, on the other hand, shifted policy to 'Socialism in one Country'. The effect, widely misunderstood, was not the abandonment of world revolution. Rather, the doctrine emphasised the need to secure the Soviet Union as the centre of world socialism, from which it could spread to other regions. In this view, the prerequisite for world revolution was Soviet security.

Meanwhile, the West in general and the US in particular enjoyed an unprecedented financial and speculative boom. Nineteen twenty-eight was a year of fabulous prosperity. On 4 December 1928 President Calvin Coolidge, sending his last State of the Union message to Congress at the end of his term, famously stated that: 'No Congress of the United States ever assembled, on surveying the state of the union, has met with a more pleasing prospect than that which appears at the present time.'

Nine months later came the Great Crash of 1929–31 which, as all the world knows, changed everything, everywhere.

The Great Crash marked the end of the Great War's aftermath, but was also the overture to the disastrous 1930s. It began in October 1929 with a crash on the New York Stock Exchange. Panic-stricken creditors called in loans, banks collapsed and so did trade. Urban unemployment soared, incomes fell. After 1931/2, everyone was mired in recession and unemployment. In Germany, there were signs of civilisational collapse. Public anger at economic misery fuelled nationalist resentment and put wind into the political sails of a riveting populist agitator named Adolf Hitler. After he came to power in January 1933 the overriding objective for the British, with hunger marches at home, soon became the appeasement of the increasingly assertive Germany in Europe, and of Japan in the East. Policy and politics were dominated by the conviction that a new war must be avoided at almost all costs. Public morale in America, Britain and France sank to new lows.

Much of Japan's trade in and with Asia and the US also collapsed, especially after 1930, when America raised tariffs on Japanese exports to the US. Japan's unemployment rose to 1 million, farm prices plunged. Of special concern was the loss of the foreign-exchange earnings that allowed Japan to buy the coal, oil, iron, rubber, even rice, that its expanding population needed. Japan now saw itself as deeply vulnerable, with national survival itself at stake. Economic and national-security problems were linked, for security required the creation of a strategically and economically self-sufficient block. If Japan's interests in Asia were going to be threatened, maybe Japan would have to start relying on its own strong right arm. Only foreign expansion could create the self-sufficient economic block required to make Japan secure.

But Chinese nationalists started to put pressure on the Japanese about their established rights in Manchuria, and the Japanese army in

China (known as the Guandong army, a special military unit established to guard the Japanese Guandong colony in southern Manchuria) grew deeply dissatisfied with Tokyo's failure to maintain the Japanese position. In fact, they wanted nothing less than national renewal, a rejection of Western cultural corruption, even a search for spiritual purity (all of which had interesting similarities with German National Socialism). Though many in Japan, even within the army, urged caution, in mid-September 1931 the Guandong army command staged an explosion on the Japanese-operated South Manchurian Railway. The army pleaded 'Chinese provocation', and found it had massive public support back home. Thousands of Japanese troops moved forward and some months later, in 1932, a 'Manchurian Independence Movement', financed by the Japanese army, established a sovereign state of Manchukuo under Japanese military protection. That gave Japan command of a major land area with 30 million inhabitants and huge mineral and agricultural resources. Shanghai also fell to the Japanese, who went on to set up puppet regimes in other regions. In Japan itself, there was a rising tide of nationalist virulence and assassinations as the slide to military rule continued. By 1936 some 1,500 junior officers and soldiers seized and assassinated several Cabinet members and generals.

Behind these passions, and fears that failure to create a self-reliant Greater Japan would be national suicide, lay the expectation that growing international tensions were making a global war inevitable. In this the Japanese were by no means alone. In other places, too, growing economic distress, popular unrest and cross-border tensions suggested that another war might be looming. Stalin was one who expected war. In 1931 he explained his industrialisation drive:

To slacken the tempo would mean falling behind. And those who fall behind get beaten. But we do not want to be beaten . . . old Russia was [continually beaten] because of her backwardness. She was beaten by the Mongol khans. She was beaten by the Turkish beys. She was beaten by the Swedish feudal lords. She was beaten by the Polish and Lithuanian gentry. She was beaten by the British and French capitalists. She was beaten by the Japanese barons. All beat her because of her backwardness, military backwardness, cultural backwardness, political backwardness, industrial backwardness, agricultural backwardness . . . We are fifty or a hundred years behind the advanced countries. We must make good this distance in ten years. Either we do it, or we shall be crushed.[12]

He was not wrong. Just ten years later, the Germans tried.

Chiang had a similarly dark view about the inevitability of war. In 1932 he spoke to the army staff college: 'How many years do we have to prepare for the Second World War? What kind of plan shall we prepare? . . . We have only five years to prepare.' He was not wrong either.

President Herbert Hoover and State Secretary Henry Stimson, for all their dislike of Japanese policies and actions on the other side of the Pacific, not only also feared war with Japan, but thought it could break out even over low-key economic sanctions. So, while America strongly sympathised with China, Washington confined itself to moral lectures. Britain and France had their hands full at home and in Europe, so no one actually opposed the Japanese. On the contrary, with the disarmament efforts of the League of Nations visibly failing, American anti-war and pro-appeasement opinion rose to fever pitch. Even when the Japanese bombarded Shanghai, and public opinion in Britain and the US became much more strongly anti-Japanese, neither country did anything. Nor did the league.

For all the strong American sympathy for China, at official as well as private levels, maintaining the post-1918, peaceful world order itself now remained a dominant American national interest in the Pacific. For the public, there now existed a League of Nations whose core principles included almost universal agreement that nations had no business waging war in pursuit of national policy. Though the US had not joined the league, this was not a principle it proposed to violate. Not that any of this stopped peace campaigners from saying, as they usually do, that 'something must be done' and demanding that Washington 'act', though without saying what that might mean as

long as America refused to intervene. In any case, American appeasement was encouraged, even compelled, by the fact that the US Army
and Navy were not remotely in a position to fight.

In January 1933 a new president who was to be one of America's
greatest leaders, Franklin Delano Roosevelt, entered the White
House. In the same month Germany acquired a new chancellor,
Adolf Hitler. Roosevelt found himself confronted by dramatically
difficult social and economic problems at home, and memorably
denounced failed financial managers as crucifying humanity 'on a
cross of gold'. Foreign conditions were also daunting. The League of
Nations system had almost collapsed. The previous year, Japan had
withdrawn from it and, perhaps more ominously still, Hitler's
Germany did the same. Under the circumstances, American anti-
war feeling became stronger than ever and it seemed only sensible to
define American overseas interests more narrowly. In the Pacific,
Roosevelt returned America to the policies of Herbert Hoover or of
his own cousin, Theodore Roosevelt, two decades earlier: appeasement and the continuation of America's strategic exports to Japan.
Some official opinion went further and was willing actually to
welcome Japanese power in China, among other things because it
would keep the Japanese busy, many Chinese might even be better off
and because more Japanese enterprise might mean more US sales.

In Britain, the public shared America's blind faith in collective
security. Through the 1930s British Cabinets were made up of men
who sincerely believed that almost no price would be too high to
avoid another war: there must 'Never Again' be the hecatombs of
World War I Flanders. The mood of the Dominions could only
encourage London, since Australia, Canada and South Africa remained strong supporters of appeasement. Hard facts pointed in the
same direction. Defence chiefs in London thought Britain weak and
collective security irrelevant. The embassy in Tokyo warned that
tension there was so great that any misstep could easily lead to war.
Furthermore, while the public continued to regard Singapore as
impregnable, the chiefs of staff said Hong Kong and Singapore were
in practice indefensible, given Britain's military unpreparedness. Even

worse, the Treasury told the government sombrely that 'today's financial and economic risks are by far the most serious and urgent that the country has to face'.[13]

In both Europe and America, therefore, there were far more pressing issues than China. That gave the Japanese freedom of manoeuvre. In April 1934 they announced that they would have to oppose any foreign military, economic or technical aid to China. Two years later, the Cabinet announced a plan to integrate the economies of Japan, Manchukuo and northern China, together with an economic penetration of South-East Asia and the establishment of unchallenged Japanese naval primacy in the Western Pacific. Then came the conclusion, with Germany, of an 'Anti-Comintern Pact' that would keep the Russians in check.

There was no real Western response. The US state department began to oppose further financial help to China. It had for long demanded to be treated as an equal, so now let it stand on its own feet. Congress even passed legislation on silver purchases that had the effect of draining silver from China and helping to produce recession there. There was little the Chinese government could do. The British and Americans had recognised the GMD administration as the legitimate government years earlier but its condition continued to have rickety and even absurd elements. The cast of GMD people and allies included Shanghai drug barons like Big-Eared Du, the boss of the Green Gang who, it was said, could command 100,000 men, and whom Chiang put in charge of the opium-suppression bureau, and Pockmarked Huang. His other supporters were equally colourful. They included warlords like the Model Governor, the drug-addicted Young Marshal or the Dogmeat General, who gave his concubines numbers instead of names because they were easier to remember, and who was rumoured to have a penis as long as a stack of eighty-six silver dollars. None of which stopped Chiang from promoting his 'New Life' movement to eliminate bad habits and drugs and combat disease. Or from continuing his patriotic insistence that China's full rights be restored, together with lost territories like Taiwan that properly belonged to China.

*   *   *

As the 1930s wore on, rural unrest continued. To be sure, for the great mass of China's hundreds of millions, life and a precarious hand-to-mouth existence went on much as it always had. Nevertheless, Communist support grew. Washington had begun by seeing the Chinese Communists as not much more than armed peasants and not worth taking seriously. Intermittent clashes between Communists and American gunboats trying to protect missionaries continued, but so did Washington's belief that the Communists would fade away once the Chinese government got round to land reform, thus removing the rural distress that was rallying peasants to Mao Zedong.

Yet the Communists were, even now, sowing seeds for future success, not only among city radicals and nationalist reformers, but more importantly among a peasantry weary of warlord exactions and oppression and even among ethnic minorities. In 1931, for example, at the first All-China Congress held in south China, the Communists pledged

> That the Chinese Soviet Republic categorically and unconditionally recognises the right of national minorities to self-determination. This means that in districts like Mongolia, Tibet, Xinjiang . . . and others where the majority of the population belongs to non-Chinese nationalities . . . they . . . shall have the right to determine for themselves whether they wish to leave the Chinese Soviet Republic and create their own independent state

or even join the USSR. Four years later Mao himself gave a pledge of such freedom and independence, promising to restore to Inner Mongolia 'the glory of the epoch of Ghengis Khan' and the 'freedom and independence enjoyed by peoples such as those of Turkey, Poland, the Ukraine and the Caucasus'.[14]

Foreign military observers also started to return from the Communist bases, impressed by the courage and discipline of the Communist soldiery. In February 1933 the American minister in China, Nelson Johnson, reported confidentially to Henry Stimson in Washington: 'The shadow of Bolshevism will lie over parts of China until a thoroughgoing program of rural economy has improved the lot of the masses and an efficient administration has produced a sense of security . . .'[15] American concern ebbed after 1934, when the Communists began their 'Long March' to escape Nationalist encirclement; but that march became legendary. It has always been celebrated as an extraordinary odyssey of bravery and hardship, ending in the back country of Yan'an, in Shaanxi, some 500 miles south-west of Beijing. That was, and remains, a poor, heavily eroded region, sparsely populated, short of food and of roads. Of the 100,000 or so Communist troops and supporters who started, what with battle casualties, sickness and desertion, only some 6–8,000 survivors reached Yan'an. But whether history really matches the legend is a question. Some of the celebrated battles of the Long March may never have actually happened; and Mao himself, far from marching 10,000 miles, is said to have had himself carried a good part of the time in a palanquin. All the same, the march was a seminal event in various ways. By 1935 Mao had emerged as the dominant leader, with subordinates and assistants but no equals. But the other survivors, too, men and women, proved to be an immensely tough, resilient and unsentimental lot. They included almost all the men destined to form the first-generation leadership of the future People's Republic of China. They became, as John Fairbank has written, the aristocracy of the revolution.

In the middle of 1935, however, the Comintern instructed Communist parties everywhere to form a united front with other anti-Fascist groups. In the following year the GMD and CCP duly proclaimed such a united front. Then came an extraordinary incident. Chiang somehow allowed himself to be captured by one of his own generals, Chang Hsueh-liang, the commander of Nationalist forces in Manchuria, who opposed Chiang's policy of fighting the Chinese Communists rather than concentrating against the Japanese. Chiang seemed to be in serious danger but various people intervened, including his wife Meiling. Money may also have changed hands. The CCP and Moscow itself called for Chiang to be freed, lest his disappearance should weaken the anti-Japanese effort and allow the

Japanese to turn north, against the USSR itself. Chiang was taken on 12 December, and on both succeeding days the Moscow papers *Pravda* and *Izvestia* hastily urged that he be set free, followed by Zhou Enlai saying much the same. Chiang was duly allowed to return home.

Japanese encroachments in China continued through 1935 and '36. The army may have reflected that the last three wars had, after all, been good for Japan. All three had produced substantial gains. These were not lessons in military moderation. Meanwhile the Chinese Communists, safely out of the way in the back country, could comfortably criticise both the US and Chiang's administration. Moscow had begun to promote the idea of a united front of all Chinese against Japan, but Mao argued for a two-front conflict against both the GMD and the Japanese; what he really wanted was that the Japanese and the GMD should fight each other, leaving his own CCP as ultimate winner. He certainly made various attempts to use the Japanese to weaken the Nationalists. He also made use of China's drug trade. During the 'Long March' through some of China's dirt-poor fringe provinces, the Communists had found there were poppy fields 'as far as the eye could see'. Once installed in their refuge in Yan'an, they grew and sold a great deal of opium, both to make money and to sell it where it would undermine the discipline of their Nationalist rivals and Japanese enemies. Later still, around the end of the Second World War, there were reports of an 'opium epidemic' in China; and much later again Zhou Enlai took a hand in organising anti-drug crusades, though with indifferent success.

American views continued to be torn between hopeful support of the Nationalist government and the conviction that the 1917 US intervention in Europe had been a mistake, not to be repeated in the Pacific now. As well, from the mid-1930s onwards, US diplomats felt that Chiang was not wholehearted about fighting the Japanese, but seemed to be holding back his best troops to deal with the Communists. Anglo-American efforts to find a reconciliation got nowhere and more fighting between the two Chinese sides seemed likely. Meanwhile, all Chinese detested American appeasement of Japan.

Stanley Hornbeck at the state department had to remind Chiang that it was not for the US to fight China's battles: US policy was meant to serve America. He did not need to point out the obvious: as long as the Japanese were drawn further into China, and provided only that China did not collapse altogether, the Japanese would be no trouble for anyone else. Only if China looked like coming under Japanese domination would there be a threat to the USA.

In fact, the American polity still made it abundantly clear that the US was simply not going to get involved in overseas conflicts. In 1935 a committee under Senator Gerald Nye held the 'Merchants of Death' Congressional hearings that led to the first Neutrality Act. It was meant to stop the president from getting the US sucked into war and authorised him to ban arms sales to belligerents. Two years later that prohibition became mandatory. To be sure, anyone – including allies like the British – could still come and buy arms or equipment in America and take it away, paying cash on the barrel-head. Advice from the American ambassador in Tokyo, Joseph Grew, repeated the old dilemma that Theodore Roosevelt had described. America, he wrote, only had two options. It could pull out of the East Asian region. Or it could insist on the old 'Open Door' but back it up by building up greater American military and naval power in the Pacific. A variant on this came in a tough and perceptive memorandum from a state-department official, John MacMurray. He had served as minister to China and taken part in the Washington conference a dozen years before. He now pointed out that Japan's assertion was a direct result of the actions of others, including the USA. It was the Americans and Chinese who had undermined the Washington system; if the US continued to ignore Japanese grievances, and tilt further towards China, there would be war with Japan. Much of the current trouble stemmed from Chinese nationalism and disunity. Japan had legitimate commercial, railway and stationing rights in Manchuria. Yet Chinese bandits and warlords had attacked Japanese people and property, though China had no chance of expelling the Japanese army. The US could either oppose Japan, or just talk. The best thing would be just to talk. Even if there were a war, and even if the US won, it would merely have to compete with the Russians instead of the Japanese for mastery of the East. MacMurray's conclusions were so awkward that they sank without trace into the archives.

Nor would the British be able to help. The reasons continued to be overwhelming. There was the absolute weakening of Britain by the First World War. On top of that came the Great Depression, the continuing long unemployment queues and concentration on social and economic problems at home. There were more intangible factors, too, having to do with will and national morale. The men who had fought in the 1914–18 war did not, at first, think it had been an unmitigated disaster. They remembered the tough times, but also the fellowship of the trenches, and the sense that they had been tested and not found wanting. Reunions of old soldiers were often cheerful. But the cheerfulness of old comrades did not reflect the damage the war had done to the very fabric of society. Their views horrified liberal opinion and, especially, mothers and wives, who found them incomprehensible and remembered only the sorrows and miseries. Moreover, the very notion that there might be another war underlined the despairing question: 'What was it all for?' The feeling that grew as time went by was one of derision for the very causes and purpose of the war. Well before the end of the century it was almost impossible to find a film or television programme that did not take the 'waste' and 'futility' of the war – any war as a given. As Hew Strachan has pointed out: 'Hindsight bred arrogance and . . . misconception.'[16] By the 1930s the effects of all this on public morale were very clear. Foreign assertion, let alone British rearmament, became virtually unthinkable. Winston Churchill was almost alone in arguing the opposite. The steady rise of German military power could only make the idea of new conflicts even more unthinkable: 'Never Again.' It would be much better to rely on reviving the League of Nations, or on the 1925 Treaty of Locarno that had been meant to settle relations among Britain, France and Germany; and especially on meeting Germany's reasonable demand that all Germans should live in a single state.

Britain therefore simply did not have the resources, or, for the moment, spirit, to sustain even a European war, let alone the possibility of a 'two-theatre' war in Europe and the Pacific. The economic and military strength needed to play a strong hand in the Far East had disappeared. It was understood that, if war did come, the fleet would defend Singapore. Yet by 1939 the chiefs of staff pointed out that if Britain and France were to face simultaneous threats in Europe, the Mediterranean and the Far East, the outcome would depend on American help. In June that year, the chiefs of staff told the government bluntly that 'without the active co-operation of the United States of America it would not be justifiable, from the military point of view, having regard to the existing international situation, to take any avoidable action which might lead to hostilities with Japan'.[17] There was no arguing with that. There would be no British defence of China.

Russia certainly did not look like taking a strong hand either, after Stalin launched the industrialisation and collectivisation campaigns that produced untold horrors for millions. By the later 1930s he would go on to launch his 'Great Purge' of the party and the army. In the process he destroyed not only the Old Bolsheviks who had come to power with him, but most of the leadership of the Red Army. Also, while the Comintern in 1935 instructed Communist parties every-where to form a united front with anti-Fascist groups, that policy was not a great success.

Then, in 1937, came a tiny incident with huge results. The Chinese armies were becoming increasingly restive. In May, the US embassy worried that their 'growing belief in their own prowess' might produce an explosion. In July some Japanese soldiers exercising near the Marco Polo bridge close to Beijing, as they were entitled to do under previous agreements, were shot at. Their commanders thought it was an assault by Chinese soldiers and counter-attacked. The Tokyo government did not want war and passed off the incident but most Japanese saw it as another sign of Chinese arrogance and Japanese retreat, and clamoured for action. There was a local agreement by the two sides at Beijing, but Chiang's government rejected it, believing that Japan was internation-ally isolated and China getting stronger. With his best German-trained divisions he attacked numerically inferior Japanese forces near Shanghai. Shortly afterwards, Chinese Nationalist planes tried to bomb Japanese ships anchored at Shanghai but hit the city instead: leaving people to blame the Japanese. The Chinese attacks failed and up to 60 per cent of Chiang's best troops were killed or wounded. At one point Chiang asked the German ambassador, Oskar Trautman, to mediate in the Sino-Japanese conflict, but nothing came of that. Meanwhile the Japanese sent fifteen new divisions to China and began a major offensive that forced Chiang to start retreating to Nanjing. Britain and Germany began to give China some aid, the Soviets recognised Chiang and the US continued to oppose the Japanese with strong words.

NANJING MASSACRE

In 1937 the Japanese army, as part of Japan's larger strategy of occupying the major cities of China's eastern seaboard, also occupied Shanghai. That proved a tough battle with much hand-to-hand fighting and heavy Japanese casualties. The fall of Shanghai made the fall of Nanjing only a matter of time. Before moving, the Japanese command issued orders threatening punishment for anyone committing 'illegal acts'.

Leaflets were dropped on Nanjing, urging prompt surrender. There was no response but Chinese troops withdrew or deserted, leaving the city in such chaos that by the time Japanese troops entered there was almost no resistance.

What followed were several weeks of murder, rape, looting and arson by Japanese troops. Why? One suspects not only Japanese racism but a combination of tiredness, frustration and a good deal of after-battle hysteria. Whatever the cause, the reports of pregnant women being obscenely killed, or of bare-chested Japanese officers wielding blood-stained samurai swords and killing men, women and children, apparently with joy, finally destroyed any sympathy Japan might have had in the West.

Nanjing became a symbol, like the bombing of Guernica by German planes in the Spanish Civil War at much the same time, which was commemorated in what is perhaps Picasso's most famous painting. In the eyes of Western opinion it made China even more an innocent victim and Japan a rogue state.*

The exact number of victims remains uncertain. Some accounts seem exaggerated. The Chinese delegate to the League of Nations at the time put the civilian toll at 20,000. A Communist Chinese newspaper put it at 42,000. One American witness, Miner Searle Bates estimated that 12,000 civilians and 28,000 soldiers had died, while another witness put the toll at 50–60,000. Modern China alleges that 300,000 or more were killed. In any case, to this day, Nanjing remains a major factor in China's resentment of Japan.

---

* Many in the West have continued to find something mysterious and frightening about 'the Japanese soul'. In the words of one Western novelist half a century after Nanjing, '. . . behind the flashing lights of Japan is something dark and very old'.

Both Chinese sides, the GMD and the CCP, now promised to co-operate in what Chiang called a triumph of national sentiment. There was even a GMD–CCP agreement that the Red Army would become the 8th Route Army, nominally under Nationalist command. However, by the start of 1938 all major Chinese cities, ports, railways and the most productive parts of north and central China were under Japanese control. They had also driven up the Yangzi, forcing Chiang's government to retreat beyond Nanjing. The battle for Chiang's capital cost the Japanese some 50,000 men and its conquest culminated in a wild Japanese massacre of Chinese men, women and children in and around the city – 'hell on earth', one American relief official called it.

Chiang now blew the Yellow River dykes, flooding thousands of square miles of China at a cost of perhaps a million Chinese dead by drowning, starvation or disease. Even that did not stop the Japanese and Chiang, followed by huge crowds – possibly millions altogether – had to retreat beyond the Yangzi gorges to Chonqing, in the back-country. The costs were very great. The GMD was now cut off from its natural roots in the coastal cities and its revenues from customs duties, not to mention opium. That had very large consequences, not just for the immediate fight against the Japanese, but for the long-term ability of the Chinese Nationalists to maintain themselves against Mao's Communists. Universities and factories were shipped to the west as well, and found life distinctly primitive. Other things deteriorated as Nationalist administrators became refugees. Morale dropped. Inflation rose. Corruption increased. The governing groups made little attempt to understand the peasantry, whose taxes and other exactions became more burdensome. All in all, the Nationalists had to deal with enormous economic and financial problems as well as with drought and food-supply difficulties. These problems were eased, but not very much, by the opening of the 'Burma Road' supply route from British-held Burma into Kunming in December 1938. Building it cost thousands of lives; but became essential once the Japanese closed the Yangzi artery.

In Chonqing, Chiang was starting to find that he and Mao in Yan'an were encountering rather similar difficulties. Each had to create and maintain a viable governing structure and encourage people's loyalty, though Mao was rather more successful in rallying popular support. He also set about organising resistance in the Japanese-held areas, at the same time as starting a guerilla war against the Japanese, with his associate Peng Dehuai in command. Mao even pursued ideas he had aired back in 1935: in 1941 the CCP set up an institute for national-minority members who, once educated and trained there, could become efficient Communist cadres working elsewhere. It was much the same pattern as Stalin's Second World War programme for recruiting and training young Germans, Poles and others who would then be able to take charge of their post-war Soviet satellites. Mao did more. He toughened the CCP organisation in ruthless style, disciplining his own people by the use of confessions, humiliation and even terror. Altogether, the war against Japan gave the CCP the cause that allowed it to mobilise the countryside and the peasantry, and to indoctrinate them with the idea of class struggle and Mao's sinified version of Marxist doctrines, 'Mao Zedong Thought'. The Communists were not better off materially than Chiang's people, but their propaganda was vastly superior. Many Western journalists became quite enchanted by the mythologies of revolution, the energy and dedication of Mao's followers and the way in which they could enlist the support, even it seemed the enthusiasm, of the peasantry. It was only much later, in 1942–4, that a few Westerners became aware of the 'black' sides of the Communist campaigning style.

The united front eroded quite quickly. There were clashes, even battles, between Communists and Nationalists. In January 1941 a Communist unit of several thousand men that had strayed too far south was ambushed and virtually wiped out by the Nationalists. It was the de facto end of the united-front effort.

As for the Japanese, by a bitter irony their gains in China turned out to drain their resources much more than to strengthen them. In time, China tied down over a million Japanese troops and most of their air force. Above all, operations in China used up huge quantities of aviation and other fuels. In fact, Japan found that the fight in China and Manchuria needed more resources than even a fully mobilised Japanese industrial base could furnish. The resources of South-East Asia therefore began to beckon, while other eyes turned north, to the resources of Siberia. If relations with the US could be kept normal, perhaps it would, after all, be possible to form an East Asian economic bloc to compete peacefully with other economic systems. Perhaps Prince Fumimaro Konoe meant no more than this when he declared that Japan must try to build 'a new order for ensuring permanent stability in Asia'. That view may have been reinforced when, in 1939, the hitherto unknown Soviet general, Georgi Zhukov – six years later the conqueror of Berlin – inflicted a bloody defeat on the Japanese at the Mongolian border.

*   *   *

For the Americans, the 1937 eruption of open war in China was a wake-up call. Japanese domination of all of China would clearly be a major change in the power balance of East Asia and the Pacific. It was not just the government that became more concerned. An experienced US Air Force officer, Captain Claire Chennault, retired from the service, went to China and became chief adviser to the Chinese air force. He also brought in American pilots to train and fly with the Chinese. Christian and missionary groups cultivated even greater sympathy for China, and there was a growing American will to restrain Japan by denying it war materials like oil and metals. As for the GMD–CCP split, some senior folk understood that even if they managed to co-operate against Japan, there would be a struggle for control of China once the war was over. In the meantime the Russians slowed down aid to Chiang and withdrew their so-called 'volunteer' pilots from China.

These East Asian difficulties came together with Soviet, German and Italian intervention in the Spanish Civil War. Roosevelt, that complex, tough and devious man, announced that, since there was now an 'epidemic of world lawlessness', the afflicted regions should be quarantined to protect the rest of the international community. Nothing much followed. The US might have the ability to put serious economic pressure on Japan, but Roosevelt and his secretary of state, Cordell Hull, continued to be wary of anything like outright sanctions.

Shortly afterwards, Japanese policy suffered three major blows. On 26 July the Americans informed Tokyo that from January 1940 they would abrogate the trade treaty between the two countries. A month later came a German-Soviet non-aggression pact which opened the door to the German attack on Poland and the start of the Second World War. It allowed Stalin to secure the Soviet Union's western marches, so that he could transfer a substantial force to guard the Manchukuo-Mongolian border against the Japanese. It also frustrated possible ideas among Western powers about leaving Germany and Russia to fight each other and left Japan without a single reliable ally anywhere.

Japan was totally unprepared for any of this and the consternation in Tokyo was real. The prime minister, Kiichiro Hiranuma, issued a famous statement on 28 August saying that 'inexplicable new conditions' had been created in Europe, and resigned. Three days later German forces crossed the Polish border. Within a year not only Poland but France collapsed and the Germans conquered almost all of Western and Central Europe as well as the Balkans. The strategic map of Europe was entirely changed and the British, isolated behind the English Channel, seemed on the brink of defeat. By the time Churchill became prime minister in May 1940, all he could do was to tell Roosevelt that when, in eighteen months, Britain came to the end of its ability to pay for weapons, he hoped the US would go on making weapons available anyway. Eventually Roosevelt did help, by the skin of his political teeth and a superb homely speech, commending to his fellow Americans his new lend-lease arrangements as being like lending a garden hose to a neighbour whose house had caught fire.

In the Pacific, the Americans started to limit the strategically vital supplies of iron ore and oil to Japan. Even now, Hull resisted any idea of doing more, let alone moving to fuller sanctions. But the broader options for Japan became stark. It could buy American economic concessions – oil and iron ore – by withdrawing from China. That would be a devastating blow to Japan's pride. It also would jeopardise food supplies and could easily provoke rebellion in Manchukuo, perhaps even in Korea. It was unthinkable. Or Japan could try to grab Siberia, which would use up more resources than Japan could spare. Or it could go for the British and Dutch as well as French possessions in South-East Asia – especially Java's oil – but that would leave Japan's communications vulnerable to interdiction by the US Navy. The European war had left the Asian colonies of the defeated Dutch and French, and even of the British, defenceless. In July 1940 even Winston Churchill had to accept a Japanese demand that he close the Burma Road for three months. So, shortly after the collapse of France in May 1940, the Japanese began to move into French South-East Asia. That new strategic geography greatly changed conditions to

China's south. It also changed things for the great British fortress of Singapore. Since Britain was barely surviving against Germany, it was clear that if Japan was going to be restrained in China or South-East Asia, it was not the British who could do the restraining.

For the Americans, if China was of somewhat secondary importance, Britain was not. After the mid-1940 battles for Britain had shown that the British would neither collapse nor negotiate with Hitler's Germany, Roosevelt became willing to send all aid short of war across the Atlantic. The obvious conclusion for American friends of China was that China needed somehow to be tied into that pro-Britain policy. The Japanese themselves made that much easier when they signed a Tripartite Pact with Fascist Italy and Nazi Germany in September 1940 to form the so-called 'Axis'. That made the wars in Europe and China, much more visibly, part of an interrelated set of problems. It became much easier for the Americans to help every power resisting the Axis. It would be even more impossible for Washington to accept any Pacific settlement without Japan's withdrawal from China. Suddenly it became politically possible to fortify the American-held islands of Wake, Midway and the Aleutians. In addition, Roosevelt tried to build up the diplomatic and other links of the 'ABCD' powers – America, Britain, China, the Dutch – to try to discourage any further Japanese move southwards, though he was deeply conscious of not having enough navy to look after both the Atlantic and the Pacific. The Chinese were going to get more American aid, too. By 1940 the Nationalists were running into trouble, not least in the air, and Roosevelt duly sent 100 American planes. He also allowed Claire Chennault to recruit American army air-force pilots as 'volunteers'. They became known as the 'Flying Tigers' and in April 1941 the president, by executive order, made them retrospectively legal.

In the meantime, the Chinese Communists began to launch attacks of their own on the Japanese in the north, but got nowhere when the Japanese launched fierce counter-attacks. GMD forces, on the other hand, together with militia units and local criminal organisations, established a presence in the Yangzi delta, that centre for food production and heavy industry. In addition, Chiang was doing more fighting against the Communists, and US diplomats became even more convinced that, far from being wholehearted about fighting the Japanese, he was holding back his best troops to deal with Mao's forces. Anglo-American efforts to find a reconciliation between the two sides got nowhere.

The Americans did, however, make large credits available to the Nationalists. In May 1941 China even became eligible for the lend-lease aid invented to help the British. American oil supplies continued to reach Japan, but amid growing criticism. China also received significant Soviet aid: that would help to tie the Japanese down in China and keep them away from Siberia. In addition, the Soviets signed a neutrality pact with Japan in April 1941.

Shortly afterwards, on 22 June 1941, came 'Operation Barbarossa', Hitler's invasion of the Soviet Union, quickly followed by stunning German advances deep into Russia and equally stunning German hauls of literally millions of Russian prisoners of war. The German advance underlined the danger of what had for some time been Roosevelt's worst nightmare, and Churchill's, too: that the Japanese might launch a simultaneous attack on the Soviet Union's eastern flank and end the war with a quick and joint Japanese-German triumph. Roosevelt immediately offered the Russians lend-lease aid. However, instead of attacking Russia, a month after Barbarossa the Japanese sailed into Cam Ranh Bay, in southern Indo-China, the prime naval base that had long been so critical to the naval strategies of East Asia (and would become even more painfully familiar to America twenty-five years later, during its Vietnam War). There were renewed fears that China might be compelled to make a separate peace with Japan. Senior Washington officials urged that Japanese assets in the US should be frozen and oil supplies entirely stopped.

The second half of 1941 produced intense discussions in Tokyo about what to do next, and almost equally intense US–Japan negotiations that failed to produce a settlement. Around mid-year the Japanese debate about whether to move and, if so, where, intensified. Any serious military effort obviously depended on oil. But Siberia offered no net oil gain. So unless Tokyo was prepared to mend fences with the US on American terms, including withdrawal from China, the alternative had to be Japanese access to oil from Java and Sumatra. In fact, Tokyo concluded, Japanese hegemony in East and South-East Asia was really the only alternative to Japanese economic decline and subservience to the European-American powers that controlled the resources Japan had to have. If the US cut off oil entirely, Japan would have to strike south. On 2 July a critical Cabinet meeting adopted a scheme to expel European power from Asia. Prince Konoe, supported by the navy and the economists, won the argument that there should be no northward attack until 'the persimmon ripened', or until, for any reason, the move had become a walk-over. Instead, what Japan should do was to move south, occupy the remainder of French Indo-China and 'Construct the Greater East Asia Co-Prosperity Sphere'.

The Americans froze Japanese assets in the US. They also turned off the oil spigot entirely: after 25 July Japan got no more American oil. Hull handed the Japanese ambassador a statement of the four principles that Japan would have to accept if it wanted good relations with America: respect for the sovereignty and integrity of all nations; non-interference in other countries' internal affairs; equality of commercial opportunity; and no change in the Pacific status quo except by peaceful means. In August Roosevelt and Churchill met at sea off the coast of Newfoundland and agreed the 'Atlantic Charter', calling for a post-war world of peace, disarmament, self-determination and free trade. A leading Japanese newspaper, *Asahi Shimbun*, condemned it as a plan for 'world-domination on the basis of Anglo-American world views', which, of course, it was.

In October, an American military mission under General John Magruder came to Chiang in Chonqing. It reported back, not by then with great originality, that Chiang wanted American lend-lease equipment not to fight the Japanese but to protect his own government against any post-war rebellion. In Tokyo, the efficient and energetic General Hideki Tojo sketched Japan's future. Now, in late 1941, the Japanese navy was probably enjoying parity with the combined Anglo-American navies in the Pacific. That parity would be short-lived, given the American naval construction programme. If Japan had to move south, the US fleet must be neutralised. If hostilities did not start by 8 December, Japan would have to wait until the spring of 1942, by which time the US would be stronger and Japan would have less oil. In October General Tojo replaced Prince Konoe as prime minister and the US ambassador in Tokyo, Joseph Grew, warned Washington that Japan might go for some dramatic move. A vastly more important piece of information, arguably decisive for the entire course of the war, went in the opposite direction, from Tokyo to Moscow. In the outstanding espionage performance of World War II Richard Sorge, a German correspondent in Tokyo who was secretly spying for Stalin, got wind of the basic Japanese strategic decision to move south. He was even able to tell Moscow that Japan would attack the Americans at Hawaii. That allowed Stalin to release Siberian divisions from his eastern front in time to take part in the great counter-attack against the Germans in front of Moscow that Zhukov launched on 6 December.

Some weeks earlier Vice-Admiral Chuichi Nagumo had already taken a six-carrier task force to sea. Objective: Hawaii. The crews welcomed the notion of taking on the 'arrogant Americans'. On 7 December, the day after Zhukov's offensive before Moscow, Tokyo launched its surprise attack on the US Navy base at Pearl Harbor, in order to secure the flank of the simultaneous Japanese invasion of British and Dutch possessions in South-East Asia. Still, the Americans were lucky. Eight battleships were lost and most of the Pacific fleet eviscerated; but the kernel of the force, the aircraft carriers, were exercising at sea and escaped destruction.

11

CHINA IN A NEW WORLD ORDER

AD 1941 to 1949

HITLER, IN ONE of the greatest follies of his career, at once decided to join Japan and declared war on the United States. Stupidity is usually easier to see once its results become evident, but here the consequences were predictable. America had been teetering on the brink of conflict for some time, but it was Hitler who made certain that there would not now be two separate wars, one in Europe and another in the Pacific. Churchill's instinctive response to Pearl Harbor was right: 'So we had won after all!'[1] after which he 'slept the sleep of the saved and the thankful'. Without delay, Roosevelt and he cut through the political and strategic complications and treated the European and Pacific conflicts as parts of a single war. However, while Germany and Japan would both have to be defeated, occupied and reformed, on the approach to that double victory, it was quickly evident that Britain would have to be secured, Japanese advances stemmed, German power contained, and an overall strategy of 'Europe First' adopted. A defeat of Japan might leave Germany free to win, while defeating Hitler would make the defeat of Japan inevitable.[2]

In the Pacific, and especially from the point of view of the leading Allied power, the United States, wartime planning had to take place in three interrelated spheres: military operations, balance-of-power considerations, and the prospective post-war order. Through a combination of increasingly massive American military and material power and virtuoso political management by Roosevelt himself, the US achieved its aims in all three fields.

In operational terms, it was obviously a condition of victory in Asia that China should not collapse and be forced to surrender to Japan. China might lose the war but had no means to win it. The China mainland campaign was therefore only a holding operation. The same was true of the British campaign in Burma. An irruption of the Japanese army into India, carrying the banners of 'Asia for the Asians', might have produced Allied disaster. As it was, the many weaknesses of the Chinese government and its armies, together with the weakness of the British, compelled the Allies to regard the entire span of the China–Burma–India campaigns as essentially defensive. To be sure, China tied down one and a quarter million Japanese soldiers and perhaps, before the end, some two-fifths of all Japanese forces, but no Allied forces within reach could hope to defeat them. They were, however, vulnerable, for they could not become self-sustaining. If Japan's home bases could be put out of action, or its sea-borne lines of communication cut, all Japanese forces overseas would wither on the vine. In the meantime, defensive operations in China and South-East Asia would make their own demands on Allied resources. It would, for instance, be necessary to keep supply lines to China open to prevent a Chinese collapse, which meant relying on the 'Burma Road'. It would also be helpful to be able to use Chinese bases for Allied aircraft to attack Japan; perhaps even to support an eventual invasion of Japan. As Roosevelt put it quite early in the war, 'We must have China to get at Japan.' Beyond that, China's principal importance for both the Allies and the Japanese was as a material or political resource that required 'talking up' China's role in international arrangements.

The core effort of Allied operations against Japan therefore turned out to be the American Pacific campaign. It was a three-pronged affair, mainly under the leadership of the US Navy. One prong was the interdiction of Japan's sea-borne supply lines to its overseas garrisons everywhere in the Asia-Pacific region. A second, perhaps of even greater psychological and political than strictly military importance, was to bring American ground and air forces under General Douglas MacArthur back to the Philippines, from which they had been expelled at the start of the war. The third, and most important, was island-hopping US forces across the Western Pacific to the point where island bases could be used to launch attacks on Japan itself. US bombers would be able, from island airfields, to bomb the Japanese home islands as the British and American air forces would bomb Germany. They might even help to launch an eventual invasion of Japan. Tokyo could see the point perfectly. Some two years later, when the Americans stormed Saipan in the Mariana Islands, the emperor's naval adviser told him tersely, 'When we lost Saipan – Hell is upon us.'[3]

The foundations of this Allied strategy were put into place almost immediately, within months of Pearl Harbor. They came in the American naval victories of the Coral Sea and, most especially, at Midway in May–June 1942. Midway Island was the strategic gateway to Hawaii, itself the key to US naval operations. The battle for it was in essence won by one chief radioman and two quite junior officers of the US Navy. The chief radioman was Harry Kidder, who began the efforts to break Japanese naval codes, starting what has been called as 'the most stunning intelligence coup in all naval history'.[4] One officer was Lt.-Cmdr. Edwin T. Layton, the Pacific Fleet intelligence officer. Helped by listening stations as far afield as Melbourne, Australia, Layton could read enemy naval messages, imperfectly but well enough to conclude that they would probably aim their next attack at Midway. The other officer was Lieutenant-Commander Wade McClusky who, by good luck, managed to bring his squadron of dive bombers over the Japanese fleet just as the decks of their carriers were helplessly covered with planes being armed and refuelled. The Japanese watched the American attack with professional admiration;[5] but the Americans sank four Japanese carriers in that battle, the imperial navy never really recovered and could never again hope for unchallenged dominance of the Pacific.

BREAKING JAPANESE NAVAL CODES

One of the decisive elements of US naval operations was the ability to read Japanese naval communications. US naval intelligence started work on breaking the Japanese navy code in 1921. It obtained a photocopy of the 'Imperial Japanese Navy Secret Operating Code 1918'. The foundations for breaking it, rather like the foundations of the modern American economy, were laid by private enterprise.

The code was a kind of dictionary with 100,000 entries that took five years to translate. But to go further, the codebreakers needed live messages encrypted in that code. That required reading Japanese radio communications, sent in a unique telegraphic code, geared to the Japanese syllabary.

Some US Navy and marine operators taught themselves, on their own initiative, to recognise and intercept Japanese radio messages. The star of the show was Chief Radioman Harry Kidder, working in the Philippines, who taught himself with the help of a shipmate's Japanese wife. Other intercept stations were created, even in Shanghai and Beijing. Later the navy set up schools for fleet radio operators.

By 1927 the Japanese code book and its updates had been translated as the so-called 'Red Book'. It became obvious that even if one couldn't read messages, important conclusions about Japanese deployments might be drawn simply from the patterns of radio traffic. But in 1930 the Japanese navy replaced the 'Red Book'. A new and more elaborate 'Blue Book' was created and it took the US Navy three years to understand a reasonable slice of it.

In 1939 the Japanese navy changed its code yet again. The Americans code-named the new one JN-25. It had much more complicated codes and transmission procedures, with huge numbers of variants. There were constant procedural changes, as well.

Still, by November 1941 various fragments of information suggested that the Japanese navy was now using large numbers of merchant ships, useful for ferrying troops; and that two Japanese navy task forces were approaching the Philippines. It was even possible to outline their composition. Even then, it was not until December 1941 that the Americans managed to decrypt a few JN-25 messages properly; they offered revealing traffic analysis.

Only on 16 March 1942 could one of the American listening stations, on Corregidor in the Philippines, issue its first complete decrypt of a Japanese message in real time. It showed the Japanese had given the code-name 'AF' to the island of Midway. That and other indicators coming through a listening station in Melbourne, Australia, suggested that the Japanese meant to launch a major thrust, probably towards Midway. That was the estimate Lt.-Cmdr. Edwin T. Layton was able to give to Admiral Nimitz.

The Americans were also able to decipher the different codes used in Japanese diplomatic radio traffic; and the Japanese do not at any point seem to have detected that any of these codes had been compromised. Naturally that gave the Americans enormous advantages. Breaking the naval codes, in particular, was critical not just in the battle for Midway but for the entire Pacific naval campaign and therefore for the entire American and Allied, including Chinese, war against Japan.

Japanese strategies were much less clear-cut, much more desperate and more risky. In fact, and astonishingly, in the entire run-up to Pearl Harbor Japanese planners had never developed a concept or design for 'victory'. In so far as they had a coherent plan, they hoped to prevail by securing the resources of China and South-East Asia, as well as creating a Pacific–East Asian empire powerful enough to make even America quail at the prospective cost of defeating it. Furthermore, that new empire hoped to enlist China and other Asians in an anti-Western crusade that would make it impractical for the Allies to carry on the conflict and compel the Americans, those 'devils in human skin', to come to terms. While that project grossly underestimated American power and resolve in the short term – not to mention the impact of Japanese cruelties in the region and beyond – in the long run it was not as unrealistic as it appeared at the time. The broad notion of liberating Asia from the white oppressors was a consistent theme in the Japanese management of their 1941–5 empire. It ranged from the invention of a 'Greater East Asia Co-Prosperity Sphere' to the cultivation of associates from Manchukuo to nationalist groupings in Indonesia and other parts of South-East Asia. It also meant deliberately humiliating foreigners in cities like Beijing as they were moved into internment. During the war, Japan failed to get more than tiny minorities of anti-European Asian nationalists to co-operate with them.[6] However, their cultivation of local nationalist feelings and people, like Soekarno, who became Indonesia's post-war president, and especially the psychological impact of their victories over the Europeans, contributed strongly to the post-war drive for decolonisation.

If designing the outlines of Allied grand strategy was relatively straightforward, balance-of-power considerations were more complex. Obviously the destruction of the Japanese military would leave a power vacuum in the Pacific. That would have to be replaced, largely by an extension of American power, and reach to the shores of the Asian continent. At the same time, America must manage to maintain Allied unity without offending anti-colonialist sentiment at home or jeopardising the US reputation in Asia and Africa as the upholder of self-determination and independence. Washington wanted the Russians to understand that they could not be allowed to dominate their old bailiwicks in Manchuria, let alone control China and East Asia; while understanding also that it was greatly in their interests to join the war against Japan, which would reduce the duration of the war and the number of US casualties.

All that overlapped with the gradually emerging designs for a post-war global order. There was not much doubt in anyone's mind, for the rest of the war and its aftermath, that in designing it the US would be in pole position. As Stanley Hornbeck, of the state department, put it: 'It will be a long, hard war, but after it is over Uncle Sam will do the talking in the world.'[7] Still, the war quickly involved a variety of allies with very different and often contradictory aims. Furthermore, Roosevelt and Churchill were careful to emphasise the multinational, *coalition* character of their war effort. It was Japan that had chosen to attack America, Britain, China and the Dutch. Not only could the ABCD label celebrate China's role as a major ally, it could thereby also help to block any future Soviet role in northern China. It was therefore imperative to create some framework for inter-Allied co-operation. The Anglo-American leaders set down its first vague shape at their 'Arcadia' conference at the end of 1941. Only much later did that sketch solidify into a shape that Roosevelt, in a moment of inspiration, christened the 'United Nations'.

Initially, the president worried about following the unhappy League of Nations precedent for setting up international organisations. But he quickly came to see that the war needed not just to be won, but to be won in ways, and on terms, that would make possible a new world order that embodied both an acceptable balance of power and a capacity to prevent future wars among major states. Setting up such a post-war order required sustained Allied unity, Stalin's full consent and, if at all possible, his trust. It would therefore need acceptance in Moscow that the defeat of Japan could not bring Soviet dominance of East Asia. No less important, the American people would have to accept some form of US participation without long-term deployment of US forces abroad. These principles formed the context for Rooseveltian policies until the end of his life.

That being so, China remained a prize, perhaps the largest single prize, of the Pacific War. In a larger historical sense, indeed, the Japanese-American war in the Pacific was perhaps nothing less than a war for China. Certainly Pearl Harbor, and America's entry into the war, must have been as much of a relief for Chiang as it was for Churchill in London.

Allied priorities, both political and military, remained unaltered, whether by a series of German and Japanese victories or by America's own early naval victories in the Pacific. The British, in particular, suffered a series of disasters, beginning with their defeats in Norway and France in 1940, followed, in mid-1942, by the fall of Tobruk in North Africa, which had Churchill dejectedly muttering 'Defeat is one thing, disgrace is another'. In fact, it was Churchill's private conviction – which he naturally took great care never to voice in public – that man for man the British were simply no match for the Germans, for whose fighting qualities he developed a growing admiration.[8] In the meantime, soon after Pearl Harbor the British suffered two further strategic disasters. Japanese aircraft conclusively demonstrated the value of air power at sea by sinking two of Britain's finest battleships off the coast of the Malay peninsula. Not only that but, contrary to almost all previous expectations, the Japanese managed to bring land and air forces southward from Indo-China and through the Malayan jungles. They were therefore able to attack Singapore from the landward side, making its great guns pointed at the sea innocuous. On 15 February 1942 Singapore, and over 100,000 men, surrendered to a Japanese force smaller in numbers but superior in military competence. Worse still, in Burma, too, the Japanese outfought the British-Indian forces. In April 1942 they finally cut the Burma Road. The consequences were more than merely military. The entire prestige and charisma on which the British empire in the East had so largely rested for a hundred years came to an abrupt end.

The cutting of the Burma Road meant that Chiang, in his fastness at Chonqing, could only receive a trickle of supplies by airlift over the Himalayan 'Hump'. He found Allied help inadequate and kept saying so virtually throughout the war. But the Chinese efforts themselves were often unremarkable. Shortly after Pearl Harbor, Roosevelt sent General Joseph 'Vinegar Joe' Stilwell to Chonqing, to be his liaison with Chiang, as well as to command all American forces in the China–Burma–India theatre and supervise the American lend-lease supply programme. Stilwell had long experience of China and considerable admiration for the Chinese people. He also thought that the Chinese, if properly trained, could be first-class soldiers. As it was, though, he thought the Chinese armies had too little training or equipment and too many officers. For their commanders he had something like contempt and despised most of their senior officers for their dishonesty and corruption. Nor did he think much of their willingness, let alone their ability, to fight the Japanese. What was needed, Stilwell thought, was a smaller, tougher, élite army. There were serious questions about Chiang's own military competence as well. He may have styled himself 'Generalissimo' but his conduct of operations was often badly flawed.

Stilwell's views of the Chinese political leadership were even less flattering. His name for Chiang was 'peanut'. He quickly concluded that the Nationalist leaders were just 'a gang of thugs with the one idea of perpetuating themselves and their machine'.[9] This may have been unkind, but was not necessarily unfair. Chiang did indeed see all alliances as temporary and tactical, his permanent aim being to stay in power so as to unify and restore China.[10] And corruption was endemic. Not surprisingly, Chiang and Stilwell did not get on and eventually Stilwell was recalled, largely at Chiang's insistence.

There were a variety of strategic and tactical disputes as well. By 1942 Claire Chennault had rejoined the US service as a major-general and his 'Flying Tigers' had become the US Army's 14th Air Force. Like some other air generals before and since, Chennault thought the air force could go a long way towards winning the war all by itself; what Nationalist China needed was an improved and expanded air force and a chain of modern airfields. Stilwell had little time for these ideas, but Chennault was an increasingly trusted adviser of Chiang, so great efforts were made to follow his advice. Hundreds of thousands of peasants were pressed into service to build roads and airfields by hand. The whole enterprise ran not just into peasant resentment but a serious shortage of Nationalist resources, including the shortage of tax collections from an already hard-hit population. It would also, in time, trigger a fierce and, from a Nationalist point of view, destructive military counter-attack by the Japanese.

If Chiang had difficulties, things were not much better on the Chinese Communist side. By 1941, attacks by the Nationalists on one side and Japanese on the other caused crises in the CCP-controlled areas. Yan'an was beset by shortages and inflation, there were major revenue problems yet stress on higher production and the need to tighten belts. That created problems of social control, which the CCP met by more intensive peasant mobilisation and indoctrination, together with the leadership's insistence that Maoist soldiers remain disciplined and even helpful to the peasantry, and must be seen to share the general privations. Other means were also used, including, where necessary, force. Opium production could be used to pay taxes. Its consumption was not encouraged among party members but opium continued to be shipped to areas controlled by the Japanese or the Nationalists for the twin purpose of earning money and weakening the enemy. In addition, Mao went on refining his sinified Marxism: 'Mao Zedong Thought'.

There was, however, one thing that the Nationalists and Communists shared. Neither, even now, fully appreciated the extent to which China's political and social frailties made it impossible to play a larger role in Allied councils or the Pacific balance, still less in the design of any future Pacific order. Nor did they see to what extent the major powers, the United States, the Soviet Union and Britain, had much larger issues to deal with than China's national interests as defined by either Chiang or Mao. As the 'self-strengthening' movement of the later nineteenth century had pointed out long ago, Beijing could not seriously hope to be influential until China had put its own economic and political house in order. In the meantime, whatever the political rhetoric, China would continue to be the object rather than the subject of Allied decisions. The Nationalists naturally used what assets they had, from the sympathies of missionaries to the more widespread perception of China as 'victim'. But nothing could really disguise the ineffectiveness of the Nationalists in the field or the maladministration and corruption of Chinese Nationalist affairs.

*   *   *

Political patterns for the war and the post-war world began to take firmer shape almost as soon as the Pacific naval and military plans became clear. Their outlines began to be filled in at the four major inter-Allied conferences of 1943. The first was in January, at Casablanca, in a meeting between Churchill and Roosevelt. Stalin declined to come, saying he was busy. (It was the last month of the titanic Battle of Stalingrad, on the Volga.) The second was a meeting of the three major Allied foreign ministers, Anthony Eden, Cordell Hull and Vyacheslav Molotov, in Moscow in October–November. The third, in November, was a meeting between Churchill, Roosevelt and Chiang in Cairo. The fourth, and most important, was a meeting in November–December of Churchill, Roosevelt and Stalin at Teheran.

In these meetings Roosevelt consistently tried to avoid the old, pre-war MacMurray conclusion about an inevitable post-war Soviet-American rivalry. At Casablanca, given the imperative need for Russian co-operation for both war and peace, and to avoid any thought in Stalin's mind that America and Britain might work for a separate peace with Germany, Roosevelt announced that Germany, Italy and Japan would have to accept 'Unconditional Surrender'.[11] He decided, too, that America must govern the post-war Pacific, surrounding Japan with a string of American bases in the Philippines, Formosa and Korea, as well as in the island chains. On the way to that end, though, an extremely costly invasion of Japan should be avoided by getting the Soviets to come into the Pacific War after Germany's surrender. Since it was also necessary to head off any future Soviet control of China, there had to be support and money for the Chinese Nationalist government as well. The elevation and celebration of China as one of the four major victor powers of the war, and prospectively one of the 'Four Policemen' of the post-war world, must also continue: America, Britain, China and the Soviet Union; in spite of Winston Churchill, who wrote to London that the inclusion of China as one of the Big Four was 'an absolute farce' and at some points, especially later in the war, called the Nationalist military failures 'grotesque'.

At Moscow matters went very much further. There would be a 'four-power declaration' about establishing a new international organisation. The Russians demurred at this additional elevation of China to great-power status but backed away when Hull warned of 'all sorts of readjustment by my government' if Moscow insisted.[12] The US itself had by then signed away all remnants of its old extraterritorial rights in China. It now did more. It replaced the old 1882 ban on Chinese immigration to the US with a quota. It even made Chinese eligible for admission to US citizenship. Then, in November, came the Cairo meeting, where Chiang could be photographed hobnobbing with Roosevelt and Churchill, and where China was brought even further into the fold. It was reconfirmed, no doubt to reassure the ever-suspicious Stalin, that there would be no peace short of unconditional surrender. It was further agreed that Korea would become independent, that China would recover all the lands she had lost ('been stolen') since 1894 and the Pacific islands that Japan had seized since 1914. To Churchill's displeasure, Roosevelt agreed with Chiang that colonialism in Asia would have to end, but the president also made it clear that the Nationalists would have to settle their domestic differences with the Communists. If Chiang accepted that Stalin should refrain from helping Mao and come into the war with Japan, he had better make some concessions of his own to the Soviets in Manchuria.

That was the overture to the meeting of the 'Big Three' at Teheran. Roosevelt was full of confidence: 'Stalin – I can handle that old buzzard', as he put it. That was going to be difficult, given the ingrained Soviet suspicions of the West, which was evident even in little things. For instance, when Molotov visited England and Churchill offered the hospitality of the prime-ministerial country residence at Chequers, the Russians brought their own bed-makers and Molotov slept with a gun under his pillow.[13] There was still the endless Soviet suspicion that the Anglo-Americans might make a separate deal with Germany; probably not least because, in the middle months of 1943, Stalin was seriously considering making his own separate deal with Hitler, which would have left America and

Britain fighting alone against Germany and Japan.[14] Roosevelt may have understood that, as well as having his own reservations about the British; in any case he remained anxious to reassure Stalin that there was no Anglo-Saxon plot to gang up on him. Stalin promptly made use of Western anxieties by suggesting that Roosevelt – as the only head of state (not merely head of government) at the meeting – should take the chair. That flattered FDR and implied an equidistant position for him between the UK and the USSR in the event that there should be differences. Roosevelt went further, pointedly meeting *à deux* with Stalin, and underlining reassurances that a 'second front' would be opened up in France as soon as possible. The two Western leaders did, however, get Stalin to confirm the promise he had made during the Moscow meeting, that once Germany had been defeated he would come into the war against Japan. He would also – this being of particular importance to Roosevelt – join in creating a new United Nations. Furthermore, he would accept Korean independence and recognise Chinese sovereignty in Manchuria. In return, he would achieve the restoration of Russia's old rights on the Chinese Eastern Railway, and acquire a warm-water port on the Pacific, the Kurile island chain and the southern half of Sakhalin.

Teheran was significant in other ways. It highlighted the shift in Western power from Britain to America. The relationship between them was always more complex, with a greater dash of rivalry in military as well as political decision-making, than was apparent at the time. Roosevelt enjoyed dealing directly with Stalin and was apt to be impatient with Churchill's and Britain's imperialism. As a despondent Churchill wrote later: 'I realised at Teheran for the first time what a small nation we are.' That American anti-imperialism brought rewards; at first, the admiration of the colonial world. Much later, however, after the war, it brought its own burdens: as the British noted, not without a tinge of *schadenfreude*,[15] the Americans inherited many of the burdens and problems that the British empire had so far dealt with. The war would indeed prove to have been, as the British historian Alan Taylor remarked many years later, the 'War of the British Succession'.

Of course that Teheran agreement did not mark, to adapt Churchill's mellifluous phrase, the end of inter-Allied debates. It was not even the beginning of the end. But it was certainly very much the end of the beginning and set the framework not just for Allied debates during the remainder of the war but for those of the early post-war world. After all, by the time of the meeting, some of the outlines of victory had begun to emerge. North Africa had been conquered. The Allies had invaded Italy and accepted its surrender in July. In Russia, the Germans had suffered a major defeat with the surrender of their entire 6th Army at Stalingrad.[16] Eventual victory seemed certain.

In the Pacific, however, there remained eighteen months of bitter and remarkably cruel fighting. There were battles for key islands, the most important being Saipan, Iwojima and, even nearer to Japan, Okinawa. Almost everywhere, Japanese soldiers and even civilians preferred death to surrender. Americans in the Pacific and English or Indian soldiers in Burma could scarcely believe their eyes. From Saipan, for instance, came film clips of Japanese women and children jumping off cliffs and everywhere Japanese soldiers died by the hundreds in suicide charges. But the women had been told that Americans would rape, torture, murder, even eat them. And the soldiers not only preferred death to the dishonour of surrender, but some harboured similar fears about having their bodies end up in Allied cooking pots. In Burma in January 1944, men of the Royal West African Frontier Force did get some Japanese troops to surrender. The reason given? The Japanese 'believed African troops ate the killed in battle, but not prisoners. They feared that, if eaten by Africans, they would not be acceptable to their ancestors in the hereafter'.[17]

Within China, the situation was highly complex. For all the official emphasis on the united front of Nationalists and Communists, the reality was that, politically and militarily, there were two Chinas. The war was therefore in many ways a three-cornered fight among Nationalists, Communists and Japanese, with each of the three

Dowager empress Cixi, the last Qing ruler (1835–1900).

Bombardment of Canton during the Opium Wars, 1856.

此物出在浙江處州府青田縣數十成羣人嚐之化為血

水官兵持砲擊之刀劍不能傷現有示諭軍民人等有

能剿除者從重懸賞此怪近見官兵逐急旋即落水逃

人便食真奇怪哉

Chinese cartoon of devilish (fire-breathing) Europeans
during the Opium Wars, 1857.

Henry John Temple,
Viscount Palmerston,
British foreign secretary
and later prime minister
(1784–1865).

The Earl of Elgin,
British commander
in China in 1857
and 1859–60.

Anson Burlingame, US diplomat, then Chinese ambassador to the West (1820–1870).

US Secretary of State John Hay, 1900.

A boxer waving
a banner, 1900.

Count Nikolai Muraviev-
Amursky, Russian
governor of eastern
Siberia, 1847–61.

Count Sergei Witte,
who negotiated the
end of the Russo-
Japanese War
(1849–1915).

Japanese naval base in the Elliot Islands during the Russo-Japanese War, 1905.

US President Theodore Roosevelt presides over the signing of the Treaty of Portsmouth to end the Russo-Japanese War, 1905.

Nanjing massacre, 1937. Japanese troops using Chinese for bayonet practice.

Generalissimo Chiang Kai-shek of China, early 1940s.

Conferees at the 1943 Allied conference in Cairo
(*left to right*: Chiang, Roosevelt and Churchill).

General Marshall, Roosevelt's envoy to China in 1946–7.

Chairman Mao and
Stalin, 1949.

US marines
head towards the
beaches of Inchon
during the Korean
War, 1950.

Chinese and Soviet
leaders: Mao and
Khrushchev, 1958.

Chinese Red Guards shout
slogans and wave the 'Little
Red Book' during May Day
celebrations in Tiananmen
Square, Beijing, 1969.

Mao and US President Richard Nixon, 1972.

A demonstrator running with a stone in his hand as the army evacuates
Tiananmen Square, 1989.

Modern Shanghai, 2000.

fighting on two fronts against both the others. What the Americans continued to want was that Chinese leaders should concentrate on fighting the Japanese and develop a strong and united China to help stabilise East Asia. It was clear that for anything like this to happen, the established Nationalist government would have to be supported. Diplomats were constantly urging economic and social reforms on it, and some conciliation between the two Chinese sides. The trouble was that, ever since Pearl Harbor, it had become increasingly and uncomfortably clear to American and British observers, by no means only Stilwell, that the population in the major GMD-controlled areas was becoming disillusioned with Nationalist rule. Reports of Nationalist corruption and brutality multiplied, while the Communists in their own regions seemed to be becoming more, and more widely, popular. They might control the smallest of the three contending areas, but they were more organised and disciplined than the Nationalists and reputed to be more honest and efficient; also, perhaps, more effectively ruthless. The Communist-sponsored and -led anti-landlord excesses were clearly designed, among other things, to commit participating poor peasants to the cause for which they had done terrible things.

On the other hand, for Washington and London the basic difficulty remained: could Mao really be trusted to co-operate with Chiang, let alone the US? After all, the Chinese Communist Party had been established with much Soviet guidance, and had since the 1920s mouthed fairly standard anti-American critiques of imperialism and capitalism. To be sure, it had, especially after Pearl Harbor, become altogether more friendly to the USA. Yet the links between Moscow and the CCP were no secret. So that, in spite of the sometimes poor wartime relations between Mao and the Russians, the question was: would Mao really be able to develop his own policies, or would he, ultimately, have to yield to Soviet control, as Communist parties did almost everywhere else?

Nothing about China was settled by the time Roosevelt, Churchill and Chiang met in Cairo, where it was agreed that after the war Taiwan and 'Manchukuo' would be returned to the Chinese government; but American policy-makers remained deeply divided. The US was obviously committed to the Nationalist government. For Roosevelt, it remained one of the 'Four Policemen' of the post-war world and an essential building block of any post-war non-Soviet correlation of forces in the Pacific. It was also an outpost of modernity. Powerful American groups, not least missionaries, continued to see that government – 'Free China' – as representing American ideals. Yet gross corruption, stifling of dissent, and disorganisation seemed to be getting worse. Most senior Americans in China and even Washington became decidedly hostile to, and contemptuous of, the Chiang government. Washington and London were horrified by reports that as many as half a million Nationalist troops were just blockading the Communists, instead of facing the Japanese army. They were dismayed by reports that supplies of food and medicines in the Nationalist areas remained inadequate; that during droughts and famines corruption actually increased; and there had even been tussles between peasants and Nationalist soldiers about who should go hungry. Yet Chonqing tried to enforce higher taxes and conscription. Meanwhile, Japanese victories in the field further undermined Chinese morale. Thousands of Chinese deserted, or just died. No wonder American officials in China thought the likelihood of civil war after Japan's defeat was large and increasing.

In the first half of 1944, the Western Allied leaders as well as the Soviets focused all but exclusively on the prospects of an Anglo-American invasion of north-west Europe, and the relationship of that to events on the Russian front, to Anglo-American operations in Italy and possible landings in southern France. On 6 June D-Day duly came and brought the Allies successfully ashore in northern France. That almost coincided with major Soviet summer offensives. In the Pacific, some nine days after D-Day, two American marine divisions landed on Saipan.

In the meantime, Roosevelt sent Vice-President Henry Wallace to Chonqing. Wallace arrived in June – just as Anglo-American forces were invading Normandy – and during a Japanese offensive. Chiang agreed to allow American military observers to travel to Mao Zedong's headquarters in Yan'an and the first observers went in July. As more US officials and journalists visited the Communist areas, they developed a high regard for them. The more they saw, the more they were impressed by evidence that the Communists were actually fighting the Japanese, by reports of land reforms in Communist-controlled areas, and by indications of popular support. Such reports strongly suggested that the Communists were much more likely than Chiang to give China what it needed and the Americans wanted. At one point Roosevelt and the joint chiefs even discussed the possibility of arming the Communists, who would be better at fighting the Japanese.

At much the same time as the Wallace trip, the airfields that Chennault had asked for became ready and could accommodate the new American heavy bombers, the four-engined B-29s. In June 1944 came their first important raid, against railway yards in Bangkok, in Thailand, quickly followed by a raid on a steel works in Kyushu, in Japan itself, and then other targets. That triggered massive retaliation. The Japanese pushed forward in China to consolidate their hold on strategic railways which they used to drive south and west to seize Nationalist airfields and even threaten Chonqing. However, by the time the Japanese reached their objectives, the B-29s had been withdrawn. They were now stationed on freshly captured Pacific islands, from which they would be able to attack Tokyo itself. The Japanese response was to try to take back the islands. That, in turn, was foiled in a wild naval engagement in which the Americans shot down so many of Japan's poorly trained new pilots that the US Navy called it 'The Great Marianas Turkey Shoot'. The Japanese navy's attempts at reassertion finally ended in October 1944 in the Battle of Leyte Gulf, in the Philippines, where the Japanese lost three battleships, four carriers and six cruisers, not to mention hundreds more pilots.

In February 1945 came the greatest of the wartime four-power conferences, at Yalta in the Crimea. The context for its decisions was the prospective post-war balance. It therefore had to settle critical issues to do with Germany and Eastern Europe, as well as with the final military moves of the war in both East and West. Roosevelt for the first time set out starkly his (and therefore also everyone else's) framework for post-war planning. In the very first plenary session he said that 'the United States would take all reasonable steps to preserve peace, but not at the expense of keeping a large army indefinitely in Europe, 3,000 miles away from home. That was why the American occupation was limited to two years'.[18] The body-language of the principals is now irrecoverable and Stalin had certainly had harsh training in hiding his feelings behind a softly spoken manner, even a trace of humour. But to both him and Churchill the long-term implications must have been instantly clear, and they shaped European politics from the outset. If the Americans were going home, any East–West balance in Europe would have to have the consent, not just the reluctant acquiescence, of Stalin, the master of what would be the overwhelming military power in Europe. It would mean confirming what could anyway not be prevented: Soviet command of Eastern Europe from the Soviet border to the already agreed Soviet zone of occupation of Germany.[19] It would also require the urgent revival of France to help prevent Soviet dominance from extending to the English Channel.

Also, in spite of much post-war mythology, while it is true that Roosevelt was tired and even ill, he was not bamboozled by Stalin or anyone else. On issues concerning Poland and Eastern Europe he gave away nothing that he was in a realistic position to deny. He had other wishes, including still that promise of Russian co-operation in the final attack on Japan, always expected to be hugely difficult and probably with horrendous Allied (and, for that matter, Japanese) casualties. Stalin duly reiterated his promise to join in the war with Japan within three months of the German surrender. The meeting also effectively ratified what Roosevelt had pursued ever since Casablanca and Teheran. Japan obviously had to be occupied and its military power destroyed. But unless China could act positively, the North Pacific would be doomed to Russo-American rivalry, just as MacMurray had foreseen. So the paradox remained: even if China was secondary to the Allied war-effort, it was logical for Roosevelt to celebrate Chiang's role as the leader of one of the 'Big Four' Allies and an essential element of the post-war international structure. Celebration came strongly at the level of publicity, political demonstration and talk. Much of it was of course pretence. China's membership of the Big Four was not a tribute to China's greatness, still less to Chinese power. It was a means of preventing the Soviet Union from using its position in North-East Asia to extend its reach far into the Pacific and Central Asia.[20]

The conference also foreshadowed the creation of the new United Nations. That organisation, the coping stone of the new hoped-for global security system, and successor to the failed League of Nations, was created at San Francisco in a fifty-nation conference that lasted from April to June 1945. It was probably the most important of the plethora of international covenants constructed in and after 1945, even though its creators once again ignored, as the creators of the league had done, Thomas Hobbes's dictum about covenants without swords being mere words. The veto that the UN Charter gave to mutually hostile groups and states meant that no 'sword' could be constructed, let alone used, except against the weak and friendless. Still, China, with strong American support, became not only a founding member but occupied one of the five permanent seats on its most important decision-making body, the Security Council. That gave China veto power over the council's decisions.

Major inter-Allied difficulties remained, for instance about keeping Soviet co-operation. The president overrode Churchill's resistance to letting the Soviets restore the old Russian sphere of influence in North-East Asia. He believed, until his death, that Stalin could ultimately be persuaded to co-operate in bringing about a united but mainly Nationalist China. He got Stalin to promise to withdraw his troops from China within three months of the Japanese surrender, even though that would give the Chinese Communists three months to establish themselves in the Soviet-occupied areas. (In the event Chiang's people asked the Soviets to stay on, partly to help keep order and partly to look after the hundreds of thousands of Japanese soldiers who were now prisoners of war. When the Russians finally did leave, in May 1946, they took with them all the industrial equipment they could lay their hands on.) Even after Roosevelt's death, Stalin told the Nationalists that he would support their government as the sole authority in China. On the other hand, in return for sidelining the Chinese Communists Stalin demanded virtually complete control of Manchuria. When Chiang demurred, Moscow agreed to settle for control of Manchurian railways plus Port Arthur and Dairen, which would give him effective control anyway.

Roosevelt, who was starting to be increasingly impatient with Nationalist ineffectiveness, had wanted Stilwell appointed to command the Chinese Nationalist forces, while continuing to work for a more effective Chinese coalition government and military. But Stilwell returned home in frustration, and in November 1944 the president sent General Patrick J. Hurley to China as his special representative. Hurley told the Chinese that America would support only the GMD government. By then Mao still had some hopes for US lend-lease aid and knew about American unhappiness with Chiang's policies. Even more Western visitors had been to Yan'an and heard Mao's assurances that the Communists were working for a united front. So that, although the Communists by now had some 900,000 men under arms and were busy with radical reorganisation in the countryside, Hurley's report remained optimistic about future CCP–GMD cooperation. The American foreign-service professionals, on the other hand, thought he was clumsy, naïve and totally underestimated the determination of the Communists and the intransigence of the GMD. Perhaps too few of them understood that the White House had never had a 'China policy'. Roosevelt, like any other president, had an American policy for China, focused on American interests and constructed on the basis of US politics and opinion. The foreign-service officers in China could suggest no new way of dealing with the power vacuum in the Pacific that would follow the defeat of Japan and Germany and the looming withdrawal of America from overseas responsibilities.

MADAME CHIANG

One of the most remarkable figures in Chinese politics in the 1940s was Chiang's wife Meiling. A striking and imperious figure, she was a woman of brilliance and steely determination, hidden behind a doll-like, flirtatious style. She came to wield considerable influence inside China as well as in the USA, and was one of her husband's more effective ambassadors. Never more so than in 1943 when she made a highly publicised tour of the United States to rally support for the Nationalist struggle.

Meiling was born in 1897 to Charlie Soong, a former Methodist missionary and Bible publisher and a political ally of Sun Yatsen. She spent part of her childhood in Georgia, and then went to one of America's most prestigious women's colleges, Wellesley. She was therefore fluent in English. She was also elegant, quick-witted and tempestuous. She was the youngest of three Soong daughters in one of China's richest families. The eldest, Ailing, married into one of the country's wealthiest banking families, the Kung, and looked after the Soongs' money. The second sister, Qingling, married Sun Yatsen, the first president of the Chinese republic; and, as his widow, was allowed to join the ranks of the Communists on her death-bed. Meiling married Sun's successor, Chiang Kai-shek, giving her direct access to power, and allowing him access to the Soong fortunes. It was commonly said of these three women that 'one (Meiling) loved power, one (Ailing) loved money and one (Qingling) loved China'.

After Sun Yatsen's death, Chiang Kai-shek became leader of the Chinese government and married Meiling in 1927. The relationship was technically bigamous, since he had not actually divorced his first wife; but her family accepted the marriage after Chiang promised to 'study Christianity'. It was a strong alliance, if a stormy one, and was widely regarded as a marriage of convenience. Many years later, after Chiang was dead, she once remarked that they had never made love. Whatever the truth, Chiang and Meiling had no children, though he came to have at least two illegitimate sons by other women.

Probably her most important public role was as her husband's personal representative in foreign affairs. Within the US, especially, not the least of Chiang's diplomatic assets was the personality of the brilliant, imperious and beautifully seductive Madame Chiang. She became widely admired, especially during the barnstorming tour of 1943, when she was accorded the honour of addressing a joint session of Congress. She knew how to handle Americans, especially American men. She was not averse to using her personal charms for political purposes. One Western visitor wrote of her 'gift of permanent elegance. Sex appeal. Quick, feminine intelligence'. It was said that when she turned up at inter-Allied conferences, wearing one of her close-fitting gowns slit up the side, a gentle whinnying sound could be heard among senior officers. She almost certainly had an affair in 1942/3 with Wendell Willkie, who was expected to be the Republican candidate for the 1944 presidential election, both during his 1942 trip to Chonqing and that 1943 US tour.

Unfortunately, she also had a tendency to think that personal admiration could translate into political influence. As Owen Lattimore wrote later: 'The value and importance of Madame Chiang has been greatly exaggerated, especially by Americans.' Stilwell, who was no fool, found her 'Quick, intelligent . . . Wishes she was a man. Doesn't think deeply, but catches on in a hurry . . . Direct, forceful, energetic, loves power, eats up publicity and flattery . . . [Historically] the Chinese were always right; the foreigners were always wrong'. The major Western leaders also found her less impressive when she and Chiang were invited to the 1943 Allied conference in Cairo. Eleanor Roosevelt remarked that she wanted to help Mme Chiang 'as if she had been my own daughter'. Yet it was a daughter who brought along her own silk sheets when staying at the White House, and insisted that they be changed — up to several times a day — if she had as much as sat on the bed. Later, when she was in New York and the president invited her to the White House for lunch with Churchill, she declined in ungracious terms.

After Roosevelt's death his successor, Harry Truman, was even less sympathetic to the Nationalists, whom he regarded as thoroughly dishonest. After he left office he told an interviewer: 'They're all thieves, every damned one of them. They stole 750 million out of the billions that we sent to China. They stole it, and it's invested in real estate down in São Paulo and some right here in New York.' Perhaps not surprisingly, Meiling and the Nationalists banked heavily on Truman's defeat, and a Republican victory in the 1948 presidential election, and were again disappointed.

After Chiang's death she made her home in New York and passed her last years there in seclusion, dying in 2003 at the age of 106.

There was one element in all this that neither London nor Washington – and perhaps not even Moscow – fully appreciated. The single issue on which Nationalists and Communists in China saw eye to eye was hostility to the 'imperialists'. After the experience of 1942–4 no senior Chinese could seriously regard the United States, or the British, as reliable in the longer term, let alone as China's friend. The Anglo-American campaigns between 1941 and 1945 may have given China security from Japanese aggression. But that was a side-effect of a much larger design. Anyway, it came after decades of Western 'exploitation'. No one in China felt that they owed the Anglo-Saxons much gratitude. Even the CCP reliance on Moscow contained a cold element of TINA (There Is No Alternative).

In the first half of 1945, the European war drew to its close. President Roosevelt died, to be succeeded by his vice-president, Harry Truman.

American and Russian armies met in the middle of Germany. Georgi Zhukov's soldiers won the race with a rival army group to get into Berlin first. Adolf Hitler shot himself in his bunker, the last German troops and their allies were rounded up[21] and Germany collapsed. In mid-year came the final inter-Allied conference, at Potsdam, just outside the now partly destroyed German capital. Not only did Stalin find himself face to face with a new president but Churchill, too, left the conference halfway through, to be replaced as prime minister by his former deputy and now political opponent, Clement Attlee.[22] By the time the conference met, Truman's advisers saw Soviet claims in China as positively threatening.

There was also the urgent question of how to induce Japan to surrender without the likely bloodbath of an invasion. This was a serious matter for the new president. It would be inexcusable not to try to finish the war quickly. The American public would greet with a roar of fury anything that looked like needless delay. Large American casualty figures so near the end would not merely have the same result but could produce, Truman was told, a collapse of American military morale. It might even, in an extreme case, create a public demand that the war be ended at once, on any compromise terms. Yet an invasion of Japan seemed likely to incur hundreds of thousands of US casualties. There seemed to be a strong Japanese army faction that wanted the whole nation to go down fighting any invader. Truman must have sighed with relief when he learned, in the middle of the Potsdam conference, that the world's first atomic test had succeeded at Alamagordo in New Mexico. It seemed that atomic weapons could be available shortly. Truman mentioned the new weapon to Stalin, who was unsurprised. One or two scientists had for years kept him secretly informed about the atomic bomb programme.

So it might be possible to shock the Japanese into surrendering peacefully. But how? Truman was warned that, while 'Unconditional Surrender' was all very well, care should be taken with the special place of the Japanese emperor, Hirohito. Nothing must be done to undermine his authority to order Japanese forces to surrender without fighting or suicide. On 26 July the Potsdam declaration duly warned that Japanese forces would face destruction if there was no unconditional surrender. The emperor was not mentioned. In Tokyo there was confusion but no sign of surrender. On 6 August Colonel Paul Tibbets of the US 509th Composite Group took off from the island of Tinian and dropped an atomic bomb on Hiroshima. Two days later came another attack, this time on Nagasaki. On the same day the Russians fulfilled to the letter their promise to Roosevelt that they would enter the war against Japan within three months of the German surrender. They declared war and Soviet troops under Marshal Malinovsky started to move into Manchuria. In the meantime, Truman's new secretary of state, James Byrnes, brought to Potsdam a fresh form of words inviting Japan to surrender, while being able to keep a constitutional monarchy and the established dynasty.

On 14 August came the famous radio broadcast by Emperor Hirohito, announcing that Japan had to 'bear the unbearable and accept' Allied terms. Just before the broadcast a group of young army hotheads invaded the imperial palace to try to smash the recorded message. They were met by a senior general who simply said 'stop this foolishness' and 'follow the imperial will'.

On the same day the Soviets and the Chinese Nationalists signed a Treaty of Friendship and Alliance in which China accepted the promises made to Stalin at Yalta, including a Soviet naval base at Port Arthur. The Chinese would recognise the independence of Outer Mongolia, a likely precondition for it to become a Soviet satellite. In return, the Soviets recognised Chinese sovereignty in Manchuria and Xinjiang and agreed not to interfere in China's domestic affairs. It quickly became clear that the real Soviet objective was to keep the Communists and Nationalists at each other's throats and prevent the emergence of a strong, unified China. For the moment, they got their wish.

Within China, the Japanese surrender made Chiang briefly into a national hero. The Communists took advantage of the new situation and deployed across north China to compel the Japanese to surrender troops and weapons to them, not to the Nationalists. (In Manchuria, the Soviet troops also made a point, when they left, of leaving huge stockpiles of weapons, equipment and ammunition to fall into Chinese Communist hands.) But the Nationalists told Japanese commanders not to surrender to the Communists. Chiang's government even instructed the Japanese to fight off Communist troops, which they frequently did. In some places, local warlords used Japanese troops for their own purposes. At the same time, both government and Communist troops moved into Manchuria. The Americans occupied Shanghai, Canton and a couple of other ports, as well as Pusan in Korea. They also decided to give the Nationalists active help and transported entire armies of Nationalist troops by sea and air into northern and north-east China, so that it could be they to whom the Japanese would surrender. In addition, the Americans moved over 50,000 of their own marines into the region, to make sure that Beijing and Tianjin could be held in the event of a Soviet advance southwards. For everyone, managing the Japanese surrender was a huge enterprise. In addition to the 1.25 million men the Japanese had in China proper, they had another 1.75 million civilians there, and more soldiers in Manchuria. At least 400,000 of them landed up in Siberian prison camps.

The whole post-war situation was by now vastly complicated. The war had indeed been a single, global strategic problem. But as soon as the fighting ended, the problems of the Pacific and of Europe became once more substantially separate. For both the Americans and the Russians the overwhelmingly most important region to be dealt with was Europe. Germany itself was the key problem, since it remained the potential future power centre of the Continent. At the same time, 'security' meant very different things in East and West. For the Anglo-Americans, the aim was construction of strong international institutions. That was bolstered by the strong social-democratic trends in post-war Western Europe; by sympathy for the enormous Russian wartime losses; and by post-war anti-imperialist views that extended some sympathy to the Soviets, who kept loudly denouncing everyone else's empire. But for Moscow, national security meant more than the physical security of the Soviet Union against a future German or Japanese revival, or even American attack. It also meant the security of the party and of Stalin himself, and the elimination of opposition. Hence harsh party and police controls were re-imposed as soon as the fighting was over. Even Soviet soldiers freed from German prison camps were promptly sent to Soviet camps since they had been 'infected' by contact with the capitalist Western world. In Eastern Europe the Russians reorganised the states their armies had liberated, as a kind of *glacis* to protect the Soviet Union. Everywhere, compliant Communist governments were installed, by persuasion or force, giving Russia just the protective belt of 'friendly' (i.e. satellite) countries that the Western powers had reluctantly conceded to Stalin at Yalta. The US also, finally, set about securing the Western half of the Continent, which the Red Army had not reached. Within three or four years the politics of wartime alliance had been replaced by confrontation.

In retrospect, it is clear why Stalin and his advisers wanted the Soviet system insulated from the West. The internal contradictions of the capitalist world were sure to become more obvious. Capitalist economies would be mutually hostile, as Lenin had long held. They would not only be unable to co-operate, they would sooner or later go to war with one another. That would certainly include conflict between the British and Americans. All that would lead to revolutionary crises and future wars, at first among the capitalists, though the Soviets could also be drawn in. On 9 February 1946, in a famous 'election' speech, Stalin explained that World War II had been no accident. It had been 'the inevitable result of the development of world economic and political forces on the basis of modern monopoly capitalism'.[23] Six years later, in 1952, he repeated that 'the inevitability of wars between capitalist countries remains in force'.

None of this prevented Moscow from seeking reconstruction credits, or dangling before American eyes the possibility that the Soviet Union might join post-war organisations and international monetary arrangements. But the Russians made difficulties in a way, and on a scale, that seemed incomprehensible to most people in

Washington and London. The explanation came in one of the most famous diplomatic documents of the post-war era, the 8,000-word 'Long Telegram' from the US embassy in Moscow. In it, the diplomat George Kennan explained the underlying reasoning and principles behind Soviet policy.[24] He explained that it would be impossible to conciliate or pacify the Soviet Union, since its world view was dictated by domestic and ideological pressures much more than by foreign speeches or events. It would pursue autarchy – and expansion. It could not be reasoned with, only contained. Here were ideological and strategic realities that were highly unwelcome to America's more idealistic post-war planners, but the telegram became one of the basic documents of American Cold War policy.

For it was also clear that anti-Stalinism would require American leadership; and that these interests and that leadership would chiefly focus in the protection of Western Europe. Events there would shape the context for Pacific affairs as well. For the US, alone among the powers, had emerged from the war hugely strengthened. By the middle of 1945 America had the greatest navy and air force in the world. After the destruction of so much German, Japanese and Russian industry, the US also had roughly half of the entire world's industrial production, not to mention technological supremacy. Together with that came a currency not only dominant in the financial world, but one that quickly became desirable cash in most of the back alleys of the globe.

The major milestones in the change from fretful East–West alliance to Cold War hostility are well known. First came the increasingly sharp divisions between the Eastern and Western occupation zones in Germany. Until the end of 1947 Western attempts to secure Soviet co-operation continued through several futile foreign ministers' conferences and difficulties over Soviet behaviour not only in Europe but in the Persian Gulf. These differences proved insurmountable. The Soviet foreign minister, still Vyacheslav Molotov and never a hard man to dislike, kept saying 'no' so often that exasperated Western officials started to call him 'The Abominable No-man'. It was the US that clung longest to the mirage of co-operation, until two major

turning-points came in 1947. One was President Truman's announcement of 12 March of US aid to the Greek government in
its resistance to Communist insurgency: 'I believe it must be the
policy of the United States to support free peoples who are resisting
subjugation by armed minorities or by outside pressures'. It was a
complete reversal of the returning isolationism Roosevelt had feared.
That was followed by the Marshall Plan for European reconstruction,
which implied co-operation, even some economic integration, in
Europe. For that very reason, it strengthened Stalin's fears and his
sense that Soviet security required territorial extension and Moscow
control. The gulf between East and West widened through the 1948
Communist coup in Czechoslovakia, the Berlin blockade and airlift,
and the West German currency reform. These were followed by the
1949 formation of the North Atlantic Treaty Organisation, the
countervailing Warsaw Pact in Eastern Europe and the political
formation of a new West German state.

For the British and French, the Second World War had really lasted
from 1938 to 1949 and there was now a passionate longing for
security and retrenchment. Governments in London and Paris found
themselves under great pressure from every quarter to dismantle their
costly empires. No less important were pressures from the Americans.
Nevertheless, both tried to restore their old spheres of influence in the
East. The British recognised that India must become independent,
but otherwise they and the French tried to behave as if very little had
happened. There were odd incidents. In Hong Kong, for instance,
the moment the war ended and the former British colonial secretary,
Frank Gimson, was released after three years' Japanese imprisonment,
he simply ran the Union Jack up the Government House flagpole, and
on his own initiative re-started colonial administration as if nothing
had happened. In Singapore, members of the Singapore Cricket Club
returned to the island and immediately began settling their outstanding club bills, which had not been dealt with in the confusion of
Singapore's surrender three years earlier. Some members even settled
the bills of others who had not survived. The French situation was

more complicated. There was the bitter legacy of the 1940 collapse, on top of the disappointments of British-led appeasement before 1939. So now France's position in the world had to be restored on a basis very different from any kind of trust in the 'Anglo-Saxons'. It was possession of the empire that underpinned France's claim to be a global power and one of the victors of WWII. Post-war France thought that, in time, there should be a single French republic with the overseas territories 'an integral part of the national community', with overseas people having their own elected members in the Paris parliament and even adopting 'a French nature'. That notion of indissoluble unity was reiterated in the 1946 Constitution of the French Union.

The only trouble was that all of this was trying, Canute-like, to stem deeper tides of European and world affairs. The French and British publics were tired of overseas obligations and neither country could remotely afford to go on propping up the old empire. Even more important forces were in play. The British and French empires, like others before them, had for long been sustained not so much by force or even money, as by prestige, respect, their own superb self-confidence and the passionate conviction that they were doing good. Not only the facts but the manner of their wartime defeats had destroyed all that. The notion of empire now merely echoed with what Shelley once called 'the memory of music fled'.

At least equally important was that legacy of Woodrow Wilson's, the desire for national self-determination and independence in the colonial territories. The claim was much more than a matter of politics. It was a moral and emotional push for self-assertion on the basis of imprecise but powerfully felt identities of race, ethnicity and religion. It had almost nothing to do with the qualities of government. It was an assertion that 'our' group constitutes a 'nation' that has a right to be governed by one of its own people, not by someone 'else'.

Not that racial or ethnic separatism were new. The war itself had accentuated ideas of racial or cultural hostility, in newly virulent forms, not only in Japan but among almost all of Japan's opponents, whether American, British, Chinese, Dutch, Filipino or Indian. Much the same happened on the Russo-German front. It also became clear that many of the emerging international economic or ideological disputes were based on just such deeper differences. In 1951, for instance, that wise Frenchman Charles de Gaulle, ruminating on the struggle between Communism and capitalism in his day, wrote that 'l'opposition communisme-capitalisme est une apparance. Au fond de tout il y a l'Asie contre l'universe des blancs. C'est une querelle sans mesure'.[25] His views about France's 1945 return to Indo-China were even more acerbic. As he wrote in June 1954, France had 'repris contact, malgré tout le monde, avec une Asie profondément soulevée et qui, sous divers étendards, rejette désormais l'Occident'.[26]

All that dovetailed with the growing hostility between the West and the Soviet Union. On China's periphery there was, for instance, Vietnam. There, too, the Japanese had broken Western authority. During the war Vietnamese independence groups, and the anti-Japanese resistance, came to be headed by another of those tough, unyielding and Paris-trained leaders of Marxist liberation movements. He was Nguyen Ai Quoc (Nguyen the patriot), soon better known as Ho Chih Minh (He Who Enlightens). A deceptively mild-mannered man of mandarin stock, he was educated at the National Academy in Hue. He then knocked about Europe, became a Communist convert in the years before, during and after World War I and joined the French Communist Party in 1920. He went on to Moscow to be trained as a Comintern agent and by 1924 returned to China to organise exiled Vietnamese radicals. He became part of a proto-nationalist Vietnamese movement formed at Canton in 1920 and had contacts with Borodin, the Comintern's China man. In 1930 his group became the Indo-China Communist Party, dedicated to the overthrow of French rule and an anti-landlord revolution at home. When most Communist leaders were imprisoned in 1931, he escaped and was condemned to death *in absentia*. Later he studied in Moscow for three years and in China for another five, from 1936 to 1941. A coalition of Vietnamese nationalist groups was then set up in southern China, under the patronage of the Chinese nationalists. It was known as the Vietminh, or the league for the independence of Vietnam. It quickly came under the control of Ho and Vo Nguyen Giap, later the brilliant commander of Vietnamese Communist forces against the French and Americans. By 1944, though, the Chinese had become wary of the Vietminh, who established a 'liberated zone' in the hills north of Hanoi. They managed to get some weapons and goodwill from the US at a time when Roosevelt's plans for Indo-China were heavily influenced, not only by American anti-colonialism, but by the president's personal dislike of the Free French leader, General Charles de Gaulle. Towards the end of the war the Allies agreed that Vietnam north of the 16th parallel should be administered by the Chinese. But on 2 September 1945 Ho Chih Minh simply proclaimed Vietnamese independence under his Vietminh, making it independent of the Chinese, of Japan and notionally of France.

Vietnam illustrated a more general problem. Local nationalisms, however much they might differ in detail from one another, were all too likely to be linked to Communism. That was, after all, what the Comintern had been all about since the 1920s, as had the Communist wartime resistance movements. Everywhere, that decisively influenced Western policies. As Winston Churchill put it in his famous 1946 speech at Fulton, Missouri: 'in a great number of countries, far from the Russian frontiers and throughout the world, Communist fifth columns are established and work in complete unity and absolute obedience to the directions they receive from the Communist centre . . . Communist parties or fifth columns constitute a growing challenge and peril to Christian civilisation.'[27]

In the Pacific the Americans, the principal Allied victors, took sole charge of Japan's occupation. On 30 August General Douglas MacArthur arrived at Atsugi naval air station near Yokohama, to take over. It was almost exactly 100 years since Commodore Matthew Perry's 'Black Ships', the representatives of the 'universal nation', had opened up Japan. Indeed, Perry's flag had been carefully preserved at the US Naval Academy at Annapolis and was specially flown out to fly over the US battleship *Missouri* during the Japanese surrender ceremonies. Now, the very manner of MacArthur's arrival won him lasting Japanese admiration. Coming into a country with hundreds of thousands of desperate, furious and resentful soldiers with guns in their hands, he stepped off his plane alone, unarmed and without escort. It was a theatrical display of courage and gave him not just admiration but an authority he never lost during his stay. Which was probably just as well, for there was much to do: Japan had lost 2 million people in the war and 8.5 million were homeless. On his flight from Australia, the general explained that his Japan policies would be guided by George Washington, Abraham Lincoln, and God (possibly in that order). The Americans also quickly made clear that, in running Japan, they would work for a radical transformation of Japan into a democracy on the US model, disbanding the imperial army and navy in the process. They would also cut out the Russians, just as, in Europe, the Russians had cut the Americans and British out of participation in the affairs of Eastern Europe, and the Americans had cut the Russians out in Italy. In fact, Stalin asked several times for a role in the occupation of Japan, but Truman refused.

There were other factors. As things settled down, the Americans acquired a hugely important strategic base on Okinawa. By 1947 MacArthur brought in a new constitution for Japan, designed by American New Dealers and containing a strongly anti-military Clause 9. Nor could the US ignore the strategic position of Korea. The Americans only began to take real notice of it in 1942, when Korean exiles came wanting to help. The Nationalist leader in exile and future South Korean leader, Syngman Rhee, warned that if the Americans did not act, there might be another Communist state in Korea. The state department's old China hand, Stanley Hornbeck, pointed out that Korea would be 'of paramount importance to Soviet Russia and China' and that Communist Koreans were being trained in the Soviet Union. A state department paper even suggested that the Soviets might come to 'occupy a dominant strategic position in relation to both China and to Japan'.[28] So a US State/War/Navy Coordinating Committee gave thought to coming 'up with a proposal which could harmonise the political desire to have US forces receive the surrender as far North as possible, and the obvious limitations on the ability of the US forces to reach the area'. Two days after the Soviet declaration of war on Japan, with Russian troops pouring over Korea's northern borders, the Americans suggested a solution. On a hot 11 August in Washington two planners, Colonel Charles H. Bonesteel and Major Dean Rusk – destined to be secretary of state a mere fifteen years later – hastily drew on a map a dividing line between American and Soviet forces. It lay at the 38th parallel, leaving Seoul in the American half. The Russians accepted, and it was roughly that line which remained the border between South and North Korea.

That division, as so often in such matters, brought problems. The end of Japanese rule in Korea encouraged a wave of renewed nationalist and anti-Japanese fervour. In the north a hitherto unknown Soviet army officer took charge and at once set about creating a new Stalinist dictatorial state with its capital at Pyongyang. His name was Kim Il-sung, another of those remarkable figures whom the tides of history bring from the most obscure origins to supreme rule. A devious, secretive, ruthless fellow, he was born in 1912 in northern Korea, joined the Manchurian Communist Youth Association when he became eighteen and was soon a partisan leader fighting the Japanese. By March 1941 Kim and a surviving band of guerrillas fled to Siberia. The Russians recruited them into the Red Army, trained them in spying and sabotage, and used them as agents. By 1943 Kim was a Soviet major and from early in 1945 was intensively trained and briefed on Korean affairs. On Stalin's personal orders, the Russians brought him back to Korea to take charge of their northern zone. The country's significance being obvious, occupation would allow them to acquire just what the Americans feared: a dominant strategic position in relation to China and Japan.

American troops arrived in Korea a month after the Soviets declared war on Japan. Any quick reunification of the peninsula seemed sure to mean a Communist government so, knowing nothing about Korea or its people, they set up a military government for their southern zone with the help of Japan's remaining colonial officials. Eventually, they decided to support Syngman Rhee, the elderly anti-Japanese rebel, as the new leader of the south.

As the division of Korea into zones of Soviet and American control congealed, Kim Il Sung, the Soviet protégé who proved to be more Stalinist than Stalin himself, was installed as North Korea's leader. Once in Pyongyang, he began to rule with an iron fist. Almost immediately, the politics of the northern and southern zones started to differ so widely that what had been a mere demarcation line became a border between two separate Korean states. By 1947 the United States transferred the sovereignty of the south to the new Republic of Korea and less than three weeks later Kim created a 'People's Republic' in the north. Each side claimed to be the legitimate government of the whole of Korea.

In China, Chiang and the Nationalist government also had reason to be more or less satisfied. Japanese troops were leaving Chinese soil. The Russians and Americans had both given assurances of support for Chiang's government and its policies of dealing with the Communists. Chiang still had forces numbering rather more than two and a half million men. So the unification of China under Nationalist control seemed a real prospect.

What, then, would happen to the Chinese Communists? To understand Mao Zedong's rise to power after 1945, one must consider not only him but the post-war views of Joseph Stalin, the senior and dominant figure of the Communist world. Mao was more than just another politician. As Ross Terrill has written: 'There was a personal fire in him . . . He was certain of himself, and of the eventual triumph of his peasant army. That – beyond mere hunger for power – gave him a will of granite.'[29] As for ideology, half a century or more later there is a widespread belief that ideologies are irrelevant to practical politics. They stem from illusions or, more simply, pretence. That is not a view that any serious observer of international affairs could afford in 1945–9.[30] It is here, in the mixture of ideology and practical state interests, that the origins of the break-up of the great wartime alliance, and the beginning of the Cold War, can be found. The position of the Chinese Communists was awkward. Some of them, though not Mao, had toyed with the idea of American support. Not until well after Roosevelt's death did it become clear that

President Truman would stick to the Rooseveltian policy of support for the Nationalists. So could Mao Zedong hope for help from Moscow? Without it, the Communists were self-evidently too weak to fight the Nationalist government. Still, there seemed no alternative to some kind of reliance on the 'Motherland of Socialism' whose great leader, Stalin, remained convinced of the inevitability of capitalist–socialist clashes. It was a policy that Mao pursued as much in hope as in expectation.

For Mao, the situation after Potsdam was complicated. Naturally he did not feel bound by the new Soviet–American agreements. Yet Mao could see that, as things stood, there was certainly no alternative to reliance on Moscow. When the Japanese surrendered, the CCP assumed a right to liberate enemy territory, especially in the north – not to mention Japanese weapons and supplies.[31] The Communists were frustrated at seeing American marines come to disarm the Japanese, and even more so by those Japanese who were under orders to surrender to Chiang. It did not help that the Americans pointed out that orders requiring the Japanese to surrender only to Chiang had been agreed with the Russians and the British. In mid-August Mao refused Chiang's invitation to come to Chonqing for talks and continued to denounce both the Americans and the Nationalists, even though he had only about 1 million soldiers, or less than half of Chiang's numbers.

Before the end of 1945 Washington and London became aware that civil war between the Nationalists and Communists in China was much closer than they had hoped. But the American military reported that remaining Japanese troops could not be removed from China without American help; and if the Japanese were still there at the start of any Chinese civil war, both sides would try to use them. That would not only be disastrous, but would surely bring the Russians deep into Manchuria. So when Hurley acrimoniously resigned in November 1945, President Truman sent America's most distin-guished soldier and public servant, George C. Marshall, as his personal representative to move matters towards a Nationalist-

Communist settlement. With two provisos: he was to support America's wartime Nationalist ally, and he must on no account accept anything that might leave China under Soviet control. Indeed he should minimise Soviet influence. General Marshall, who had been Roosevelt's armed-forces chief of staff throughout the war, saw that Washington's hopes for a peaceful unification of China depended entirely on co-operation between, and compromise by, the two Chinese sides. That would be doubly difficult to secure as long as the US gave military aid to Chiang, but Truman was not prepared to abandon the Nationalist regime.

Marshall's mission began well. Nationalists and Communists accepted his rulings during the move of Nationalists troops into Manchuria, and in the first two months of 1946 the two sides worked out elements of a political/military settlement. In February both sides even agreed to troop reductions. All the same, armed clashes continued in many places. So did political intrigues, for the two Chinese sides had learned for decades to distrust one another. Marshall managed to raise aid money for China in the US. However, in April 1946, as the Russians started to withdraw from Manchuria and the Communists moved in, conflict resumed. There were on-again-off-again efforts to maintain a truce, while the Americans continued to think it essential to preserve Chiang's position. At the end of June, Washington announced a new agreement with the Nationalists on a cease-fire in Manchuria and the supply of large amounts of military aid. Not surprisingly Chiang, now believing that the US had no alternative to supporting him, decided on an all-out campaign to crush the Communists. Mao, seeing that the Americans would not abandon Chiang, ordered the start of an anti-American campaign. By mid-year Marshall could see that as long as US aid to the Nationalists continued, there was no hope for peace. So Washington accepted an embargo on arms to China and Marshall started to disengage US marines. Anti-Western feelings grew and there were attacks on Americans. By the end of October both Marshall and the US ambassador agreed, and Washington accepted, that further mediation was hopeless. A month later the marines finally left China and a month after that Marshall left as well, to become secretary of state in January 1947.

That was the background to further developments in China. It is true that Chiang's problems were numerous rather than precise. But the carelessness and inefficiencies of the Nationalist administration were on full display. There was serious mismanagement of finance. Inflation soared as the government resorted to printing money. Corruption and speculation increased, and there was a sharp rise in food prices. Taxation and requisitioning grew in rural areas while bureaucrats in the cities made themselves comfortable. There was much robbery and many scandals about the return to rightful owners of property that had been seized by the Japanese. In the Communist areas there was a fairly ruthless programme of land reform, including strong populist appeals to poor peasants who, together with all kinds of thugs, were given their heads in kangaroo courts or lynch-mobs, directed against local gentry or landlords. It was not a pretty scene and large numbers of people were killed. Not until the end of 1947 did Mao begin to restrain this mob rule.

As for Chiang, he seriously overestimated the extent to which the West would try to bail him out. He especially failed to understand two critical points. First, there was the basic geo-political fact that China was still very weak, still the object rather than a real subject of Allied policy-making. Second, he was seriously wrong in his estimate, not just of American intentions but of the uses and limits of American power. George Kennan, the Soviet expert, became head of policy planning in the state department and argued that China was not an industrial power, would not become one for a long time, and could therefore not threaten the United States or its essential interests. Truman understood that events within China were beyond the reach of American power and that China was anyway not high on the list of American national interests. The US might be prepared to use military power to protect Western Europe or the Middle East, but it was not willing to become engaged on the East Asian mainland.

Consequently, between 1947 and 1949 the chief focus of the Administration remained the reconstruction and protection of

Western Europe. In China, America invested little diplomatic and political capital. To be sure, much American opinion continued to regard the US as China's champion. But underlying strategic calculations had changed. Under Roosevelt, it had been that the Soviets were a potential threat to US interests, while China could not be; hence a revived Nationalist China could help contain Soviet influence and power. But Chiang's China had shown itself to be unreliable and ineffective. 'Containment' would have to come mainly from the US positions in Japan and Korea. Yet there remained much Congressional support for aid to Chiang, and criticism that the Administration's insouciance about the Chinese Communists contradicted the broader need to deal with Soviet imperialism, and the growing hostility in Europe and North America to all things Communist.

So Truman did from time to time help Chiang in minor ways: it was more important to conciliate Congress than to avoid irritating the Chinese Communists. But the Nationalists wanted more than Washington was willing to concede and moved closer to the Republican opposition in Congress. Chiang himself claimed that if he were eventually defeated it would be because the US denied him the aid he needed. He continued to believe that his Republican friends were bound to win the forthcoming 1948 presidential election after which the US would come to his rescue. When it was Truman who was returned to the White House, Republican critiques of the Administration's China policies became even less restrained.

As for the CCP, American officials had long ago forecast that civil war would increase their dependence on the Soviet Union. Mao had welcomed American diplomatic and military representatives during the war and he kept up connections with a few Americans later on. But in general, he came to resent and feel betrayed by them. He thoroughly distrusted General Marshall's efforts at mediation, especially when they came together with American help to Chiang's troop movements into Manchuria. 'It was the first time for us to deal with the US imperialists,' he said later. 'We didn't have much experience. As a result, we were taken in. With this experience, we won't be cheated again.'[32] But it was above all ideology, a particular view of the world, that convinced him that the US was the chief opponent of the Chinese Communist revolution. He came to regard himself as the legitimate heir of Marx, Lenin and Stalin and, after them, the leading Marxist-Leninist theoretician and leader of his day. More practically, he admired the Soviet industrialisation efforts and was not worried about its human costs, any more than he was worried in later years about the human costs of socialism in China. He thought that Soviet ideas could usefully be adapted to Chinese conditions. 'Democratic centralism' was just what he needed.

Together with that came, with him as with Chiang, that traditional incomprehension of China's real role in the world and a thorough failure to understand how America and its government functioned. Accustomed to his own style of governance, he seems genuinely to have thought that any pronouncement by senior Americans, whether odd Congressmen or even editorials, reflected the opinions of the White House and the president. Nor did he really accept that China might be less than central in the politics and strategy of the globe, or in America's perceptions; or the reasons why the United States might ultimately allow its ally, Chiang, to be ousted from power. After all, the Americans had intervened before, in the Boxer rebellion of 1900 and in Russia in 1918 in an effort to defeat the Bolshevik revolution. Why would they not intervene more forcefully to stop the CCP now? Here were ideas that Stalin encouraged, warning that a clash with the US might arrive suddenly, unbidden. By 1949 Mao thought, quaintly, that if the US did intervene against the Chinese Communist revolution and, in effect, seize China, 'the United States would possess all of Asia . . . [and] US imperialism could concentrate its forces on attacking Europe'.[33]

Against that background, the three years after the Japanese war were painful for the Chiang regime and its American supporters. At the time of Japan's surrender the Nationalist forces were twice the size of their Communist rivals. They had strong support from the United States in equipment, supplies and transport and held most of China including, once the Japanese had left, most of the major cities. Yet even with such advantages they managed to lose the now-inevitable civil war. They got wrong almost everything that could be got wrong, whether in administration or war. The economy, the currency and questions of inflation were mishandled, often grossly, while taxation and other government demands, as well as corruption, grew further. The government alienated large sections of the population, including the majority of the peasants. Too often, civil and military leaders alike displayed a combination of arrogance and incompetence. For instance, Nationalist commanders made virtually no attempt to fraternise with the locals in their areas of operations, and scarcely listened to local leaders. Even worse was the gross mishandling of currency reform of 1948. The reform produced not only misappropriation but inflation, to the point where the street value of money might halve in a day. Nothing could have been more calculated to produce popular distress and resentment. Meanwhile, the Communists won shoals of supporters with their programme of land reform.

In the field, the Nationalists allowed themselves to become badly overextended in ways that made them vulnerable to Communist tactics. In truth, Maoist 'People's War' only really worked in north China up to 1944. Military leaders like Lin Biao and senior political commissars like Deng Xiaoping preferred regular troops and regular mobile warfare. Chiang's generals still insisted on holding cities and neglected the areas in between, allowing the Communists to mobilise and organise the countryside, especially in the north and north-east. Before long, the Maoists owned Manchuria and the north. As Nationalist morale began to crack, desertions multiplied, arms and equipment were abandoned and losses led to further exhaustion. The Communists also received greatly superior grass-roots intelligence, demoralised their opponents and were increasingly able to arm and rearm themselves with American weapons and equipment taken from the Nationalists.

1948 was a story of continuing disaster for the government, with thousands of Nationalist troops deserting and other units destroyed, especially in Manchuria. Communist forces began to move from their northern bases down into central China. Nationalist morale and cohesion gave way further as it became evident that Communist strength was greater than the Nationalists or the Americans had understood. By the start of 1949 it was clear to almost everyone that the Nationalists were on the brink of collapse and whole divisions, even armies, began to desert or change sides.

When the Communists finally encircled Beijing early in 1949, the Nationalist commander surrendered with all his troops, rather as some Ming generals had surrendered to the Manchus in 1643/4. Again like those predecessors, he and others like him received honourable positions in the new regime. The Maoists entered the city in their captured American-supplied trucks, led by American-made tanks; while Chiang and the remnants of his forces retreated to the old pirate stronghold of Formosa (Taiwan), carrying whole museums of national treasures with them, but still claiming to be the true government of China, still promising to return and reclaim their country. But it was Mao who had the new flag of the People's Republic of China raised over Tiananmen Square on 1 October.

12

THE NEW EMPEROR

AD 1949 to 1976

A FEW WEEKS LATER, he was in Moscow. Communist Chinese rhetoric had for long been strongly hostile to the West, suffused with all the familiar verbiage about an American 'imperialism' and 'occupation' of China. As early as 30 June Mao announced his policy of 'leaning to one side' in the new great confrontation between East and West

By this time the Cold War divisions of the world had firmed up. The Americans, true to their traditions, viewed this as much in moral terms as in terms of power. That confusion of power and principle, of interests and morals, continued to be both the strength, and the Achilles heel, of US policy. It was also based on the assumption that no stressful foreign policy could count on American public support unless it was based on 'making the world safe for democracy'. It was no accident that President Harry Truman, in his inaugural address of 20 January 1949, spoke, as several of his predecessors had done, of America's objective as a world in which all peoples should be free to choose their own government. Or that the wise old British ambassador, Sir Oliver Franks, observed that Truman's new secretary of state, Dean Acheson, had 'come to believe that the United States had an appointment with destiny, from which there was no easy way out but for the nation to lead and bend its whole energies to ordering the world'.[1] President Eisenhower later echoed the same themes when he proclaimed that the defence of freedom was one and indivisible, and American policies were an extension of America's moral responsibilities.[2] Yet for all the rhetoric about ordering the world, the very scope and scale of American economic and political ascendancy meant that the US had perforce become something of a status-quo power: committed to 'containing' Communist power, to the support and protection of Western Europe and the new United Nations Organisation.

In the meantime, Stalin had transformed Eastern Europe into a series of Communist-ruled satellite states and this was the context for Mao's visit to Moscow, which lasted for two months. He had long wanted to meet Stalin, and Stalin's reaction to the Chinese visit, though businesslike, was at times effusive, even emotional. He mentioned his own past downgrading of the Chinese Communist Party and admitted that the CCP had been right to go its own way. 'I sincerely hope that the younger brother will one day catch up with and surpass the elder brother' and 'I do not like to be flattered by others. But I am often flattered. This annoys me. What I have said today, that is, that the Chinese Marxists have become mature, and that the Soviets and the Europeans should learn from you, is not flattering you. I am telling the truth'.[3] He conceded that he had made mistakes in dealing with China and apologised for having doubted Mao's ability to achieve victory. 'We know that we have made ourselves a hindrance to you . . . we may give you erroneous advice as the result of lacking understanding of the true situation in your country' and he went on to suggest that 'I hope that China will take more responsibility in helping the national and democratic revolutionary movements in colonial, semi-colonial and subordinate countries'.

He also demanded, and got, an excellent deal from Mao. Moscow secured Mongolian independence under Soviet guidance, the continuation of the Russian role in managing the Manchurian railway and Soviet basing rights at Port Arthur until 1952 (later extended to

1955). Mao also had to agree to forming joint-stock companies to develop the minerals of Manchuria and Xinjiang. All of which gave the Soviets an assured friendly power along that long and vulnerable Asian frontier. It also created a huge Sino-Soviet bloc, dominated by the USSR, to command the entire Eurasian land mass from Berlin to the Sea of Japan. Mao, too, got what he most wanted from the visit. On 14 February 1950 the Chinese and Russians signed a thirty-year Treaty of Friendship, Alliance and Mutual Assistance that was directed overtly against a Japan that was sure to revive in time, and by fairly obvious implication also against the United States. It made Soviet power into China's shield. Mao also received $300 million in long-term credits but no promise of military assistance, though Chiang on Formosa was talking about re-invading the mainland. The treaty was welcome in Beijing: it was the first time any Western power had undertaken to give China substantial financial, technical and other aid. It was also the first time that a major Western country had signed a political and strategic alliance with China.

It was therefore clear that the end of China's civil war would have dramatic effects outside as well as inside China. America's British allies quickly and pragmatically recognised the People's Republic on 6 January 1950, not least in order to safeguard their crown colony of Hong Kong. For the Americans things were more difficult. For one thing, in spite of earlier probes, Mao did not seem very interested in coming to terms. He would rather exploit American hostility as a rallying cry both at home and in the global Communist family; and claim, often meretriciously, the leadership of a number of revolutionary and national-liberation groups. American leaders noted that the Chinese Communists were not only behaving badly towards individual Americans remaining in China, but continued to be loudly hostile to the US in general. Resistance in Washington to any deal with them was so passionate that it seemed best to wait for tempers to cool before making any moves towards Beijing.

In any case, Chiang and his people had for years been recognised and supported as the legitimate government of China by the entire international community. On Formosa, they remained on Chinese soil, claiming still to be fighting the civil war. They were the government holding the 'China' seat at the UN. They were America's allies. It was not clear when, how and under what circumstances it would be proper, let alone wise, to transfer recognition (and UN membership) to the new, effective rulers of China without creating general suspicions that US friendships were unreliable.

For Truman, the situation was further complicated by fierce domestic criticism that America had 'lost China'. So in August the government published documents and papers showing that events there, and the results for Soviet power, had been beyond America's control. Nevertheless, in January 1950 the president reaffirmed the old Allied declarations of Cairo and Potsdam that Formosa was part of China. He added that the US would stay out of the Chinese civil war, and that while it would give economic help, there would be no military aid to the Chinese Nationalists. His secretary of state went much further. Dean Acheson was a quintessentially 'East Coast Establishment' figure. Tall, moustached, dapper and witty, a product of Yale and Harvard Law School, he was well able to handle the intellectual fisticuffs of his new post. He had served as under-secretary of state in Truman's first term and now recalled that he arrived at the state department 'just in time to have him [i.e. Chiang] collapse on me'.[4]

He understood that the new geo-strategic triangle in East Asia consisted of the US, the Soviet Union and China. In that context, he took a long view, though he knew that Mao had abandoned all hope of US co-operation. As Acheson explained only a few months after Mao's triumph: 'The very basic objectives of Moscow are hostile to the very basic objectives of China.'[5] Even after the outbreak of the Korean War in mid-1950, the US National Security Council continued to think that America's foremost objective in Asia should be to detach China from its Soviet alliance.[6] In the meantime, Acheson thought, the collection of Communist power in East Asia did not actually threaten the security of the USA, whose defensive perimeter did not include China or Taiwan or even, by seeming implication, South Korea.

Acheson was attacked at home, preposterously, by Senator Joseph McCarthy, chairman of the Senate Permanent Subcommittee on Investigations. McCarthy accused him of not just being 'soft on Communism' but very likely a hireling of the Kremlin. Acheson saw much further than his populist accusers. His view was quite consistent with the principles of the old 1946 Kennan analysis: if China could be prised loose from the Soviet alliance, 'containment' of the USSR would score a major success.

Therefore, while the Americans wanted to continue to protect Chiang, the new realities would have to be recognised; but how could relations be established with the victorious Maoists? Especially since Mao was wary, well aware that US policy would try to divide him from Stalin.

Barely half a year after Mao's triumph that entire question of recognition, and much else, became irrelevant. On 25 June 1950, large and well-armed North Korean armies invaded South Korea. The Korean situation had for some time been messy and dangerous. Leftist dissidents launched, and lost, a bloody rebellion in the South. But the key question for the North and China was: if we attack, what will America do? Would conflict spread? Washington had accepted the Communist victory in China and the Sino-Soviet alliance. Why would Washington now get excited about the Korean peninsula? In March 1949 the American commander in the Pacific, General MacArthur, publicly placed Korea outside the American defence perimeter. Later that year Truman withdrew all US military forces from there. More impressive still, Dean Acheson, speaking at the National Press Club in Washington, explained that the West's defensive perimeter 'runs along the Aleutians to Japan and then goes to the Ryukyu [islands]' and from there 'to the Philippine Islands'.[7] That excluded Korea. He added that if there were attacks elsewhere it would be for 'the entire civilised world' under the UN to help out the local resistance. It was exactly the kind of offshore strategy that Presidents Eisenhower and Nixon were also to use later. No wonder the Soviets, the Chinese and even Kim Il-sung were astonished that the US, after not fighting for China, would go to war over a small tongue of land poking out into the Sea of Japan.

In any event, Kim Il-sung persuaded Stalin to agree, cautiously and reluctantly, that he could try to take over the South. Kim said Communism would gain a huge strategic victory, the US would not intervene and he could anyway occupy the South before any intervention could take place. Stalin was attracted by the idea of a united and Communist Korea, not to mention Soviet access to Korean warm-water ports. Still, he said, Kim would have to rely on help from Mao if things went wrong. He sent arms and advisers, including three Soviet major-generals, but that was all. In Beijing there was hesitation; but Mao, the combative revolutionary roman-tic, wanted violence, blood and for China to display Communist solidarity. He overrode dissenting views and seconded a few battle-hardened Koreans from the Chinese People's Liberation Army (PLA) to help the North Korean attack.

For the West, the danger was obvious. Not just for Japan and the Pacific balance, but in Europe as well, there were fears that the Korean offensive was just a prelude to a wider assault on the non-Communist world. Truman at once sent US forces to help the South. Within days the UN Security Council voted that members should help South Korea. The Soviet delegates, in a monumental diplomatic misjudgement, were not present to veto the US proposal. A week later, still without Soviet participation, the council established a UN expeditionary force for Korea. That gave South Korea's defenders the imprimatur of a UN banner. Twenty other countries sent troops to help the US.

Truman did more. For his generation of leaders one of the basic lessons of international relations was the Munich conference of 1938. Then, Czechoslovakia had been abandoned to Germany in the interests of peace. Now, everyone thought they understood that failure to resist aggression would only mean resistance in worse circumstances later. It was one of the few points on which successive Democrat and Republican secretaries of state, Dean

Acheson and John Foster Dulles, entirely agreed. It followed that if Communist power was to be contained, it would have to be contained around the entire Communist periphery, in Germany, in the Middle East, in South-East Asia as much as in Korea. Kennan had been right to argue, as early as 1945–6, that there would be constant Soviet probes of the periphery of the non-Communist world. This new conflict extended Cold War concerns from Soviet and pro-Soviet behaviour in Eastern and Central Europe all the way to the Yellow Sea and the Western Pacific. Korea was clearly just one more probe of Western boundaries and resolve. So, as well as sending American troops to Korea, Truman moved the US 7th Fleet to the Taiwan Straits, to prevent an attack from the Chinese mainland on Taiwan. He declared that any Communist occupation of Formosa – and destruction of what America still recognised as the legitimate Chinese government – would be a threat not just to US forces but to the entire Pacific area.[8]

For Mao, the situation now looked dangerous. Was America trying to reverse the verdict of the Chinese civil war? The fears deepened when Chiang, a short month after Truman's announcement, offered the Americans 33,000 troops for the Korean campaign. Developing American strategies underlined these fears. The South Koreans and Americans were driven back to the south coast, around the port of Pusan, whereupon MacArthur staged a landing 200 miles behind the enemy lines, cutting their lines of communication and supply. Within two weeks the Americans killed or captured half the North Korean troops and drove the remainder back to their starting lines along the 38th parallel. Were the Americans, the Chinese wondered, about to try to reunite Korea by force? And establish American power on the very borders of, or even inside, China's chief industrial base in Manchuria? In spite of several Chinese warnings, the Americans did drive all the way north to the Sino-Korean frontier and MacArthur made his own unauthorised arrangements with Chiang. He said openly that the war should be taken into China itself. The result was that 300,000 Chinese, carefully labelled 'volunteers', to avoid the notion that China was making war on the United States, crossed secretly into Korea. They achieved total surprise and threw back the Americans and their allies. The war went on, though General Omar Bradley in Washington had tried to reassure the British: 'We all agree that if the Chinese Communists come into Korea, we get out.' Finally, in 1953, the two sides achieved a cease-fire line that became a frontier virtually along the original border.

The war may have ended in stalemate, but its consequences were far-reaching for everyone.[9] Mao had helped to begin the war even though China needed few things more than peace and reconstruction after the turmoil of the previous decades. Instead, he aroused twenty years of American hostility. Before the war, he had been on the brink of occupying Formosa, which he could probably have done without much difficulty. Now Taiwan was a formal ally of the United States. The war had been a godsend for Mao's old enemy, Chiang Kai-shek. Stalin had probably hoped to embroil Mao against the West and to win a cheap Communist victory. Instead, he found himself in a long, world-wide struggle against a more heavily armed America.

The results were particularly dramatic for Japan, which became an essential strategic and economic base for the United States. Supplying American needs in Korea was a major trigger for Japan's entire post-war economic revival, since American military spending, together with billions in economic aid, was the fuel for what later became the Japanese economic 'miracle'. No wonder that some Japanese called the war their economy's 'divine wind' (kamikaze), in memory once more of the violent storm that had wrecked that Mongol invasion of Japan centuries earlier. In addition, in September 1951 the Americans finally signed the peace treaty with Japan that formally ended the Pacific War. Six months later they ended the occupation of Japan as well. Even rudimentary Japanese defence forces were created in the early 1950s. For Koreans that outcome was bitter, since post-1945 relations with Japan remained blighted by memories of earlier Japanese occupation.

For Washington itself, the Korean War produced one irresistible temptation and three powerful conclusions. The greater the war's implications of a global contest between irreconcilable ideologies, the greater the temptation and need to interpret the conflict in moral terms. After Korea, that conjunction became even more powerful. The first conclusion was that the Chinese Communists must now be regarded as equal partners with Moscow in a world-wide Communist alliance; one with considerable ideological dynamism, and with friends and supporters in most parts of the world. The Soviets had therefore won a huge victory in China, adding a vast country to a united, even monolithic, Communist bloc. While America, Britain and France had been busy consolidating the Western zones of occupation of Germany, fending off Stalin's challenge to the Western position in Berlin and to pro-Western governments in France and Italy, the Communists had successfully struck the West in the rear, in East Asia.

Secondly, the war triggered massive US rearmament and militarised the whole of 'Containment'. Until 1949/50 the Cold War was centred in Europe and Allied forces in Germany were, under the new umbrella of the North Atlantic Treaty Organisation (NATO), deployed to guard against an assault by Soviet tank divisions across the North German Plain. In the same year came the first Soviet atom-bomb test, followed by the extension of an American 'nuclear umbrella' over Western Europe. Then, in 1953, came the development on both sides of yet more destructive thermonuclear (fusion) bombs. Not only that, but two months before the North Korean offensive the president had received the famous National Security Council planning document 68 which spoke of an imperialist, untameable and inherently aggressive Soviet Union that had already subjugated China, and had Europe next on its agenda. The document, inspired by the views of George Kennan, was written by Paul Nitze. He was a businessman rich enough to be able to devote his life to public service, serving under every president from Franklin Roosevelt to, eventually, George Bush and becoming one of America's wiliest arms-control experts.[10] For him and others, Korea further blurred the boundaries between an extension of Communist power by inter-state aggression and one by domestic changes or civil war, as had happened in China. It even made abruptly clear that the US had inherited Japan's geo-political burdens in the North-East Asian region. As Kennan himself commented, 'It is an ironic fact that . . . we have fallen heir to the problems and responsibilities the Japanese had faced and borne in the Korean-Manchurian area for nearly half a century . . .'[11]

Thirdly, the war vividly demonstrated the limitations of using military power and the risks of wider conflicts. Most particularly, it was evident that the United States must never again be involved in a land war on the Asian mainland, and especially not against China. It was a conclusion that would largely determine the outcome of a very different American war, fifteen years later, in Vietnam.

For the People's Republic, the Korean war had shown that the new China was not to be trifled with. The alliance with the USSR and the partial and costly successes of that war had, between them, demonstrated that a new era in China's long history had indeed begun. After 100 years of turmoil, China had acquired a new, tough and ruthless government, once more highly centralised, determined to re-establish a strong unitary state after a century of 'shame and humiliation'. It was ruled by a trinity of the party (the most important), the People's Liberation Army and the government. The three structures were not separate and had a broad base. There was a hierarchy of committees and controls, culminating in a tiny leadership group with, ultimately, a single imperially dominant figure in charge. To be sure, when Mao came to power the leaders of the Chinese Communist Party (CCP) had given very little thought to how they might actually administer China; and large numbers of old officials, possibly 2 million, were at first left in place with all their talents and experience.[12] But it soon became clear that membership of the CCP was now the only path to advancement, even security. Military leaders were invariably also members of the party and quite often would serve as provincial administrators. The CCP, which in 1947 claimed to have some 2.7 million members, grew by 1959 to 14 millions.

There was great stress on mass organisation, with indoctrination through training programmes at all levels, with the pervasive presence of the secret police and security services safeguarding everything against nationalist remnants, unreliable elements and the ever-present dangers from abroad. The whole was further sustained by thought control. The bottom line was party dominance, with party cadres in command of everything and cruel national campaigns against any evils of thought and conduct. Thought reform was itself a mixture of appeals to idealism, of propaganda and a judicious admixture of terror.[13] It was a continuing 'campaigning' style of social development, with the whole apparatus of the state, and popular masses, being focused from time to time on dealing with selected target groups, notably the 'bourgeois' or so-called 'rightists'. That process began almost immediately with mass arrests and executions of undesirables. The combination of class struggle and the airing of local grievances had begun in 1946 and continued strongly in the first four years of Communist Party power. Western estimates suggest that large numbers, possibly up to two and a half millions, were killed in this process of land reform, violent class politics, and the erosion of family pieties and cohesion. The result, as always when 'freedom' means social fragmentation, left individuals without the old family support and increasingly reliant on the state. Outsiders, Christians, Moslems, Buddhists were brought under state control and foreign missionaries were once again either expelled or gaoled.

The new government moved to collectivise agriculture, not only for ideological reasons but because of its commitment to self-sufficiency and fears about uncertain food supplies. The effect was to politicise control of the countryside and the peasants under a new, largely self-selected, local élite of ambitious party cadres. That further increased rural China's dependence on the state. For instance, there was a vast new grain monopoly that regulated growth, prices and distribution. Inflation was met by tax increases and, as early as 1950, the establishment of firmer central economic and monetary controls. Not even language was neglected. Partly to promote literacy, the government simplified the beautiful but complex pre-1949 style of Chinese writing and resolutely pushed the replacement of local dialects and even languages by the new centralising language of Mandarin, which had originally been only one of several dialects. As the Europeans had discovered for themselves in the eighteenth and nineteenth centuries, few things unify a people more than standard dictionaries and a common language.

The nation-building effort also meant modern industry and modern education and skills. That relied, in the first instance, on the heavy industries that the Japanese had created in Manchuria, but then on Soviet help and advice in industrial construction. To be sure, in 1945/6 the Russians had taken away maybe half of Manchuria's industrial equipment. Nevertheless, China now depended strongly on the Soviets for help with industry, infrastructure development, technology, communications and trade. Soviet influence was also strong in town planning and higher education, with concentration on scientific training and the establishment of a Soviet-style system of higher education – and the dispatch of thousands of Chinese students to the USSR. For some years the Russians behaved with considerable generosity. In addition to granting China major credits, they sent large numbers of technicians, and vast amounts of technology and blueprints, especially to help build and run Chinese industries. In 1955 they not only evacuated Port Arthur but transferred to Beijing the Soviet share of the joint-stock companies formed to exploit Xinjiang minerals. It is true that Soviet aid also meant Beijing's acceptance of Soviet political leadership. Still, starting in 1954, many thousands of Soviet industrial experts came to China, helping to build China's industries, with special emphasis on investment in heavy industry. Naturally much of what was done was copied wholesale from old Soviet models.

There was help in all kinds of military matters, including the dispatch of advisers. That continued after the 1953 armistice, when China's wartime losses meant that it needed even more Soviet help for the People's Liberation Army. Around 1955 Mao seems to have decided to build his own atom bomb and by 1957 Moscow even secretly agreed to help this embryonic nuclear-weapons programme and to send a prototype atom bomb. In the meantime, the Chinese were very much aware that the Russians were their only protection against any American attack, something to which they were acutely sensitive after the Korean War, which the party used to destroy pro-American groups, especially among intellectuals.

In no ancient society, set in its ways and habits, are the effects of changes, even ones as seemingly sweeping as these, quite as simple or clear-cut as they look at first sight. The revolution was a decisive step in China's adaptation to Western ideas and practices. Yet the country also remained oddly unchanged from its condition centuries earlier, for instance during and after the decline of the Ming dynasty. The Marxist-Maoist insistence on the unity of theory and practice fitted almost seamlessly into the traditions of Confucianism. Chinese people were still poor and frugal, afflicted by turmoil, and there were again – even more so – arguably too many of them. There was even a fresh surge of population growth, strongly encouraged by Mao, who believed it would make China stronger.

Society still relied not on the individual but on the collective to decide what should be done or even thought. The revolution itself carried many echoes of the imperial past. There were intriguing parallels between the 'times of troubles' that had preceded the rule of Qin Shi Huangdi, of Sui Wendi, certainly of Hongwu and of the Qing, and the 'time of troubles' that had afflicted China for the first half of the twentieth century. If, in 1949/50, the new regime killed many hundreds of thousands of people, it was not notably more bloodstained than previous changes of imperial regime had been. It was also clear that a new Mandate of Heaven had been conferred on a leader the nature of whose power made him, in short order, a new emperor in all but name. The cult of Mao, which soon developed and grew to monstrous proportions in the 1960s, was in many ways just another version of the cult of the old emperors: everything came to depend on his will, including the fate of even the most eminent favourite. Confucian teachings about the dutiful subordination of the individual still allowed the supreme leader to do outrageous things. Once again, any challenge to the emperor's authority might mean death.

In policy terms, too, the new regime displayed much of the old determination to conquer nature and the rivers – as in the 'Three Gorges' project for damming the Yangzi – the same ruthless disregard for life in the pursuit of 'higher' ideological and social aims, the same tug-of-war between outward- and inward-looking policies. The desire to learn and use foreign ideas and inventions ran once again in parallel with the old distrust of foreigners who had now spent a hundred years exploiting China and would, if they could, go on disturbing the Chinese order.

There was also, albeit in a somewhat new guise, the old desire to re-establish the ideal coincidence of China's culture and territory. That, underpinned by simmering resentments about the wrongs China had suffered, meant a fierce determination to reclaim all the lands that had once been under Chinese control. Of course it meant 'reunification' with Taiwan. It also meant a determination to hold Tibet and quash any sign of separatism, perhaps for strategic reasons as much as for Chinese nationalist ones. Tibet may have been, and remained for the West, a land of romance and mystery. Yet, with the exception of the period 1900–30, it had for some centuries been, if not part of China, at any rate in considerable measure under Chinese influence, at times even authority.[14] Such considerations led to the October 1950 invasion of Tibet, and the campaign of 'liberation' that followed. The same impulses meant, sooner or later, claims on the northern borders with the Soviet Union. That involved the return of some lost lands and a strengthened hold on regions like Xinjiang with its oil and minerals, even though no Chinese national administration had really governed there since 1911 and by 1950 Xinjiang had closer ties with the Soviet Union. There was tough repression of minority ethnic and Moslem groups especially, later on, around the nuclear development and testing region. Large military detachments were stationed in Xinjiang, which was also used as a dumping ground for

MAO ZEDONG'S PRIVATE AFFAIRS

The more Mao became the dominant, unchallenged leader of his party and country, the more imperial he became in his attitude to women and sex. He seems to have groped for something like the immortality of which (as noted in chapter 1) Daoist manuals of the eastern Han period had spoken and which connected that search with having sex as often, and with as many women, as possible.

Mao seems to have striven for the same kind of thing. Throughout his life, according to his doctor, he was intensely interested in many varieties of sex and his own potency, having had his first sexual experience as a teenager with a pretty, twelve-year-old village girl.

He also attracted deep and lasting affection. His third and last wife Jiang Qing, for instance, had had a stellar theatrical career in Shanghai even before they met – probably in Yan'an in 1939 – and seems then to have been deeply in love with him almost for the rest of his life.

But he also needed time to retreat from politics and to relax with simple women for brief encounters when he felt like it. Once in power, he was constantly surrounded by groups of young women. He had a voracious appetite, especially for young and innocent ones, though it did not matter if a woman he wanted was married. No one was forced, but they did not need to be. The women were almost always willing and the husbands of those who were married don't seem to have objected. In fact, they were often promoted. The women were, of course, carefully screened before coming anywhere near Mao, among other things to make sure that they were properly filled with admiration of the great man and an almost religious wonder at the huge honour being done to them. One remarked: 'The chairman is such an interesting person. But he cannot tell the difference between one's love of him as a leader and love of him as a man. Isn't that funny?' Perhaps that is why a number of them seem to have offered to bring along their younger sisters for his (and their) pleasure.

Yet he often treated his women with callous ruthlessness. He had some unusual personal habits. He never cleaned his teeth, merely rinsing them, in peasant fashion, with green tea. The result was that they often looked as if they were covered in green paint. He usually refused to see a dentist and by the time he reached the age of seventy most of his back teeth had fallen out. Moreover, once he came to the old imperial residence in Zhongnanhai in Beijing, he ceased to wash, merely allowing himself to be rubbed down with hot towels. Which meant, among other things, that his genitals were never properly cleaned; he merely announced grandly that 'I wash myself in the bodies of my women'.

Though he quite early contracted a lesser venereal infection, he refused to have it dealt with, caring nothing about passing it on to his partners. 'If it's not hurting me,' he said 'then it doesn't matter.' He remained a carrier until the end of his life. Yet for most of the women, a connection with him was a matter of vast pride and status, and to be infected by him was itself a badge of honour. They claimed to derive a variety of pleasures from him. Especially in his later years, he indulged in Daoist sexual practices such as withholding his own ejaculation, allowing him to go on and on while deriving satisfaction and renewal from his partners' reactions and secretions.

In other ways, too, his habits with them were imperial. He had a special large wooden bed made for him – with one side higher than the rest to cater for his sexual exploits – that was carried on his private train and set up wherever he was. It was even airlifted to Moscow when he was there.

Especially when in Zhongnanhai he spent much time in bed – as often with piles of books as with a woman – and might not dress for several days at a time. But twice a week dances were organised, with a room just off the dance floor, where his huge bed was installed and where he could 'rest' – often with young women he had just danced with. And there was a similar room, opulently furnished, just off the Great Hall of the People, to which he could withdraw.

large numbers of criminals who could populate an archipelago of forced-labour camps. There and in Mongolia there was a steady influx of Han Chinese. By the mid-1950s only about 15 per cent of the 7.5 million people of Inner Mongolia were Mongolians. All of these efforts had the backing of a refurbished People's Liberation Army of some 2.5 million regulars with, quite soon, a professional officer corps.

On the whole, then, the Korean War and the new Sino-Soviet alliance did establish China, for the first time in modern history, as a major player in its own right on the broader international scene. China had become a major partner in a solid anti-Western Eurasian bloc. It claimed an additional role: the support and even leadership of revolutionary forces in Asia and beyond. In 1954 Zhou Enlai announced China's Five Principles of Peaceful Coexistence – mutual respect for sovereignty and territorial integrity; mutual non-aggression; non-interference in one another's internal affairs; equal and mutual benefits; and peaceful coexistence. But some Western opinion chose to misinterpret it as merely underlining China's vocal support for colonial revolutions, with China itself a model for such liberation.[15] Fairly obviously, these views heavily contributed to the desire, which China shared with all other major states, ancient and modern, to dominate, if not control, its own periphery.

The new government brought a new turn in yet another ancient cycle. From at least the time of the Tang (618–907), certainly the Yang (1279–1368), the Ming (1368–1644) and the Qing (1644–1912), the advent of a new dynasty had been preceded not just by imperial weakness but by foreign disregard, even contempt, for China's weakness. Also in each case the assertiveness and power of the new dynasty brought fresh foreign respect for its views and interests. So it was again now. That conjunction of Chinese policy and revolution in the Asian colonies confronted the West in general, and the US in particular, with painful choices. The Americans very much retained their strong anti-imperialist traditions. There had long been heavy pressure on the British to give independence to India, on the Dutch to 'free' Indonesia, and on the French about the future of their empire. There would consequently have been confusion after 1945 even if the Americans had been sure what should actually be done with ex-colonies like India, Vietnam or Hong Kong. To be sure, the Indian sub-continent was partitioned into independence by 1947, at Moslem insistence and after vast bloodshed. As for Hong Kong, the state department had long wanted to have the British hand the colony over to Chiang's China. In 1941 the suggestion was that Hong Kong be sold to China with the US Treasury meeting the cost. In 1943 Roosevelt said it should be handed over as a gesture of goodwill. At the 1945 Yalta conference he suggested to Stalin that it should become a free port. In the event, the British disconcertingly just took it back.

Nowhere were these choices more important than in Vietnam. There were difficulties about returning it to the French after the Japanese surrender, but in practice there seemed no alternative. Growing friction ensued between the restored French colonial authorities and the Communist/nationalist Vietminh of Ho Chih Minh, culminating in an armed insurgency led by Ho and Vo Nguyen Giap. For the Americans, the dilemmas were clear. Ho and Giap were getting decisive help from China, and would get more as time went by. Furthermore, it had become axiomatic among Western governments that almost no coherent Communist groups or parties existed anywhere that were not allied with or subservient to the Soviet Union. By the time Truman left office at the beginning of 1953 these considerations produced the domino theory: the idea that if one South-East Asian country fell, others would be toppled over in their turn. On the other hand, if Indo-China was critical, and if the trouble there was ultimately caused by China, America might have to tackle China itself – which was simply not possible after the Korean experience. It might be true that, in the long term, Vietnam could revert to its traditional fears about the China threat, while China and Mao could harbour quite similar fears about the Soviets. But it was the domino theory that seemed immediately relevant to the obvious energy of Communist movements around the world.

As Washington saw it, therefore, whatever the historic suspicions between China and Vietnam, the Vietminh were now controlled from Beijing and therefore ultimately by Moscow. And a Communist/nationalist alliance from Mosow, via Beijing, into Vietnam and beyond to the growing Communist groupings in South-East Asia could pose strategic dangers of the first order. Yet opposing the Communists in Vietnam, and defending French Indo-China, flatly contradicted American anti-colonialist principles. Furthermore, although the French formed their three colonies of Laos, Cambodia and Vietnam into 'Associated States' within the French Union, they were obviously not independent; whereas making them independent and sovereign could hardly be done without also granting sovereignty to France's North African possessions of Morocco, Tunisia and Algeria. By 1950 the US administration cut this Gordian knot and decided that Indo-China had simply to be kept non-Communist. That meant supporting France in its war, but at the same time urging the grant of independence to follow.

Wise or not, dealing with the Indo-Chinese Communists proved enormously difficult and expensive. The Americans gave massive aid to the French: by 1952 they were covering three-quarters of the cost of the war. The French sent out one of their most brilliant commanders, the tall, hawk-nosed General de Lattre de Tassigny. But he was a sick man and the others were much less able. Towards the end John Foster Dulles even threatened direct American intervention, declaring that 'the imposition on Southeast Asia of the political system of Communist Russia and its Chinese Communist ally by whatever means would be a grave threat to the whole free community'.[16] But by this time, much had changed. Washington found itself alone when allies, especially the British, refused to join in. China was not keen on another direct confrontation either, fearing another war with America so soon after the Korean armistice of 1953.

As has often been said, a guerrilla army wins as long as it can avoid losing; a conventional army is bound to lose unless it wins decisively.

Yet there is no essential ground on which the guerrilla army can be pinned down and worn out. The French not only suffered from that basic difficulty but made fundamental strategic errors. They had nowhere near enough men to hold the whole country against hit-and-run raiders. If they concentrated forces at population centres, the Vietminh would own the countryside. If they tried to protect the villages, the Vietminh would attack selected towns. The French knew they could not win a guerrilla war, but did think that they could win a set-piece battle. So they tried to bring matters to a head when, towards the end of 1953, they sent an élite force of twelve battalions to a strategically minor dot in the country's north-west, called Dien Bien Phu. The idea was to tempt the Vietminh into a regular battle and defeat them in time to influence the next great-power conference at Geneva. In the event, the Vietminh managed to bring up 60,000 men, many of them men of suicidal bravery. They also had decisive Chinese artillery support. That included two dozen 105-millimetre guns – with much longer ranges than the French had expected and therefore able to cover the French air strip – and anti-aircraft guns and gunners as well. Defence was therefore hopeless. After a heroic resistance, what was left of the 15,000-man French garrison had to surrender.[17] It also became known that when the last French commander in Vietnam, General Navarre, was appointed, the prime minister told him that his job was 'not to destroy the Vietminh or to win the war; it is to create the conditions for an "honourable way out"'. No wonder the French officer corps felt betrayed and that no one could explain why French soldiers should get killed so that France could withdraw.

In France, public support for the war collapsed – General de Gaulle himself described the French as 'the most fickle and unmanageable people on earth'. The French accepted a Soviet proposal for a new Indo-China conference at Geneva, and the British foreign secretary, Anthony Eden, made a point of drawing China in. The outcome was that France simply withdrew from the whole region. Not that Ho got the full national independence he sought. Instead, Vietnam was divided along the 17th parallel, supposedly pending internationally supervised elections. It was stalemate, for the Vietminh were not strong enough to continue the war without support. The Americans continued to think that Indo-China was a key to the global balance of power. China wanted to support Communism, but was privately dubious about having a united Indo-Chinese power on its southern borders. Ho Chih Minh and his people spent the next few years gathering their forces for another try at Vietnam's unification.

The mid-1950s also saw the first rumblings of serious discontent in the Sino-Soviet relationship. It had, of course, been clear from the start not just to Acheson but to the major Western intelligence services that Sino-Soviet differences would surface at some point and that it would be very much in the West's interests that they should. 'Proletarian internationalism' was just verbiage. Unfortunately that did not answer the practical question about when and how those differences might occur. In the event, the first turning-point came as early as 1953. In March that year, Stalin died. Two difficulties arose at once. His successors could see that his structures of command, both within and without the Soviet Union, would have to be changed. That was bound to mean some 'de-Stalinisation' and greater local (i.e. national) responsibility and leadership, which brought some dilution of Communist unity and consequent tensions with China. Worse still, from China's point of view, was the fact that the Russians behaved as if the leadership of the Communist world had simply come down, by a kind of apostolic succession, to the new post-Stalin leaders. But that was to reckon without Mao's vision of his own standing, and his rejection, bordering on paranoia, of anyone else's claim to authority.

Mao had been willing, in view of Stalin's personality, power, history and prestige, to defer to him as the unquestioned head of the global Communist family. He accepted Stalin as the legitimate heir of Lenin and, through Lenin, of Marx. After Stalin, though, the next leader of the Communist world should obviously not be a crude, mercurial and uneducated peasant like Nikita Khrushchev. It should be he himself, Mao, the founding emperor and theoretician. In no sense was Mao – who saw himself as a historic revolutionary figure – prepared to take second place to, let alone orders from, the dumpy bureaucrat, with no standing as theorist, who now governed in Moscow. Not only that but in August 1953 the Soviets tested their first thermonuclear bomb. Stalin's successors, who saw the test, concluded at once that while atomic war might, just, have been sustainable albeit with vast losses, a thermonuclear war would mean the destruction of civilisation. For the Chinese, that view was an inexcusable abandonment of the historic task of world revolution. Not all of this was visible to the world, but to the French, Cartesian logic suggested as early as 1954/5 that at some point Moscow might even become China's grand adversary and the defender of the West against the 'yellow world'.[18]

Mao was even less willing to forgive Khrushchev for his entirely unexpected posthumous critique of Stalin in 1956. From Khrushchev's point of view, Stalinism without Stalin was unsustainable and the Soviet regime needed to change. For Mao, an open critique of Stalin harmed the entire global Communist cause by denigrating its great leader. It might even weaken the position of other leading figures, including Mao himself. It would play into the hands of the imperialists, 'helping the tigers to harm us'. Worse still, in the same year the Russians entertained, in Moscow, the very 'revisionist' heretic who had left the Soviet bloc in 1948, Marshal Tito of Yugoslavia.

Khrushchev increased aid for China, but Beijing continued to complain that Soviet support for China's own interests and wishes was entirely inadequate. It was bad enough that American aid to Taiwan's separatism continued, but in 1953 the new US president, Dwight Eisenhower, announced that the US 7th Fleet, still in the Taiwan Straits, would no longer interfere with Chiang's efforts to liberate mainland China. There were Nationalist bombing and commando raids against the mainland coast, while American defence aid to Taiwan gradually became more overt. In December 1954 the Americans even signed a mutual defence treaty with Chiang's 'Republic of China', which the US and many of its friends continued to recognise as the legitimate government occupying the China seat in the United Nations. In fact, throughout the 1950s Washington gave to that 'Second China' economic aid at around $250 million per annum, while enforcing a trade embargo against the Communists.

Then there was the business of nuclear weapons. By the later 1950s the Soviets could point to brilliant examples of scientific and technological progress, including not only the 1953 development of the hydrogen bomb but the testing of an intercontinental ballistic missile (ICBM) in August 1957, followed, six weeks later, by the successful launch of the Sputnik satellite. These successes caused great alarm in America. The threat of an adverse 'missile gap' with the Russians became a major factor in the 1960 presidential election, which brought John F. Kennedy to the White House. Not only that, but in November 1957 Mao paid his second and last visit to Moscow for the fortieth-birthday celebrations of the Bolshevik revolution. It was the last time he travelled anywhere outside China. At that very time a second Soviet satellite was sent aloft. Mao was delighted and announced in his oracular way that 'the East wind is prevailing over the West Wind'. Here was a great chance to vanquish the capitalists. These notions supported rather than detracted from Mao's old enthusiasm for the power of mass mobilisation and human enthusiasm in overcoming obstacles. The key to development, in this view – and equally, the key to successful defence in the nuclear age – was the will and the energy of the entire country. However, Khrushchev had served at Stalingrad. He may have been a tough Communist apparatchik, but the memories of that dreadful, inhuman battle, and of Russia's horrendous wartime losses, were burned on his memory. He had now seen nuclear tests, and could imagine the result of using such devices in war. He was therefore increasingly cautious about using his nuclear advantage against the West. Mao was contemptuous of these Soviet fears: 'If the worst came to the worst and half of mankind died, the other half would remain while imperialism would be razed to the ground and the entire world would become socialist.'[19] He may even have meant it.

All of which coloured Mao's Moscow trip and put him in a bad temper. He treated some of the finest examples of Russian culture with the deliberate resentment of an ignorant peasant. Nevertheless, it was during Mao's stay in Moscow that a secret agreement was signed under which the Soviets promised to help China to acquire nuclear weapons, even to hand over a sample bomb. And over the next two years the Russians gave China technical help on matters from uranium mining to missile programmes.

Other profound differences remained and turned out to involve basic issues of Communist belief and practice. The Soviet leader was so impressed by the power of nuclear weapons that he even started to argue that the old Marxist principle of the inevitability of war was out of date. In an era of weapons of mass destruction, prudence pointed to peaceful coexistence with the West. For Mao this was simply a betrayal of Moscow's international socialist obligations, and in 1960 he openly challenged the whole idea of peaceful coexistence; especially now, after the dramatic Soviet successes in weapons and technology, which should be the basis for strategic superiority over the USA and made nuclear war, which was anyway inevitable, also winnable. It was all of a piece with Moscow's refusal to back Beijing on other issues. Mao continued to fret, most especially about any possibilities of Soviet-American accommodation; but Khrushchev remained entirely unwilling to subordinate the Soviet Union's fundamental interests to clamour from the radical and internationally inexperienced Chinese junior partner.

There were other problems in and near China. In Vietnam, the Americans had begun to be involved, at first to help the South look after the hundreds of thousands of Northern refugees who fled after the 1954 Geneva conference.[20] However, by the end of the decade there was much evidence of Northern-sponsored guerrilla and assassination campaigns in the South, whose suppression began to involve the Americans. By 1962 they were shipping arms to the South Vietnam authorities; two years later still, they began to bomb targets in North Vietnam. Meanwhile, in 1959 there was an armed rebellion against Chinese occupation in Tibet that was brutally suppressed. Many Tibetans died in bitter fighting and the Tibetan spiritual leader, the Dalai Lama, fled to India, where he was given sanctuary. There were also large anti-Chinese riots in Indonesia with thousands of Chinese killed or injured.

There were new difficulties inside China, too, as people continued to migrate with settlers, volunteers and prisoners into various border regions. In some places, locals were appeased by being given 'Autonomous Region' status. In 1957/8 Mao's government invited frank public comments on what the government was doing ('Let a hundred flowers bloom'). The leadership got much more than it had bargained for and the result was disastrous for all concerned. The new political masters were, for the most part, poorly educated, ignorant and suspicious of the outside world, strongly geared to both xenophobia and anti-intellectualism. They found all their prejudices confirmed by the disloyalty, especially of intellectuals and professionals. Mao himself remained, to the end of his days, vindictively distrustful of them. The result of the invitation to frank comment was therefore that several hundred thousand people, mostly professionals, were simply dismissed as 'rightists'. Yet they were precisely the trained minds the new masters would have needed to help them avoid some of the monumental errors of the next decade.

Mao, whose personal moods now often had a decisive influence on policy, was horrified by criticisms and opposition and started to plunge China into fresh turmoil. As the 1950s went on, he had become worried not only by shortcomings in agriculture but by a supposed loss of China's revolutionary energy and a deplorable tendency towards mere imitation of Soviet examples in social and economic matters. What was needed was 'continuing revolution', with all Chinese becoming, at one and the same time, 'red and expert'. A new social revolution was needed to galvanise the people, hasten China's development and overtake Moscow as socialism's champion. That drive culminated in the 'Great Leap Forward', a gigantic experiment in social engineering and mass mobilisation; a frenzied drive for both industrialisation and rural reform, into which all the dynamism and energy of the Chinese people was poured. Mao, with his usual marvellous inability to admit mistakes – not to mention his increasingly imperial personal habits[21] – wanted to raise agricultural productivity, to reclaim land and expand local industrial production, mainly through self-sacrificial mass enthusiasm. He was convinced that the enthusiasm and energy of the people, once harnessed, could compensate for technological backwardness, in industry as much as in war.

So men were dragooned into the countryside to work on huge irrigation projects by mere muscle power. Co-operatives were collected into communes. Even family life took on a military hue. Industrial progress was promoted to order, and simply by the use of vast numbers of ordinary folk. It was also directed towards exports, to buy capital goods for domestic investment. A huge People's Militia was formed, allegedly of some 220 million people. Old buildings, even Beijing's ancient city walls, behind which its citizens had felt secure, if confined, were destroyed in the revamping of urban settlements. Indeed, much of old Beijing was simply razed, to be replaced by vast new, soulless, Stalinoid – and often structurally dubious – high-rise buildings. Mao even pushed forward Sun Yatsen's old idea for damming the Yangzi, a notion from which would evolve the later 'Three Gorges' dam project. (It, too, remains a grandiose project all too likely to prove a human, ecological and not least economic disaster – especially once the river behind the dam begins to silt up.) At the same time, there was an even closer interweaving of the party and the PLA. Many Western enthusiasts cheered it all. The French philosopher Jean-Paul Sartre thought Mao's Great Leap Forward was 'profoundly moral'.

In fact, the results were chaotic and extraordinarily harmful. The growing internal turmoil may have provided endless and picturesque fascination for Western intellectuals, students and journalists, but the reality was grim. The peasantry trusted Chairman Mao and remained docile, as it had always done. But fake reporting led to absurd claims of increased production, for instance of grain, when the reality was that food shortages began to appear as early as 1957. By 1958 it became clear that actual grain production was not much more than half the officially reported figures. Even then, with government requisitions based on the reports, grain exports to the Soviet Union were increased to pay for more heavy machinery. Oil, steel and machine-tool production did increase, but in general it turned out, quite predictably, that enthusiasm was not enough and faith could not, after all, move mountains. While resources had, for instance, been poured into small-scale local industry, including a million or so amateur 'back-yard' steel furnaces, created in the 'battle for steel', most of what was produced was useless.

By 1959 criticisms were gathering force. Mao's response was fierce, but the wild optimism of the leadership could not hide the disastrous consequences of policy failures, especially in agriculture. Food production declined markedly while the farmers were busy making revolution, and in 1959/60 matters were made much worse by bad weather. Production dropped further while reports to the centre talked of a doubling of production; indeed, by 1960 the country's Gross National Product had declined by something like one-third. At the same time, urbanisation outgrew industrial expansion, unemployment increased and even communes began to return to co-operative arrangements. There were huge famines between 1959 and 1961 in which some 30 million people or more died – quite possibly the greatest man-made famine in history – quite apart from those many others whose lives were shortened by the privations of the 'Great Leap'. In short, the 'Leap' was a disaster, a 'man-made catastrophe' proving only that revolutionary enthusiasm was no substitute for halfway decent economic planning.

The results of all this were too devastating to leave no political residue. For many in the higher leadership Mao had been shown to be fallible – even if efforts were made to keep starved corpses out of sight. Worse still, internal disagreements about policy, and Mao's imperial punishment of dissent, undermined the old unity of the leadership, and its former freedom of debate. In 1959 Mao simply sacked his old associate Peng Dehuai, who had criticised the Great Leap, and replaced him with Lin Biao. What had still been a collegial revolutionary leadership group was being reduced to a single man's dominance.

The Great Leap even had important implications for China's relations with everyone else. The traditional Chinese belief that all foreigners are barbarians, when topped off with Maoist Marxism-Leninism, merely strengthened the inherited Chinese sense of superiority. Now, there was the contrast between Soviet models and the fierce Maoist search for 'new' methods of development that actually revived classic imperial habits of using masses of peasants to build dams or roads by hand. The Chinese actually claimed to have devised a novel path to socialism, that did not need to follow the Soviet model; that challenged Moscow's ideological pre-eminence, and leadership role, in the Communist world; and there was deep anger in Moscow.

Nikita Khrushchev visited Beijing in 1958 and again in 1959, largely to try to restore Sino-Soviet amity. But he thought the Great Leap was folly, and said so. He even described Mao as a romantic deviationist, yet also tried to get Mao to promise not to attack Taiwan and to create a joint Sino-Soviet fleet for the Pacific. Mao treated him like an emperor dealing with a tribute-bearer. A fleet? Certainly, with 'his ships and our captains'. The Soviet purpose, Mao understood, 'is to control us'. In 1958 the Chinese began again, as they had done in 1954, to bombard the Nationalist-held offshore island of Quemoy, and did so without even consulting Moscow. When questioned, Mao said provocatively that China–Taiwan issues were simply a domestic matter. But Khrushchev could see that Mao was not just trying to sabotage the Soviet attempts to come to terms with the Americans but threatening to be able, at any time, to start a fight over Taiwan that the Russians might have to finish. Khrushchev was obviously neither able nor willing to subordinate vital Russian interests to Chinese threats and clamour. Matters only became worse when Mao kept repeating that neither the rockets nor the weapons could rescue imperialism or prevent the proletarian revolution; or when, in a border dispute

between China and India, which had become an important and
friendly Soviet contact with the Third World, Moscow decided to
remain neutral. On all these matters both sides, Chinese Communists
and Russians, were deeply convinced that the other was, in effect,
abandoning the true Communist faith.

The upshot was that by 1959 the Soviets went back on their
promise of nuclear support and a sample bomb. They also withdrew most of their advisers working in China and cancelled some
600 major projects and contracts. They even took away the blueprints. The split had, as such major developments always do, many
causes. Old ethnic differences remained. There were grievances
over armaments and Soviet technical help. There was Beijing's
obvious attempt to capture the leadership of the global revolutionary movement. Even more basic were Soviet worries about
Chinese fundamentalism and willingness to use force. Indeed, once
the Chinese acquired nuclear weapons, they might start something
that would involve Moscow.

For the United States, there were growing concerns about the
nuclear balance with the Soviets, culminating in the 1962 Cuban
crisis. The discovery that the Soviets were secretly installing medium-
range, nuclear-capable missiles in Cuba began what arguably became
the most dangerous confrontation of the entire Cold War. It terrified
both sides. Understandably, neither Washington nor Moscow was
remotely willing to allow China issues to intrude. Shortly after the
crisis ended, Beijing fiercely denounced the outcome – withdrawal of
Soviet missiles from Cuba and US missiles from Turkey – as a
humiliating Soviet retreat in the face of imperialist aggression.

The crisis led to greater efforts at crisis management by the two
superpowers, plus Britain, starting with the 1963 Nuclear Non-
Proliferation and Partial Nuclear Test Ban treaties, both of them
at least partly inspired by concerns about China. Beijing forcibly
objected to both as a blatant attempts to frustrate others, like China,
trying to provide adequately for their defence. That view was
underlined by China's explosion of its own first nuclear device in
October 1964.[22] This evidence of China's entry to the nuclear-

weapons club hugely increased its prestige and strengthened Beijing's claims to be a leader of Third World radicalism and liberation. Within the global Communist movement, the emergence of two divergent centres of Communist power made it possible for local Communist parties to be more independent by playing one centre off against the other.

Meanwhile there was the life and spectacular death of President John F. Kennedy and his social and administrative 'Camelot', followed by the solid domestic-policy triumphs of his successor, Lyndon Johnson. For the US, the rest of the decade was dominated by the traumas of the Vietnam War. America became committed lest an ostensibly monolithic Communist threat would see Vietnamese or Chinese columns marching all over South-East Asia. China played her carefully passive but ultimately decisive role, becoming, arguably even more than Hanoi itself, the chief cause of America's bitter defeat. The prime reason was not so much Chinese aid to North Vietnam, important though it was to have some 50,000 Chinese soldiers there, mostly serving in anti-aircraft mode or keeping the railway lines to China in good order. It was the American determination, after the Korean War, never again to risk a land war against China on the Asian mainland, which ensured that nothing was ever done, or even attempted, that might provoke Chinese intervention. The fundamental point became evident as early as 1965, when the US and the People's Republic took steps to avoid any direct confrontation. For example, the Americans promised that their aircraft would try to avoid Chinese airspace. Mao was not trustful: he ordered the dispersal of industry to remote valleys in China's far west and south-west, as a precaution against air attack. These arrangements created an untouchable North Vietnamese sanctuary for America's enemies, so virtually guaranteeing a US defeat, with all its large consequences.

In the 1950s and early 1960s, British and French policies had ceased, with some exceptions like British involvement with Malaya and Singapore, to be much concerned with China or even with South-East Asia. In 1956 the new government of Egypt nationalised the Suez Canal which had, for a century, been the vital commercial waterway between the Mediterranean and the East. Britain and France objected bitterly and conspired with Israel to invade the canal area. They were foiled, largely by US opposition.[23] The crisis cruelly underlined the end of their global roles and the British had two reactions. They concluded that they must never again be seriously at odds with America. In other matters they relapsed into a kind of sulky post-imperial depression. The French, by contrast, decided they must never again rely on Anglo-Saxon support. By 1957 they signed the Treaty of Rome, together with West Germany, Italy, Belgium, Holland and Luxemburg, creating the European Economic (and other) Communities, a decisive step towards the economic and political organisation of Western Europe, very largely under French leadership.

In this environment, what were the Americans and the West Europeans to make of the Sino-Soviet relationship? In spite of much speculation, most government advisers remained of the view, certainly until 1964, that Moscow–Beijing differences might still be a mere family spat. Many scientific, technical and economics links remained. The Soviets were still China's largest trading partner. They had not cut off oil supplies to China. If political or strategic push came to shove, they would continue to make common cause against the Western world. Only de Gaulle, and to some extent his German opposite number, the West German chancellor Konrad Adenauer, saw further. In 1958 Adenauer contacted Dr Kissinger, the adviser to Richard Nixon, the probable next Republican president, to argue forcibly that a break between the Soviets and China was inevitable. He was not believed.[24] De Gaulle saw as early as 1960 that, with rising tensions between Russia and China, the Russians might try to mend fences with the West.

In fact, the early 1960s saw several crises that, taken together, would even more fatally weaken the old Sino-Soviet alliance. One was the Cuban missile crisis itself. Also in 1962 came a fresh border war between China and India along their Himalayan frontier, which the

Chinese won quickly and decisively. Beijing objected loudly to the flow of Soviet military assistance to India, including the supply of jet engines and even some jet aircraft.

China objected even more – little information is available – about small Sino-Soviet border clashes in Xinjiang that came together with a list of Chinese claims against the Soviets in Central Asia. In these regions, the pressures of China's overpopulation were once again making themselves felt. The Soviets, for their part, decided that the old 1689 Treaty of Nerchinsk had been negotiated 'under duress' and that its border arrangements were therefore invalid. To China's barely disguised anger, Khrushchev not only refused Chinese claims for territorial restitution on the Sino-Soviet border but extended credits to India and went to visit Washington. There were also differing Chinese and Soviet attitudes to the situation in Vietnam, where US help to the South was still increasing. By 1964 these various doctrinal and practical differences were starting to affect the cohesion of the whole international Communist movement.

Even more important were developments within China. The People's Republic was beginning the approach march to a further bout of social and political hysteria that would end up involving upwards of 100 million people. More evidence had seeped upward into government about how bad the country's economic situation really was, how devastating the famines at the start of the decade had been, how wretched morale was in the countryside, and how often party cadres had abused their positions while under pressure from higher authority to meet absurd regional and national production quotas. A clean-up campaign began both in local administration and to re-educate the people in the virtues of selflessly building socialism. Industrial production slowly rose. Normal administration took hold. Yet it took until 1965 for agricultural output to return to 1957 levels.

Even so, the restorations left Mao most unhappy. For one thing, as he began to move against his critics he had to sweep away doubts and opposition, a matter doubly irritating to a man whose word had for so long been law. For another, restoration brought pragmatism, and a growth of bureaucracy, that were entirely at odds with Mao's own romantic but also ruthless impulses. For him, China was once again in danger of following the old imperial patterns of government – from the top down. The Maoist revolution was losing impetus, the party was becoming ossified and party bureaucrats were 'taking the capitalist road' – a deadly accusation. It was hard to deny that it all represented a denial of his vision of mass action, of governance by continuing struggle. Mao was always enchanted with himself and to accept these developments would undermine not just his revolution but his own vision of himself and his place in history. Perhaps, too – who knows? – for a man who had been on campaign all his adult life, he found the prospect of piecemeal administration tedious and hankered after the scent of fresh battles. What was needed was the renewal of revolutionary spirit in every generation, fresh emphasis on egalitarianism, the power of mass mobilisation, rebellion against anything smacking of the old order. It was also necessary to strength- en the admiration of the people for his own person. So he staged the almost incredible spectacle of himself swimming across the Yangzi.[25]

Lin Biao, the army commander and veteran of Yan'an days, began to intensify indoctrination in the People's Liberation Army, praised the supreme leader to the skies and encouraged study of the new 'Little Red Book' of Mao's aphorisms. Ideas of revolutionary stead- fastness, of sacrifice and self-reliance were re-emphasised. Nor was Lin Biao alone. He was joined by Mao's last wife, Jiang Qing, a former actress who had strong connections among Shanghai intellectuals and concentrated on cultural politics. In 1965, Lin Biao went on to declare that the peoples of the Third World would defeat the advanced capitalist nations. This was widely interpreted in America as open Chinese support to revolutionary movements. It was even thought, in alarmist circles, to be a warning that China might intervene in Vietnam. In Indonesia, too, the Communist Party (PKI) seemed on the brink of power and staged a coup, reinforcing Western fears of a disciplined Communist axis of power from Beijing through both Vietnams into Indonesia. In the event, the Indonesian army eliminated the Communists almost immediately, with massive slaughter. Nevertheless, the broader fears, and the knowledge that the

Soviets and China competed in supporting North Vietnam with arms, advice and other help, contributed to Western fears about South-East Asia that produced a greatly increased American combat presence in Vietnam. By the end of 1965 some 180,000 US troops were serving there, creating new potential dangers to southern China.

Now Mao began to move more fully into what he and his supporters called the 'Great Proletarian Cultural Revolution' (though wicked tongues in the West contended that it was neither great, nor proletarian nor cultural nor, in fact, a revolution). Finding more opposition within the CCP, and unwilling to listen to anything except applause, he sought support outside the party. His desire for violent revolutionary renewal led him to emphasise mass meetings, public excitement and especially reliance on students and disgruntled young urban people to attack the establishment. As the movement got increasingly out of hand, it produced turmoil and growing public hysteria. The revolutionary radicals spread unrest and students in secondary schools issued arm bands declaring the wearers to be 'Red Guards', whom Mao encouraged to 'learn revolution by making revolution'. There may, eventually, have been 10 million of them. But as violence gathered pace, Mao simply said: 'Who are against the Great Cultural Revolution? American imperialism, Russian revisionism, Japanese revisionism, and the reactionaries.'[26] Schools and universities were closed to make room for revolution. Youthful Red Guards rampaged through the streets waving 'Little Red Books' of Mao's sayings. Mao himself began to review gigantic parades of Red Guards, their ranks swelled by millions of young people from schools and universities from all round the country, all of whom were given free travel. His pronouncements – though never by public oratory: he never aired his rough, provincial accents – had a nice line in invective and he excited them. Very soon the destruction of property and of lives gathered pace.

Everything old and established was in danger, from buildings to people. Tens of thousands of officials and middle-class people, including elderly professionals, were beaten, and sent into the countryside to carry night soil and learn from 'the people'. The daughter of Deng Xiaoping, himself sacked from his senior party posts, reports that at Peking University, where she studied, her brother was tortured and crippled and 'a student . . . had nails driven through his kneecaps, silvers of bamboo shoved under his fingernails, his fingers broken by pliers. Then he was tied in a gunnysack, kicked downstairs and beaten almost to death'. Meanwhile the president of the university was hung by his thumbs from a rafter and tortured to extract a confession that he was a 'false Communist'.[27] All traces of private property, let alone private economics, were attacked. Intellectuals and others were thrashed, taught to lick their own blood from the ground, frequently executed or beaten to death. Often a victim would have his tongue cut out, so that he could not, at the last moment, shout something politically incorrect to the mandatory crowd. Others committed suicide – which was classified as a betrayal of the party and its revolution. Hundreds of thousands died. The police were told not to interfere; if people were beaten to death 'it's none of your business'. Tens of millions had their lives shattered.

Anyone who had a Western education, or dealings with the West, was assaulted and humiliated. Thousands were imprisoned. Art collections and libraries went up in flames or were stolen. Mao himself, always in the habit of 'acquiring' books he wanted, is thought to have acquired thousands of old works in this way before having himself, with breathtaking insincerity, photographed against a study wall filled with them so as to enhance his reputation for scholarship. Some things were preserved: on Zhou's orders a whole division of troops was stationed in the Forbidden City to prevent looting and destruction. But millions of young people, and folk from the countryside, went on destroying art objects and buildings, and to attack and sadistically humiliate teachers, parents and others.

The central target of the campaign was the CCP itself. The party was purged, even at the highest ranks, as Mao's wife Jiang Qing and her radical groups conducted witch-hunts and staged attacks on Mao's own establishment. Not unlike Stalin, who through the 1930s had purged the entire old party leadership that had come to power with him, Mao now declared a kind of war on the leadership that had survived the Long March. He used their ingrained party loyalty and discipline against them, the conviction that insistence on personal rights was selfish and anti-social. Altogether, some 60 per cent of party officials were eventually purged.

From the point of view of the outside world, things became so bad that it was almost impossible for any foreign government to do normal business with the Chinese. In August 1967 Red Guards took over the ministry of foreign affairs, destroying records and disrupting everything. Foreigners were beaten up and there were huge meetings to condemn foreign things and people. Red Guards invaded the British mission and sacked it[28] as well as attacking other diplomats. Relations with several countries were broken off. The foreign minister, Chen Yi, was forced to engage in self-criticism before several thousand chanting and jeering students, with Zhou Enlai, no less, presiding. Such foreign-affairs business as could be done at all went through Zhou's office. China's ambassadors abroad were withdrawn, except one, in Cairo. Instead, radical diplomats were sent out and made their embassies centres of revolutionary propaganda and help to local Communist parties. Occasionally, 'capitalists' trying to visit an embassy would be attacked with sticks.

Inevitably, some of the Red Guard fervour became focused on their fellow guards, as uncoordinated groups ended up fighting one another in a frenzy of accusation and destruction. It was only in 1967/8 that the PLA, which had so far only protected critical installations and people, including nuclear facilities, had finally to be called in to restore order, often by force. Even then, it was not until around mid-1968 that Mao disbanded the Red Guards, large numbers now themselves sent down to the countryside to learn from the peasants. China was to suffer considerably from having a whole generation of young people caught up in the frenzies of revolution and missing out on education and training. More importantly, the effect of the Cultural Revolution, and its destructive effects on the personnel and institutions of government, meant an effective transfer of authority to the still-disciplined and functioning PLA. By the time the Cultural

Revolution ended, it had shattered the unity and perhaps the confidence of the party. After 1969 there had to be a major effort to rebuild it and restore economic production.

In the overheated atmosphere of this Great Proletarian Cultural Revolution, the interpretation of Sino-Soviet relations also underwent a critical shift. China's principal and most dangerous enemy had so far been identified as the chief capitalist power, the USA. By 1967 the Soviet Union was being labelled as an equally and perhaps, given its revisionism, even more dangerous enemy. This was fighting talk. The alliance with Moscow was fractured. Things started to look even blacker with the Soviet invasion of Czechoslovakia in 1968, triggered by the decisions of a new, more liberal and reformist administration in Prague which, in Moscow's view, endangered Communist ascendancy in the country. Especially alarming was the Russian justification of this invasion, which invented the idea (promptly labelled the 'Brezhnev doctrine', after the Soviet leader, Leonid Brezhnev) that the Soviet Union had not just the right but the duty to intervene in any country where the achievements of socialism were under threat. Given China's own talk of Soviet heresy, was it not all too likely that the Russians would take that doctrine as justification for intervention in China, too?

China's sense of isolation and danger was further sharpened by three other and quite disparate issues. First, there was growing evidence of China's economic backwardness, underlined, for instance, by the startling economic boom of China's old nemesis, Japan. It was fuelled by several factors, all foreign to China's recent experience. One was progressive tariff reductions in Japan's world markets as the pressures for protectionism eased in many places. Another was the consistently low cost of raw materials. Then there was Japan's possession of a tame workforce, with labour costs kept low, in part by the need to absorb the 6 million Japanese who had returned from China, Korea and elsewhere. There was also a move towards capital-intensive activities like electronics and petrochemicals. A second issue for China was population growth. In spite of the huge loss of life of the Great Leap and the Cultural Revolution, the 1950s and 1960s were, overall, a period of quite rapid population increases. In fact, this crowding was making rapid industrialisation more difficult. The sparsely inhabited lands of China's north-west, as well as former Chinese regions in the Soviet Far East, were obvious targets for the growing numbers of workers and settlers. That raised yet another, and ultra-sensitive, issue: the reuniting of all the lands that China had lost during the previous century and a half. That meant not only the matter of Xinjiang's borders but of parts of the Soviet maritime provinces acquired by the czars. There were even suggestions that the Amur basin had been an 'integral part' of China as long as two and a half millennia before. It was an explosive set of claims.

The third issue was growing military tension with the Russians. In March 1969 came the sensational spectacle of fighting on the Sino-Soviet border. With the partial exception of the Soviet suppression of Hungary in 1956, it was the first time that 'fraternal' socialist countries had openly fought each other. Chinese troops ambushed some Soviet patrols on Damansky (Chenbao) Island at the confluence of the Amur and Ussuri rivers on China's north-eastern borders. The Russians retaliated and massively reinforced their entire frontier with China. By 1971/2 the Soviets had some forty-four divisions on that border. They even deployed tactical nuclear weapons to deter the Chinese, who had followed up their own first atomic explosion by developing thermonuclear devices three years later, and who began in 1969 to deploy their first-generation nuclears in Manchuria. Henry Kissinger remarked later that the Russians had tried to sound out the Nixon administration on whether the US would stand by if the Russians 'took out' the Chinese nuclear facilities before their weapons became deployable, but had been refused. If there were such discussions, they developed no further.

This border clash was the culmination of two extraordinary decades in Chinese foreign affairs. Between 1949 and 1969 China had been in dispute, often conflict, with almost everyone. It had done battle in

Ussuri Clash

In March 1969 the world was startled to find that the two great socialist powers, the Soviet Union and the People's Republic of China had begun to fight each other on the Ussuri River boundary in north-east China. The clash occurred on an island in the river, called Damansky (Russian) or Zhen Bao (Chinese).

There were, in fact, two clashes, on 2 March and 15 March. In the first, it seems that around 300 Chinese élite troops ambushed a Russian patrol and killed nineteen of them. By 15 March each side had several thousand troops in the area and the fighting on the island may have involved up to 500 Chinese and 200 or more Russians, backed by a couple of dozen tanks.

It seems clear that the Chinese prepared carefully for the confrontation and in the first clash heavily outnumbered the Russians. But the reasons for the affair remain unclear. Border disputes were nothing new and there had been minor confrontations for weeks and months. Various explanations for this armed incident seem possible. One is that it was another Maoist attack on Russian 'revisionism'. Another, perhaps more plausible, may have been a need to rally Chinese opinion and people after the turmoil of the Cultural Revolution. Whatever the real reason, one major result was a huge Russian military and missile build-up along the border.

1950–3 with the United States and South Korea, fought India twice, had forcibly suppressed Tibet and Xinjiang, been seriously at odds with the Mongols, remained in a state of cold war with Taiwan and had even deployed troops against the Americans in the Vietnam War. Now, in 1969, it was in armed conflict even with its putative elder brother, the Soviet Union. It was a remarkable record, due to be further extended by clashes with South Vietnam over the South China Sea in 1974, a Chinese invasion of Vietnam in 1979, and small clashes over the Spratly Islands in 1988. Even more remarkable was the fact that by the end of the 1960s, while boundary treaties had been signed with Burma, Mongolia, Pakistan and others, China was also in some danger of conflict with both superpowers. That Beijing feared possible American attack was not new. But for years it had been taken for granted that the Soviet Union would help to fend off the worst of China's dangers. Now Beijing itself had not merely broken that link but was almost at daggers drawn with everybody. Not only Zhou but even Mao seems to have seen that this was a set of risks too far.

However, for the Russians and even more so for the Americans, the situation in China offered new opportunities. It would be logical to replace two decades of simple East–West confrontation with the greater subtleties of triangular politics. The US, for instance, needed China's help to end the Vietnam conflict and to deal with the Soviets. The aim now, as the president's National Security Advisor Dr Henry Kissinger put it, would be for Washington to have better relations with Moscow and Beijing than these two had with each other. One could then use a Sino-American understanding to press the Russians further towards *détente* and nuclear-arms control. For it was clear that earlier arms-control agreements could not stem the growth of great-power nuclear-weapons arsenals. Mutual deterrence might not be enough to avoid war, whether by miscalculation or accident, as both sides deployed more missiles and developed multiple warheads. By the later 1960s both sides even developed anti-missile systems that might, eventually, undermine the principle of deterrence. President Johnson tried to open negotiations with Brezhnev before the 1968 Soviet invasion of Czechoslovakia made it politically impossible for him to go further. But the next president, Richard Nixon, brought matters to a successful conclusion in the 1972 nuclear-arms-limitation and anti-ballistic-missile agreements, signed in Moscow.

Here was the context within which lesser problems, even the important matter of Sino-American relations, could be developed. There was no single turning-point. But one important change came in 1968 when Lyndon Johnson's announcement that he would not run for re-election to the presidency made it clear that America's sole remaining aim in Vietnam was to get out. It was even clearer that China was in a position to help. Beijing was no less eager to move away from a simultaneous confrontation with the two super-powers. In subtle and indirect ways, the two sides sent signals to each other. There were pointed Chinese references to the Soviets as an equal threat and the fact that China did not have, and did not intend to have, any troops outside its own borders. The Americans sent signals of their own, also privately. Confidential Sino-American talks resumed in Warsaw. In 1969 the Americans started to relax trade restrictions. By 1971 there was a highly publicised invitation to American ping-pong teams to play the Chinese. The Americans finally ended their trade embargo of China. And Henry Kissinger secretly flew to Beijing to prepare for a visit by the president himself. The prospect of Sino-American accommodation naturally alarmed Moscow, and helped to produce those first major nuclear-arms-control agreements. On the other hand, these treaties, and the general Soviet-American accommodation they implied, greatly alarmed the Chinese, encouraging Sino-American accommodation even further.

In the meantime, the military clashes on the frontier did more than fuel Chinese anti-Soviet feelings. The story, duly embellished, suggested that the People's Liberation Army was heroically saving the entire populace. Lin Biao's prestige soared, compounding Mao's problems. He began to feel that his purges might have been overdone. The party needed to be rebuilt, and criteria of ideological purity dropped. He also thought that the role of the military ought to be reduced and Lin had become too prominent. At any rate Lin began to find himself undermined in arcane ways and he may have harboured thoughts of unseating Mao. Various plans came to nothing but in the end Lin's plans were given away by his own daughter, Dodo, to Mao's guards.[29] By late 1971 he was dead. It seems that Lin, his wife, son and others tried to flee by air to the Soviet Union, and that his plane crashed. In 1972 Premier Zhou Enlai explained baldly that Lin had in reality been a renegade and a traitor. Once again the party accepted the supreme leader's word and decision without question. Mao was by now above mere politics, utterly untouchable and virtually beyond criticism: perhaps the latest towering figure in a long line of emperors and the founder of something very much like a new Communist Party dynasty. In fact, he displayed many of the same characteristics as the founding Ming ruler, Hongwu (1368–98). There was much the same ruthless-ness and intolerance of criticism, the same wish to centralise all decision-making in the hands of the supreme ruler, the same notion that his word was law, the same God-like attributes.

Then came a major sensation. In February 1972, President Nixon himself flew to Beijing, the first American president ever to visit China. Before going, he was briefed that China's greatest worries were, in order, American protection of Taiwan, a possible revival of Japanese military power, and the problem of divided Korea. The president was advised to raise issues of human rights and trade; and there should be mutual Sino-American assurances about not seeking hegemony in Asia. By the time Nixon left, the two sides had set up a relationship which fell short, but not far short, of full diplomatic relations. It was elegantly outlined in the 'Shanghai communiqué' of 1972, which provided a road-map for Sino-American relations for the next decade. It recorded the different views of the two sides. The Americans said that the US 'acknowledged' and 'does not challenge' the view of all Chinese that 'there is only one China', but insisted that any disputes (e.g. between Beijing and Taiwan) must be resolved only by peaceful means. The document mentioned that 'normalisation' should be promoted. It was so carefully balanced that partisans in both Beijing and Washington would have had no difficulty in misunderstanding it.

China came to replace Taiwan in the 'China' chair at the United Nations. Following the old myth of China as an unlimited market, American businessmen began to flock to China almost immediately after the Nixon visit. In 1969 Chinese exports to the US had totalled $5 million; by 1973 the total was $700 million. Some eleven months after the visit an American withdrawal from Vietnam was agreed; and

Mao had reached his own conclusions about the war. The Americans, he remarked to one foreign ambassador, had never really been serious about Vietnam. After all, what great power abandons a serious conflict after suffering a mere 58,000 dead?

If President Nixon's China visit came to be seen as perhaps the greatest single foreign-affairs triumph of the Nixon–Kissinger regime, it was also the greatest – perhaps even the single – serious foreign-policy achievement of China in the Maoist era. It was a priceless gift, not just to the 78-year-old Mao but to China itself, that the president of the greatest power in the world had come to China, not quite cap in hand but, symbolically, rather like a bearer of tribute to the emperor. No wonder that Mao approved of Nixon. Rightists, he said, were predictable. If any Chinese citizen, by the end of 1971, still doubted the sheer magnificence of Chairman Mao, and the grandeur of his achievement in restoring China to its proper eminence at the heart of world affairs, the visit of the American president converted him. It was a curious reversal of history. In 1840 the British had fought China mainly on the issue of state equality. In the 1980s it was China, newly emerged from the inward-looking constraints of the Mao era, which put foreign acknowledgement of China's status virtually at the head of its foreign-affairs priorities.

The effects of these realignments went far. The Chinese wanted the North Vietnamese to go on fighting the Americans but the war ended with a fudged peace and the US in domestic turmoil. America and North Vietnam signed a peace accord in Paris in which no one believed. In it, both parties guaranteed that 'the South Vietnamese people's right to self-determination is sacred, inalienable and shall be respected by all countries'. Furthermore, the South Vietnamese 'shall decide themselves the political future of South Vietnam through genuinely free and democratic elections under international supervision'.[30] Not long afterwards the North Vietnamese army overran the South. Ironically, the North Vietnamese victory also served to sharpen their political and other disagreements with China, which the war had disguised. A few years after the North Vietnamese had marched into the Southern capital of Saigon, they found themselves at war with China.

These events gave China a still larger role in South-East Asia. The Vietnamese, historic enemies of the Khmer, invaded Cambodia and pillaged much of it. The Chinese, for cold balance-of-power reasons, supported the resistance of the admittedly murderous Khmer Rouges with advice, money and weapons. The Americans encouraged that, too, since it was the Soviet Union that was supporting the Vietnamese.

Whether by coincidence or not, soon after the Lin Biao affair Mao began to deteriorate. When Kissinger visited Beijing again in 1973, he still found that Mao 'exuded greater concentrated willpower and determination than any leader I have encountered' (except de Gaulle[31]). But the old man understood, a little mournfully, how little even his titanic efforts had been able to change the age-old habits of China and the Chinese. He never gave up, of course. He allowed, even encouraged, the Shanghai group headed by Jiang Qing – the 'Gang of Four' – to dominate culture and media and much of the tone of politics. In 1973 Zhou Enlai's cancer flared up, but even then he accepted Mao's refusal to let him have modern Western treatment – to make sure that Zhou would die before he himself did. Which Zhou achieved in 1976.[32] Another old hand was then brought back into a top administrative role. It was Deng Xiaoping, that tough and experienced survivor of the Long March, who would eventually become Mao's successor. He may have been victimised by the Cultural Revolution, but character begets power and he was too able and dynamic to be abandoned. He now became vice-chairman of the party, only to be imprisoned once more by Jiang Qing's group, who insisted on being more Maoist than Mao. It was a turmoil that continued to reflect the tensions between Mao's pitiless revolutionary romanticism – his doctor had frightening tales of his monstrous personality[33] – and the practical needs of China's rapidly growing population. They remained essentially unresolved until 1976. In June that year, Mao had another stroke and began to fail badly.

Then came major earthquakes and storms. A quarter of a million people were killed in just one quake east of Beijing. All of which was traditionally supposed to be nature's way of heralding the death of an emperor. Once again the signs proved to be true. Shortly after midnight, on 9 September, Mao Zedong, the heir of the great emperors of the past,[34] who was no longer able to move or speak, drew a deep breath and died.

13

REASSERTION

AD 1976 to 2001

M AO LEFT CHINA in considerable danger.
While he was busy 'making revolution', China had become exposed, economically and strategically. At the core of everything was, once again, China's continuing population growth. Its people, around 400–450 millions in 1945, had grown rapidly and would triple to 1.2–1.3 billions by 2000. Such masses needed to be fed, and given homes and work. With some 80 per cent of Chinese still living on farms, mostly at subsistence levels, China's poor agricultural productivity created fresh famines and a need to import food – without the viable exports to pay for it. Food security alone would require rapid economic growth, but the economic disasters of the Great Leap and the Cultural Revolution left China an economic and technological backwater.

Neither had Mao's 'revolutionary diplomacy' achieved much. The ploy to make China a swing state between the US and the Soviets had only benefited the US, which was indeed now on better terms with Beijing and Moscow than these two were with one another. Moreover, now that the US had left Vietnam, America had become much more important to China than China was to America: China's economic reconstruction required nothing so much as peaceful borders plus modernisation and technology at home. America was a major potential source of both.

That did not, however, deal with the growing dangers of Soviet political and military encirclement. The Russian build-up on the Chinese border continued and by 1980 included the new SS20 mobile and multi-warheaded nuclear missiles, capable of a 3,000-mile range. China therefore found itself directly affected by, but without voice in, the nuclear-arms-control discussions that were a central strand of Soviet-American relations in the 1970s and most of the 1980s. Each superpower had to consider not only its opponent's arsenal, but the effect of Chinese weapons on the balance between them. Attempts to limit the European deployments of the new Soviet SS20s, or of their controversial Western counterparts, were complicated by the question of whether Soviet missiles deployed in the Far East, and pointed at China, should be included. After all, being mobile they could easily be moved to Europe. Or again, Soviet-American discussions dealing with submarines inevitably had consequences for China's coasts and coastal cities, which were wide open to sea-borne attack.

On the other hand, it was clear to the Chinese leaders that the strategic relationship between the USSR and the US had become so complicated, and both sides were so fearful of any clash, that barring some unforeseeable accident a nuclear conflict was highly unlikely. It was even less likely that China would be directly involved if it did occur, especially while it retained a minimal deterrent of its own. China therefore had room for political manoeuvre.

There were also growing Chinese frictions with Russia's ally, Vietnam. Traditional ethnic antagonisms reasserted themselves, and as Vietnam's ties with Moscow strengthened, China saw that its ancient regional dominance might be threatened by a strong neighbour in the south and especially by a Soviet-Vietnamese encirclement. In November 1978 Moscow even signed a Treaty of Friendship with Vietnam that brought Soviet naval and air units to the erstwhile American base of Cam Ranh Bay. A month later the Vietnamese invaded Cambodia to overthrow the Chinese-backed rule of the Khmer Rouges and install their own puppet regime. Two months later again, the Chinese sent 100,000 troops to launch a limited, 29-day border war against Vietnam, to 'teach the Vietnamese a lesson'. What it really taught was that the Chinese troops, especially anything less than their very best formations, were not very effective against a tough, experienced and battle-hardened opponent; and, more importantly, that the Soviets would not risk a larger war for the sake of supporting their Vietnamese allies. The Chinese were badly mauled.[1] Still, they remained assertive. By the late 1980s Vietnam and China each deployed several hundred thousand troops on border protection, and there was some cross-border harassment.

In the meantime Beijing began quietly to co-operate with the US, even though it regretted the decline in American power and will under President Carter. In 1978 Carter sent his National Security Advisor to Beijing and moved to formal US diplomatic relations with China. Shortly afterwards Deng Xiaoping himself was trying on ten gallon hats in Texas; and China raised no objections to the signature, in 1979, of the Soviet-American SALT II arms-control treaty.

The US and China also developed common concerns about Islamic fundamentalism, which boiled over in 1979 into the overthrow of the shah of Iran. This eruption threatened to bring instability to the entire Middle East, and the oil supplies on which Western economies depended. Fundamentalist groups seized sixty-nine American embassy staff in Teheran as hostages and attacked US missions from Libya to Pakistan. Even closer to China, in neighbouring Afghanistan, there was another Moslem rebellion, this time against the pro-Soviet government in Kabul. In December 1979 the Soviets sent in troops to quell the trouble, and by spring 1980 had some 100,000 soldiers in the country. The Chinese saw this as a Soviet plan to outflank Western Europe, a major step to seizing control of the Gulf and extending Soviet hegemony deep into Asia. Afghanistan remained, as it had been in the nineteenth century, geo-politically vital – even more so by the end of the twentieth century, given Central Asia's role in global oil and gas supplies. So the Americans, also fearing that the Russian move, and America's expulsion from Iran, heralded a further Russian push towards the oil of the Persian Gulf, reacted sharply and gave the anti-Soviet forces arms and other help. Once again, American and Chinese interests dovetailed, for China had to consider two dangers. Soviet dominance of Central Asia would be a direct (and highly traditional) threat to China's western borderlands. Yet the religious enthusiasm of the anti-Soviet Islamic guerrillas, the Mujahedeen, posed an almost equal threat to the tranquillity of the Islamic peoples of western China. While the Soviet presence in Afghanistan had to be opposed, so must any radical Islamic influence in places like Xinjiang.[2]

A year after according formal recognition in 1979, Carter sent his defence secretary, Harold Brown, to China and agreed to transfer advanced technology and military support equipment. The Chinese also agreed to put into Xinjiang a US listening post, manned by Chinese, to monitor Soviet missile tests. It would replace Iranian posts lost with the fall of the shah. By the mid-1980s, and after President Ronald Reagan's 1984 visit to Beijing, Sino-American understandings seemed reasonably firm. There were substantial economic ties, a flow of technology to China, a modest degree of diplomatic and military co-operation, even some sharing of intelligence on Soviet military activities. Much else also changed. The US agreed to give China most-favoured-nation trading status and ended the old US–Taiwan defence treaty. American aid to the island declined, and Beijing promised to work peacefully for reunification with Taiwan. China and the US, wanting to limit Soviet influence in South-East Asia, even supported the genocidally murderous Khmer Rouges in Cambodia. They effectively recognised the grisly Khmer Rouge leader Pol Pot as the legitimate leader of the country. Even after the Khmer Rouges were driven from the capital Phnom Penh, they sent him military supplies through Thailand. In the meantime, in 1984, and after five years of negotiations, Beijing agreed with London that Hong Kong would revert to Chinese sovereignty in 1997 – when it would be allowed much autonomy and to keep the capitalist system for half a century.

American co-operation with China extended to other regions, even Africa, where the West learned that Marxism and nationalism in the ex-colonies could be entirely compatible. Especially the Leninist version of an all-powerful state run by a single party might have been tailored to the wishes of their dominant castes. In any event, the Chinese began to oppose Marxist and Soviet-backed entities. Although they had no great interest or stake in Africa, they denounced Cuban intervention there and even supported an anti-Communist insurgency in Angola.

POL POT

Even in the long twentieth-century list of mass killings and brutalities committed in the name of Communist and national-liberation ambitions, Pol Pot occupies a special place.

He was born Saloth Sar in an up-country Cambodian village, probably in 1928. At the age of six he went to live with a brother in Phnom Penh in the royal household. There he was influenced by Buddhist precepts and two years later went on to a Catholic primary school, where he learned French and something of Western culture.

In 1949 he travelled on a government scholarship to study in Paris and became one more in the long roster of developing-country revolutionaries who, like Zhou Enlai and Deng Xiaoping in China, received their intellectual training there. The point is uncertain, but it seems possible that Pol Pot, like many others, was captivated by the nihilist strands in the existentialist philosophy of Jean-Paul Sartre, which was all the rage in Paris at the time and became profoundly influential throughout Europe and beyond.

In any event, it was in Paris that he got his introduction to Communism and joined the French Communist Party. Four years later, in 1953, he returned to Cambodia. Within a month he had joined the Communist resistance, becoming a member of the Indochina Communist Party (IHC) which was dominated by Ho Chih Minh's Vietminh.

A year later, the government of Prince Sihanouk won a national election. Pol Pot became a teacher in a private college but also a recruiter for the Communists. When the government began an anti-Communist crackdown, Pol Pot took to the jungle near the Vietnamese border, where he spent the next seven years.

During that time the Communists began their 'approach march' to power by recruiting and building their strength and discipline. Their cause was helped by the fact that the Cambodian government was weakened by North Vietnamese military attacks. When the Vietnamese achieved a major victory in 1971, the Communist Khmer Rouges could take over whole regions. Finally, in early 1975, the Khmer Rouges prevailed. They entered Phnom Penh on 17 April and within twenty-four hours ordered the evacuation of the whole city. The story of that evacuation has become legendary: men, women and children, young and old, the sick and the well – at any rate those who were not killed in the process – had to march into the countryside. People with education, social standing, former officials, were liable to be killed out of hand. Evacuation was ordered in other cities as well. Perhaps 2 million out of a population of around 5 million were sent into the countryside. There was no provision for food or care of any kind: many people starved to death and others were routinely killed in what became known, much later, to the outside world as the Cambodian 'killing fields'.

In the meantime Pol Pot was prime minister of Cambodia, renamed Kampuchea. In August 1976 he launched a Four Year Plan for the collectivisation of agriculture and the nationalisation of industry. The country would rely on agricultural exports to finance its economy. The result was untold misery. Thousands died in the paddy fields. In a replay of the brutalities of Stalin's collectivisation campaign in the Soviet Union at the beginning of the 1930s, and of Mao's Great Leap, crops badly needed to feed the people were marked for export. As if malnutrition and starvation were not enough, the Khmer Rouges compounded the misery by insisting on the use of traditional Cambodian medicine. Pol Pot also started an interrogation centre where well over than 20,000 men, women and children were tortured to death.

In the meantime, skirmishes with Vietnam continued. At the end of 1977 the Vietnamese began to make real advances into Kampuchea. A year or so later, by January 1979, Vietnamese forces finally reached Phnom Penh. The Kampuchean government fled by train and Pol Pot was taken by helicopter to Thailand. For the next nineteen years he remained in exile in the Thai jungle – without harassment, let alone trial – and died in 1998.

By the end of the century Cambodia had barely begun to recover from the disasters of Pol Pot's rule. The human – even more than the economic – cost of the Pol Pot episode had been too great. Not until 1999 did Cambodia have its first full year of peace for three decades and even then, in the later 1990s, any economic advance had been halted by civil violence, political struggles and regional economic difficulties.

For all these foreign concerns, however, the men who tried to fill the Mao-shaped hole in Chinese politics were forced to see that the beginning of wisdom, whether in matters of domestic welfare or international influence, was still economic reform at home. At first, Mao's heir-apparent, Hua Guofeng, tried ham-handedly to revive the country with old-fashioned, Soviet-style stress on heavy industry and detailed central planning. That could not last. Even had the approach been desirable, post-Mao China entirely lacked the managerial expertise or the infrastructure to make it work. It became evident that the old Maoist search for self-sufficiency was fruitless and China would, on the contrary, have to be integrated into the international trading and economic system. By 1978, both the Maoist radicals around his widow, Jiang Qing – who were arrested soon after Mao's death – and Hua, were sidelined and new patterns in both party and state started to become clear.

The man who then took charge was Mao's old protégé, Deng Xiaoping. A tough, stocky, diminutive little Sichuanese, he had gone to France as a student worker aged sixteen and had an early education as fitter and turner in French workshops and factories. Zhou Enlai recruited him into the fledgling CCP in 1924. That launched the little man, in a constant boil of energy, on a distinguished career as political commissar and party general secretary under Mao. Now, as a member of the original revolutionary generation, who had survived both the Long March and the Cultural Revolution, he had the personal authority of decades-long personal connections in the highest reaches of the party and, no less important, the senior military. He was something of a force of nature and his throw-away remarks were usually more decisive than long expositions from others. Like Zhou before him, Deng was a pragmatist, given to careful analysis. He could see the essentials – that China's state socialism was massively inefficient – and duly focused on reform at home as the basis for all progress.

He could see that this must mean a huge, complex and, this time, quite fundamental programme of industrial, technical, military and educational modernisation. Only a few years earlier, in April 1974, Deng had declared before the United Nations General Assembly: 'in the final analysis, political independence and economic independence are inseparable' and 'a developing country that wants to develop its national economy must first of all keep its natural resources in its own hands and generally shake off the control of foreign capital'. Yet he also saw quite quickly that 'to achieve genuine independence a country must first lift itself out of poverty. It should not erect barriers to cut itself off from the world.'[3] Growth would depend, in large part, on creating domestic middle-class purchasing power to fuel activity.

The complexities, not just economic but rather political, social, even ideological, were daunting and entailed nothing less than another social revolution.

The problem obviously was how far one could dismantle the Maoist system without undermining the whole basis and legitimacy of China's post-1949 political structure. The reform of China's entire industrial base, and catching up with modern Western machinery, products, production methods and education, would mean a huge and hugely delicate change from the old reliance on inefficient and uncompetitive state-owned industries. It would require a whole new category of modern and export-capable light industries and manufacturing. The import of Western and Japanese goods and capital, technology, manufacturing expertise and financial know-how would have to be encouraged. China would need a stable and reliable currency. It would also have to rely on foreign trade for the import of the essential raw materials, energy supplies, machinery and know-how, and on export earnings to help finance it all. The Chinese industrial work-force, accustomed to the famous 'iron rice-bowl', was untrained, lazy and tied up in bureaucracy. So the role of inefficient state-owned enterprises would have to be reduced and industrial decision-making shifted to smaller units, even to enterprise autonomy. At the same time, there must not be intolerable unemployment or welfare problems and the 'commanding heights' of the economy must continue to be controlled by the state. Agriculture, especially, must be sustained and modernised. By 1981 there was even a fairly forthright critique of some parts of the Maoist record, especially the disaster of the Cultural Revolution. Nevertheless, the Communist party regime, and its ultimate control of the state, must of course be maintained: indeed that maintenance was an indispensable requirement for the carrying-out of the reform programme in the first place.

Deng went to work, starting in 1978, under the slogans of 'Seek truth from facts and practice is the sole criterion of truth' and 'Opening and Reform'. He simply stood the old order on its head and declared that economic construction would in future take precedence over class struggle. He even opened the door to a limited free market, private ownership of property, and more foreign trade. There would also be a much greater welcome to foreign investment. The underdeveloped and rural Chinese interior would remain closed to foreigners, but the coastal regions, with some 200 million people, would be increasingly integrated into the global system. For millions of former Red Guards, now rather older, Deng's commercialism directly contradicted everything they had previously been taught, with numbing repetition, to hold dear. The programme started in 1979 with the creation of four 'Special Economic Zones' in southern cities, where foreign investment was encouraged, especially for export production. The zones were insulated from the rest of the country by barbed-wire fences and fierce dogs. Other cities were added later and Hainan Island even made a tax haven for foreign capital. By 1992 Deng's 'Southern Tour' again emphasised the significance of the 'Special Economic Zones' on the coast, which increased China's reliance on foreign trade and interdependence with foreign economic partners.

There were other intriguing facets to the programme. Foreign investment and foreign contacts began to come in from, and through, Hong Kong and Taiwan, and connections with the rich and powerful overseas Chinese communities were welcomed. Much more was involved here than formal ties of interdependence: there was a common culture with common, well-understood customs. Not only did that make greater use of Taiwan's notable entrepreneurialism but it seemed possible that the stronger and more productive these trade and investment links became, the weaker might become the Taiwanese drive for full political independence – something that China was committed to resisting, if necessary by armed force.

Many in the West thought that with economic modernisation, openness (what Gorbachev was later to call 'glasnost') and globalisation – not to mention greater 'democracy' – China would develop an irresistible momentum for change towards a Western-style liberalism: China would become 'more like us'. That is not what happened. The party remained dominant, even while the reform programme was dramatically successful. To be sure, Deng faced heavy opposition, not least from groups in the state sector and the economic ministries who wanted to concentrate on development on the Chinese mainland. Other commentators argued that far from needing liberalisation, China needed a stronger and more intrusive state. Occasionally, anti-foreigner nationalism was even accompanied by fierce and racist anti-foreigner views, quite reminiscent of some of the anti-foreign-missionary diatribes of the 1870s and '80s.[4] Even for proponents of reform, there were qualifications. Deng himself conceded that, once China's doors were opened, 'flies and insects' would come in. Others accused him and his new policies of betraying Marxism-Leninism, but he was impervious to criticism and brushed off the charges. 'It does not matter whether a cat is black or white, as long as it catches mice,' he repeated, and, 'To set out to be rich is glorious.' The old key-point schools, which admitted students solely on merit and which had been abolished during the Cultural Revolution, were brought back. Once again, as in the 1890s, a wave of Chinese students travelled abroad to study, especially economic, scientific and medical subjects.[5] In the decade 1978–88 some 50,000 of them left to study at foreign universities, two-thirds of them in the US.

For most Western businesses, that turn away from self-suffi-ciency, and opening to the international economy, revived all those nineteenth-century dreams and mirages of a limitless Chinese market and untold riches awaiting bold traders and entrepreneurs. But large numbers, including major Western corporations like Shell, Exxon, British American Tobacco and the German utility RWE, found that senior Chinese had little understanding of the outside world, let alone of the kinds of government–business relations to which they were accustomed in the West. Some had to walk away when the Chinese simply shifted the previously agreed – and contracted – goal-posts. Many smaller investors simply lost their shirts and few, except ones with close ties to Chinese mercantile families, made anything like the profits they had expected.[6] Not everyone understood that high Chinese officials rarely believe that foreign firms deserve much return for their investments. As one

Western businessman remarked: 'Anyone who thinks China is an easy market is in the wrong business.'

Nevertheless, Deng's reforms changed the dynamics of East Asian politics and trade. China very quickly became not just the largest but the most economically dynamic developing power in the history of the world. Albeit starting from a very low base, in the quarter century from 1978 China's Gross Domestic Product multiplied by five. Foreign trade surged: one of the more dramatic aspects of the new policy became the flood of Chinese textiles on to world markets.[7] China sold billions of dollars' worth of arms to both sides in the Iran–Iraq war of the 1980s, and to Saudi Arabia, and weapons-related know-how went to others, including Pakistan. Especially useful was adding value to imported goods, which could then be profitably exported again, in the process also training the Chinese work-force. As early as 1994 firms financed from abroad seem to have furnished around 30 per cent of China's exports, mostly of products assembled from imported parts.

The Chinese reforms also had important spin-off effects for others, like the Japanese. Their 'economic miracle' had, from the 1960s, been based on some highly traditional factors. The Japanese government took a strongly interventionist role, especially through its powerful ministry for international trade and industry. In favoured sectors there was preferential tax treatment. The government liked industrial concentration and, above all, the focusing of labour and capital on growth through exports. That produced ten huge foreign-trade cartels that, between them, accounted for more than half of Japan's exports. It was a logical reversal of Japan's pre-1941 policies. Then, the Japanese had sought to dominate the sources of the raw materials their industries needed. Now, the alternative had to be to sell manufactured goods to foreign markets to earn the money to buy the food, fuel and raw materials that Japan had to have. The Americans played a major role in Japan's economic revival. By the middle 1980s they were buying over a third of Japan's exports which amounted, in turn, to over one-fifth of America's total imports.

DENG XIAOPING

Deng Xiaoping, the 'Second Emperor' of the CCP 'dynasty', was born in 1904 in Szechwan province and died in 1997 of Parkinson's disease.

At the age of sixteen he sailed to Marseilles – travelling steerage – and spent five years in France. He took odd jobs as a fitter and fireman; and in 1924, under the guidance of senior folk like Zhou Enlai, joined the brand-new Chinese Communist Party. Two years later he left for Moscow, where he studied Marxism, especially at Sun Yatsen University (in Moscow) where he was in the same class as Chiang Kai-shek's eldest son, Chiang Ching-kuo. By 1927 he was back in China, where he spent some years organising and commanding Communist groups. His first wife died shortly after giving birth to her first child. His second wife left him after he came under political attack in 1933.

During the 'Long March' of 1934/5 Deng served as director of the political department and then as the political commissar of the First Army Corps. Once the war with Japan began in 1937, Deng became the political commissar of one of the three divisons comprising the Eighth Route Army. And in 1939 he married for a third time, in front of Mao's Yan'an cave dwelling.

After the 1939–45 war he found himself a member of the leading group of the CCP around Mao and in 1956 was appointed general secretary of the party.

In 1966 he was disgraced in the purges of the Cultural Revolution and remained out of power until 1969. His family was harassed and victimised as well, his son being crippled. He returned to office in 1973 and was dismissed by the radicals once more a year or two later. But by 1976 he was back as vice-president of the CCP and in 1978, two years after Mao's death, became China's 'Paramount Leader'. At which point he stood the old order on its head by declaring that economic construction would in future take precedence over class struggle. He therefore became the chief architect of the dynamic Chinese modernisation programme.

Deng's reforms in China fitted in with many of these developments. Japan could draw on China's oil and raw materials, while selling technology and manufactures to China in return – not to mention investing money. In 1979–83 Japan provided roughly half of China's foreign credits; in 1985–7 Japan's direct investment in China soared from $100 million to $2.2 billion; and by 1985 China had become Japan's second-largest trading partner after the USA. In 1980 Japan overtook the Soviet Union as the world's second economic and industrial power, and a few years later it replaced even the US as the world's first financial power in a period of huge American foreign borrowings.

The spill-over benefits of Chinese growth were not confined to Japan. The four 'Asian Tigers': Hong Kong, Singapore, South Korea and Taiwan, whose economic 'miracles' had begun earlier, also benefited. All of them, not coincidentally, shared the Confucian inheritance and culture that emphasised things like the importance of family, self-discipline, hard work, thrift and respect for hierarchy. As Japan became more prosperous, partly on the back of China's growth, South-East Asia's low-skilled and low-cost workers could undercut the Japanese in producing the same kinds of goods. By the 1980s, as their work-forces became more skilled, they even began to compete in areas like computers. They, like the Japanese, emphasised export-led growth. When that contributed to major trouble, in the 1987 Asian financial crisis, China again helped them (and itself) with steadying monetary and exchange-rate policies.

Then, at the end of the 1980s, came three developments, entirely unrelated to each other, that between them substantially changed the relationship between China and the outside world. One was the tough demonstration, by Deng and his colleagues, of the limits to permissible dissent. The second was the sudden and unexpected collapse of the Soviet Union and of European Communism. The third was the huge shock of the 1991 Gulf war.

Within China, reform had made room, among other things, for more open expressions of public opinion. As Mao might have put it, a hundred flowers of popular dissatisfaction began to bloom: with pollution, corrupt local government, even the party dictatorship itself. Students had staged demonstrations before, and there had been other expressions of opinion, for instance in the 1979 'Democracy Wall' postings. But in 1989 a further protest movement, this time by millions, came to a head in Beijing and some eighty other cities. The protests had two elements. The demand for moral purity was largely a replay of the traditional role of Chinese intellectuals, even of the traditional Confucian critique of the ruler: 'speaking truth to the emperor'. But there was more to it. The dissidents were encouraged by the beginnings of reform in Eastern Europe and the Soviet Union; and the excitement came to a head with the visit to Beijing of the reformist Soviet leader, Mikhail Gorbachev, in mid-May. When he arrived hundreds of workers, intellectuals, even policemen and soldiers, poured into Tiananmen Square to join dissident students there. After he left, a quarter of a million people gathered round the huge figure of the 'Goddess of Democracy' they had built, modelled on the Statue of Liberty in New York. Posters were waved saying 'Deng must go', alongside others with Gorbachev's face and banners in Chinese, Russian and English saying 'Democracy is our Common Dream . . . In the Soviet Union They Have Gorbachev. In China We Have Whom?'

No wonder the grim old men who had survived the Long March thought what was now at issue was a challenge to the very basis of state authority, and of the party to which they had given their lives and for which they had sacrificed wives, children, friends. Weakening the party would loosen the very cement that was making China a coherent state. While openness and reform were desirable and necessary, the new Cultural Revolution that the young reformers threatened, with its consequences in confusion and the undermining of authority, would be intolerable. So the leadership's usual talent for subtlety went by the board. The moment Gorbachev had left Beijing for Shanghai the party leader, Zhao Ziyang, who favoured accommodation with the dissidents, tried to resign, and was refused (but sacked anyway after the crackdown). Troops were brought in from distant provinces and on 4 June 1989 the People's Liberation Army assaulted Tiananmen Square and shot down youthful demonstrators who were demonstrating against corruption, trying to liberalise the regime and broaden its base. Possibly 1,000 or more civilians died in or near Tiananmen Square – in full view of foreign television cameras. Throughout China, the demonstrations were violently suppressed and resistance crushed.

The lessons for Chinese society were clear. Whatever the reforms, China would continue to have a ruthlessly authoritarian regime. Much would be allowed to the new literate and enterprising classes. Exchanges of ideas, especially in commercial, technical and scientific fields, even the more esoteric aspects of sociology, were fine. Enterprise and making money were even better. But no threat to the state or its operational mechanism, the party, would be tolerated, and no grouping that might challenge the party's hold on power would be allowed to flourish.

In the outside world, and especially in the West, public outcries were deafening. Human-rights and other groups were horrified. Governments and international organisations imposed sanctions and both the US and Europe put arms embargoes in place. None of that lasted for long. Privately, decision-makers and business could see that China and its newly booming economy was much too tempting a partner for reckless emotionalism. Moreover, it was clear that verbal protests would achieve nothing. Not much more than a century earlier, Palmerston had fought two successful wars against China, largely in defence of the principle of sovereign equality of states. China had then spent decades painfully transforming itself from an imperial network of provinces into a coherent modern nation, and was now well able to use those same principles of sovereignty in its own defence. Western pressures on 'human rights' not only had nothing to do with the imperatives of Chinese politics, but could be presented as simply a revival of Western imperialism, this time in garments of law likely to appeal to Western political and public opinion. Deng and his prime minister, Li Peng, continued China's flat refusal to allow foreign interference in China's internal affairs. So by

1990 or so, Europeans and Japanese resumed relations and the Bush (Senior) administration refused to go back on the arrangement for China's most-favoured-nation trading status that Carter had accepted. The successor Clinton administration did the same in 1993 and 1994, not least because it also wanted China's help to rein in North Korea's dangerous nuclear-weapons project. In late 1994 the North Koreans finally agreed to freeze the programme (though it later turned out they had done nothing of the kind). As for Japan, both the emperor and Prime Minister Kaifu visited China. The British prime minister, John Major, also came.

For most people in the West, Chinese affairs were in any case soon overshadowed by the entirely unexpected collapse of the Soviet Union and its empire. Beijing noted it with amazement, and the separatism of the various Soviet republics with real alarm.

In Moscow, the great break came, as these things so often do, with a change of personnel, indeed of generations. In March 1985 young Mikhail Gorbachev became general secretary of the Soviet Communist Party, and leader of the Soviet Union, in succession to a generation of the old Soviet warhorses. Unlike most of his recent predecessors, he was well educated, having taken a law degree at Moscow University. (His influential wife, Raisa, was herself a doctor.) He built a reputation as an enemy of corruption and inefficiency long before he became the top leader. Almost from the start he imposed significant reforms in the interests of making the system work more efficiently. He could see that if the Soviet Union was to survive, productivity would have to grow and so would consumer demand. Hence the two key phrases of the Gorbachev era: 'glasnost' (openness) and 'perestroika' (reform). But shifting serious resources to the civilian economy must mean cutting defence spending. He therefore began to liquidate the war in Afghanistan, which had cost so much blood and money. Even more important, he began to seek an end to the arms race with the West.

At the core of this search for an end to the arms race were once again questions about nuclear weapons. The more so because the new American president, Ronald Reagan, in power since 1981, had begun a massive build-up in almost every category of arms, including research and development on anti-missile defences. Gorbachev could see that Russia had no hope of matching this, and the technological arms race could only worsen the Soviet economic crisis. Fresh arms-control talks began. They included promising but ultimately fruitless discussions about a total elimination of nuclear weapons; but by 1987 the two sides agreed to do away with intermediate-range missiles from Europe and on outlines for fresh limits on strategic forces.[8] The agreements included a Soviet undertaking to eliminate its SS20s in Asia. In addition, both sides announced unilateral cuts in arms and defence spending for their opposing alliance systems in Europe, NATO and the Warsaw Pact.

Even these arms agreements were much less important than the political turmoil in Eastern Europe caused by Gorbachev's moves away from established verities and towards reform. No less important was his view that these Eastern European allies had become liabilities, not least economically. The result was that, starting in 1989 and with Poland in the van, the Eastern Europeans abandoned their Communist political system and its leaders. Poland was, of course, in a strong position, given the traditional power there of the Catholic Church, together with the new popularity of a powerful labour movement named Solidarity. The Hungarians, with a temerity unheard-of since their 1956 revolution, authorised the formation of opposition parties, opened the hitherto closed frontiers with Austria and in January 1990 even had the effrontery to ask the Soviets to remove their troops from Hungarian soil. The Czechs did much the same and the famous dissident and writer Vaclav Havel became the country's president. Even earlier the Romanian strong man Nicolae Ceaușescu and his wife had been executed by the military.

It was Germany that remained the fulcrum of Soviet and American concerns in Europe. Here the old order began to crumble with the opening of Hungary's frontier with Austria – which allowed large numbers of East Germans to travel via Hungary and Austria to seek refuge in West Germany. A tumult of change followed. The wall separating East from West Berlin was opened and East Germany held free elections in which the Communists were decimated. There was more. Since 1945 everyone had assumed that the Russians would never allow East Germany to escape their control. It was, after all, the most powerful of Russia's European satellites and the area where Russia stationed some of its strongest and most modern forces, to fend off NATO and keep Eastern Europe in line. Now Gorbachev made it clear that Moscow would no longer maintain its position there by force. Not only was that shift utterly unexpected, but it opened up a further and equally unexpected consequence: the reunification of East and West Germany,[9] with all its heavy economic costs for Germany and its large and long-term consequences for Europe and the entire East–West balance.

As the Soviet Union lost control of its European satellites or abandoned its clients in the Third World, the political system of the Soviet Union itself began to disintegrate. Gorbachev's own reforms began to loosen his grip. A new parliamentary-style institution merely opened him to free and public criticism from opposition groups on national television. Long-ignored grievances became the subject of nation-wide debate, while economic decline accelerated, with the Soviet GNP dropping no less than 2 per cent in 1990, growing foreign debt, and declining oil, coal and farm production. In a larger sense, the Soviet Union had probably sickened and died over several generations from its many shortcomings. Its fossilised economy, riddled with corruption, was quite unable to meet the demands of the modernising world. It had long been a private joke in NATO that the USSR was just a kind of 'Upper Volta with rockets'. Long-suppressed national discontent reared its head in many of the Soviet Union's old non-Russian republics, but Gorbachev's failed attempt to force the Baltic republics back into line by military force only made matters worse. When the USSR finally disintegrated, its constituent societies mutated back into their pre-existing states, in the form of Russia and some fourteen other republics. A bluff, hard-drinking populist named Boris Yeltsin became the president of Russia even

while Gorbachev remained president of the new and more federal
union of Soviet socialist republics that had been created to replace the
old centralised Soviet Union. At the end of 1991 Gorbachev resigned,
dissolved the Communist Party, and vanished from the political
scene, leaving the citizenry to worry about fresh economic and
political turmoil. It was the end of the Leninist and Stalinist state
that had so largely dominated European and world affairs for most of
the century.

That Soviet collapse abruptly changed the contours of great
power politics. For twenty years, many had expected that the global
dominance of two superpowers in contention would be followed by
a time when half a dozen powers – including China, India and
others – might dominate in collegial or at least balance-of-power
fashion. Instead, what now began was a period of unique and
solitary American ascendancy in global affairs. Whether in military
power, market dominance, technological clout or, in Joseph Nye's
happy phrase, the 'soft power' of diplomacy, science, production,
films, television, art, literature or fashion, the United States had, for
the moment, no competitor. It became, in a colourful French
phrase, 'the hyperpower'. With that, the dangers of a global nuclear
conflict faded. Attention also focused on the global economic,
industrial and technological changes that gathered pace during
the 1980s and '90s – many of which also centred on, or originated
in, the United States. Global television and media-driven mass
populism substantially changed the terms of politics and social
arrangements, even structures. In technology, changes came in
largely unpredicted forms centring on new, instant and virtually
uncontrollable means of communication through which personal,
strategic, technical, financial and commercial information could
flow. Above all, there was the development of the ultimately
American-controlled internet,[10] which could transmit, at the touch
of a button, not just information but money from or to any part of
the world. Together with that came mobility of many kinds of
assets, including manufacturing and service capabilities, trying to
balance among markets, currencies and differential labour costs. All

of which began to change the terms of international competition, not just in industry and economics, but in education, skills, and military affairs. The growing gap between American and even European capabilities in all these fields created consternation in Europe when it became evident that it might even liberate the US from dependence on allies.

China had not been directly involved in these Soviet dramas, but the issues and concerns they produced for Beijing were many, and none were simple. It was, for instance, no trivial matter that America no longer needed China as a counterweight to the USSR. After 1989, China maintained friendly relations with Moscow. The Soviet evacuation of Afghanistan, and of other points on China's periphery, like Mongolia and Indo-China, eliminated dangers to China's northern, southern and western frontiers. The break-up of the Soviet Union removed an even more comprehensive threat that had loomed over China for two or three decades. All that permitted major reductions in China's ground forces. Economic relations were cultivated at both local and national levels – by 1993 China was Russia's second-most important trading partner – and most of the border definitions were quietly agreed. The two sides even forged reasonable defence relations, with China buying advanced equipment from the Russians, not least jet fighter aircraft and advanced submarines. On the other hand, there was the question, made more acute by the Tiananmen affair, whether the collapse of the Soviet Communist Party might turn out to be a precedent for the weakening, or worse, of the CCP. Similarly, the way some ex-Soviet regions now distanced themselves from Russia was not an unmixed blessing: it could easily encourage other separatist tendencies and any disintegration of the new Russian Federation could create more dangerous foci of instability on China's frontiers. Meanwhile, the Americans tended quietly to support President Putin's sometimes hard-fisted efforts to restore and strengthen Russia. Neither Beijing nor Washington could fail to see that, if and when Russia recovered, it might once again become a key balancing factor between them.

The waves of economic and technical change also affected every aspect of military affairs and operations. The collapse, by eliminating the second nuclear-armed superpower, drastically diminished the danger of a major nuclear war and therefore the importance of nuclear weapons in the calculations of the major powers. The consequence was greatly increased attention and effort in non-nuclear fields, especially the hi-tech developments on which the Americans, in particular, had for some time concentrated under the heading of the 'Revolution in Military Affairs (RMA)'. The first major demonstration of its devastating effectiveness came in the 1991 Gulf war. The speed and decisiveness of the American-led victory in Arabia demonstrated how the military determinants of power had changed and that almost everyone else was now second-class. Beijing had to accept that the greater part of the People's Liberation Army was badly out of date – and would remain so for a long time. Not only that, but the citizen militia of many millions, on which Mao had relied, would be useless.[11]

The government therefore found itself in a series of interlocking difficulties with respect to each of the three chief pillars of state power: the ability to provide security and welfare for the people, and the very legitimacy of the governing structure.

The approach to the military reforms that had become essential was driven by several considerations. China remained broadly secure against a land invasion: China's vast land forces could credibly threaten to swamp an invading army. The collapse of the Soviet Union, the rise of the US to hyperpower status and the 1991 Gulf war reduced the political and deterrent value of nuclear weapons and focused attention on new conventional conflicts, new arsenals of precision weapons and especially on domestic morale.[12] Furthermore, growing difficulties over North Korea, Japan and Taiwan suggested that China's strategic focus must shift from the traditional business of northern borders to the Pacific. While China had no hope of matching America's command of hi-technologies within the foreseeable future, it might have to fight limited local or regional wars under hi-tech conditions. That would mean concentration on command, control and intelligence, as well as air and sea capabilities, rather than an almost exclusive focus on land warfare. China therefore began to indicate that it wanted a capacity to operate in the Western Pacific, as far beyond China's shores as 'the first island chain'. This was defined as a line running from the Ryukyu isles to Taiwan, the Philippines and parts of Indonesia. It may or may not be an accident that this closely echoed Dean Acheson's 1950 pre-Korean War definition of America's essential strategic interests in the Western Pacific.

The obvious difficulty was that China's own defence-industry base was quite inadequate to develop and maintain the systems involved. The result was heavy expenditure, rising soon after that 1991 Gulf war, on the purchase of modern weapons, including ships and aircraft, from Russia and Israel. China maintained its very small force of around twenty intercontinental missiles and a few hundred medium-range ones, and paid attention to developing shorter-range weapons that could cover targets in Taiwan, the Philippines, even Japan and Vietnam. Together with that came work on logistics, training, co-ordination and administration. Training became a special feature, especially for officers and non-commissioned officers. A major force reorganisation came in 1998, especially of procurement, quality control, research, development, and, by no means least, intelligence. At much the same time, the armed forces were told to abandon their huge corpus of business activities – for years these had ranged from manufacturing to running brothels and even smuggling. Above all, the modernisation programme needed money and in the decade to 2000 China's defence budget doubled. Even that seriously understated real spending. China's official defence budget in 2000 was around $14.7 billion. But the Americans thought the People's Liberation Army was probably spending at least three or four times more than that. Even so, Chinese defence spending remained very small by comparison with others, especially the USA.

In the meantime, though, China's old social controls began to loosen with subtle shifts in public morale and politics. After the Tiananmen affair of 1989, and the spectacle of the people's army shooting at the people, relations between the party and the people could never be quite the same again. The old Communist enthusiasms and certainties were further undermined by the new economic and social policies of the Deng regime. For all but a tiny minority, even within the ranks of the party itself, passionate belief in the old Maoist verities evaporated, as did willingness to sacrifice for the sake of the 'Revolution'. Instead, the leadership mobilised fresh waves of injured nationalism. Moreover, enthusiasm for nationalist feelings and claims now came together with enthusiasm for personal enrichment. Nationalism and economic growth became the new ideology of the state and the new source of the party's legitimacy. That fettered government to the fulfilment of economic promises as well as to those nationalist ambitions. Economic and technical development had to provide the foundations on which all elements of modernisation could be built. Yet the great economic progress of the 1990s was not accompanied by political or social reforms of any consequence. It seemed possible that the results, in the new century, would be difficult to cope with.

Recognition of the difficulties in combining rapid growth, and its inevitable volatilities, with the maintenance of firm control, led to changes at the top of the party. While Deng remained the unchallengeable supreme leader, the governing group of old men agreed on a new party leader in the person of the conservative mayor of Shanghai, Jiang Zemin. He came from a middle-class family, had been well schooled in traditional Chinese subjects and European literature, topping it all off with university training as an electrical-machinery engineer. He was the first of the 'third generation' of leaders to reach the top of the party, men who were not veterans of the Long March or even of the war against the Nationalists. However, he had seen enough, in war and especially in his party bailiwick of Shanghai, to make him a thorough moderniser. Under Deng and Jiang, China experienced through the 1990s not only spectacular growth, at breakneck speed, but an elaboration of China's international economic ties. That further helped to produce startling advances in China. Between 1978, when Deng first set the country on the path to reform, and the end of the century, China grew by around 9–9.5 per cent p.a.[13] In the 1980s and 1990s average incomes in China multiplied by four, and by the year 2000 China's GDP, on standard measures, placed it sixth in the world,[14] with 40 per cent of it claimed by services.

Unsurprisingly, money and investment flooded into China; not only from banks and multinational corporations but from or through sophisticated overseas Chinese. American and European investment tended to concentrate on China's domestic market and a Chinese middle class that was growing rapidly in numbers and purchasing power. Car manufacturers like VW, Peugeot, General Motors, DaimlerChrysler and others invested in China. Great financial firms came too: Goldman Sachs opened its doors in Shanghai. East Asian investors, on the other hand, tended to focus on China as a base for labour-intensive exports to the rest of the world. By 2003/4 foreign investment, zero in 1978, had reached a total of some $448 billion.[15] Soon after 2000 inward foreign direct investment was running at, or more than, $40 billion per annum, while China was itself becoming a significant foreign investor, in particular the second-largest foreign holder (after Japan) of US Treasury bonds. Chinese firms were also going further afield under orders from the government, buying access to raw materials and energy, entering into hi-tech industries or even starting to build global brands of their own. All these processes expanded the pool of Chinese managerial competence. It grew even further with the doubling, in the later 1990s, of China's tertiary student population and the return of Chinese graduates from overseas.

In the US and Europe, between 1982 and 2003 merchandise imports, from China grew by 20–21 per cent a year. That meant changing the relative prices of assets, capital and labour for large parts of the world, even influencing interest rates and keeping down bond yields. Especially important was the increase in China's importance to its neighbours. China's share of South Korean exports, for example, rose from zero in 1980 to 20.5 per cent in 2003; and in the same period its share of Japan's exports went up from just under 4 per cent to 13.6 per cent. The nature of Chinese exports also changed, from concentration on labour-intensive products like consumer durables to becoming the world's third-largest exporter of electronic equipment and a seller of information-technology products. Nor did Beijing neglect innovation. In the decade 1991–2001 applications to China's patent office multiplied by five.

Naturally by 1990 China had also become a large importer of raw materials and energy. China started to import oil in 1993. Nine years later it was importing 70 million tons and, according to Beijing estimates, expected to import 150 million tons by 2010 and 250–300 million tons by 2020. China's coal consumption was also expected to double between 2001 and 2025. The political effects of such flows were very large. They have also focused attention on China's massively wasteful use of energy: by the opening of the twenty-first century Chinese consumption of energy per unit of output was anything from three to ten times as high as in the industrialised countries. Growing oil consumption also forced China to try to diversify its sources of supply, for instance by investing in Africa and South-East Asia. Saudi Arabia, too, started to court Chinese custom for oil in exchange for goods and military hardware. Of course, these oil-supply routes were still guarded by the US Navy.

China finally joined the World Trade Organisation (WTO) in December 2001 with average Chinese tariffs quickly dropping from 41 per cent to 6 per cent. At the same time, everywhere in the last two decades of the twentieth century rhetoric about free trade barely disguised the reality of managed trade in a dense web of deals and bargains among corporations and governments, driven largely by government-defined national interests and social policies. Moreover, it was estimated by the turn of the century that almost half of, for example, American exports and imports were traded not on the open market but within corporations and their affiliates. Such groupings could shift materials, components, production and work in ways that hardly showed up on national, let alone international, statistics. Even the much-discussed American trade deficit with China was partly illusory. The growing practice of American firms to outsource work and deliver products to world-wide markets through foreign affiliates meant that unknown numbers of sales listed as Chinese exports, even of sales within the US to American customers, were in fact US affiliate sales and products.

A governing factor in all this was the question of currencies. In 1994 China reorganised its currency markets and pegged its currency, the yuan, to the US dollar. That made China, for many purposes, part of the dollar world. At the same time, the low fixed exchange rate gave important advantages in trade with the US and in other, US-dollar denominated trading regimes, not only to Chinese traders but to other Asian countries that aligned their own currencies with the yuan. As Chinese trading and currency earnings rose, large quantities of Chinese (and, for that matter, Japanese) reserves were parked in US Treasury bonds. Such an anchor to the world's premier trading currency would avoid exchange-rate volatility while earning secure, reasonable and internationally credible real rates of return and, in addition, help to prop up US domestic spending, not least on imports from China itself. That access to the US market also gave China large trade surpluses to balance what would otherwise have been deficits in its overall trade.

Inevitably, growth and expansion came together with weaknesses. By the end of the century China had developed bulging over-capacity in areas like steel and automobiles and huge over-investment in infrastructure. Moreover, financial affairs everywhere were much affected by the new, globalised means of information and transmission. In the 1990s, that promoted startling growth and cheapened credit while encouraging consumption and speculation, not least in real estate. In the US, the surge in share prices of the late 1990s boosted the holdings of US households by $7 trillion over a mere four years followed by a boost of the value of US homes by another $5 trillion. Non-financial problems also grew. Trade in goods meant huge increases in shipping, much of it under uncontrolled flags of convenience. By the end of the 1990s US ports alone handled some 60,000 port calls by ocean-going ships of all kinds. Many of them might have crews from any part of the world, whose members could often bypass over-stretched American immigration officials, while the ships themselves carried more containers than could be thoroughly scanned or inspected. The implications for national security were large. Not only that, but the world's shipping lanes continued to be infested by industrial-scale piracy, especially in South-East Asian waters and the South China Sea.[16] But China had tougher controls than most. The presence of several million people in various kinds of labour or punishment or rehabilitation camps underlined these points. So did the executions of hundreds, perhaps thousands, of malefactors each year.

On the other hand, the country's public finances and government statistics remained a largely opaque mess. Western estimates suggested that, while government revenues over the 1980s and '90s ran at around 30 per cent of GDP, a great deal of revenue may have been collected but was not listed in the budget figures and did not reach government coffers. Instead, it remained in the uncontrolled hands of local officials. The result was the near-collapse of public finance in many counties and towns, so that additional revenue had to be extracted from farmers, often by coercion. Furthermore, the banking system turned out to be a quite inadequate base for a flourishing entrepreneurialism. It was clumsy, bureaucratic and burdened with very large quantities of non-performing assets, especially those in the state-owned sector. At the same time, government involvement in banks and business was massive. The state continued to control most of the peaks of the economy, from energy, mining and telecoms to transport, textiles, health care and much of the retail sector. The private sector itself had close ties to the state; and many of the firms that came to be listed on the Hong Kong Stock Exchange were in reality subsidiaries of big state corporations and were therefore merely capital-raising exercises. Furthermore, as many foreigners discovered to their cost, joint ventures with government entities were best avoided. For Chinese officials 'upholding China's interests' was a top priority, and foreigners were regularly cheated. In the words of one foreign trader, 'the overall system is almost incompatible with honesty'. At all levels, records were apt to be doctored, and agreed factory and staff conditions ignored.

Above all, the entire regulatory system remained arbitrary and entirely unpredictable. It was even, rather as in the imperial era, subject to the whims of provincial or local officials – which is why wise investors made a point of never relying on the law but rather establishing good links with the CCP. Property rights were highly uncertain. A particular source of complaint by foreigners was China's cavalier way with the intellectual property, including patents, on which so much of the modern hi-tech and service economies depend. According to calculations by the US Trade Representative's office in 2004/5, some 90 per cent of the software on Chinese PCs, of the music on CDs and films on DVDs, was pirated. The government, foreigners said, was indifferent.

No less important was the fact that economic growth encouraged a revival of rampant corruption, enthusiastic fraud, embezzlement, counterfeiting and criminality of various kinds. Given the blurred lines between public and private wealth created by privatisation, membership of the party opened the way to corrupt riches for some, including the families of high party cadres. Corrupt dominance could be exercised in collaboration with violent criminal gangs who could keep villagers and others in line. More and more of this was reported on Chinese websites and even the press, but none of it was much changed by the occasional disgrace or even execution of offenders. Indeed, criminal gangs flourished. The Triad system, that global network of ancient and secret criminal societies, grew further both in China and the global Chinese diaspora. Before the end of the century there were suggestions that there was no business of any size in Hong Kong that did not have some Triad investment. In the 1990s China seems also to have become a major drug consumer, producer and transit point for international trafficking, much of it fuelled by the new electronic means of moving international capital.

By the end of the century, then, and despite weaknesses, China had discovered how to become rich while remaining an authoritarian police state. Yet the exchanges of information essential for entrepreneurialism and growth also brought an unprecedentedly free exchange of news and views between individuals and even with the outside world. Foreigners had started to flock to China. Some came to invest, often in the form of joint ventures. Others came for tourism. That became an important source of foreign-currency earnings and, as in imperial times, a way of impressing the world with China's grandeur. It also became impossible to stop more open discussion of issues as the regime's ability to control reporting and comment proved to be highly imperfect. That did not stop the authorities from trying,[17] especially since China found itself dealing with an increasingly censorious Western world which had developed a much more arrogantly intrusive view of others. Yet closing journals and imprisoning editors often did more to stimulate than to limit discussion, even though reading critical Western reports could earn the reader a spell in a forced-labour camp.[18] Nor did attempts to monitor or filter internet facilities, or suspend search engines, help much, though the government was said to use up to 30,000 police to do the monitoring. That loosening of controls, and the general turn towards Western ideas, could hardly help increasing the influence of foreigners, especially of Americans, in the higher reaches of Chinese society.[19] In any case, how could trade, investment, productivity, flourish without creating room for markets, incentives, creativity?

No less important was the rise of religious groupings, notably Buddhists and especially Protestants. There were said to be tens of millions of Protestants, including even party officials. There was ethnic discontent, too, especially in the western regions and among Moslems. The state met that by controls, bans on several hundred Buddhist temples and Christian churches, and attacks on priests or Tibetan monks and nuns.[20] No less striking was the rise of the Falun Gong spiritual society.[21] It was founded in 1992 by Li Hongzhi, a minor park policeman and practitioner of traditional breathing exercises said to improve health and give long life, as well as improved spiritual understanding. It made its first public appearance, entirely without warning, on 25 April 1999, when members used the new means of electronic communication to assemble anywhere from ten to

Falun Gong

Falun Gong is a spiritual practice, with some beliefs akin to those of Daoism and Buddhism, that purports to improve the bodies, minds and spirits of its practitioners. It is also a huge movement which, albeit unpolitical — indeed, its teachings forbid political involvement — has reached a size and organisation that has alarmed Chinese authorities and led to severe repression.

Falun Gong went public in 1992 through the efforts of Li Hongzhi and quickly became popular not only in China but world-wide. For seven years it flourished under the general supervision of the Chinese Communist Party and in 1998 a state-owned television station in Shanghai claimed that it now had between 70 and 100 million members in China alone.

But government and party became concerned in April 1999 when some 10,000 Falun Gong members assembled in Beijing, quietly and without warning, to sit on the ground and meditate in protest against alleged mistreatment of their fellows by the police. A few months later the government, obviously alarmed by the size and organisation of the group, and now convinced that it sought political power, began a nation-wide programme of Falun Gong suppression. The head of the Communist Party, Jiang Zemin, personally began to use the media, including the party newspaper *People's Daily*, to condemn the group. The authorities clearly saw the dispute as one for science and materialism, against superstition and idealism. That created a variety of difficulties, since several tens of thousands of party members also belong to Falun Gong.

In fact, the party's distrust is not so much of idealism as of any grouping so large and disciplined, and therefore constituting a potential threat to the party's dominance and control of society. Both the Taiping rebellion of 1850 and the Boxer rebellion of 1900 began with strong religious impulses. If history is cyclical, as Chinese have always believed, the pattern might repeat itself.

> Sensitivities are increased by the fact that Chinese society is in any case undergoing culturally disruptive changes in the whole process of modernisation.
>
> There has, in fact, been no sign that Falun Gong, as a group, has political ambitions. Which has not prevented police from adopting very harsh measures indeed against its members, including imprisonment, beating, torture and even execution.

sixteen thousand members, quite suddenly, outside the party headquarters in Beijing's Forbidden City. They sat there for fifteen hours, murmuring, passive and evidently impossible to scare away, seeking legal permission to publish their tracts and books. They also asked for the freeing of some dozen Falun Gong members who had been arrested the day before in a northern city. When Premier Zhu Rongji met their leaders he was astonished to find that the protesters included high officials and party members. The party reacted with its usual ruthlessness against anything that might smack, however faintly, of an alternative centre of power. Falun Gong was banned as superstitious and treasonous.[22] Thousands of adherents were imprisoned, tortured and even killed, yet there have, since then, been suggestions that Falun Gong may have some 30–50 million members. As one writer puts it, 'What Beijing fears is not so much Falun Gong itself but what it represents – the underlying problems and instability in Chinese society.' The party leaders understood very well that in the past such sects had threatened dynasties, or even helped overturn them.

More fundamentally still, population increase, combined with industrial growth and pollution, created serious shortages of water, clean air and land. According to the ministry of water resources, in 2003 China consumed four times as much water per unit of GDP as the world average. Many villages found themselves drought-ridden as water was diverted to favoured places like Beijing. Moreover, the water problem was greatly aggravated by the problems of pollution and waste management. Some 80 per cent of China's waste water was untreated and three-quarters of China's lakes had become polluted. About one-third of China was also thought to suffer from severe soil erosion. Too much land was appropriated for construction. Air pollution was made much worse by China's massive and inefficient use of hydrocarbons. In 1999, of the ten cities with the worst air pollution in the world, nine were in China. Pollution alone, according to the World Bank, was costing China almost 8 per cent of GDP. Alongside that were huge and growing problems of health care. Under Mao, 90 per cent of country people had had access to subsidised health clinics. By the late 1990s, 90 per cent of country people and 60 per cent of people in cities had no kind of health insurance and the World Health Organisation ranked China's health system as 144th in the world.[23] There were also huge disparities in health care between different regions, with the poor western regions having the worst health and education services.

All of which was certain to put question marks against the role of the party itself. Belief in Maoism might decline but the party continued to propagate his heritage which was, after all, the taproot of the party's authority. On the other hand, the very economic reforms needed for growth eroded the role of the institutions that were the base of the party's power, even though small groups of smart young party members remained at key points of many large enterprises. In any case, corruption and local official collusion remained, and most Chinese thought party members would just use their power for personal gain. By the end of the century there were, in fact, startling signs of discontent. There were official crack-downs on 'public intellectuals' who said uncomfortable things. There was a sharp rise in the number and size of public protests. According to police figures there were some 87,000 in 2005 compared with 10,000 a decade earlier.[24] To be sure, most were spontaneous local protests against official extortion and corruption, and could often be defused by economic concessions to the demonstrators. Still, the protests against land appropriation mattered. According to the UN Development Program, by 2001/2 some 50 million people had been thrown off their land with little or no compensation.

None of this unrest or dissatisfaction was likely to threaten the party's monopoly of power, backed by demonstrated willingness to use all the powers of the police and armed forces to make sure that there was no organised political opposition. Civil society, certainly in any Western sense, remained underdeveloped. All the modern means of hi-tech communication and intelligence that might be used to inform and rally dissidents were, obviously, even more fully available to the state. And yet dissent, unless reasonably dealt with, could also undermine national security. The 2003 Gulf war only reminded the leadership, in case a reminder was necessary, that countries whose society has been allowed to rot can be easily defeated in war.

In any case there were many ways of containing unrest. One was, obviously, by distributing growing wealth. Another was greater decentralisation of the economic and much other decision-making that was anyway necessary on economic grounds. Local officials could change or subvert Beijing's decisions in the interests of local conditions or people. Some of that went back more than two millennia, to the very beginnings of the Chinese imperial bureaucracy. Even strong emperors had always found it hard to control local officials and by the 1990s it was all happening again. It was hard, now, to control local officials who, together with private enterprise, tried to bring new vitality to the industries of their own regions, especially with major projects. Conversely, soon after 2000 the government tried to use administrative measures to slow down economic overheating. But curbs on bank lending proved very unpopular and less effective when more decisions had been turned over to local or provincial control. In any event there were very large sums of private money flowing around the system, quite beyond the control of the centre. Growing prosperity and education meant a growing middle class with increased purchasing power and demands.

Blaming foreigners naturally helped. Deng pointedly countered Western outrage about the Tiananmen affair, as well as Western views about economic interdependence, by saying that there was a Western strategy to subvert the rule of the Chinese Communist Party in peaceful and evolutionary ways. But the leadership would not allow the agenda for China's rapid economic development to be subverted. So the authorities tried to capture the gains of interdependence with the outside world, while rejecting the political implications, including a deeper involvement of foreigners in the Chinese economy. They tried, above all, to avoid any danger that China might come to depend on others. Foreigners' motives were certainly suspect. By the 1990s the key to the party's hold on power had obviously become a more open economy to furnish growing prosperity for most Chinese; but that must not be allowed to tie the hand of the leadership.

Other difficulties were less easily controlled. The central leadership itself was experiencing problems, especially through the steep decline in the charisma and intrinsic authority of the post-Deng generation of leaders. Deng himself, before leaving office, set out new and more stable leadership-succession arrangements. After he died in 1997, he was duly followed by Jiang Zemin, who had been party general secretary since 1984. In the fall of 2002 Jiang, by then seventy-six years old, was in turn replaced and there were other major changes in the party politburo, whose make-up became more technocratic. The party's new general secretary was Hu Jintao, a young, smooth, sartorially Westernised administrator, intelligent and well educated but with no obvious ideology or new and far-reaching ideas about China's world role. Born in 1942, he had held senior provincial jobs. In 1985 he had been the party's youngest provincial leader, in Guizhou province. In 1988 he took over Tibet, where he duly crushed pro-independence protests and at one point declared martial law. At the highest levels, though, he was a neophyte. Now, in 2003 and a year after becoming general secretary and so becoming, together with President Jiang, joint leader of China, he succeeded Jiang as president, too. In 2004 Jiang, then aged seventy-eight, also resigned as chairman of the Military Commission, again in favour of the now-62-year-old Hu. The new man duly declared 'Western-style democracy' unsuitable for China and set about being tougher on dissent while starting to reform the state banks and the stock market.

However, neither Jiang nor Hu could claim anything resembling the personal prestige of the older generation of leaders, let alone of a near-mythical figure like Mao Zedong. Still less could either claim anything comparable to Deng's long-standing and intimate links among the senior military.

By the turn of the twenty-first century, therefore, the new leaders, supported and backed by increasing numbers of well-educated economists, technocrats and administrators – not to mention well-connected and sympathetic overseas Chinese businessmen – remained acutely aware that all their aims for domestic cohesion and welfare, not to mention China's clout in the world at large and even their own power, continued to depend on economic growth and modernisation – and even on trying to spread prosperity from the coast and its Special Zones to the often poverty-stricken interior.

Against that background, China's view of its role in the world proceeded from, as it were, a concentric circle of interests, rather as that of the old empires had done. The principles were not obscure. China saw the world, entirely unsentimentally, as a highly competitive system of independent states among which relations would be arranged by a balance of power. There was deep suspicion of interdependence as anything other than a mechanism for enhancing one's own advantages, and total disbelief in the myths of multi-culturalism. In that context, China would, of course, remain 'in-dependent', meaning unaligned. It would proceed on the basis of 'comprehensive national power', a principle with clear echoes of the old Soviet idea of 'correlation of forces' – the idea that an effective policy must weigh all aspects of national power: diplomatic, military, artistic, literary and other elements of what has become known as 'Soft Power'.[25] In managing its affairs, China would have assets ranging from historic reputation or long-established cultural or political ties, to the full range of economic, diplomatic and military power. All supported, as always with Chinese external policy, by China's proverbially boundless patience. But not yet supported by other essential elements of national power, especially the thoroughgoing reform and modernisation of China's military establishment that the economy was now making possible, so that both the economy and an effective military would be available to restore China's international influence.

At the core of policy lay two considerations. One was the need to manage the political and strategic environment so as to maintain an overwhelming concentration of attention, effort and resources on China's own massive domestic problems. The other was the restoration and maintenance of China's own territorial integrity, defined with endless reiteration as the claim to any territory or waters that any Chinese ruler may have controlled, however briefly and however long ago. Emotions on such issues have often been inflamed by the continuing tones of injured nationalism in Beijing.[26] Sometimes the claims could be met in agreeable fashion. In 1997, for instance, the British returned Hong Kong to China with no more drama than a rain-drenched parade, a lowering of the Union Jack and a speech by the Prince of Wales. That, and the reassertion of Chinese sovereignty in Macao, were surely major foreign-policy achievements for the regime. Another was the assertion, even by new domestic laws, of control over any potentially oil-bearing region of the South China Sea.[27] The Indonesians and Vietnamese already had oil companies prospecting there, but such a Chinese claim could be left on the record for years or decades, only to be revived long afterwards as a 'historic right'. Similar claims exist in other areas, for example over the Senkaku/Diaoyu Islands in the East China Sea, which Japan also claims.

Above all, there was the always the neuralgic question of Taiwan, which China insists is merely a renegade province of the one indivisible China. The issue became particularly sensitive during the early and middle 1990s when a growing independence movement on the island began to argue for separate international standing. In many places the claim was thought reasonable. Taiwan was, and remains, an economically successful, orderly democracy of something over 20 million people and, the argument has run, should be able to run its own independent affairs. By contrast, Beijing has consistently tried to isolate Taipei internationally. It has kept a close and suspicious eye on efforts by Taiwan leaders to use informal visits to build relations with Asian and North American statesmen. In late October 2004 the Taiwan president, Chen Chuibian, remarked that 'in Taiwan, a country of 36,000 kilometres' coastline with effective government and a sound political system, sovereignty is vested with the people'.[28] There was an immediate response from Beijing, which repeatedly warned that on this vital issue of sovereignty it would use force. In 1996 China even fired some missiles into the sea not far from Taiwan, but calmed down when the US sent two carrier task forces into the vicinity, to signal its continuing commitment to Taiwan's defence against any unprovoked attack. Although by 2000 or so the PLA probably lacked the forces to take on Taiwan, it staged exercises on the mainland coast, simulating an invasion of the island. A few years later Taiwan was planning a new constitution, while China was veering between hints about lowering the temperature and acquiring the means to launch a 'decapitation strike' at Taiwan. The United States, for its part, has consistently discouraged Taiwan from moving away from the concept of 'One China' and been most reluctant to prejudice the interdependent Washington–Beijing relationship. Such difficulties and threats have certainly contributed to China's defence build-up.

There was also China's old habit of territorial expansion, not by force of arms but by demographic reach. Latter-day examples have been Tibet, and Xinjiang, where China fears pan-Turkic and pan-Islamic subversion. Ethnic or religious ties are not controllable. One response (in spite of the regions' water shortages and discouraging climates) has been a migration of Han Chinese that cannot fail to swamp local cultures and communities. There has been a strong clamp-down in both areas, perhaps especially in Xinjiang, which houses some Chinese nuclear-development facilities. Not only was the influx of Han people designed to submerge the locals, but the region has become an archipelago of punishment and labour camps ruled by the Xinjiang Construction Corps, which answers directly to Beijing. Xinjiang's huge oil and gas reserves, and cotton, have been

developed and in September 2004 came the start of a new 620-mile
pipeline to bring more oil across eastern Kazakhstan into western
Xinjiang. The eight million Uighurs, who historically dominated
Xinjiang, have become a minority in their own 'Autonomous Republic', where the best jobs and goods have gone to the Chinese. In
the ancient city of Kashgar, in the Uighur heartland, traditional mud-
brick houses have been razed to make room for apartment blocks for
ethnic Chinese. Sporadic rebellions, for instance in 1990 and 1997,
were met with repression, which merely intensified after the events of
11 September 2001 in the USA. There has been much anger about
the establishment of an Uighur government-in-exile in 2004 in
America. Indeed, China began to define as 'terrorist' anyone who
thinks 'separatist thoughts' and to denounce any disturbance as
'splittism' and/or counter-revolutionary, stimulated by 'foreign
sources'. There are notable similarities between these tactics and
those that the emperor Qianlong employed in Turkestan and with the
Mongols some three and a half centuries earlier. Equally of course,
once the Chinese become the majority in any such region, China can
argue for the rights of local majorities. By such methods China has
achieved a significant expansion of its effective territory since the
declaration of the People's Republic in 1949. Not surprisingly, some
Western commentators have said that the Chinese empire is a multi-
cultural entity held together by force.

There is also the ambiguous situation of Central Asia, beyond the
borders of Xinjiang and Tibet. The 60 million locals in ex-Soviet
Central Asia have shown themselves very conscious of the fact that
Sino-Soviet clashes occurred a mere two decades after the Chinese
took over Xinjiang, and they have fears of their own about Chinese
expansionism. According to unofficial estimates, by 2004 there were
as many as 300,000 Chinese – mostly merchants – in Kazakhstan
alone. Kazakhstan, Kyrgyzstan and Tajikistan have all become
nervous about the flood of Chinese migrants, encouraged by
China's economic boom, coming into Xinjiang and liable to seep
further west. The Kazakhs in particular have become wary about
the new rail and road links in western China, lest they become

springboards for Chinese expansion into the sparsely peopled regions of their country. Several Central Asian states, notably Kyrgyzstan, Kazakhstan and Tajikistan, in seeking a policy of Chinese restraint, have shown that they wish to strengthen links with Beijing. Obviously, they are acutely aware of the ancient principle that strong empires always wish to control, even occupy, weak or potentially volatile borderlands.

Beyond that, there is China's growing regional influence. It has begun to affect not just cultural affairs but to make China a focal point of regional trade and investment, and to influence industrial development and military planning. Beijing has established close economic and even political ties with South Korea. China and India, on the other hand, continued to see one another as an economic competitor, a spur to development and an unavowed, but often deeply felt, potential threat. These various links and influences China has sometimes used to frustrate other 'outsiders', including the US. By the end of the century, the most acute problem in North-East Asia remained North Korea and its nuclear-weapons programme. It posed a direct danger to North-East Asian countries and the USA, and seemed likely to stimulate rearmament elsewhere, even in Japan. The American view – following North Korea's failure to deliver on previous agreements – was that Pyongyang must move towards disarmament before it could expect economic aid. The Chinese and South Korean view, however, was that encouragement to economic reform would itself be part of a pacification programme, would encourage North Korea to be more co-operative and might even encourage, in the US phrase, 'regime change'. A North Korean collapse, on the other hand, might lead to a reunified and strong Korea. Indeed, even short of collapse, any kind of economic or military crisis could bring a flood of North Korean refugees pouring across China's borders. The Chinese therefore tried to demonstrate what reform and modernisation could achieve. They even invited senior North Koreans to visit China's new research-and-development hub for international companies.[29] Before the end of the century it had become widely accepted that China was the key player in seeking a peaceful resolution of the issue, while North Korea remained confident that it could rely on Chinese and South Korean aid to prop up its miserable economy.

Relations between Japan and China have always been complex. On the one hand, Japan has given China many tens of billions of yen in aid, and invested billions more in technology and production. Indeed, in the 1990s Japan became China's major source of advanced technical equipment. During the later stages of the Cold War, Beijing welcomed signs of growing Japanese strength and self-defence efforts as a restraint on the USSR. In the 1990s, though, China reverted to seeing Japan as a chief long-term threat[30] to itself. Beijing became sharply critical of Japan's growing role in Asian affairs, though both countries had common interests, for instance over North Korea. The government, and the Chinese public, noted reviving Japanese nationalism and self-confidence with alarm. Chinese opinion, strongly encouraged by government and the domestic media, continued to browbeat Japan by emphasising its misdeed in the 1930s and '40s. There was anger at Japan's failure to show sufficient contrition, while the Japanese saw themselves as victims of Allied misdeeds at Hiroshima and Nagasaki. There were further Chinese worries about US–Japan defence co-operation or the strengthening of Japan's technologically much superior defence forces, itself largely the result of growing North Korean dangers and the expansion of China's military, naval and air power. Beijing has even criticised Japanese efforts to 'infiltrate, control and exploit' the Chinese economy. Shortly after 2000 these attacks on Japanese national confidence began to encourage a decided backlash and reassertion in Japan.

South-East Asia has for many centuries been a region with strong cultural, strategic and economic links with China. It is also one in which Chinese and Indian interests meet. The South-East Asian grouping of states, ASEAN, has developed a strategy to constrain either of them from exercising dominance in the region, or the South China Sea. ASEAN members have allied themselves with China in resisting Western 'human rights' pressures but failed to get China's agreement for a multilateral regime for the South China Sea. Uncertain whether America would stay involved in South-East Asia, they adopted Gulliver tactics: enveloping China not only in trading and tourism arrangements but in multiple regional and exchange organisations and arrangements. By 2004 a number of these states were even organising an East Asian summit meeting, proposed by China, one of whose announced purposes was to exclude the West in general and the United States in particular. Or again, it has been widely conceded that if anyone could influence the military regime of Myanmar (Burma) it must be, for all its softly, softly approach, China. Even more clearly, from the 1980s onwards, China worked hard to eliminate any remaining Russian influence in Cambodia. In the words of US President Carter's former National Security Advisor, Zbigniew Brzezinski, 'There is no doubt that China is quietly creating a very successful Chinese co-prosperity sphere in East Asia. The countries of the region increasingly are paying China due deference, something to which the Chinese graciously respond' – just as, one might add, the old emperors behaved towards tribute-bearers.

Beyond these more immediate concerns, China's global position has been rife with uncertainties and ambiguities. China became assertive and, conscious of growing economic clout, began to stress its rights and its desire to resume its classical leading role in East Asia, and as one of the world's great powers. Though it refused most distant involvements, by the end of the twentieth century it had achieved growing international influence and respect at every level. It was accepted by the major powers as an important, indeed necessary, participant in global financial, trading and political arrangements. In the words of a 1999 study by the US Council of Foreign Relations, 'no significant aspect of world affairs is exempt from its influence.'

After a long period in which Beijing distrusted multilateral approaches as limiting its own freedom of manoeuvre, it started in the 1990s to see such networks as possible instruments of national policy. In 1995 the official party newspaper, the *People's Daily*, spoke of the United Nations as the 'largest and most authoritative intergovernmental organisation in the world [with] unique powers'. A mere thirty years earlier, albeit during the Cultural Revolution, it had spoken of the UN as a 'dirty international political stock exchange, in the grip of a few powers'. (It did not discuss whether both descriptions might not be true.) In any case, Beijing continued to resist those effects of globalisation that blurred the distinction between the domestic and international realms. It continued to reject globalisation's tendencies to state fragmentation. So that, while Beijing pursued closer links with Arabian oil producers, the Han Chinese have, since the terrorist attacks in the United States, become more suspicious and disdainful of Moslems, even those living within China's borders.

China has therefore tried to spread its diplomatic net, and its 'soft power' and cultural appeals, far and wide. By the mid-1990s China had joined or tried to join a raft of international organisations, especially economic ones like the WTO and the Asian Development Bank. It joined the 1968 Non-Proliferation Treaty, shortly afterwards halting nuclear tests. It has been evident that where Beijing joined an international regime, it acted to maintain, not to transform it. Even the UN Security Council seat was used mostly in unobtrusive ways. China also raised its political visibility with high-level visits abroad, well beyond Asia, and its cultural role with tours by colourful artistic groups and gymnastic and sports teams. Criticisms were apt to be brushed off, again, as new versions of imperialist attacks on China's national integrity.

At the same time, given its tremendous domestic problems, and especially its large new transnational dependencies, it was not surprising that China showed no desire to be an international trouble-maker and kept its head conspicuously below the parapet on most major international issues that did not directly affect it. There was, for instance, the marked consolidation of the European Union in the decade from the mid-1980s, and the creation of a common European currency, the 'Euro'. There was active Western intervention in the Balkans, the results of which were often extremely odd. For instance, the NATO campaign in the Serb province of Kosovo, allegedly to prevent Christian Serbs from 'ethnically cleansing' Moslem Albanians, quickly led to ethnic cleansing of most of the Christian Serbs by Moslem Albanians and the creation of an expensive NATO military protectorate. Or there was European diplomatic assertion in Iran and the Gulf, or the dispatch of troops to Afghanistan.[31] By the start of the new twenty-first century over 50,000 – at times 100,000 – European troops were serving outside Europe, albeit mostly in peace-keeping missions.

In all of this, Beijing remained silent, or at least disengaged. The Europeans' own interest in China was almost exclusively as a market and a target for investment by major firms like Siemens in Germany and Alcatel in France. China, in its turn, saw Europe mainly as a market or a source of finance. Soon after 2000 Germany had become China's fifth-largest trading partner and France an important supplier of technology. Although Europe imposed an arms embargo after the 1989 Tiananmen affair, within a decade the French got their EU partners to agree that the embargo was an anachronism. If either side saw the other as a natural partner in forming possible counterweights to the American hyperpower and its historic tendencies to unilateralism, that was not much apparent by 2000 or so.

It was, though, China's relationship with the United States that was at the core of Chinese foreign-relations policy and plans. Both sides might find each other vital partners for the maintenance of peace in Korea, the Taiwan Straits and the South China Sea, for co-operation in the UN Security Council, and curbing the spread of nuclear weapons. Both Jiang Zemin and, after him, Hu Jintao went to some lengths to maintain equable relations with Washington. Both expressed appreciation for US efforts on trade, and Jiang even managed an invitation to President Bush's ranch in Texas.

Nevertheless, both sides also understood that China wanted to take back its 'rightful' role as the dominant power in East Asia; and that, in the long term, China might develop the potential not just to challenge America in the Pacific but perhaps even to challenge America's global primacy. For the time being, American support for China's development was essential for China's trade and finance flows, and to maintain the generally stable environment that China needed. But the relationship could not be one of simple friendship, let alone alliance, for the doubts about America and its intentions were real. Beijing welcomed the advantages of the American economic links, but could also see the dangers of possible dependence. It could welcome the American contribution to the stability of the East Asian region, and take on board American declarations about welcoming a 'strong, peaceful and prosperous China', without abandoning its belief that a fundamental American aim was to weaken and delay China's rise and to force it to play by international rules formulated by the West, without China's say-so. Jiang and Hu could play down China's global ambitions, and leaders like Prime Minister Wen Jibao could emphasise the peaceful nature and intentions of that rise, as he did in a major speech in New York in 2003. But in Beijing, behind closed doors, Hu Jintao could point out that America had

> strengthened its military deployments in the Asia–Pacific region, strengthened the US–Japan military alliance, strengthened coop-eration with India, improved relations with Vietnam, established a pro-American government in Afghanistan, increased arms sales to Taiwan, and so on. They have extended outposts and placed pressure points on us from the East, South and West. This makes a great change in our geopolitical environment.[32]

The Chinese, for their part, also understood that the American stress on democracy and human rights, whatever its other justifications, was much more than just a way of embarrassing China in the eyes of the international community (not unlike the way in which China was trying to embarrass Japan by harping on its pre-1945 transgressions). It was also, as we have seen throughout the last three chapters, a facet of the perennial American tendency to grope for moral and legalistic principles as the basis for foreign affairs, even for some general institutional, or generally accepted legal structures between states as the proper way to manage differences of custom and interest (even though such arrangements must not limit American sovereign self-determination). Inevitably, China has strongly resisted such attempts at interference, on the basis of alien standards, as a way of intervening in China's internal affairs and an attempt to influence, perhaps even to manage, changes in China's political structure. Equally naturally, China has tried to constrain American wishes and claims in Asia, so long as this could be done without causing major repercussions, whether military or in the US Congress.

Where such a mixture of contradictory views and profoundly interlocking interests might lead remains, at the beginning of the twenty-first century, in the lap of the future.

14

TOWARDS THE FUTURE?

'HISTORIES,' THAT PERCEPTIVE historian, Simon Schama has written, 'never conclude, they just pause.' In thinking about relations among the world's powers, the start of the twenty-first century is a deceptively neat place for such a pause. In retrospect, it may prove to have been more deceptive than neat; particularly since the constellations of world politics and power are showing signs of important and potentially dramatic change.

At the start of the twentieth century world politics centred on Europe. That focus remained dominant, as demonstrated in the secondary importance of East Asia in World War II. There followed the establishment, for four decades after 1945, of a reasonably secure balance between two superpowers. Its end saw the emergence of the United States as the single 'hyperpower', uneasily playing a key role in three somewhat separate regions that came to dominate world politics at the end of the century: Europe, the Middle East and East Asia.

American economic, political and military supremacy temporarily disguised the fragilities of that pattern. But US ideas of world order, resting on the conviction that America was not just another power but a special state with a manifest destiny, on the universal appeal of

American ideals and the policing of that order by US power, had already by the end of the twentieth century begun to run into difficulties. Such ideas mandated an interventionism that meant retreat from institutions of global governance, even a United Nations which seemed slow and inadequate. That helped to undermine further the principles of state sovereignty and clear control of borders and territory, which were in any case being subverted by new transnational interests and groups in migration, economic globalisation or crime. As American power – even 'soft' power – entered a period of decline relative to the growing political and cultural self-confidence of other centres, like the major European powers, the implementation of universalist American ideas began to run into resistance, both among allies and within the US itself. US economic and financial dominance also started to weaken. Indeed, by the turn of the century the US ceased to be a dominant exporter of goods and capital; in fact, it became the only major imperial power on record to be a major debtor.

Even more fundamental challenges for all countries stem from science and technology. The internet and other means of instant global communication are altering society's relations with government, whatever the attempts to control them. They enhance the importance of the 'soft' revolution in which knowledge is replacing physical resources as the driver of economic wealth. By 2002 or so, some three-quarters of the value of publicly traded US companies was in the form of intangible assets. Yet the global money and flows systems on which all this is based might disappear very quickly. These novel patterns of the world economy, themselves strongly encouraged by American ideas, policies and inventions, also helped to emphasise the destabilising side of new, globalised manufacturing, trading and monetary systems. With the destruction of Communism and the creation of huge new sources of inputs and production, the old established economic formulae no longer work. With the entry of billions of Asians into the world economy, no one can calculate the full extent of the global labour market that may become accessible. For example, China and India are paying increasingly massive numbers of people not only to manufacture but to develop innovations. Therefore, as the pressures for globalisation become more powerful and less controllable, those societies which led the march to globalisation, including Japan and America, might also become its victims. The new forces have accentuated inequalities of wealth within as well as between states. While these forces have increased aggregate wealth measured in conventional GDP forms, they have also tended to decouple such aggregates from individual welfare, creating important instabilities of jobs and income for families. Personal and social fears and insecurities have grown in many countries. By 2005, the US National Intelligence Council began to ask whether the global trading order could, for instance, survive the rise of China.

In the future, furthermore, new technologies will also change energy supplies and consumption, building design, and vehicles. Novel kinds of weapons, including nuclear and other weapons of mass destruction, will become available to small groups. Bio-technology might produce even larger changes: there are already signs that sections of the Western scientific and medical communities are prepared to farm the bodies of individuals for spare parts, whether in the interests of science or for profit.[1]

It may nevertheless be a mistake to make too much of this too soon. Dominant patterns of power have always had their difficulties and the American claim – in effect – to run, or at least direct, the world could hardly avoid running into problems. All imperial powers eventually decline and so, in due course, will that of America; but perhaps not yet.

How will China fit into this no longer 'bipolar' or 'unipolar' world? Its relations with the outside world will, of course, to a large degree be determined by what happens within China itself; and for all the tumultuous events of the last two centuries, there is much about modern China that is redolent of its past. Mao himself spoke the truth when he remarked mournfully to Henry Kissinger how little change, for all his revolutionary efforts, he had been able to achieve. Although history is obviously not just a replay of times past, it is interesting to think about the period from the late nineteenth century to 1949 as just another 'time of troubles', of the kind that has afflicted China repeatedly in the intervals between one dynasty and another; and to think of Chinese governance over the half-century since 1949 as merely the establishment of a new kind of dynasty. For all the differences between personalities and their different historical periods, the career of Mao has intriguing parallels with that of another dynastic founder, the founding Ming emperor Hongwu. Both men came from a peasant background. Both came to govern the empire by dint of battle, hard work and ruthless determination. Once in power, each came to centralise governance in his own hands. In each case, the ruler's word came to be law: for Hongwu's, from the time he ascended the throne; for Mao's, only by the 1960s. Each of them achieved God-like personal status in the eyes of the populace and became the wholly dominant figure in the politics and administration of the China of his day. Some, albeit more limited, dynastic similarities continue when one thinks of their successors. Hongwu was followed, after a short interval, by the forceful, yet lesser, figure of Yongle, as Mao was succeeded, after a short interval, by the powerful but much less overwhelming figure of Deng Xiaoping. Deng was, in turn, followed by rulers of declining personal ascendancy, in the figures of Jiang Zemin and Hu Jintao as, after Yongle, the imperial throne was occupied by smaller personalities.

Even the fundamental problems of successive dynasties have strong echoes in the half-century of the Mao 'dynasty'. If the Tang, Song, Ming and Qing dynasties were, each in turn, undermined by the interlinked problems of population growth, central administration, and borders, China had not surmounted these difficulties by the year 2000 either. China's population tripled after 1945. Never in the history of the world has anyone tried to govern some 1.3 billion or more people from a single centre and it remains far from clear how, or even whether, it can be done. The social, economic and policy dilemmas with which this population explosion has confronted this (or any other) Chinese leadership are unlikely to be easily or quickly resolved.

At the same time, while China has accepted – recently even insisted upon – modern concepts of state sovereignty, there is not much evidence that the ancient and deep-rooted Chinese sense of cultural and civilisational superiority has weakened, let alone disappeared. Partly as a result, China and the Chinese can be easily, even unreasonably, sensitive to anything that looks like a slight or an injury. Which does not prevent the Chinese state from being as ruthless with its own citizens as with outsiders, whether individuals, corporations or countries.

Let us glance briefly at possible futures under six headings: demography, governance, economics, China's role in the fields of science and technology, its relations with its borderlands, and most especially its possible place in the global balance of power.

The matter of population, which has been China's strength but also weakness, seems very far from resolution, and the problems it presents are becoming more acute. The 'one child' policies introduced around 1980 were often circumvented from the start,[2] and often relaxed. Indeed, one deputy minister has said that by 2020 China will have 1.5 billion people.[3] Occasional efforts to control births have accentuated difficulties. China talks about 300 million births avoided over the last thirty years; but that also means 300 million fewer young to care for a quite quickly growing population of old people that will have to be taken care of by someone, somehow. No wonder that the government soon after 2000 made children legally responsible for their parents' pensions (making the children's employment critical not only for themselves but for the more extended family). In the meantime, single children growing up without siblings might, in their turn, produce children who will grow up without brothers, sisters, cousins, aunts or uncles, all with potentially devastating effects on the family structures which have been the foundation-stone of Chinese society since time out of mind. It has also been estimated that the working-age population may peak in 2009 at some 925 million but decline to 835 million by 2024.

Presumably there would have to be a marked increase in productivity to cope with such changes. That may pose special problems, given the apparently worsening environmental problems to be mentioned shortly.

Further difficulties stem from the fact that Chinese families have always wanted sons, who carry on the family name, inherit property and will look after parents, rather than girls, who need a dowry and will look after other folk. As more people can afford ultrasound scans and even more have abortions, that preference for boys has skewed sex ratios. A normal sex ration – reflecting the greater longevity of females – is 105 boys to 100 girls. In China the ratio, at the time of writing, is 118 to 100. The results are serious. It is said that by 2020 China can expect to have at least 23 million single men who have no hope of finding a wife. There are already many stories of men simply kidnapping women, perhaps from other provinces. In some places, especially in the poorer peasant regions, a single woman may be acquired, through kidnapping or purchase, by a group of brothers and serve as wife for all of them.

Population pressures also permit, where they do not actively encourage, illegal migration, by preference to Japan, the US and latterly Britain. This has reached such a stage that illegal migrants from Fujian province, for instance, can on arrival in the West expect to link up with substantial networks of Chinese from the same region.

None of these trends will necessarily last, but they seem likely to help determine the short- and even medium-term future.

How might the Chinese government cope with these and the other problems of Chinese growth and social turmoil? The central force in Chinese politics and executive government remains the Communist Party. It continues to be the dominant panel of the governing triptych of party, army and state. Its tentacles reach into every capillary of Chinese society and the economy. For all the dramatic evidence of China's economic dynamism, it remained true well after 2000 that the entire private sector lived in the shadow of the state. China's business cycles continued to be driven by a state sector indifferent to low returns. The party and the state continued to control most of the peaks of the economy, including energy, transport, health, education, banking and telecoms. The state still owns nearly 60 per cent of China's fixed capital stock and some 80 per cent of the chief executives of state enterprises are appointed by the party. Less than 10 per cent of the banking market's credit has continued to go to private enterprise, many of whose businesses are mere reincarnations of old state-owned enterprises and many of whose entrepreneurs are themselves former officials. These patterns seem sure to remain in place, at least for the time being, especially given the party's absolute refusal to tolerate any conceivable rival for national power. Effective political, social and economic debate, and the strengthening of the current developmental authoritarianism, necessarily happen within that party.

At the same time, in China, as everywhere, television changes the nature of politics, making the screen into reality and emphasising the role of personality, while the internet can produce increased cacophony. Dealing with the particulars of such an increasingly complex society and economy, with its growing inequalities, will increase the pressures for greater decentralisation of policy and decision-making. It may accentuate in-fighting within the party and government bureaucracies. That cannot fail to erode internal party command and control, and emphasise the politics of personality and intra-party and regional bargaining. The freedom of manoeuvre claimed by provincial and local officials also goes back to imperial times, but is hard to square with the unity, sense of common purpose, even discipline, of a secretive and essentially Leninist party structure. In any case, the cohesion of the party is threatened by the spread of rampant corruption – itself, once again, a phenomenon with a very long history, far back into the days of imperial China. Foreigners, whether individuals, corporations or governments, will still have to find their own way as best they can through the jungles of competing authorities.

Unquestionably the greatest single threat to the system stems from contradictions between Communist dogma and discipline as against the needs of entrepreneurial capitalism and the rivulets of energetic dissent that run, as always, beneath the Chinese surface. Now that the erosion of Maoist verities at home, and the collapse of Communism abroad, have left prosperity and nationalism as the chief criteria for the legitimacy of the Chinese Communist Party, the needs of economic growth contradict many of the claims to power of the party which that growth sustains. It is all very well to say that prosperity has come to depend on releasing dynamism and creativity, on decentralisation at home, and growing links with the outside world, but economic growth and technical innovation are always disruptive to established systems. Fast growth inevitably creates volatilities, as it did in Britain in the late eighteenth century or in Germany and Japan after 1918. The global links of business, technology, information and trade must constrain national policies in novel but awkward ways. So must the mobility of money. Many of the most important Chinese manufacturing facilities are largely the creation of foreign investment.[4] Additional pressures must arise from new ideas, from the outside world, from tourism, or from scientific and technical developments. They will create, in modern form, the very dangers of disruption against which the old emperor warned back in 1717. At the same time a legal system able to encourage innovative economic activity cannot continue to be a mere creature of political power but must be able to provide independent, clear and firm rules.

How, then, can the organisational discipline of a Leninist state be maintained? How can the corruption, which is a mortal threat to the party, be coped with? And how can the essential position of the party be combined with the development of capitalism without, as President Jiang Zemin almost admitted, falling into the political black hole that swallowed the Soviet Union? Some Chinese leaders understand the need for political reform and public participation. One minister has even remarked that 'the faster the economy grows, the more quickly we will run the risk of a political crisis if the political reforms cannot keep pace'.[5] Other difficulties stem from those restive minority nationalities, like Uighurs or Tibetans, or the grinding poverty of a peasantry which may now be only a few minutes' drive away from glittering city affluence, its penury made even less bearable by the constant evidence of television.

No wonder that, in the face of cruder Western demands that China reform itself along Western lines, Jiang explained wearily that the only result of trying to introduce Western-style parliamentary democracy would be that 'Chinese people will not have enough food to eat [and] the result will be great chaos'. Or that his successor Hu has equally rejected the Western democratic example. They are not alone. The Chinese Academy of Social Sciences has been at pains to argue that the efforts at reform in the former Soviet Union and Latin America were 'major disaster areas of neo-liberalism'.

In some ways even worse, there is the environmental degradation, the pollution and soil erosion, even shortage of water in villages and the countryside. Erosion, desertification and urbanisation have halved the amount of usable land over the last half-century and replanting trees has not so far restored the old balances. Yet no Chinese ruler is likely to forget how often in the past emperors have been undone by peasant rebellions.

For all that, growth seems certain to continue for some time at record rates.[6] China is trying hard to become less dependent on foreign companies, foreign standards and foreign inventions. For now, the employment by international firms of China's low-wage labour tends to increase unemployment in rich countries while helping foreign companies achieve record returns on capital and giving rich-country consumers greater spending power. At the same time, that growth draws people from the Chinese countryside to the new economic centres, where serious labour shortages in higher-skill areas fuel demands for higher pay. Such flows of people have produced a virtual collapse of health-care systems, with life expectancy probably falling (in the process possibly somewhat relieving the looming pensions problem). China's environmental problems, the World Bank has suggested, may cost China around $170 billion per annum. Yet China is building new cities, industries, dams and roads for millions of cars without much regard for pollution, other environmental issues or even water supply. There is not enough water in many places. China also remains a vastly growing consumer of power but an inefficient user of carbon fuels; and, consequently, a major driver of increases in world oil consumption and prices – which, in turn, can damage just those economies which are China's best customers and sources of technology. Foreigners continue to pursue the old dream of a vast new Chinese market and of vast new profits even though these have, so far, signally failed to materialise. Foreign investment flows into China continue at a rapid clip,[7] though it is not possible to untangle the ownership of most Chinese companies and few foreign joint ventures have been, or look like being, hugely profitable. The country has substantial overcapacity in some areas and is riddled with banking scandals, while also aiming to be a major overseas investor. These investments will give China a greater political role across the world, one unconstrained by fashionable Western concerns about human rights or the nature of local governments. By 2005 China also moved towards currency flexibility with a managed float, opening the way for a rise in the yuan against the dollar. Some financial experts argue – even if the wish should prove mainly father to the thought – that if and when China also liberalises capital controls, the yuan is likely to join the dollar, yen and possibly the euro, as the world's fourth major reserve currency.[8]

Irrespective of such growth, tensions and challenges, it would be a mistake to expect a revolution in China tomorrow morning. There is no visible, let alone organised, alternative to the overwhelming role of the party. Barring a major split in the party or a massive failure of the security forces or even a flare-up of anti-Japanese nationalism, the more China decentralises or localises, in whatever fashion and for whatever reason, the more this uniquely placed organisation is likely to be an essential cement of China's polity and society. In any case, while some people may remember the 'democracy wall' experiments of 1979, Confucian notions of benevolent government and obedience to authority remain dominant. Under the brittle carapace of modernity the ancient principles of Chinese civilisation remain, including the priority accorded to family and community over the individual, and acceptance of the idea that sacrifice may sometimes be necessary.

The general bias towards authoritarian-led consensus is traditional, as is the absence of any concept of loyal opposition. The quest for a successful marriage of all that with 'modernity' is far from over. In any case, the authorities will continue to confront difficulties with the tried and tested rallying cry of the dangers from crude or malevolent foreign policies and powers. They will also rely on China's deep-rooted defensiveness in the face of foreign criticism.

Even so, neither history nor the tides of early twenty-first-century affairs suggest that any one political party, or form of political organisation, is likely to endure. Sooner or later it is sure to change its nature. The internet, and the 'blogosphere', might make possible a cultural revolution not stemmed by most available forms of official censorship. A breakdown of the current system is not impossible. The number and force of local protests could grow further. Religious and quasi-religious groups may gather adherents. The party's grip might slip. More likely, though, may be the erosion and decay of existing patterns, even in the context of formal maintenance of the single party, the unitary state and its major structures. Such changes happen all the time: we need only think of the shift, in several major states like Russia or even France or Germany, and in a mere half-century since 1950, from representative towards mass populist democracy. What would emerge in China it is impossible to say. Perhaps a further growth of regional and provincial self-assertion. That might, just possibly, culminate in something like a break-up of Chinese unity. It has, after all, happened before. There might then be another 'time of troubles', with unpredictable consequences not only for the Chinese people but for their neighbours.

What about the international role of this China? It continues to see itself as, beyond question, special: a subtle and brilliant culture claiming by right a seat at the world's top table. There is much to sustain this view. China remains an ancient and in many ways fascinating civilisation, comprising within a single nation state around one-fifth of the world's people. It has also been exceptionally competent for many centuries in the art of political and diplomatic theatre, persuading others that because it is self-confident, large and populous, it is also a great power, entitled to tell the world on emerging from two centuries of weakness and trauma, as King Henry V said to Falstaff: 'presume not that I am the thing I was'.

In that search for power and status, China has two strong cards. One is the way in which China continues to cast its spell on foreigners. The other, always China's strongest diplomatic card, is patience. For the time being, China is ambitious but vulnerable, with a sense of grievance but self-confident to the point of arrogance, already a major regional player and moving up the scale. Even now, China has a growing international presence and her demographic and economic growth tempts many to think that China might become a serious rival to the United States, as Garnet Wolseley forecast over a century ago. Yet, for the time being, it lacks the means to achieve anything of the sort, and will continue to lack them for quite some time. Per head of the population, most of its people are very poor. The social and political structure is backward. China lacks serious global financial and, in many respects, general economic clout. It is far from having an organised and co-ordinated economic, industrial or investment policy, even at home, let alone for operations overseas. It remains technology-dependent, not a technology leader. Nor does it have much 'soft power' beyond its immediate periphery. For all the widespread fascination with the brilliance of Chinese art, theatre and dance and, of course, development, China's lifestyle has not yet encouraged much imitation elsewhere. The new Chinese middle classes, and especially the new rich, show every sign of wanting Western ways of living, to listen to Western music and see Western films. In contrast, few people in Western capitals want to live by the rules of Chinese culture and in Chinese ways. Nor does China pose any ideological or religious challenge to the West, and since the decline of Maoism has shown no desire to do so. It has no ideology to spread. Still less does it yet possess a truly up-to-date military or naval power with a serious capability for power projection. It does not even have – or at least has not articulated – a clear, coherent and plausible vision of its own future international role.

In reality, then, China is a medium power, albeit one very likely to become a significant global actor eventually. For the time being, it would be a mistake to confuse the possibility of a great China tomorrow with the realities of China today. It has accepted the shift, in not much more than a century, from an empire at the core of its own world order to being, formally, a modern Western-style nation state. Since the death of Mao its external policies have often been pragmatically shrewd and may well remain so. For the time being, this new China will go on concentrating on its borderlands or, to use the Russian expression, its 'Near Abroad'. Even on the issue of Taiwan's return to the motherland, Mao told Nixon when they first met: 'We can do without them [i.e. Taiwan] for the time being, and let it come after 100 years.' Although more recently Prime Minister Wen Jibao stressed that unification was 'more important than our lives', that did not imply a time-frame, either. Possibly, economic links between Taiwan and the PRC will make formal political unification less relevant, especially should the PRC itself decentralise further. Beyond that, Beijing will continue to insist on every jot and tittle of its other territorial claims, on imperial firmness in dealing with renewed restiveness, especially among Moslems, in and around China's western periphery.

In Korea, China will try to avoid various almost equally undesirable developments. One would be a collapse of North Korea leading to a torrent of refugees fleeing across the Chinese border. A second would be a new Korean war. Another is the emergence of a strong, reunified Korea that would, almost certainly, be America's ally. A fourth is the emergence of North Korea as a nuclear weapons state. In the meantime Beijing will also try to combine the maintenance of its very valuable industrial and other economic links with North Korea while also, possibly half-heartedly, coping with the money-laundering and drug-trading that North Korea conducts with and through China.

China will also try to strengthen its influence in South-East Asia, where it will have to cope with much deeply embedded sinophobia, engendered by long experience of Chinese expansionism and economic penetration. India, too, will pursue growing trade and exchanges with China while remaining, strategically, disengaged and wary. Beyond that,

China has, very sensibly, ceased to involve itself in international revolutionary activities. Instead, it has decided that its national interests are best served by a posture of general support for international stability.

As for major power relationships, Japan's relations with China remain highly sensitive. The Chinese government's use of nationalism and patriotism as a rallying cry at home has also fuelled anti-Japanese and anti-American sentiment in the population. Massive flows of Japanese aid or investment, and repeated Japanese apologies for the past, have done little to stem the accusations and the official hectoring. All that comes together with a certain Chinese triumphalism now that China has resumed its role as perhaps the leading power in East Asia. At the same time, China also fears what a revived and rearmed Japan might do at some point in the future; these fears are fed by Japan's involvements in the Middle East and growing co-operation with the US Navy. Together with that comes Sino-Japanese competition for energy and raw materials as well as for influence, regionally and beyond.

The endless Chinese criticisms, at a time of general revival of Japanese national pride, have produced a predictable reaction in Japan. Younger Japanese seem to resent the country's continual acceptance of wartime guilt, and many Japanese seem attracted by a more nationalist alternative to the existing pacifist state. Tokyo seems less and less inclined to back down over the territorial issues, such as who owns what on the high seas or the sea-bed, especially energy rights on or around various offshore islands. Although the Japanese public has not been keen for the country to loom large on the international scene, the government will surely continue to wean the country further away from extreme pacifism and a merely complacent reliance on United States power. Indeed, the stronger China becomes and the more it seems to threaten Taiwan, the closer Japan's links with the US are likely to become. Japan's armed forces, especially air and navy, small but of excellent quality, will continue to modernise. Japan is already unwilling to be simply pacifist in relation to missile threats from North Korea. Its naval co-operation with the US in the Pacific is likely to go further and even its neutrality in the event of armed clashes over Taiwan cannot be taken for granted. Yet the Chinese and Japanese economies remain highly complementary; and useful economic links between the two seem sure to continue, though perhaps not to the point of making Japan more vulnerable than necessary to Chinese moods. Japan will compete with China in space programmes, and there has been some talk of a pan-Asian union, to include Japan, China and Korea but not the US, that might help dilute and restrain China's power. Even so, and although the United States is sure to act as pacifier, the possibilities of serious friction between China and Japan should not be underestimated.

European interest in China and the Pacific region has grown, in part as an inevitable component of increased European assertiveness in the world. The major European states believe that their own economic health might depend in part on seizing opportunities in East Asia. That means not just trade and investment, but accommodation with a power whose trade has rapidly grown and whose markets and low labour costs appear to offer limitless opportunities, as does its growing middle class. Beyond that, the British, Germans and French – driven as always by the perennial Western illusion that it is the West's duty to organise the world – think China is likely to be important in dealing with the stability of South and South-East Asia, the proliferation of weapons of mass destruction and the environment. Since the later 1990s, and especially following the return of Hong Kong to China, European officials and Chinese leaders have beaten paths to one another's doors. Nevertheless, the strongly inward-looking tendencies of contemporary Europe will prevent it from becoming a serious – as distinct from occasionally vocal – collective player in eastern-hemisphere affairs. That seems likely to remain true unless and until the European Union becomes an operational political and strategic unit, as it has already, at times fitfully, become a trading entity.

The role of the Russian Federation remains, as it has been for some years, one of the more important and unanswered questions for the international system. That Russia will, strategically and politically, revive after years in the doldrums, is certain. The question is when and how. For the time being, Russia is basing its reviving international clout largely on its energy reserves, which are a matter of acute interest to

China and the industrial world, and over which the central Russian government has increasingly direct command. For the time being, Russia seems to want to balance between China and the West. Although Wen Jibao spoke at one point – a shade wistfully, perhaps? – of a possible India–Russia–China axis, until further notice everyone will have to accommodate to the reality of US supremacy. For the foreseeable future, both Beijing and Moscow seem likely to have a greater stake in good relations with the US than in good relations with one another. Still, Russia remains China's principal supplier of advanced weaponry, though not much that China is buying looks like being at the same technical level as American arms and equipment. By 2005 the two countries even mounted sizeable joint manoeuvres. As against that, history suggests that frictions will rarely be far below the surface. New Sino-Russian difficulties seem sure to arise, including over access to Siberian oil reserves and the routing of the necessary pipelines. There may also be fresh border problems, partly stemming from the movement of large numbers of people from China into the Russian Far East. That continues to be fuelled both by Chinese population pressures and by severe labour shortages in the Russian Pacific regions.

It is therefore the United States that is, and looks like remaining for quite some time, central to China's foreign links and dealings. Washington remains China's chief foreign interlocutor, the key power in the Pacific and guarantor of regional stability, a key market for China's exports and foreign investment, as well as a chief source of investment, technology, science and monetary stability. The inter-dependence of the two economies is substantial. Even China's most popular and prestige gains, like entry to the World Trade Organisa-tion and the allocation of the 2008 Olympic Games to Beijing, would have been difficult without American goodwill. It is the development of the Sino-US relationship which will clearly largely decide the future balance of the entire eastern hemisphere.

Other things being equal, and assuming reasonable good sense on all sides, accommodation seems likely to continue. Each side has taken some care, over several decades, to define its offshore interests in the Pacific, or in South-East Asia, in ways that abut upon, rather than conflict with, the interests of the other. Even on Taiwan, American policy now strongly discourages any drive for independence and supports the island's accommodation, perhaps even a good deal of economic integration, with the People's Republic. Both the US and China have a major stake in each other's peaceful development and prosperity. Neither has essential interests strongly in danger from the other, at least so far. If America has been willing to accept some co-operative forms of engagement with China, China has had to accept that America is determined to contain some Chinese aims and ambitions, and that China's military build-up has no hope of matching the American one, either in quantity or quality. Indeed, since the late 1990s the US has conducted in the Pacific the greatest military build-up in the world since the start of the Cold War in 1947. It is true that some important problems remain: for instance, regarding Japan, to whose alliance the US is committed while China remains deeply suspicious of Tokyo. Yet even here, a Sino-American understanding that is comfortable with the position of Japan seems entirely conceivable. The interests of others are obviously also in play as well: Western and Japanese investors, for instance, will continue to see the state of Sino-American relations as an important guide to the extent of their involvement in China.

Open Sino-US conflict seems quite unlikely, barring only some unexpected folly from Taiwan. Since the Korean conflict, both China and the US have displayed great care to avoid anything of the kind and there is no reason to think that they will take less care in future. It is not clear what either side would have to gain from conflict, or how it could hope to gain it. How could 'success' or 'victory' even be defined for either side?

The trouble might be that policy is not always driven by 'reasonable good sense'. In the affairs of nations it is always a mistake to rely too strongly or exclusively on logic and sober calculation of interests and benefits. Misinformation and miscalculation play important and often decisive roles. So do embedded national prejudices or the gusts of popular passions that can erupt as suddenly and destructively as a Caribbean hurricane. Not only are the US and China by no means powers of equal capacity and clout, but ignorance and misunderstandings about one another are widespread on both sides. In China nationalist sensitivities, even xenophobia, are very much alive and even at times encouraged by official warnings of foreign hostility. There have been official accusations that the US has fomented revolutions in Central Asia, Ukraine, Georgia and has directly attacked Chinese interests and people. US human-rights agitation will continue to seem a not-so-subtle interference in Chinese affairs; and while a virulent nationalism may have its uses for the Chinese government, it could also get out of hand. The general misunderstanding of America remains profound and helps to perpetuate distortions of history and to accentuate unreasonable sensitivities and anger about imagined slights or hostility.

In America, the general public tends not to be well informed about China, beyond newspaper or television reports and tourist impressions, but seems content to judge China by the criteria and rules of US domestic affairs and politics. Trade and human-rights issues play a large and often disproportionate role. American administrations have some difficulty in making cautious and pragmatic use of US ascendancy while Congress and the public retain old and deep-seated illusions, such as the idea that American definitions of democracy or human rights are universally loved. Such beliefs continue to influence the moralistic tone of US policy and, together with American legalism, underpin notions of the United States as moral guardian and the major law-enforcement agency of world order. These ideas have led, and will lead again, to treating states and groups with which the US has differences as immoral, or law-breakers, or both.

Difficulties can also be created by overestimating the importance of economics and trade in the affairs of peoples and states. It is almost as if the old virus of nineteenth-century Marxism, the idea that economic forces are the ultimate determinants of national and international life, had erupted again after a period of quiescence. It is a view that is full of peril if it ignores the forces of politics and psychology, of pride and ambition, insecurity and fear, of jealousy, of national and group identity and cohesion, which have, in the end, usually been dominant in the affairs of states. For the time being, it seems, belief in the overriding importance of economic relations accentuates the indignation of many Americans at what they regard as Chinese economic and financial trickery and the continuing patterns of large-scale Chinese espionage and theft of American intellectual property and know-how.

It is true that none of that has stopped the US from developing a more careful policy of engagement with China. Beijing, for its part, will surely continue to concentrate on its vast domestic problems. China understands that it lacks the means or the purposes to undermine American military and technological pre-eminence, or its organising role in the Pacific, from which China also benefits. Nevertheless, significant dangers might yet arise, not only over Taiwan but over such things as any Sino-Japanese clash that could involve the US. Or from the rapid and large-scale modernisation of China's armed forces, undertaken with the avowed intention of producing a capability to attack US forces if necessary.

At the start of the new century it is therefore not clear how far America can take its 'democratic mission' without running into active, and counter-productive, political resistance; or how far changes in the international economy, or in China itself, will shape American political and strategic choices. China obviously continues to believe that the steady growth of its international standing will carry its own lessons for everyone. And America still seems torn between the view that China could in time become America's most important geopolitical rival – which therefore needs to be contained – and the belief that market-driven economic growth will, of itself, compel democratic moderation in China.

There are only two things that can be said with complete confidence. First, no pattern or structure of power or of relations lasts very long. America itself will change. US dominance of the Pacific and beyond will alter. How China develops, whether it becomes a more equal partner of America, or else a competitor, equally depends on a myriad decisions not yet made, or even formulated, each of them attended by the inevitability of unintended consequences. Secondly, and finally, since all dreams of the future are mere artefacts of the present, the only absolute certainty is that the unexpected is out there somewhere, brooding and waiting to pounce. And, as the American writer Philip Roth says somewhere, history is really only the path by which the unexpected becomes the inevitable.

NOTES

1. Creation: From Origins to the Qin

1 The original five were millet, glutinous millet, wheat and barley, legumes and hemp seeds. Rice, corn and others followed.

2 In fact, they seem to have had advanced jade-carving techniques and fairly advanced textile crafts.

3 Even his dates, let alone his precise writings, are uncertain. Modern estimates suggest that he lived sometime between 600 and 200 BC.

4 None of which made the Daoists other-worldly, even as they searched for immortality. One Daoist manual of the Han period argued that the Yellow Emperor had become immortal after sleeping with 1,200 women; and the sage Peng Zhu is said to have lived to a ripe old age by having sex with 10–20 girls every single night.

5 Daughters, by contrast, were raised for their future husbands. At marriage, the bride became part of the groom's family (and subject to the authority of his mother). The groom's 'bridal gift' was more or less intended to repay the bride's parents for the cost and effort of having raised her.

6 Kings were not good insurance risks. On one occasion a messenger brought the young king – not yet emperor – an enemy's head in a box and a map showing territory that another ruler wanted to give him. While he looked, the man pulled out a poisoned knife and struck. The king managed to dodge behind a pillar and, though hampered by his court robes, eventually pulled his own sword and wounded the attacker, who was promptly killed.

2. From the Han to the Sui

1 For instance, through the efforts of the Confucian scholar Dong Zhongshu. Wudi even allowed an imperial academy to be set up to train Confucian officials.

2 By the end of the dynasty it had produced a criminal code in no less than 960 volumes.

3 What they examined was not training in job qualifications but rather, as in the French and British higher civil services of the nineteenth and twentieth centuries AD, cultural attainment, character and intellect.

4 Although there were, and remain, mutually unintelligible dialects in Chinese, in its written form there are fewer regional variations. For centuries, people who could not understand each other's speech could nevertheless recognise the same standard set of Chinese characters (even though there are various styles of calligraphy, some of which are lovely and can reflect the character of the writer). That allowed books to be copied and helped to produce a common general culture. Over time, the writing system spread to Japan, Korea and Vietnam, too, where many books came to be written in classical Chinese instead of in the local language.

5 The first recorded use of paper, made from mulberry bark, seems to have been around AD 100 by a court eunuch who was promptly given high honours by the emperor. Paper-making was declared to be a state secret and revealing it to enemies meant death. It was not until some six centuries later that the Persians imported Chinese paper to use in state documents, and knowledge of how to make it took another half century to cross borders. See Bahiyyih Nakhjavani, *Paper*, London, Bloomsbury, 2004, pp. 231–2.

6 The Yilou, who had earlier called themselves the Sushen, lived in what is now northern Liaoning and parts of Heilongjiang province. They were ancestors of the Manchus who, some eighteen centuries later, became rulers of China.

7 Quoted in Arthur Waldron, *The Great Wall of China: from history to myth*, Cambridge/New York, Cambridge University Press, 1992, p. 35.

8 These horses, with their lovely light red-gold colour, were later named, after a nineteenth-century Russian traveller, Prejevalsky's horse.

9 Pliny the Elder, *Natural History* 6:54.

3. High Culture and Collapse: The Sui, Tang and Song

1 Trans. in Witter Brynner, *The Jade Mountain*, New York, Knopf, 1929, p. 305.

2 In the meantime, the Tibetans created a written language and imported Buddhism, the first Buddhist monastery being built in AD 779.

3 Even the crusaders benefited. Contact with civilised Islam introduced them to luxurious textiles, to spices, even to the use of soap. It seems likely that it was also these contacts that first brought notions of courtly love to the ladies of Europe.

4 Like the Christians, who came later, the Buddhists had great difficulty in expressing their new concepts in the language and the characters already in use for older ideas that the population understood in the old way.

5 From AD 600 or so, more Japanese came to China, whether to trade or get copies of Buddhist scriptures.

6 The council sent Nestorius into exile. His followers abhorred image worship, denied the doctrine of purgatory or the practice of confession, and asserted that nothing outside the Bible is essential to salvation.

7 Some scholars argue that as late as the twentieth century the Chinese population of 400 millions was governed by a mere 20,000 officials; but with 1.25 million degree holders helping to run local affairs.

8 In the 1960s disgraced intellectuals were still being sent to carry night soil in the countryside and 'learn from the people'. See Ch. 12 below.

9 Joseph Needham, *Science and Civilization in China*, Cambridge, Cambridge University Press, 1971, vol. 4 Pt. 3, p. 476.

4. The Coming of the Mongols

1 Once, when Ghengis was still just Temujin, some surrendering tribal leaders who had captured their overlord, released him before reaching Temujin's camp. When they admitted as much, Temujin replied: 'If you had laid hands on your own khan . . . I would have executed you and all your brethren, for no man should lay hands on his rightful lord. But you did not forsake him and your hearts were sound.'

2 Marrying brothers' widows was not peculiar to the Mongols. It had already been customary among the Hittites 2,000 years earlier.

3 The tale was recorded some centuries after Ghengis's death, and may well be mythical. At minimum, it says something about the reputation for cunning and deviousness he left behind.

4 There has, of course, always been a close link between the lust for sex and for blood.

5 The effects of these Mongol habits have been oddly far-reaching. Around the turn of the twenty-first century, an Oxford population geneticist made calculations based on the fact that y-chromosomes are passed on, virtually unchanged, from father to son through the generations. They suggest that almost 8 per cent of men living in the region of the former Mongol empire – some 16 million males – carry almost identical y-chromosomes, implying a single genetic lineage. This particular lineage has been found in only one population outside the former Mongol empire – in Pakistan. It seems plausible to assume that the Mongol habit of slaughtering much of the male population of the regions they conquered, and the acquisition of their women, contributed to the dominance of this y-chromosome strain.

6 Possibly a reference to the commander's fabulous golden tent.

7 Their leader, the 'Old Man of the Mountain', beguiled young men, with the aid of girls, wine and hashish (hence 'hashishiyun' from which comes 'assassins') to kill his opponents at whatever cost to their own lives.

8 It is from Abbasid Baghdad that we have inherited words like alchemy, algebra, nadir and zenith.

9 In fact, the Mongols ruled Tibet through the lamas, who were even allowed to preach lamaist religion to the Mongols themselves.

10 Another version is that the adolescent prince died, leaving his baby brother as the surviving Song male. To escape the Mongols, a senior adviser took the baby prince in his arms and jumped into the sea.

11 It has been suggested – though there is no proof – that Europe's Black Death of 1348-9 might have arrived by caravan from the bubonic plague that decimated China in 1331-54

12 The Mongols were tolerant of a variety of religions. The Nestorian Christians had made many converts, not least among the Central Asian tribes, like the Keraits, that provided many of the princesses given in marriage to Mongol princes.

13 The text, translated from the Persian, is in Christopher Dawson (ed.), *The Mongol Mission*, New York, Sheed and Ward, 1955, pp. 85-6. However, another monk, Brother Benedict the Pole, renders the phrase '. . . I shall know you as my enemy' as 'I shall know for certain that you wish to have war' (Dawson p. 84).

14 See *Journey of William of Rubruck to the Eastern Parts of the World 1253-55: as narrated by himself; with two accounts of the earlier journey of John of Pian de Carpine*, trans. from the Latin and ed. with an Introduction by William Woodville Rockhill, London, printed for the Hakluyt Society, 1900. The original Rubruck manuscript seems to have been lost, but two or three contemporary manuscript copies are in the Parker library of Corpus Christi College, Cambridge.

15 Who is on record as having made a marvellous silver liquor dispenser for the Great Khan and his international guests. It was designed to serve, simultaneously, wine, rice wine, honey-based mead and the Mongols' own qumiss, fermented mares' milk.

16 Shortly after his death, this material was translated into Syriac, a language of eastern Christians, but both the original and the translation disappeared. Sauma's remarkable mission was known only through brief references in archives of the Vatican, France, and England – until the Syriac manuscript resurfaced in Persia (Iran) in 1887.

5. The Ming, South Sea Barbarians and Missionaries

1 He was the third Ming emperor, after taking the throne from his nephew.

2 When the Chinese reached Bengal, they were enchanted to find a giraffe that had been sent as a gift from the king of Malindi. They persuaded the Malindi ambassadors not only to offer the animal as a gift to the Chinese emperor, but to send for a second giraffe. Zheng He presented both to his emperor when he returned to Beijing in 1415.

3 Roughly: 'those who are absent are always in the wrong'.

4 One of its more famous tales has to do with the withdrawal of the Moors from Granada. When its last Moorish king, Boabdil, looked back at the city he was leaving, he burst into tears. His mother was pitiless: 'Yes: weep like a woman for a city you could not defend like a man.'

5 Actually, Diaz and da Gama were not quite the first. According to Herodotus, a Carthaginian captain had sailed around Africa long before, taking two years to do it but sailing from east to west, unlike the Iberians, who then sailed from west to east.

6 Father Martín was an influential man and even recommended to King Philip II that he should go and conquer China. Fortunately for Spain, Philip refused any such madcap adventure.

7 Cited in C.M. Cipolla, *Guns, Sails and Empires: Technological Innovation and the Early Phases of European Expansion 1400-1700*, New York, Pantheon, 1965, p. 120.

8 Yet he may have been loved. For all his hatred of Mongols and stress on Chinese norms, when he died no less than 38 of his 40 concubines chose to follow Mongol precedents on the death of a ruler, and committed suicide.

9 See the capsule on 'Eunuchs' in Ch. 6.

6. Manchus and Russians

1 As a grand strategy, it was similar to that adopted by Stalin in Eastern Europe in 1945: creating a broad *glacis* against possible future attacks from the West.

2 As late as the 1842 the British, in their campaign in China, noted that the Chinese (Han) troops distrusted their own Manchu comrades (whom the British referred to as 'Tartars') as mere foreigners.

3 The saying comes from Voltaire's ironic reference to the unlucky British Admiral Byng, who was shot in 1757 for failing to beat the French off the island of Minorca. I am indebted for the reference to my editor, Bill Swainson.

4 The tale of Yangzhou continued to fuel anti-Manchu resentment among the Han into the mid-1800s.

5 Just 300 years later China's first post-Mao paramount leader, Deng Xiaoping, tried much the same appeal to consolidate loyalties to his social and economic reforms: 'It is glorious to be rich'.

6 Louis Le Conte, *Nouveaux Memoires sur l'état present de la Chine*, Paris, J.L. de Lorme, 1697.

7 Just before he died, the pope made him a cardinal.

8 For instance, Father Louis Le Couplet, *Tabula Chronologica Trium Familiarum Imperialium Monarchiae Sinicae*, Paris, 1686.

9 This process of double translation must have caused multiple difficulties, then and later. Language moulds, and is an essential component of, national character and is essentially untranslatable without a subtle and deep understanding of the other party's cultural context. As Wittgenstein once said: 'The limits of my language are the limits of my world.'

10 The Jesuits took much of the credit for the conclusion of the treaty, which helped to produce Kangxi's 1692 edict of toleration.

7. Europeans, Missions and Trade

1 For instance, F.M. Arouet de Voltaire, *Catechisme Chinois* (1764), vol. 1 of the *Dictionnaire Philosophique*, (1764), Paris, Librairie Garnier Frères, 1936.

2 It has been estimated that, roughly between 1400 and 1800, China's grain supply multiplied by six.

3 Ping-ti Ho, *Studies in the Population of China 1368–1953*, Cambridge, MA, Harvard University Press, p. 281.

4 By 1850 China's numbers had grown further, to some 400–50 millions.

5 Quoted again in a memorial to the emperor in 1835; cited in Michael Greenberg, *Britain's Trade and the Opening of China 1800–1842* (1951), New York, Monthly Review Press, 1979, p. 45.

6 Cited in Greenberg, op. cit., p. 42, fn. 5.

7 One Ming official history described, in great detail, the Portuguese method of boiling and eating Chinese children.

8 It seems unlikely that they remained chastely solitary. In Chinese cities, there were somewhat separate groups of courtesans and prostitutes catering to different social classes. By the 1820s the groups with the highest standing, the courtesans, were, rather like Japanese geishas, companions and entertainers at dinners and banquets, by no means necessarily available for sex, though they might be. There was a clear distinction between them and lower-class girls. In the same period in India, most British men took mistresses, creating in the process an entire new class of Eurasian people. There was anyway, in many places and among many Westerners, a tendency to prefer compliant local mistresses to demanding Western wives. It is a tendency with echoes into the twenty-first century.

9 It was the Königlich Preussische Asiatische Handelskompanie. It organised five sailings to China but without great result.

10 Whence it would normally be taken overland, across Mexico to the Caribbean, and sent by the annual Spanish treasure fleet to Spain.

11 According to comparative tables published by the Bank of England, the AD 2002 equivalent is some £42,800,000.

12 John W. Foster, *American Diplomacy in the Orient*, New York, Houghton Mifflin, 1903, pp. 56–7.

13 Hosea Ballou Morse, *The Chronicles of the East India Company, trading to China 1635–1834*, Cambridge, MA, Harvard University Press/Oxford, Clarendon Press, 1926–9, vol. 2, Appendix G, p. 232.

14 Alain Peyrefitte, *The Collision of two Civilisations; the British Expedition to China 1792–94* (trans. J. Rothschild), London, Harvill/HarperCollins, 1993, p. 1 fn. 2.

15 Aubrey Singer, *The Lion and the Dragon: The Story of the First British Embassy to the Court of the Emperor Qianlong in Peking 1792–1794*, London, Barrie and Jenkins, 1992, pp. 180–1.

16 There may have been more to this than the typical Chinese refusal to acknowledge that the Europeans were better at anything. As noted in Chapter 5, for Chinese infantry fighting off attacking horsemen from the top of northern walls, bows and arrows served well enough. In any case, few peasant conscripts

were capable of using guns; and as late as 1842, even élite Manchu troops tried to fight the British with a sword in each hand. See my *Opium, Soldiers and Evangelicals*, London, Palgrave, 2004, p. 135.

17 Weaknesses that reinforced suspicion of the mission. Before it left Beijing the Canton viceroy was told to make visible military preparations before Macartney's arrival. The British were 'habitually truculent' and 'bullying' and should not be allowed to stir up trouble on the coast because Beijing had refused their requests. Singer, op. cit., p. 103.

18 In 1842, the year when the first Anglo-Chinese war ended, the firm's net profit was $130,000 (according to US Department of Labor figures, that represents almost 1.75 millions in 1991 dollars). Cf. Delano letter to Sturgis 6.4.43, Forbes collection, Baker Library, Harvard.

19 One comment on the modern situation is in William Langewiesche, *The Outlaw Sea: A World of Freedom, Chaos and Crime*, New York, North Point Press, 2004.

20 G.W.F. Hegel, *Lectures on the philosophy of world history: Introduction, reason in history* (trans. H.B. Nisbet; with an introd. by Duncan Forbes), Cambridge, NY, Cambridge University Press, (1975) 1980, pp. 199–200.

21 Roughly: 'exist only on paper, which tolerates anything'.

22 His *Voyage Round the World* was published in St Petersburg 1810–14, with an English edition, in two volumes, in 1813.

23 Jiaqing's edict in E. Backhouse and J.O.P. Bland, *Annals and Memoirs of the court of Peking (from the sixteenth to the twentieth century)*, Boston, Houghton Mifflin/London, Heinemann, 1914, pp. 387–8.

24 The first shipment of tea from Assam, in northern India, does not seem to have reached England until 1837.

8. The Mandate of Heaven Dissolves

1 Peyrefitte, *The Collision of two Civilisations*, op. cit., p. xix.

2 Some of those Frenchmen had, under the command of the Comte de Grasse, fought the British at Chesapeake Bay and Yorktown, giving decisive help to the American victory in the War of Independence. Later, on 1 September 1785 John Jay recommended to the Continental Congress that Paris be thanked for the courtesies shown to the Americans by the French at Canton. Diplomatic Correspondence 19.9.1783 – 4.3.1789, pp. 767–8.

3 Some of them used to meet in the rooms of D.W.C. Olyphant in the Canton 'factories'. They became known, irreverently, as 'Zion's Corner'.

4 Quoted in Jonathan Spence, *The China Helpers: Western Advisers in China 1620–1960*, London, Bodley Head, 1969, p. 38.

5 Otto von Kotzebue, for example, wrote about his explorations, very much for the czar, in *A Voyage of Discovery into the South Sea and to Behring's Straits; in search of a north-west passage, undertaken in the years 1815,16,17 and 18 in the ship Rurik* (2 vols.), London, printed for Sir Richard Phillips and Co., 1821.

6 Quoted in Immanuel C.Y. Hsü, 'The Great Policy Debate in China, 1874: Maritime Defense v. Frontier Defense', *Harvard Journal of Asiatic Studies* 1964–5, p. 222.

7 Anyway, the devoutly Presbyterian Napier basically thought the Chinese were ignorant heathens and was astonished to find that they thought him an unlettered barbarian.

8 Charles Greville, *The Greville Memoirs 1814–1860* (ed. Lytton Strachey and Roger Fulford), London, Macmillan, 1938. Entries for 24.8.1840 and 13.11.1840.

9 François Guizot, *Mémoires pour servir à l'histoire de mon temps* (nouv. edn.), Paris, Michel Lévy frères, 1872, vol. 7, p. 309.

10 But the company's trade mark continued to be accepted by everyone as a hallmark of quality, even on contraband.

11 One *tael* = 1.2 ounces of pure silver.

12 Quoted in Maurice Collis, *Foreign Mud, being an account of the opium imbroglio at Canton in the 1830s and the Anglo-Chinese war that followed*, London, Faber and Faber, 1946, p. 207.

13 Not long afterwards Lin was dismissed in disgrace. He was calmly philosophical. 'Shifting the blame for political failure on to others,' he remarked, 'is a permanent feature of political life.'

14 I have discussed this in detail in my *Opium, Soldiers and Evangelicals*, London, Palgrave, 2004.

15 Chinese Repository vol. XI, 1842, pp. 274–89.

16 Lecture in Boston, in the *Baltimore Niles Weekly Register*, vol. 61 (1842), pp. 326–30.

17 Still, there was time to relax. One British officer, Major-General Lord Saltoun, was fond of playing the violin, so he brought along an aide who could accompany him on his cello.

18 Lin even asked Parker to check his, Lin's, letter to Queen Victoria (which was never delivered) and to translate parts of Vattel's *Law of Nations*.

19 Earl Swisher (ed.), *China's Management of the American Barbarians*, New Haven, Yale University Press, 1953, p. 137.

20 Memorial to the emperor, 4.4.44, in Swisher, op. cit., pp. 142–4.

21 Quoted in Frederic Wakeman Jr., *Strangers at the Gate: Social Disorder in South China 1839–1861*, Berkeley, Cal., University of California Press, 1966, pp. 88–9.

22 One visitor to Australia noted that the Chinese were the best gardeners 'the best workmen, the best cooks and the most honest and law-abiding people'.

23 This sense of fighting for unselfish reasons is not confined to British motives in 1840, 1857 and 1860 in China. It also plays a part in British and American views of their roles in World War I. Here is President Woodrow Wilson addressing Congress on 8 January 1918: 'What we demand in this war is nothing peculiar to ourselves.' Cf. John Whitley Chambers (ed.), *The Eagle and the Dove: The American Peace Movement and United States Foreign Policy 1900–1922*, Syracuse, NY, 1991, p. 131. A very similar rhetoric of universal benevolence has run through America's twentieth and twenty-first century wars in Korea, Vietnam and both Gulf conflicts.

24 Theodore Walrond (ed.), *Letters and Journals of James, eighth Earl of Elgin* (with a preface by Arthur Stanley), London, J. Murray, 1872, p. 212.

25 During the fighting the local American commander, Commodore Josiah Tatnall, paid a visit to his friend, the wounded British admiral James Hope. While he was at it, his boat's crew helped to work the British guns and Tatnall used his steamer to tow into action several barges of British marines who could make no headway against the tide. Afterwards, he simply explained that kinsmen had been in trouble and 'blood is thicker than water' and that he'd 'be damned if he'd stand by and see white men butchered before his eyes'. The secretary of the navy approved.

26 H. Cordier, *Histoire Generale de la Chine*, Paris, Paul Guethner, 1920, pp. 121-3, quotes a dispatch of 15.2.60 from the Duke of Montebello, the French ambassador in St Petersburg, citing remarks from Prince Gorchakov, the Russian foreign minister.

27 Foreign minister to Baron Gros 21.4.60, in Cordier, op. cit., pp. 124-31.

28 Quoted in Spence, *The China Helpers*, op. cit., pp. 74-5.

9. Collapse and Revolution

1 When the captain of his ship had the impertinence to attack three Danish ships inside Chinese territorial waters, the minister, Guenther von Rehfüs, had to wait for two years before being received at court.

2 Tsungli Yamen to the US envoy, Mr Low, 28.3.71, US Foreign Relations 1871, Washington, DC, USGPO.

3 Consul-General at Shanghai G.F. Seward to Secretary of State W.H. Seward 14.10.68, US Foreign Relations 1870, p. 337.

4 Henry Wheaton, *Elements of International Law: with a Sketch of the History of the Science*, Philadelphia, Carey, Lea & Blanchard, 1836.

5 Some copies survived, though. The tale is told by E.R. Hughes in his *The Invasion of China by the Western World*, London, Adam and Charles Black, 1937, pp. 107-8. Hughes wrote that his own copy of the diary was finally published in Chengtu (Chengdu) in Szechwan in 1897.

6 Jeffery G. Barlow, *Sun Yat-sen and the French 1900-1908* (China Research Monograph No. 14), Center for Chinese Studies, Institute of East Asian Studies, University of California, Berkeley, 1979, p. 9, quoting records of *The management of barbarian affairs of the Ch'ing dynasty from beginning to end* (80 vols.) Beijing, 1930.

7 The US minister to China, Frederick F. Low, blamed the French chargé d'affaires in Beijing, Count de Rochechouart, for raising the spectre of war. He thought the count was 'ambitious and unscrupulous, even for a Frenchman. His actions are controlled entirely by passion, prejudice and personal ambition' and he had made a lot of money out of exaggerated compensation claims to the Chinese. Dispatch of 21 June 1870 to Washington.

8 That is one variant of a large number of guesses. The Chinese memorandum to the 1909 International Opium Commission at Shanghai gave provincial

consumption estimates varying from 2 per cent of the population in Manchuria to 50 per cent in Anhui and 50 per cent of all males in Yunnan. International Opium Commission, Report of the International Opium Commission (1909), vol. 2 pp. 62–6. Professor Alfred W. McCoy suggests 13.5 million addicts (i.e. not merely smokers) around 1900 in 'Opium History 1858–1940', Recreational Drug Information website.

9   Since the German Reich had not yet been formed, Burlingame spoke and wrote as the envoy of the Chinese emperor, to Bismarck as chancellor of the North German Confederation.

10 Quoted in Spence, *The Search for Modern China*, op. cit., p. 215.

11 The Cologne paper *Kölnische Zeitung* of 25.7.94, quoted in the *North China Herald* 7.9.94.

12 Buying modern ships and weapons was one thing. Organisation and training were something else. Until 1900, in Chinese armies, weight-lifting and archery still counted in qualifying examinations for officer candidates. S.D. W. Putjata, *China's Wehrmacht*, Vienna and Leipzig, 1895, pp. 27–33. Also Kurt Bloch, *German Interests and Policies in the Far East*, New York, 1939.

13 There were three major loan agreements, each for L15 million. One was by some French and Russian banks and two by the Hong Kong and Shanghai Banking Corporation and the Deutsch-Asiatische Bank. All three were secured on China's customs revenues.

14 Which, as the British historian A.J.P. Taylor contemptuously pointed out 'turned out to be useless as a naval base. It provided only a bathing beach for the ratings of the China squadron'. *The Struggle for Mastery in Europe 1848–1918*, Oxford, Clarendon Press, 1954, p. 376, n. 2.

15 When William II heard of the murders he ordered the German naval squadron, then at Shanghai, to sail to Kiaochow and show 'with unscrupulous brutality' that the German emperor was not be trifled with. He wanted his ships to 'augenblicklich nach Kiautschou zu fahren, die dort befindliche Ortschaft zu besetzen . . . und wenn nötig mit brutalster Rücksichtslosigkeit den Chinesen gegenüber zu zeigen, dass der deutsche Kaiser nicht mit sich spassen lässt' ('immediately to sail to Kiaochow, to occupy the place and, if necessary, to show the Chinese with the most brutal ruthlessness that one cannot play games with the German emperor' (author's translation). Johannes Lepsius, Albrecht Mendelssohn Bartholdy, Friedrich, Thimme (eds.), *Die Grosse Politik der Europäischen Kabinette; Sammlungen der Diplomatischen Akten des Auswärtigen Amtes*, vol. 14, Berlin, 1924, doc. 3686, p. 67.

16 It was a phrase that became famous, in Kaiser Wilhelm's speech of 1901 to the North German Regatta Association in C. Gauss, *The German Kaiser as shown in his Public Utterances*, New York, Charles Scribner's Sons, 1915, pp. 181–3.

17 George Nathaniel Curzon, *Problems of the Far East*, London, Longmans Green, 1894, p. 238.

18 Robert Hart's comment on Li was that 'he is industrious and cheerful but . . . as to his real proclivities etc, he talks as if he thought England alone to be trusted and acts as if in Russia's pay!'

19 *The Times* of 30 July 1900 reported him as saying: 'Just as the Huns a thousand years ago, under the leadership of Attila, gained a reputation by virtue of which

they still live in historical tradition, so may the name of Germany become known in such a manner in China . . .'. That seems to be one reason why, in the First World War, the British referred to the Germans as 'Huns'.

20 The total allied force sent to China, numbering some 42–44,000, seems to have included Americans, Austrians, Belgians, British (and Indians), Dutch, French, Germans, Italians, Japanese and Russians. Hart commented with interest that 'the Japanese show up better than the others for deftness, discipline, organisation and endurance'. Letter of 18 August 1900 to E.B. Drew.

21 Including that thirty-nine years' worth of interest, the actual payment seemed likely to be 980 million *taels*.

22 Published in *McClure's Magazine*, February 1899 and republished in *Rudyard Kipling's Verse: Definitive Edition*, New York, Doubleday, 1929.

23 Stephen Kinzer, *Overthrow: America's Century of Regime Change from Hawaii to Iraq*, New York, Times Books, 2006.

24 The British, for instance, sent one of their more remarkable imperial soldiers. Ian Hamilton, born in Corfu, had fought on the north-west frontier of India, Afghanistan, Burma, in the Sudan and the Boer War – and was to fail, tragically for the British, when put in command of the Gallipoli campaign of 1915.

25 The boy remained in his palace but never again played a role. After a storm-tossed life he died in 1967 as a clerk or gardener in the People's Republic.

10. The Dragon as Pawn

1 The largest contingent of these Japanese, as early as 1883, was that of prostitutes.

2 John K. Fairbank and Merle Goldman, *China, a new history*, (enl. edn.) Cambridge, Mass, Belknap Press of Harvard University Press, 1998, p. 260.

3 Winston S. Churchill, *The World Crisis* (4 vols.), vol. 2, 1915, New York, Scribner, 1929, pp. 1–2.

4 See Robert Lansing, *Self-determination: a discussion of the phrase*, Washington, 1921.

5 It was founded in 1919 as Moscow's instrument for dealing with affiliated Communist parties around the world, ones committed to implementing Comintern policies; which were, in practice, decided by the Soviet Communist Party.

6 Jung Chang and Jon Halliday allege that he had a 'love of blood-thirsty thuggery' from an early age. *Mao: The Unknown Story*, London, Jonathan Cape, 2005.

7 Not because the British were unpopular. The Tibetans actually found them much easier to deal with than the Chinese. 'When one has known the scorpion,' they said, 'the frog seems divine.' Even very much later there were oddly magical echoes of Tibetan friendliness. In the 1930s a British diplomat met the latest incarnation of the Panchen Lama in Beijing. The Panchen said they had met before. The diplomat, who had never been to Tibet, was puzzled, but later discovered that he bore a striking resemblance to a certain George Bogle, who

had been the first British visitor to Tibet in 1774 and had met the then Panchen Rimpoche, with whom he was much taken. Patrick French, *Tibet, Tibet, A Personal History of a Lost Land*, London, HarperCollins, 2003.

8 In fact, Wellington Koo wanted more. He wanted to use international law to undermine the old doctrine of *rebus sic stantibus*, so as to have laws and treaties thought valid only while the circumstances that had produced them did not change: a very traditional Chinese view.

9 For the compradors, it was said, even the foreigners' farts were fragrant.

10 Owen Lattimore, *China Memoirs: Chiang Kai-shek and the war against Japan*, Tokyo, University of Tokyo Press, 1990, pp. 137-8.

11 Cited in Spence, *The China Helpers*, op. cit., p. 195.

12 J.V. Stalin, *Problems of Leninism*, Moscow, Foreign Languages Publishing House, 1953, pp. 454-8.

13 Quoted in Michael Howard, *The Continental Commitment*, London, Temple Smith, 1972, p. 98.

14 Quoted in Walker Connor, 'Ethnology and the Peace of South Asia', *World Politics*, October 1969, pp. 62-3.

15 Johnson to Stimson 13 February 1933.

16 Hew Strachan, *The First World War*, vol. 1, Oxford/New York, Oxford University Press, 2001, p. 331.

17 Quoted in Howard, *The Continental Commitment*, op. cit., pp. 132-3, 139.

11. China in a New World Order

1 Winston S. Churchill, *The Second World War* (6 vols) (new edn. rev. reset), London, Cassell, 1949, vol. III, p. 539.

2 As the US Chiefs of Staff put it: 'notwithstanding the entry of Japan into the war, our view remains that Germany is still the prime enemy and her defeat is the key to victory. Once Germany is defeated, the collapse of Italy and the defeat of Japan must follow.' Robert E. Sherwood (ed.), *The White House Papers of Harry Hopkins: An Intimate History* (2 vols.), London, Eyre and Spottiswoode, 1948-9, vol. I, p. 449.

3 Quoted in Carl Hoffmann, *Saipan: The Beginning of the End*, US Marine Corps Historical Division, 1950, p. 36.

4 John Keegan, *Intelligence in War: Knowledge of the Enemy from Napoleon to al-Quaeda*, London, Hutchinson, 2003.

5 Gordon Prange, Donald Goldstein and Katherine V. Dillon, *Miracle at Midway*, New York, McGraw-Hill, 1982, pp. 260-3.

6 Although, for example, there was a small Indian nationalist force fighting with the Japanese, that was dwarfed by the (British) Indian Army. This was composed entirely of volunteers and, with some 2 million men under arms, was probably the greatest volunteer army the world had ever seen.

7 Quoted in Christopher Thorne, *The Issue of War: States, Societies and the Far Eastern Conflict of 1941-1945*, New York, Oxford University Press, 1985, p. 25.

8 Roy Jenkins, *Churchill: a biography*, New York, Farrar, Straus and Giroux, 2001, p. 680–1.

9 Quoted in Christopher Thorne, *Allies of a Kind: the United States, Britain and the War against Japan 1941–1945*, New York, Oxford University Press, 1978, p. 181.

10 He set out his principles in his 1942 book *China's Destiny*, a mixture of principles from military life with elements of traditional morality together with American Methodism.

11 Which would also finesse the need for the Allies to agree among themselves on surrender terms. Trying to negotiate those would certainly have caused enormous difficulties.

12 Herbert Feis, *Churchill, Roosevelt, Stalin: the war they waged and the peace they sought*, Princeton, Princeton University Press, 1957, p. 211.

13 When Churchill's horrified butler reported his find to the prime minister, he was quietly told just to leave things as he had found them.

14 There were mutual soundings through Stockholm.

15 An untranslatable German word, meaning pleasure at the misfortunes of others.

16 Its commander, Field Marshal Paulus, surrendered on 31 January. The story of the campaign is brilliantly told in Antony Beevor's *Stalingrad*, London, Viking, 1998.

17 A. Heywood and F.A.S. Clarke, *The History of the Royal West African Frontier Force*, Aldershot, 1964, pp. 385–6.

18 Martin Gilbert, *W.S. Churchill* (8 vols.), London, Heinemann, 1966, vol. 8, p. 1180.

19 Which later became the state of East Germany, and lasted until German reunification in 1990.

20 After the war some people argued that Roosevelt had betrayed China at Yalta. But he had no way of preventing Russian armies from moving into Manchuria, any more than he could have prevented them from marching into Poland. Long before Yalta the Chinese government had asked the US to help them make arrangements with the Russians, but gone on to make rather more concessions to Moscow than the Americans had advised.

21 The German war-effort, too, was conducted by something like a multinational coalition. Perhaps the most spectacular example was the deeply multinational composition of the *Waffen SS* (armed SS) divisions that some Allied soldiers considered to be the finest troops on either side. Among the very last defenders of Berlin as the Russians moved in were the remnants of French SS formations.

22 Loss of office may have been a shattering blow, but Churchill recovered. Sometime later he had a few American Mormons to dinner at his country house, Chartwell, and invited them to share his brandy after the meal. The senior Mormon frowned and explained that drink like this combined the bite of a viper and the kick of an antelope. Churchill smiled blissfully. 'All my life I've been looking for a drink like that.'

23 Robert V. Daniels (ed.), *A Documentary History of Communism* (2 vols.) (rev. edn.), Hanover, NH, University Press of New England, 1984, pp. 137–8.

24 *Foreign Relations of the United States*, op. cit., 1946 vol. VI, p. 696, Washington, USGPO. The document is conveniently summarised in Mr X,

'The Sources of Soviet Conduct', *Foreign Affairs*, July 1947. Frank Roberts from Britain's Moscow embassy was telling London much the same.

25 'The conflict of Communism and capitalism is just a show. At bottom it is Asia against the universe of the whites. It is a dispute without end' (author's translation). De Gaulle letter of 14 January 1951 to his nephew Bernard. Charles de Gaulle, *Lettres, notes et Carnets, Juin 1951–Mai 1958*, Paris, Plon, 1985, p. 177.

26 'Resumed its links, contrary to world opinion, with an Asia that has risen strongly and, under various flags, flatly rejects the West' (author's translation). Letter of 7 June 1854 (in *Lettres, notes . . .*, op. cit., p. 209) to Jean Sainteny who, after being a wartime Resistance leader, served from 1946 as a senior French official in Indo-China.

27 Churchill, by then a private citizen, cleared the text before delivery with President Truman and Prime Minister Clement Attlee.

28 Quoted in Bruce Cumings (ed.), *Child Conflict: The Korean-American Relationship 1943–1953*, Seattle, University of Washington Press, 1983, p. 13.

29 Ross Terrill, *Mao, A Biography* (rev. and expanded edn.), Stanford, Stanford University Press, 1999, p. 459.

30 Its power has nowhere been more clearly explained than in some works of fiction. One of the best is Arthur Koestler's *Darkness at Noon*.

31 It has been suggested that the Russians secretly handed some tens of thousands of Japanese prisoners of war over to the Chinese Communists, to train their army and create an air force for them, perhaps even to fight for Mao. Cf. Chang and Halliday, Mao op. cit.

32 He Di, 'The Evolution of the Chinese Communist Party's Policy towards the United States 1944–1949', in Harry Harding and Yuan Ming (eds.), *Sino-American Relations 1944–1955: A Joint Reassessment of a Critical Decade*, Wilmington, Del., Scholarly Resources, 1989, p. 40.

33 Zhang, Shu Guang, *Deterrence and Strategic Culture: Chinese-American Confrontations 1949–1958*, Ithaca, Cornell UP, 1992, p. 21.

12. The New Emperor

1 Quoted in Max Hastings, *The Korean War*, London, Michael Joseph, 1987, p. 59.

2 Inaugural Address 20 January 1953 in *Public Papers of the Presidents of the United States: Dwight D. Eisenhower*, 1953 vol., Washington, USGPO, 1960, p. 7.

3 Shi Zhe, 'With Mao and Stalin: Reminiscences of Mao's Interpreter, Pt. II: Liu Shaoqi in Moscow', *Chinese Historians* 6, Spring 1993, p. 84.

4 Dean Acheson, *Present at the Creation*, New York, W.W. Norton and Co., 1969, p. 257.

5 Executive Testimony, 29.3.50, US Congress, Senate Committee on Foreign Relations. *Historical Series: Review of the World Situation 1949–50*, Washington, USGPO, 1974, p. 273.

6 NSC 48/5, *Foreign Relations of the United States, 1951*, vol. 6, Washington, USGPO, pp. 35, 37.

7 Acheson, *Present at the Creation*, op. cit., p. 357.

8 Statement by President Truman issued 27 June 1950, in Harry S. Truman, *Years of Trial and Hope 1946–1952, Memoirs*, vol. II, New York, Doubleday, 1956, p. 339.

9 It had odd side-effects, too. In Korea, the practice of circumcision did not start until 1945 and did not become widespread until the arrival of so many Americans, who became Koreans' models, apparently in body as well as mind.

10 For his own account, see Paul H. Nitze, *From Hiroshima to Glasnost: At the Center of Decision*, New York, Grove Weidenfeld, 1989. Also Ernest May, *American Cold War Strategy: Interpreting NSC 68*, Boston, MA, Bedford/St Martin's, 1993.

11 G. Kennan, *American Diplomacy 1900–1950*, Chicago, Chicago University Press, 1951, pp. 51–2.

12 The government also gave a good deal of freedom to experiment to local and regional leaders, consolidating into general 'policy' whatever worked best.

13 Even short of terror, much of this was a continuous form of personal pressure which some writers suggest had results not unlike those of the Roman Catholic practice of confession leading to forgiveness; or, alternatively among Baptists, to believers being 'born again'.

14 The current (2004) Dalai Lama, the spiritual leader of Tibet, may have spent decades of exile in India. But when he was very small, his family seems to have spoken Chinese at home.

15 The Western impression was strong but may have been mistaken. Zhou's speech may just have been an attempt to mend fences with local nationalist governments.

16 Sir Robert Thompson, *Revolutionary War in World Strategy 1945–1969*, New York, Taplinger, 1970, p. 120.

17 Many of the defenders were German foreign legionnaires. Having little to lose, and as ready to die as anyone else, they insisted on getting up early so that they could have their hot coffee before they went out to get killed. The literature on the campaign is large. One good recent book is Martin Windrow, *The Last Valley: Dien Bien Phu and the French Defeat in Vietnam*, London, Weidenfeld and Nicolson, 2003.

18 The Journal *Défense Nationale* published several pieces along such lines, e.g. issues of May 1954 and February 1955.

19 Suart Schram, *The Political Thought of Mao Tse-tung* (rev. and enl. edn.), New York, Praeger, 1969, pp. 408–9.

20 As a 'back channel' security measure, the American and Chinese ambassadors at Warsaw started occasional talks.

21 For instance, Mao travelled around the country in his personal eleven-carriage train. During his trips all traffic along the entire rail line was stopped and stations cleared of people. The train moved only while he was awake and stopped whenever, day or night, he chose to sleep.

22 A year earlier, in 1963, President Kennedy asked Assistant Secretary of State Averell Harriman to explore with the Soviets what their attitude would be if the US launched a preventive nuclear strike against Chinese nuclear facilities.

23 The US secretary of state, John Foster Dulles, felt that the British action at Suez was a betrayal: a senior British minister, Harold Macmillan, had assured him privately that nothing much would happen.

24 Henry Kissinger, *Diplomacy*, New York, Simon and Schuster, 1994, pp. 588–9.

25 It was even more miraculous for anyone who, studying the pictures, could see no sign of swim-strokes by a chairman who seemed to be standing up in the water.

26 Jerome Chen, *Mao Papers: Anthology and Bibliography*, New York, Oxford University, 1970, pp. 24–5.

27 Deng Rong, *Deng Xiaoping and the Cultural Revolution* (trans. Sidney Shapiro), New York, Bertelsmann, 2005, p. 85. Many of the methods of harassment and torture seem strikingly reminiscent of the National Socialist pogroms against Jews and others, especially after 1938.

28 The second-in-command of the British mission at the time (later ambassador), Percy Cradock, has given a colourful account of the sacking, and the harassment of staff, in his *Experiences of China*, London, John Murray, 1994, Ch. 6.

29 This is the version in Chang and Halliday, Mao, op. cit.

30 Agreement on Ending the War and Restoring Peace in Vietnam, 27.1.1973, UN Treaty Series 935, 52, 55.

31 Henry Kissinger, *Years of Renewal*, London, Weidenfeld and Nicolson, 1999, p. 144.

32 But he took time, not long before he died, to send a message to the guardians of Confucius's tomb, telling them to close the gates and defend the temple, for the Red Guards were coming.

33 Li Zhisui, *The Private Life of Chairman Mao*, London, Chatto and Windus, 1994.

34 As he himself well understood, and said to Richard Nixon: *RN, Memoirs*, New York, Grosset & Dunlap, 1978, p. 558.

13. Reassertion

1 Not for the first or last time, the Chinese were casually indifferent to human losses. The British diplomat Percy Cradock tried to commiserate with a senior Chinese minister about the loss of some 20,000 young men. The minister just laughed. 'We have a lot more,' he said.

2 Unfortunately for both the US and China, help sent to the anti-Soviet guerrillas included some 20,000 young Saudis, men who would return home with military skills and also start to believe, like one of their leaders, a certain Osama bin Laden, that dedicated Islamic fighters could defeat a superpower.

3 *Selected Works of Deng Xiaoping*, vol. 3 (1982–92), Beijing, Foreign Languages Press, 1994, p. 201.

4 See Geremie Barmé, 'To screw foreigners is patriotic: China's avant-garde nationalists', *China Journal*, July 1995, p. 209.

5 It soon became well understood among foreigners that the way to ensure that one's business would flourish was to arrange for a son or nephew of the most important party secretary, Chinese CEO, or regional military commander, to be accepted at a Western, especially American 'Ivy League', university.

6 One striking account of how to lose money in China – even when trying to invest in an apparently sure-fire business like the Shanghai Greater Unison Condom Factory – is Tom Clissold's *Mr China*, London, Constable and Robinson, 2004. Of course the notion of sophisticated financiers losing money to shrewd local 'hayseeds' is far from new. Other warnings can be found in James McGregor, *One Billion Customers: Lessons from the Front Lines of Doing Business in China*, New York, Free Press, 2002. See also Mark Kitto, 'That's China', *Prospect*, April 2006.

7 Carrying echoes, perhaps, of the way in which the old Mogul empire in India had once upon a time based its wealth on carpets and textiles.

8 The detailed agreement was signed in July 1991 with Reagan's successor, President George Bush Sr.

9 It was 'unification' rather than 'reunification' since Germany had never before been truly unified, except during the period 1933–45. By no means everyone, even in Germany, let alone elsewhere, expected it to happen or welcomed it when it did. But it was not a development that any German could decently oppose, or even fail loudly to welcome, once unification became practical politics.

10 America not only created the internet but controlled, and controls, the key physical infrastructure that makes it work. It also has authority over the body that controls the internet's protocol numbers and the domain-name system of addresses.

11 There was, of course, the argument that if an invader, especially an American one, found himself littering the Chinese countryside with half a million or a million dead, he would simply recoil in horror. However, that was hardly a basis for sound strategic planning.

12 Both the 1991 and the 2003 Gulf wars demonstrated that in this matter the US was vulnerable. Both showed that the increasingly professionalised army required by the new arsenals was also increasingly divorced, personally, socially and in ideology, from the broad body of citizens in whose names the battles were fought. Which also meant growing civilian anxieties, especially in the West, about fighting shown in real time on television, and largely unreal distinctions between fighters and 'innocent civilians'.

13 That was three times the growth rate of the USA, albeit starting from a very low base.

14 On purchasing-power parity comparisons, it was second.

15 Much of it was probably money from inside China, seeking the tax advantages accorded to foreign firms.

16 See, for instance, William Langewiesche, *The Outlaw Sea*, op. cit.

17 For instance when the US vice-president, Dick Cheney, visited China in 2004, Chinese press reports of his addresses were heavily censored, with references to Taiwan and North Korea removed.

18 One Western estimate suggested that by 2004 these camps contained some 4–6 million people, being subjected to 'administrative correction' and 're-education through labour'.

19 Not just its higher reaches, either. Around the turn of the century a Western correspondent interviewed a Young Pioneer during a ceremony to celebrate Mao's 110th birthday. 'We learn from Mao,' said the youngster 'that you can always achieve your goal if you struggle and work hard enough.' 'And what is your goal?' 'To go to America.'

20 Not that Beijing always won. In 1989 the 10th Panchen Lama died. In 1995 the Dalai Lama, in secret collusion with a Tibetan abbot, agreed on, and proclaimed, the 11th incarnation of the Panchen Lama. The Chinese abducted the child and his parents and appointed their own Panchen. The Dalai's nominee was never seen again but the Chinese version was scorned and later fled.

21 See, for instance, Maria Hsia Chang, *Falun Gong: The End of Days*, New Haven, Yale University Press, 2003.

22 The party may condemn Falun Gong as an 'evil cult' that idolises its leader as God and brainwashes its followers to become 'new men and women', but that also seems a fair description of Maoism in a country where Mao thought continues to be taught at every level of the education system.

23 By Western standards, living conditions, whether in factory workers' dormitories or for many university students, were dreadful. There might be eight people in one small room sharing four bunks.

24 Some reports say that, in 1990–2005, 7,000 policemen died on duty, with 1,000 killed and 30,000 injured in deliberate attacks.

25 The phrase was invented by Professor Joseph Nye of Harvard in his *Bound to Lead: The Changing Nature of American Power*, New York, Basic Books, 1990.

26 For example, vast numbers of Chinese appear to believe that in May 1999 NATO aircraft, in their campaign against Serbia, bombed the Chinese embassy in Belgrade on purpose and not by accident – even though no plausible motive has ever been suggested. Similarly, millions of Chinese seem to believe the absurd idea that when a US Navy reconnaissance aircraft suffered a mid-air collision with a Chinese fighter over the South China Sea in April 2001, it was a case of the lumbering US transport aircraft deliberately ramming the much faster and agile jet fighter.

27 In later years, firms like Exxon reported that the prospects there were actually poor.

28 Quoted in the *Economist* 16.10.04, p. 71.

29 In 2004 the Germans actually managed to open the first foreign cultural centre in North Korea, in the shape of the Pyongyang Goethe Institute.

30 Cf. Allen S. Whiting, *China Eyes Japan*, Berkeley, Cal., University of California Press, 1989.

31 Where German special forces found themselves welcomed as fellow Aryans.

32 Quoted in Andrew Nathan and Bruce Gilley, *China's New Rulers: The Secret Files*, New York, New York Review Books, 2000, pp. 207–9.

14. Towards the Future?

1 It is not outrageous to speculate that if – or when – it becomes possible to clone human beings, all human relationships might change profoundly.

2 Parents have found many ways. For instance, if a couple have a second child no more than a couple of years or so after the first, they might bribe a doctor to issue a birth certificate for the second child with the same birth-date as the first – making the two, officially, 'twins'.

3 See the interview of China's deputy minister for the environment, Pan Yue, with the German magazine *Der Spiegel*, issue of 7 March 2005. All such predictions are, of course, speculative. Some demographers argue that world population growth has been declining since the end of the 1980s and even in the developing world will reach replacement-level fertility around 2035. The reasons are mysterious. Whatever they may be, could China remain immune from them?

4 By 2004 American estimates were that two-thirds of the value of Chinese products was imported.

5 See note 3 above.

6 A word of general caution may also be in order. Growth is everywhere measured in terms of GDP. But in a period when economies are more driven by knowledge and services, do GDP figures mean just what they did in the days of manufacturing?

7 By 2004 cumulative totals of inward FDI flows seem to have reached US$560 billion or so.

8 Professor Fred Hu of Beijing University makes this argument in the *Financial Times*, 3 August 2005, p. 11. He is a managing director of Goldman Sachs.

SELECT BIBLIOGRAPHY

Amyot Joseph, *Art militaire des Chinois* (publ. by M. Deguignes) (Joseph de Guignes), Paris, 1772.

Anderson, Benedict, *Imagined Communities: Reflections on the Origin and Spread of Nationalism*, London, Verso, 1991.

Anson, G., *A Voyage round the World in the years 1740–44*, compiled from his papers and materials by Richard Walter, London, Milner, 1832.

Ashley, Evelyn, *The life and correspondence of Henry John Temple, Viscount Palmerston, by the Hon. Evelyn Ashley* (2 vols.), London, R. Bentley & son, 1879.

Backhouse, E. and J.O.P. Bland, *Annals and Memoirs of the court of Peking (from the sixteenth to the twentieth century)*, Boston, Houghton Mifflin/London, Heinemann, 1914.

Banno, Masataka, *China and the West 1858–1861, The Origin of the Tsungli Yamen*, Cambridge, Mass., Harvard UP, 1964.

Barlow, Jeffrey G., *Sun Yat-sen and the French 1900–1908* (China Research Monograph No. 14), Center for Chinese Studies, Institute of East Asian Studies, University of California, Berkeley, 1979.

Bau, Mingchien Joshua, *The Foreign Relations of China: A History and a Survey* (rev. enl. edn.), London, Nisbet & Co, 1922.

Baum, R., *Burying Mao: Chinese Politics in the Age of Deng Xiaoping*, Princeton, Princeton University Press, 1994.

Beale, Howard K., *Theodore Roosevelt and the Rise of America to World Power*, Baltimore, Johns Hopkins Press, 1956.

Beasley, William, *The Meiji Restoration*, London, Oxford University Press, 1973.

Bell, Herbert C.F., *Lord Palmerston* (2 vols.), London, Longmans Green, 1936.

Bernstein, Richard, *Ultimate Journey*, New York, Knopf, 2001.

Berridge, Virginia, *Opium and the People* (rev. edn.), London/New York, Free Association Books, 1999.

Biraben, J.R., 'Essai sur l'évolution du nombre des hommes', *Population*, Jan.–Feb. 1979.

Black, Conrad, *Franklin Delano Roosevelt: Champion of Freedom*, London, Weidenfeld and Nicolson, 2005.

Bloch, Kurt, *German Interests and Policies in the Far East*, New York, 1939.

Bobbitt, Philip, *The Shield of Achilles: War, Peace and the Course of History*, New York, Knopf, 2002.

Booth, Martin, *The Dragon Syndicates: the global phenomenon of the triads*, New York, Doubleday, 1998.

Bourne, K., *The Foreign Policy of Victorian England 1830–1902*, Oxford, Clarendon Press, 1970.

Boxer, C.R., *South China in the Sixteenth Century, Being the Narratives of Galeote Pereira*, Fr. Gaspar da Cruz O.P., Fr. Martin de Rada O.E.S.A. (1550–75), London, Hakluyt Society, 1953.
    The Portuguese Seaborne Empire 1415–1825, Manchester, Carcanet, 1991 (orig. London, Hutchinson, 1969).

Burghardt, G.E., *Kleine Missions-Bibliothek*, vol. III, Bielefeld, 1860.

Burnett, John S., *Dangerous Waters: Modern Piracy and Terror on the High Seas*, New York, Dutton, 1992.

Buruma, Ian, *Inventing Japan 1853–1964*, London, Weidenfeld and Nicolson, 2003.

Bush, George W., *The National Security Strategy of the United States*, Washington, The White House, September 2002.

Buzan, Barry, *The United States and the Great Powers: World Politics in the 21st Century*, Cambridge, Polity Press, 2004.

Buzan, Barry and Rosemary Foot (eds.), *Does China Matter?* London, Routledge, 2004.

Cambridge History of China (genl. eds. Denis Twitchett and John K. Fairbank), Cambridge/New York, Cambridge University Press, 1978–98.

Chambers, John Whiteclay (ed.), *The Eagle and the Dove: The American Peace Movement and United States Foreign Policy 1900–1922* (2nd edn.), Syracuse, NY, Syracuse University Press, 1991.

Chang, Maria Hsia, *Falun Gong: The End of Days*, New Haven, Yale University Press, 2003.

Chen Chi, *Die Beziehungen zwischen Deutschland und China bis 1933*, Hamburg, Institut für Asienkunde (Institute for Asian Studies), 1973.

Chen Jian, *China and the Cold War*, Chapel Hill, North Carolina Press, 2000.

Ching, Julia and W. G. Oxtoby (eds.), *Discovering China: European Interpretations in the Enlightenment*, New York, University of Rochester Press, 1992.

Churchill, Sir Winston Spencer, *The Second World War* (6 vols.), (new edn., rev. reset), London, Cassell, 1949.

Cipolla, C.M., *Guns, Sails and Empires: Technological Innovation and the Early Phases of European Expansion 1400–1670*, New York, Pantheon, 1965.

Clayton, Anthony, *The Wars of French Decolonization*, London, Longman, 1994.

Collis, Maurice, *Foreign Mud, being an account of the opium imbroglio at Canton and the Anglo-Chinese war that followed*, London, Faber and Faber, 1946.

Constant, Charles Samuel de, *Les mémoires de Charles de Constant sur le commerce à la Chine* (ed. Louis Demigny), Paris, SEVPEN, 1964.

Cordier, H., *Histoire Génerale de la Chine* (4 vols.), Paris, Paul Guethner, 1920.

Costin, William C., *Great Britain and China 1833–1860*, Oxford, Clarendon Press, 1937.

Council on Foreign Relations, *Council on Foreign Relations Task Force on Chinese Military Power*, New York, Council on Foreign Relations, 2003.

Couplet, Fr. Louis, *Tabula Chronologica Trium Familiarum Imperialium Monarchiae*, Sinicae, Paris, 1686.

Cranmer-Byng, J.L., *An Embassy to China: Lord Macartney's Journal 1793–1794*, in *Britain and the China Trade, 1635–1842*, London/New York, Routledge, 2000, vol. 8.

Crowley, James, *Japan's Quest for Autonomy: National Security and Forign Policy 1930–1938*, Princeton, Princeton University Press, 1966.

Cumings, Bruce, *The Origins of the Korean War* (2 vols.), Princeton, Princeton University Press, 1981–90.

Cunnynghame, Arthur, *An ADC's Recollections of Service in China*, London, 1844.

Curzon, George Nathaniel, *Problems of the Far East*, London, Longmans Green, 1894.

Dallin, David J., *The Rise of Russia in Asia*, New Haven, Conn., Yale University Press, 1949.

Dalloz, Jacques (trans. Josephine Bacon), *The War in Indo-China 1945–54*, Dublin, Gill and Macmillan, 1990.

Daniels, Robert V. (ed.), *A Documentary History of Communism* (rev. edn.), Hanover, NII, University Press of New England, 1984.

Davies, J.F., *The Chinese, A General Description of the Empire of China and its Inhabitants* (2 vols.), London, Charles Knight, 1836.

Dawson, Christopher (ed.), *The Mongol Mission: Narratives and letters of the Franciscan Missionaries in Mongolia and China in the Thirteenth and Fourteenth Centuries* (trans. by a nun of Stanbrook Abbey), New York, Sheed and Ward, 1955.

Dennett, Tyler, *Americans in East Asia; a critical study of the policy of the United States with reference to China, Japan and Korea in the 19th century*, New York, Barnes & Noble, 1941.

Dermigny, Louis, *La Chine et l'Occident: le commerce à Canton au XVIIIe siècle, 1719–1833*, 3 vols., Paris, 1964.

Djilas, Milovan, *Conversations with Stalin*, New York, Harcourt Brace and World, 1962.

Dower, John W., *War Without Mercy: Race and Power in the Pacific War*, New York, Pantheon, 1986.

Embracing Defeat: Japan in the Wake of World War II, New York, Norton, 1999.

Dunne, George H., SJ, *Generation of Giants: The Story of the Jesuits in China in the last Decades of the Ming Dynasty*, London, Burns and Oates, 1962.

Eberhard, Wolfram, *A History of China*, Berkeley, Cal., University of California Press, 1977.

China und seine Westlichen Nachbarn, Darmstadt, Wissenschaftliche Buchgesellschaft, 1978.

Fairbank, John K., *The United States and China* (4th edn.), Cambridge, MA, Harvard University Press, 1979.

The Chinese World Order: Traditional China's Foreign Relations, Cambridge, MA, Harvard University Press, 1968.

Fairbank, John K. and Merle Goldman, *China, A New History* (enl. edn.), Cambridge, MA, Belknap Press of Harvard University Press, 1998.

Feis, Herbert, *Churchill, Roosevelt and Stalin: the war they waged and the peace they sought*, Princeton, Princeton University Press, 1957.

Fewsmith, Joseph, *China since Tiananmen*, Cambridge, Cambridge University Press, 2001.

Foreign Office (UK), *Foreign Office confidential papers relating to China and her neighbouring countries 1840–1914, with an additional list 1915–1937* (compiled by Lo Hui-nim), The Hague/Paris, Mouton, 1969.

Foreign Relations of the United States (series of official documents), Washington, USGPO, (annual).

Foster, John W., *American Diplomacy in the Orient*, New York, Houghton Mifflin, 1903.

Gallagher, Louis J., SJ, *China in the Sixteenth Century: The Journals of Matthew Ricci, 1583–1610*, New York, Random House, 1953.

Gaulle, Charles de, *Lettres, notes et Carnets, Juin 1951–Mai 1958*, Paris, Plon, 1985.

Gelber, Harry G., *Nations out of Empires*, London, Palgrave, 2001.
Opium, Soldiers and Evangelicals. London, Palgrave, 2004.

Gernet, Jacques, *China and the Christian Impact, A Conflict of Cultures*, Cambridge, Cambridge University Press, 1985.

Gilley, Bruce, *Tiger on the Brink; Jiang Zemin and China's New Elite*, Berkeley, University of California Press, 1998.

Goldstein, Melvyn C., *The Snow Lion and the Dragon: China, Tibet and the Dalai Lama*, Berkeley, University of California Press, 1997.

Goodman, David S.G. and Gerald Segal (eds.), *China Rising: Nationalism and Interdependence*, London, Routledge, 1997.

Graham, Gerald S., *The China Station: War and Diplomacy 1830–1860*, Oxford, Clarendon Press, 1978.

Greenberg, Michael, *Britain's Trade and the Opening of China 1800–1842*, (Cambridge, Cambridge University Press, 1951) New York, Monthly Review Press, 1979.

Greider, William, *One World, Ready or Not: The Manic logic of Global Capitalism*, New York, Simon and Schuster, 1997.

Greville, C.C.F., *The Greville Memoirs; a journal of the reigns of King George IV and King William IV* (ed. Henry Reeve) (3 vols.), London, Longmans Green, 1874.

Grew, Joseph, *Ten Years in Japan*, New York, Simon and Schuster, 1944.

Grunfeld, A. Tom, *The Making of Modern Tibet*, Armonk, NY, M.E. Sharpe, 1987.

Guizot, François, *Mémoires pour servir à l'histoire de mon temps* (nouv. edn.), Paris, Michel Lévy frères, 1872.

Hackett, Roger F., *Yamagata Aritomo in the Rise of Modern Japan 1838–1922*, Cambridge, MA, Harvard UP, 1971.

Harrison, John A., *The Founding of the Russian Empire in Asia and America*, Coral Gables, University of Miami Press, 1971.

Henriot, Christian, *Prostitution and Sexuality in Shanghai, a Social History 1849–1949* (trans. Noel Castelino), Cambridge, Cambridge University Press, 2001.

Hevia, James, *Cherishing Men from Afar: Qing Guest Ritual and the Macartney Embassy 1793*, Durham and London, Duke University Press, 1995.

Howard, Michael, *The Continental Commitment*, London, Temple Smith, 1972.

Hsü, Immanuel C. Y., *The Rise of Modern China* (5th edn.), New York, Oxford University Press, 1995.

Hughes, Ernest Richard, *The Invasion of China by the Western World*, London, A. & C. Black, 1937.

Huntington, Samuel, *The Clash of Civilizations and the Remaking of World Order*, New York, Simon & Schuster, 1996.

Hyma, Albert, *The Dutch in the Far East: a history of the Dutch commercial and colonial empire*, Ann Arbor, George Wahr, 1942.

Iriye, Akira, *Origins of the Second World War in Asia and the Pacific*, London, Longmans, 1987.

Israel, Jerry, *Progressivism and the Open Door: America and China 1905–1921*, Pittsburgh, University of Pittsburgh Press, 1971.

Jenkins, Robert Charles, *The Jesuits in China, and the Legation of Cardinal de Tournon*, London, D. Nutt, 1894.

Jenkins, Roy, *Churchill: a biography*, New York, Farrar, Straus and Giroux, 2001. *Franklin Delano Roosevelt*, London, Macmillan, 2003.

Jocelyn, Viscount, *Six Months with the Chinese Expedition*, (2nd edn.), London, J. Murray, 1841.

Johnston, Alastair Iain, *Cultural Realism: Strategic Culture and Grand Strategy in Chinese History*, Princeton, Princeton University Press, 1995.

Jung Chang and John Halliday, *Mao: The Unknown Story*, London, Jonathan Cape, 2005.

Kao, John, 'The Worldwide Web of Chinese Business', *Harvard Business Review*, 71, 1993.

Kennan, George ('Mr X'), 'The Sources of Soviet Conduct', *Foreign Affairs*, July 1947.

Khodarkovsky, Michael, *Where Two Worlds Met: The Russian State and the Kalmyk Nomads 1600–1771*, Ithaca, Cornell UP, 1992.

Kierman, Frank A. and John Fairbank, *Chinese Ways of Warfare*, Cambridge, MA, Harvard University Press, 1974.

Kim, Samuel S. (ed.), *The International Relations of Northeast Asia*, Lanham, MD, Rowman and Littlefield, 2003.

Kirker, James, *Adventures to China: Americans in the Southern Oceans 1792–1812*, New York, Oxford University Press, 1970.

Kissinger, Henry A., *The White House Years*, London, Weidenfeld and Nicolson, 1979.

Kotzebue, Otto von, *A Voyage of Discovery into the South Sea and Bering straits . . . in the years 1815–1818* (2 vols.), London, 1821.

Krusenstern, Adam Johann von, *Voyage round the world in the years 1803, 1804, 1805 and 1806* (trans. Richard Hoppner), London, 1813.

Lane, George, *Ghengis Khan and Mongol Rule*, Westport, Conn., Greenwood Press, 2004.

Langewiesche, William, *The Outlaw Sea: a World of Freedom, Chaos and Crime*, New York, North Point Press, 2004.

Lattimore, Owen, *Inner Asian Frontiers of China*, London, Boston, Beacon Press, 1962.

China Memoirs: Chiang Kai-shek and the war against Japan, Tokyo, University of Tokyo Press, 1990.

Le Conte, Fr. Louis, *Nouveaux Mémoires sur l'état present de la Chine*, Paris, J.L. de Lorme, 1697.

Lee, Thomas, H.C. (ed.), *China and Europe: Images and Influences in the Sixteenth to Eighteenth Centuries*, Hong Kong, Chinese University Press, 1991.

Lepsius, Johannes, Albrecht Mendelssohn Bartholdy and Friedrich Thimme (eds.), *Die Grosse Politik der Europäischen Kabinette: Sammlungen der diplomatischen Akten des auswärtigen Amtes* (40 vols.), Berlin, Deutsche Velagsgesellschat für Politik und Geschichte, 1922 et seq.

Leutner Mechthild, (ed.), *Deutschland und China 1937–1949*, Berlin, Akademie Verlag, 1998.

Li Zhisui, *The Private Life of Chairman Mao: the memoirs of Mao's personal physician*, New York, Random House, 1994.

Lombard, Denis and Jean Aubin (eds.), *Asian Merchants and Businessmen in the Indian Ocean and the China Sea*, Oxford, Oxford University Press, 2000.

Lu Yan, *Re-understanding Japan: Chinese perspectives 1695–1945*, Honolulu, University of Hawaii Press, 2004.

Lukin, Alexander, *The Bear Watches the Dragon*, New York, Armonk, M.E. Sharpe, 2003.

Ma, Laurence J.C., *Commercial Development and Urban Change in Sung China (960–1279)*, Ann Arbor, Department of Geography, University of Michigan, 1971.

Macdonald, Sir Claude, *The Open Door and British Informal Empire in China 1895–1900*, New York and London, Garland Publishing, 1987.

MacFarquhar, Roderick (ed.), *The Politics of China: The Eras of Deng and Mao*, Cambridge, Cambridge University Press, 1997.

MacFarquhar, Roderick, and Michael Schoenhals, *Mao's Last Revolution*, Cambridge, MA, Harvard University Press, 2006.

McNeill, William H., *The Pursuit of Power: Technology, Armed Force and Society since AD 1000*, Chicago, University of Chicago Press, 1982.

The Age of Gunpowder Empires 1450–1800, Washington, American Historical Association, 1989.

Mahan, Alfred Thayer, *The Influence of Sea Power Upon History 1660–1783*, Boston, Little Brown, 1890.

Malek, Roman (ed.), *The Chinese Face of Jesus Christ*, St Augustin, Institut Monumenta Serica, Nettetal, Steylar, 2002.

Malek, Roman, and Arnold Zingerle (eds.), *Martino Martini SJ und die Chinamission im 17, Jahrhundert*, St Augustin, Institut Monumenta Serica, Nettetal, Steyler, 2000.

Mancall, Mark, *Russia and China, Their Diplomatic Relations to 1728*, Cambridge, MA, Harvard University Press, 1971.

China at the Center: 300 years of foreign policy, New York, Free Press, 1984.

Manz, Beatrice Forbes, *The Rise and Rule of Tamerlane*, Cambridge, Cambridge University Press, 1989.

Marshall, Robert, *Storm from the East: From Ghengis Khan to Khubilai Khan*, Berkeley, Cal., University of California Press, 1993.

Martin Jones, David, *The Image of China in Western Social and Political Thought*, London, Palgrave, 2001.

Martini Martino SJ, *Bellum Tartaricum, or, The conquest of the great and most renowned empire of China, by the invasion of the Tartars ...* (trans. into English), London, printed for John Crook, 1654.

Michael, Franz, *The Origin of Manchu Rule in China*, Baltimore, Johns Hopkins Press, 1942.

Milton, Giles, *Nathaniel's Nutmeg*, New York, Farrer, Straus and Giroux, 1999.

Mohr, Friedrich Wilhelm, *Fremde und deutsche Kulturbetätigung in China*, Münster, 1926.

Montesquieu, Charles Secondat, Baron de, *L'esprit des lois*, Paris, 1748.

Morgan, David, *The Mongols*, Oxford, Blackwell, 1986.

Morse, Hosea Ballou, *The International Relations of the Chinese Empire* (3 vols.), London, New York, Longmans Green, 1910–18.

Nathan, Andrew J., *China's Transition*, New York, Columbia University Press, 1998.

Nathan, Andrew J. and Robert Ross, *The Great Wall and the Empty Fortress*, New York, W. W. Norton, 1997.

Needham, Joseph, *Science and Civilization in China*, Cambridge, Cambridge University Press, 1954.

Nye, Joseph S. Jr., *Bound to Lead: The Changing Nature of American Power*, New York, Basic Books, 1990.

Ouchterlony, John, *The Chinese War*, London, Saunders and Otley, 1844.

Pelcovits, Nathan A., *Old China Hands and the Foreign Office*, New York, American Institute of Pacific Relations, 1848.

Petech, L., *China and Tibet in the Early XVIIIth century* (2nd edn. rev.), Leiden, E.J. Brill, 1972.

Peyrefitte, Alain, *The Collision of two Civilisations: the British Expedition to China 1792–4*, London, Harvill, 1993.

Polo, Marco, *The Book of Ser Marco Polo*, London, J. Murray, 1926.

Prange, Gordon W., *At Dawn We Slept: The Untold Story of Pearl Harbor*, New York, McGraw-Hill, 1981.

Prange, Gordon W., Donald M. Goldstein and Katherine V. Dillon, *Miracle at Midway*, New York, McGraw-Hill, 1982.

Preston, Diana, *The Boxer Rebellion*, Cambridge, Cambridge University Press, 1995; New York, Berkeley Books, 1999.

Pritchard, Earl H., *The Crucial Years of Anglo-Chinese Relations 1750–1800*, Research Studies of the State College of Washington, Washington, Pullman, 1936.

Putjata, S.D.W., *China's Wehrmacht*, Vienna and Leipzig, 1895.

Roberts, J.M., *The Triumph of the West*, London, Guild Publishing, 1985.

Robinson, Thomas, and David Shambaugh (eds.), *Chinese Foreign Policy: Theory and Practice*, Oxford, Clarendon Press, 1994.

Rockhill, William Woodville (ed.), *The Journey of William of Rubruck to the eastern parts of the world 1253–1255; as narrated by himself; with two accounts of the earlier journey of John of Pian de Carpine* (trans. from the Latin and edited, with an introductory notice, by W. W. Rockhill, London, printed for the Hakluyt Society, 1900.

Rossabi, Morris, *Voyager from Xanadu: Rabban Sauma and the first journey from China to the West*, Tokyo/New York, Kodansha International, 1992.

(ed.) *China among equals: the Middle Kingdom and its neighbours, 10th–14th centuries*, Berkeley, Cal., University of California Press, 1983.

Rowbotham, Arnold H., *Missionary and Mandarin: The Jesuits at the Court of China*, Berkeley and LA, University of California Press, 1942.

Rywkin, Michael, *Russia in Central Asia*, New York, Collier Books, 1963.

Schlesinger, Arthur M., *War and the American Presidency*, New York, Norton, 2004.

Segal, Gerald, 'Does China Matter?' *Foreign Affairs*, September–October 1999.

Serge, Victor, *Memoirs of a Revolutionary 1901–1941*, London, Oxford University Press, 1963.

Serruys, Henry, *The Mongols and Ming China: Customs and History* (ed. Francoise Aubin), London, Variorum Reprints, 1987.

Shambaugh, David, *Modernizing China's Military: Progress, Problems and Prospects*, Berkeley, Cal., University of California Press, 2003.

Sherwood, E. Robert (ed.), *The White House Papers of Harry Hopkins: An Intimate History* (2 vols.), London, Eyre and Spottiswoode, 1948–9.

Sinor, Denis (ed.), *The Cambridge History of Inner Asia*, Cambridge, Cambridge University Press, 1990.

Smith, Adam, *An Enquiry into the Nature and Causes of the Wealth of Nations* (4th edn.), London, A. Strahan and T. Cadell, 1789.

Snow, Edgar, *Red Star over China* (1st rev. and enl. edn.) (1937), New York, Bantam Books, 1978.

Spate, O.H.K, *The Spanish Lake*, Minneapolis, University of Minnesota Press, 1979.

Spence, Jonathan, *The China Helpers; Western Advisers in China 1620–1960*, London, Bodley Head, 1969.

'Opium Smoking in Ching China', in Frederic Wakeman Jr and Carolyn Grant (eds.), *Conflict and Control in Late Imperial China*, (selected papers presented at a conference at the East–West Center, Honolulu, in June 1971), Berkeley, University of California Press, 1975.

The Search for Modern China, New York, Norton, 1990; 2nd edn. 1999.

Staunton, Sir George, *An authentic account of an embassy from the king of Great Britain to the emperor of China* (2 vols.) (2nd edn., corr.) London, G. Nicol, 1798.

Stephan, John J., *The Russian Far East: a History*, Stanford, Cal., Stanford University Press, 1994.

Stöcker, Helmuth, *Deutschland und China im 19. Jahrhundert; das Eindrigen des deutschen Kapitalismus*, Berlin, Rütten und Löning, 1958.

Strachan, Hew, *The First World War* (vol. 1), Oxford/New York, Oxford University Press, 2001.

Sun, Yuli, *China and the Origins of the Pacific War 931–1941*, New York, St Martins, 1993.

Sutter, Robert G., *China's Rise in Asia: Promises and Perils*, Lanham, MD, Rowman and Littlefield, 2005.

Swisher, Earl (ed.), *China's Management of the American Barbarians*, New Haven, Yale University Press, 1953.

Taylor, A.J.P., *The Struggle for Mastery in Europe 1848–1918*, Oxford, Clarendon Press, 1954.

Temperley, H.W.V., and L.M. Penson, *Foundations of British Foreign Policy from Pitt (1792) to Salisbury (1902)*, Cambridge, Cambridge University Press, 1938.

Teng Ssu-yu, *China's Response to the West: a documentary survey 1839–1923*, Cambridge, MA, Harvard University Press, 1954.

Terrill, Ross, *Mao, a biography*, Stanford, Cal., Stanford University Press, 1999. *The New Chinese Empire: and what it means for the United States*, New York, Basic Books, 2003.

Thorne, Christopher, *The Issue of the War: States, Societies and the Far Eastern Conflict of 1941–1945*, New York, Oxford University Press, 1985.

Tirpitz, Grand Admiral Alfred von, *My Memoirs* (2 vols.), New York, Dodd Mead & Co, 1919.

Toland, John, *The Rising Sun: the decline and fall of the Japanese Empire, 1936–1945*, New York, Bantam Books, 1971.

Torday, Laszlo, *Mounted Archers*, Edinburgh, Durham Academic Press, 1997.

Tuchman, Barbara, *Stilwell and the American Experience in China 1911–1945*, New York, Grove Press, 2001.

Tyler, Christian, *Wild West China: The Taming of Xinjiang*, London, John Murray, 2003.

Ure, John, *The Cossacks*, London, Constable, 1999.

Van Alstyne, Richard W., *The United States and East Asia*, London, Thames and Hudson, 1973.

Van Gulick, R.H., *Sexual Life in Ancient China: A Preliminary Survey of Chinese Sex and Society from ca. 1500 BC till 1644 AD*, (Sinica Leidensia, vol. 57), Leiden/Boston, Brill, 2003.

Väth, Alfons, SJ, *Johann Adam Schall von Bell SJ, Missionar in China, Kaiserlicher Astronom und Ratgeber am Hofe von Peking 1592–1666: ein Lebens – und Zeitbild* (new edn.), Nettetal, Steyler, 1991.

Wakeman, Frederic Jr., *Strangers at the Gate: Social Disorder in South China 1839–1861*, Berkeley, University of California Press, 1966.

Waley-Cohen, Joanna, *The Sextants of Beijing: Global Currents in Chinese History*, New York, Norton, 1999.

Walrond, Theodore (ed.), *Letters and Journals of James, Eighth Earl of Elgin*, (with a preface by Arthur Stanley), London, J. Murray, 1872.

Washington Treaties: Conference on the Limitation of Armament 1921–22, treaty between the United States, Belgium, the British Empire, China, France, Italy, Japan, the Netherlands and Portugal, regarding principles and policies to be followed in matters concerning China, signed at Washington, 6 February 1922, Washington, US Government Printing Office, 1925.

Wheaton, Henry, *Elements of International Law: with a Sketch of the History of the Science*, Philadelphia, Carey, Lea & Blanchard, 1836.

White, Gordon, *Riding the Tiger: the Politics of Economic Reform in Post-Mao China*, London, Macmillan, 1993.

Whiting, Alan, 'Chinese Nationalism and Foreign Policy after Deng', *China Quarterly*, June 1995, pp. 295–316.

Will, Pierre-Etienne, *Bureaucracy and Famine in Eighteenth-Century China* (trans. Elborg Forster), Stanford, Stanford University Press, 1990.

Wills, John E. Jr., *Embassies and Illusions: Dutch and Portuguese Envoys to K'ang-hsi 1666–1687*, Cambridge, MA, Council on East Asian Studies, Harvard University, 1984.

Windrow, Martin, *The Last Valley: Dien Bien Phu and the French Defeat in Vietnam*, London, Weidenfeld and Nicolson, 2003.

Wolseley, Garnet Joseph (Field Marshal Viscount), *The Story of a Soldier's Life* (2 vols.), Westminster, Archibald Constable and Co., 1903.

Woodcock, George, *The British in the Far East*, London, Weidenfeld and Nicolson, 1969.

World Bank, *The East Asian Miracle: economic growth and public policy*, New York, NY, Oxford University Press, 1993.

Young, L.K., *British Policy in China 1895–1902*, Oxford, Oxford University Press, 1970.

Yü Wen-Tang, *Die Deutsch-Chinesischen Beziehungen von 1860–1880*, Bochum, Brockmeyer, 1981.

Zhai Qiang, *China and the Vietnam Wars 1945–1975*, Chapel Hill, North Carolina Press, 2000.

Zhang Shu Guang, *Deterrence and Strategic Culture: Chinese-American Confrontations 1949–1958*, Ithaca, Cornell University Press, 1992.

Zhang Yongjin, *China in International Society since 1949: Alienation and Beyond*, Oxford, St Antony's College; New York, St Martin's Press, 1998.

Zhou Yongming, *Anti-Drug Crusades in Twentieth Century China: nationalism, history and state building*, Lanham, MD, Rowman and Littlefield, 1999.

INDEX

A NOTE ON THE AUTHOR

Harry G. Gelber read history at Cambridge before going on to do a PhD at Monash University in Australia. He has taught international politics at Boston University, Harvard, the LSE, Yale and Monash. From 1975 until 1992 he was Professor of Political Science at the University of Tasmania and remains Professor Emeritus there. Most recently he has been Visiting Fellow, Center for European Studies, Harvard University (2004–2006) and Visiting Fellow, Department of International Relations, London School of Economics (2001–2004). His many books include *Nations out of Empires* (2001) and *Opium, Soldiers and Evangelicals* (2004). He lives in Australia, from where he travels regularly to the USA and Britain.

Designed in 1792, the Bulmer types are named not after their designer, William Martin, but after the English printer William Bulmer (1757–1830) who produced an edition of Shakespeare for King George III and also printed the work of the engraver Thomas Bewick. In 1928 Morris Fuller Benton created revivals for American Type Founders. Originally, Martin's type was the English answer to the sharp, fine letterforms of Italy's Bodoni and France's Didot type foundries. But the Bulmer types did more than imitate the starkness of the modern-style Didot-Bodoni types. By condensing the letterforms, giving the strokes higher contrast, and bracketing the serifs slightly, Martin made his typefaces both beautiful and practical.